T0414008

Trade and Finance in Global Missions (16th–18th Centuries)

Studies in Christian Mission

The titles published in this series are listed at *brill.com/scm*

Trade and Finance in Global Missions (16th–18th Centuries)

Edited by

Hélène Vu Thanh and Ines G. Županov

BRILL

LEIDEN | BOSTON

Cover illustration: Imago primi saeculi Societatis Iesu: a prouincia Flandro-Belgica eiusdem Societatis repraesentata. Published in 1640 by Antuerpiae: Ex officina Plantiniana Balthasaris Moreti. In the public domain.

The Library of Congress Cataloging-in-Publication Data is available online at http://catalog.loc.gov

Typeface for the Latin, Greek, and Cyrillic scripts: "Brill". See and download: brill.com/brill-typeface.

ISSN 0924-9389
ISBN 978-90-04-44417-1 (hardback)
ISBN 978-90-04-44419-5 (e-book)

For Ante, Christophe and François

∵

Contents

Acknowledgments

It has taken time to complete this book after the conference at which some chapters were presented as short papers, because we wanted completely re-worked chapters rather than telegraphic conference drafts. We also wished to include contributions from colleagues who did not attend the conference, but whose works would provide a wider perspective on the subject.

In the first place, we thank the *University of Bretagne-Sud*, the *Centre Alexandre Koyré* (CNRS/EHESS) and *Centre d'Etudes de l'Inde et de l'Asie du Sud* (CNRS/EHESS), who were the main financial supports for the conference, "Conquering New Markets. Trade Routes, Conversion and Missions" held in Paris at the *Centre d'Etudes de l'Inde et de l'Asie du Sud* (CNRS/EHESS) in 2016. The *Institut universitaire de France* was our financial support for the publication.

Along the way, many researchers and technical staff helped at various moments. We thank Antonella Romano, who was among the organizers of the Paris conference. We also thank the commentators at the conference: Charlotte de Castelnau-L'Estoile, Pierre-Antoine Fabre, Marie-Lucie Copete, Corinne Lefèvre. We also thank those who were not able to contribute chapters for their participation and stimulating discussions.

We thank Nadia Guergadj for making maps; Margaret Whibley for copy-editing and "Englishing" most of the texts.

Maps

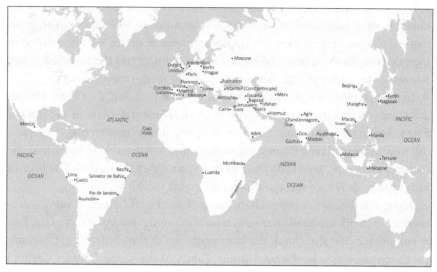

MAP 1   World map

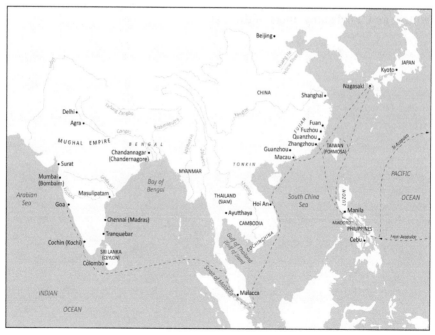

MAP 2   Asia (with trade routes of the great ship of Macau and of the Manila Galleon)

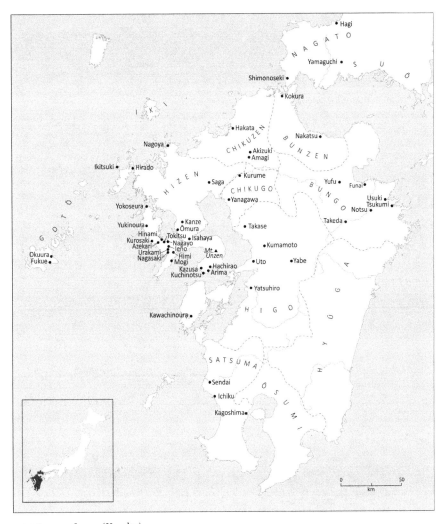

MAP 3   Japan (Kyushu)

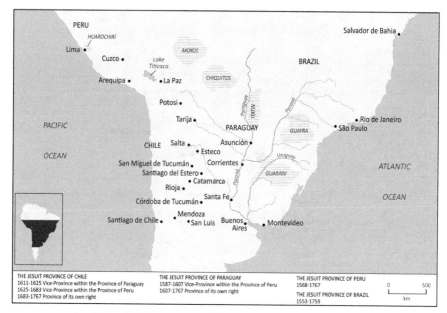

MAP 4   South America (Jesuit provinces)

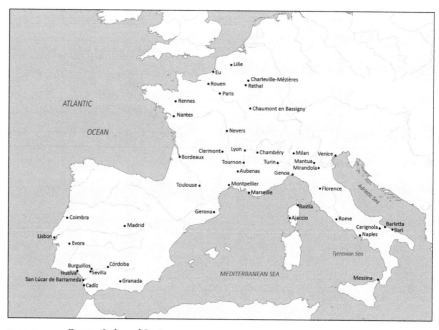

MAP 5   France, Italy and Spain

Illustrations

Abbreviations

ACDF	Archivum Congregationis pro Doctrina Fidei, Rome
AGI	Archivo General de las Indias, Seville
AGOCD	Archivum Generale Ordinis Carmelitarum Discalceatorum, Rome
AHN	Archivo Histórico Nacional, Madrid
AMEP	Archives des missions étrangères de Paris, France
APF	Archivio Storico de Propaganda fide, Rome
ARSI	Archivum Romanum Societatis Iesu, Rome
ASV	Archivio Segreto Vaticano, Rome
BA	Biblioteca Ambrosiana, Milan
BA/JA	Biblioteca da Ajuda/*Jesuítas na Ásia*, Lisbon
BNE	Biblioteca Nacional de España, Madrid
BUG	Biblioteca Universitaria de Granada
DI	Documenta Indica
HJ	*Historia de Japam*
JapSin	*Japonica-Sinica*
MEP	Missions Étrangères de Paris
n.d.	no indication of date
n.p.	no indication of place
RAH	Real Academia de la Historia, Madrid
SC	Scritture riferite nei Congressi
SO	Sanctum Officium
St.St.	Stanza storica

Notes on Contributors

Tara Alberts

is Senior Lecturer in Early Modern History at the University of York (UK). Before joining the Department of History in 2012 she held a Research Fellowship at Jesus College, Cambridge, and was a Max Weber Fellow at the European University Institute, Italy. Her research explores encounters and exchanges between Europe and Asia between c.1500 and c.1700. She published *Conflict and Conversion. Catholicism in Southeast Asia, 1500–1700* (Oxford: Oxford University Press, 2013) and co-edited with D. R. M. Irving, *Intercultural Exchanges in Southeast Asia. History and Society in the Early Modern World* (London: Bloomsbury, 2013).

Ariane Boltanski

is Associate Professor in history at University of Rennes II, France. She is a specialist of the Ancien Régime in France. Her current researches explore pious foundations in France and Italy during sixteenth and seventeenth centuries.

Ryan D. Crewe

is Associate Professor at the University of Colorado, Denver. He is a specialist of colonial Latin America and the Pacific world. He is interested in the politics and economics of religion in early modern colonization, transoceanic migrations and exchanges, and cross-cultural interactions. He recently published *The Mexican Mission. Indiginous Reconstruction and Mendicant Enterprise in New Spain, 1521–1600* (Cambridge: Cambridge University Press, 2019).

Rômulo da Silva Ehalt

is JSPS International Research Fellow at Sophia University, Japan. He is a specialist of the Jesuit mission in Japan. He recently defended a PhD entitled "The Jesuits and the Problem of Slavery in Japan" (Tokyo University of Foreign Studies).

Fabian Fechner

is Postdoctoral Fellow at Fernuniversität in Hagen, Germany. He is a specialist of the Jesuits in Paraguay during the 17th and 18th centuries. He published his PhD thesis on this topic in 2015 (*Entscheidungsprozesse vor Ort. Die Provinzkongregationen der Jesuiten in Paraguay (1608–1762)*. Jesuitica. Quellen und Studien zu Geschichte, Kunst und Literatur der Gesellschaft Jesu im deutschsprachigen Raum 20. Regensburg: Schnell & Steiner, 2015).

Claudio Ferlan

is Researcher at the Italian-German historical Institute in Trent, Italy. His current research explores the historical concept of Patchwork Religion as a spiritual experience characterized by the coexistence of elements from different traditions, religions, exoteric and spiritual movements. He published several books, including *I Gesuiti* (Bologna: Il Mulino, 2015).

Sébastien Malaprade

is Associate Professor at the Université Paris Est-Créteil/CRHEC, France. He is a specialist of the social and economic history of Spain in the Early Modern period. He recently published *Des châteaux en Espagne. Gouvernement des finances et mobilité sociale au XVIIᵉ siècle* (Limoges: PULIM, 2018).

Hélène Vu Thanh

is Associate Professor at the University of Bretagne-Sud/Institut universitaire de France, France. She specializes on the study of missionaries in and around Japan in the 16th and 17th centuries. Her recent research focuses on the funding of the Japanese mission from a local and global perspective. She published *Devenir japonais. La mission jésuite au Japon (1549–1614)* (Paris: Presses universitaires Paris-Sorbonne, 2016).

Christian Windler

is Professor of Early Modern History at the Department of History of the University of Bern. His interest in cross-cultural encounters first resulted in a book on intercultural diplomacy, entitled *La diplomatie comme expérience de l'Autre. Consuls français au Maghreb (1700–1840)* (Geneva: Librairie Droz, 2002). His most recent book is *Missionare in Persien: Kulturelle Diversität und Normenkonkurrenz im globalen Katholizismus (17.–18. Jahrhundert)* (Cologne; Weimar; Vienna: Böhlau, 2019), which is an in-depth investigation of interactions within global Catholicism from the viewpoint of missionaries in Safavid Persia.

Ines G. Županov

is Senior Research Fellow at the *Centre National de la Recherche Scientifique in Paris*, member of the *Centre d'études de l'Inde/l'Asie du Sud* (CNRS-EHESS) and currently posted at the *Centre for Social Sciences and Humanities*, New Delhi. She is a social/cultural historian of Catholic missions in South Asia and has also worked on other topics related to the Portuguese empire. In addition to two other books, her latest monograph, cowritten with Ângela Barreto Xavier, is *Catholic Orientalism, Portuguese Empire, Indian Knowledge, 16th-18th centuries* (New Delhi: OUP, 2015). Her most recent edited volume is *Oxford Handbook of the Jesuits* (New York: OUP, 2019). She has co-edited 10 books and her articles in various languages are published in edited books and journals (*Annales, Representations, Indian Economic and Social History Review, Archives de sciences sociales des religions, Journal of Early Modern History, Journal of Economic and Social History of the Orient, RES: Anthropology and Esthetics*, etc.).

CHAPTER 1

Preface

Ships of Dreams

Hélène Vu Thanh

> After divine grace, what helped us most in making Christians, was the Ship ...[1]

∴

Most missionaries of the modern era would have approved of General Acquaviva's statement when first setting eyes on the new lands they hoped to evangelize, after a long uncertain voyage from which they would, in all likelihood, never return. In this time of widening European horizons, when the "four parts of the world" came to be tied together, the ship became a prominent and versatile symbol, widely used in literature, especially religious literature. The authors of the *Imago primi saeculi* gave it extensive representation in the numerous engravings illustrating the book, which was published in Antwerp in 1640.[2] The book was drafted by Jesuits and their students of the Flemish province to commemorate the Society of Jesus's hundred years of existence. It was as much a homage to the Society's founders as a celebration of the spiritual and material achievements of its members over the century, with a particular emphasis on the order's missionary vocation. From the moment of its publication, the *Imago* was attacked by the Jesuits' enemies: both Protestants and Jansenists denounced the Society's arrogance as well as its casuistical methods. Here is not the place to relate the history of the work or its reception, but it seemed essential to us to highlight the significance of the emblems illustrating the book's

---

1 Words attributed to Acquaviva in 1585 and quoted by Philippe Lécrivain, *Les missions jésuites. Pour une plus grande gloire de Dieu* (Paris: Gallimard, 1991), 2.

2 *Imago Primi Saeculi Societatis Iesu Flandro Belgica Eiusdem Societatis Repraesentata* (Antwerp: Officina Plantiniana, Balthasaris Moreti, 1640).

© HÉLÈNE VU THANH, 2021 | DOI:10.1163/9789004444195_002

six sections.[3] Among them, the image of the ship caught our attention, to the point where we picked it for the cover of the present book.

The ship as an emblem features a dozen times in the *Imago*. The ship symbolizes happy auspices, connected to the missionary vocation of an order founded to bring the word of the gospel to the remotest corners of the world, and echoes Christ's mandate to his apostles: "I shall make you fishers of men."[4] The ship was the providential tool that allowed the missionaries to reach those corners. They braved the elements and the monsters then thought to roam the oceans, with most passengers falling prey to all kinds of terrors and temptations.[5] It was the place where personal virtues could be tested, owing to the harrowing trials experienced during the voyage, as described at length by Francis Xavier in his letter dated November 5, 1549 and addressed to his Jesuit brethren. The founder of the Japanese mission relates the voyage from Malacca to Kagoshima and all the storms he sailed through, which led him to ponder divine grace, temptation and trust placed in God, in whose name the missionary was destined to great achievements.[6] The trials he had to go through were an opportunity to work toward his own salvation, and more importantly, the salvation of the souls to whom he was to bring the word of God. The ocean space thus became the vector for the spreading of the faith and the umbilical cord between the old and new Christian lands. In the process, the ship became a symbol of the mission itself and of the promise of future conversions, in search of which missionaries were ready to face all kinds of adversities, be they spiritual or physical.[7]

It is thus no surprise that the ship found a special place in the imagination of early modern religious men. The evangelical missions cannot be dissociated from this first globalization, as Serge Gruzinski coined it, in the context of which the circulation of men, goods and ideas found unprecedented scope,

---

3 See G. R. Dimler, "The *Imago Primi Saeculi*: the Secular Tradition and the Seventeenth-Century Jesuit Emblem Book," *Thought* 56 (1981): 433–38; Marc Fumaroli, "Baroque et classicisme: L'*Imago primi saeculi Societatis Iesu* (1640) et ses adversaires," in *L'Ecole du silence. Le sentiment des images au XVI* siècle (Paris: Flammarion, 1994), 365–95; John W. O'Malley, ed., *Art, Controversy and the Jesuits: The Imago Primi Saeculi (1640)* (Philadelphia: SJUP, 2015).

4 Matt. 4: 19. See the emblem in *Imago*, 177, representing a fisherman to illustrate "Lucrative poverty."

5 *Imago*, 943–48. On the Jesuit mission at sea, see Liam Matthew Brockey, "Largos caminhos e vastos mares. Jesuit Missionaries and the Journey to China in the Sixteenth and Seventeenth Centuries," *Bulletin of Portuguese/Japanese Studies* 1 (2000): 45–72; Delphine Tempère, "Ce voyage que l'on ignore: la mission jésuite en mer au XVII* siècle," in *Contrabandista entre mundos fronterizos,* ed. Nicolas Balutet et al. (Saint-Denis: Publibook, 2010), 1–18.

6 *Monumenta Xaveriana,* tome 1 (Matriti: Augustin Avrial, 1899–1900), 603–606.

7 See the emblem in *Imago,* 574.

mostly along sea lanes.[8] A fact sometimes neglected: the making of a globalized Catholicism owed much to the profit-driven development of navigation.
The routes of conversion used by the missionaries were none other than the
trade routes linking Europe, the Americas and Asia. In their search for new
markets and products (spices, sugar, silk), the Europeans opened new routes or
found their way into existing ones, always on the lookout for profit-making opportunities. The missionaries followed in their wake; they too in search of new
markets of their own. They hoped to regain contact with old Christian communities in Africa and India, but above all, to found new Christianities. It would
be a mistake to oppose the concurrent quests for profits and souls driving this
two-faced expansion. The merchants were deeply concerned with their own
salvation, and they also understood that the missionaries could be key allies
in opening up new commercial opportunities, owing to their linguistic and
diplomatic skills. Conversely, the missionaries remained deeply dependent on
the merchants for the transportation of men, funds, supplies and letters across
the globe. Well aware that there could be no evangelical mission without the
help of merchants, the missionaries were keen to attend to the dynamics of
sea trade. Francis Xavier thus wrote, in another letter dated November 5, 1549,
and addressed to António Gomes, that the *sine qua non* for the evangelization
of Japan was to draw Portuguese merchants to East Asia with promises of great
profits.[9] He even suggested that a *feitoria* (factory or trading post) be opened
in Sakai, then Japan's central trading hub, and that pepper be bought in small
quantities to maximise the gains. While Francis Xavier stopped short of suggesting that the Jesuits could fund their missions through trade, in his plan
the spiritual and commercial expansion to Japan would go hand-in-hand. This
would become a hallmark of the Society of Jesus, as his successors would not
only work to maintain close links with European merchants, but also become
involved in all sorts of lucrative activities, from the Americas to Asia, in order
to meet their needs and those of their converts. In the process, however, the Society came to be identified as a wealthy institution, attracting fierce criticism
from the other missionary orders, in particular the Mendicants.

The Society was well aware of this danger, as illustrated by the emblem on
the cover of this book, entitled *"Paupertas sapiens."*[10] On the roaring sea, the
ship is heaving dangerously. Men on board are jettisoning crates of goods to
lighten the vessel, as the look-out scans the horizon, hoping for signs of more

---

8   Serge Gruzinski, "Les mondes mêlés de la Monarchie Catholique et autres *connected his-*
       tories," Annales Histoire Sciences Sociales 56ᵉ année/1 (2001): 85–117.

9   *Monumenta Xaveriana*, 648–50.

10   *Imago*, 175. Literally "Wise poverty," and subtitled "let them perish, lest they destroy."

SS. Cosmas & Damianvs confirmatæ Soc. Præstites.

Felicibus auspiciis.

ILLUSTRATION 1.1   Felicibus auspiciis (under happy auspices), *Imago Primi Saeculi* (1640), 46

clement weather. The emblem is followed by a short poem on the necessity of parting from wealth so as to drive the storm away, which concludes: "From time to time loss has to be endured for a profit. Thus wealth is well thrown overboard lest it cause destruction."[11] This emblem seemed to serve as a response to two of the *Imago*'s other emblems, also featuring a ship: one the symbol of the happy auspices under which the Jesuit order was founded (illustration 1.1);[12] the other emphasizing the dangers of ambition, with waves threatening to engulf the ship (illustration 1.2).[13]

In order to fulfill God's will and the destiny ascribed thereto, the vessel that was the Society of Jesus needed firm hands at its helm, whose strength derived

---

11   Translated from Latin in O'Malley, *Art,* 449.
12   *Imago*, 46.
13   *Imago*, 197.

ILLUSTRATION 1.2   Ambitio periculosa (dangerous ambition), *Imago Primi Saeculi* (1640), 197

from the observance of vows, chiefly that of poverty. The emblem was thus also a response to the Jesuits' critics: the vow of poverty had been taken on board and guaranteed the ship's safe journey. Conquering new markets certainly was the great enterprise of many European who left for other continents. But, as the *Imago* reminds us, the missionaries' quest remained focused on the conquest of souls, for therein lay their true profit.

Bibliography

Primary Sources

Imago Primi Saeculi Societatis Iesu Flandro Belgica Eiusdem Societatis Repraesentata. Antwerp: Officina Plantiniana, Balthasaris Moreti, 1640.

Monumenta Xaveriana, tome 1. Matriti: Augustin Avrial, 1899–1900.

Secondary Sources

Brockey, Liam Matthew. "Largos caminhos e vastos mares. Jesuit Missionaries and the Journey to China in the Sixteenth and Seventeenth Centuries." *Bulletin of Portuguese/Japanese Studies* 1 (2000): 45–72.

Dimler, G. R. "The *Imago Primi Saeculi*: The Secular Tradition and the Seventeenth-Century Jesuit Emblem Book." *Thought* 56 (1981): 433–38.

Fumaroli, Marc. "Baroque et classicisme: L'*Imago primi saeculi Societatis Iesu* (1640) et ses adversaires." In *L'Ecole du silence. Le sentiment des images au XVIe siècle*, 365–95. Paris: Flammarion, 1994.

Gruzinski, Serge. "Les mondes mêlés de la Monarchie Catholique et autres *connected histories*." *Annales Histoire Sciences Sociales* 56e année/1 (2001): 85–117.

Lécrivain, Philippe. *Les missions jésuites. Pour une plus grande gloire de Dieu.* Paris: Gallimard, 1991.

O'Malley, John W., ed. *Art, Controversy and the Jesuits: The Imago Primi Saeculi (1640).* Philadelphia: SJUP, 2015.

Tempère, Delphine. "Ce voyage que l'on ignore: la mission jésuite en mer au XVIIe siècle." In *Contrabandista entre mundos fronterizos,* edited by Nicolas Balutet, Paloma Otaola, and Delphine Tempère, 1–18. Saint-Denis: Publibook, 2010.

CHAPTER 2

Profit and Souls in Global Missions (16th–18th Centuries)

An Introduction

Hélène Vu Thanh and Ines G. Županov

1 Economic Globalization and Catholic Missions: Reconciling Commerce and Religion in the Early Modern Period

Starting in the late fifteenth century, the Iberians began projecting their power towards the four corners of the world. While the Spanish quickly concentrated most of their efforts on the appropriation of precious metals from the Americas through large-scale conquest, Portuguese expansion, with more limited territorial ambitions, was essentially driven by the desire to control African and Asian riches, such as gold, spices and slaves, through commercial domination. Europe's main powers followed in the fierce struggle for the control of major trade routes and the profits derived from the circulation of global goods.[1] In this contest, states, and increasingly, prominent private interests, evolved various strategies, the most salient of which was the trade company.

That expansion was matched by the growth of Catholic faith, soon to be reinvigorated through the Council of Trent (1545–1563). As Vasco de Gama's sailor/convict, João Nunes, famously put it when he reached Calicut in 1498, Europeans were on a quest for "Christians and spices." The quote is interesting for the way it combines, without ascribing precedence to one or the other, the Iberians' economic and religious objectives. In contrast, historical research has generally tended to divorce and oppose these two aspects of European expansion. Leading scholars on the Portuguese presence in Asia, for instance, side either with a religious or commercial hypothesis in explaining its genesis.[2] It is only recently that such a dichotomy has been seriously challenged, notably by Giuseppe Marcocci, who has demonstrated how fundamental the association

---

1 Studies on global goods and material culture have proliferated these last years. See for example Giorgio Riello, *Cotton: The Fabric that Made the Modern World* (Leiden; Boston: Brill, 2003) and Anne Gerritsen and Giorgio Riello, eds., *The Global Lives of Things. The Material Culture of Connections in the Early Modern World* (London; New York: Routledge, 2015).

2 See Vitorio Magalhães Godinho, *L'Économie de l'empire portugais aux XVᵉ et XVIᵉ siècles* (Paris: SEVPEN, 1969).

between the two objectives was in Portuguese imperial thought.[3] Such a trend is not specific to Portuguese history and can be observed also in the historiographies of the early modern Spanish, Dutch, English and French empires.[4]

1.1   *Connecting Histories of Missions*

The historiography of the early modern apostolic missions has been similarly demarcated and disconnected: while its renewal in recent years has seen new perspectives emerge on the dynamics of conversions and the circulation of knowledge, investigations into the interplay between economic and missionary expansion have been few, especially when compared to the number of seminal works published over recent decades on economics and religion in the ancient and medieval periods.[5] To be fair, the missionaries themselves kept reaffirming the necessity for keeping matters of faith and wealth strictly separate, quoting from Matthew: "You cannot serve both God and Mammon."[6] It is easy to overstate the implications of such a pledge in the pre-industrial era, when there was no notion of "economy" as a distinct, autonomous domain of human activity, and when reflections on sacred and profane matters went hand-in-hand. In more practical terms, there is no lack of sources demonstrating the many ways missionaries became involved in productive, commercial and financial activities. Such sources include accusations of self-enrichment levelled against religious orders, particularly the one most closely associated with overseas evangelization, the Society of Jesus—these accusations eventually contributed to

---

3 Giuseppe Marcocci, *A consciência de um império. Portugal e o seu mundo (sécs. XV-XVII)* (Coimbra: Imprensa da Universidade de Coimbra, 2012).

4 See for example Paolo Broggio, *La teologia e la politica: Controversie dottrinali, Curia romana e monarchia spagnola tra Cinque e Seicento* (Florence: Leo S. Olschki, 2009); Dana Agmon, *A Colonial Affair: Commerce, Conversion, and Scandal in French India* (Ithaca, NY; London: Cornell University Press, 2017).

5 On religious missions, see for example Charlotte de Castelnau-L'Estoile et al., eds., *Missions d'évangélisation et circulation des savoirs, XVIe-XVIIIe siècles* (Madrid: Casa de Velázquez, 2011); Ronnie Po-Chia Hsia, ed., *A Companion to Early Modern Catholic Global Missions* (Leiden; Boston: Brill, 2018); Ines G. Županov and Pierre-Antoine Fabre, eds., *The Rites Controversies in the Early Modern World* (Leiden; Boston: Brill, 2018). On economics and religion during late antiquity, see Peter Brown, *Through the Eye of a Needle: Wealth, the Fall of Rome, and the Making of Christianity in the West, 350–550 AD* (Princeton, NJ: Princeton University Press, 2012). For the Middle Ages, see Constance Hoffman Berman, *Medieval Agriculture, the Southern French Countryside, and the Early Cistercians: A Study of Forty-Three Monasteries* (Philadelphia: The American Philosophical Society, 1986) and Jacques Le Goff, *La Bourse et la vie: économie et religion au Moyen Âge* (Paris: Hachette, 1986). See also Nicole Bériou and Jacques Chiffoleau, eds., *Économie et religion. L'expérience des ordres mendiants (XIIIe-XVe siècles)* (Lyon: Presses universitaires de Lyon, 2009).

6 Matthew 6:24.

the order's downfall in the eighteenth century, but they were already feeding into anti-jesuitism by the mid-sixteenth century.[7] In Portuguese Asia, a proverb hence advised to "guard your wife from the friars, but watch your wallet with the Jesuits," revealing the prevalence of the stereotype of the missionaries' wealth.[8] The many forms of their involvement in economic activities thus need to be systematically inventoried, although without disconnecting them from the spiritual aims of the order: conversion to Christianity remained the ultimate purpose for the religious who chose to leave Europe for distant, and more-or-less inhospitable lands, which in some cases had hardly been visited, let alone colonized, by Europeans. Their economic and missionary activities must be understood together, as they informed each other in various ways.

Most obviously, the missionaries—and not just the Jesuits—invested in economic activities in order to secure the material support required for their proselytizing activities. A typical case is presented by the Dominicans, who, as soon as they reached the Zambezi in the late sixteenth century, sought to acquire land before turning to trade for their survival, since the Portuguese Crown's donations proved too limited.[9] How did the missionaries reconcile such activities, which meant relying on complex, changing global economic networks, with their evangelical purpose? What role did they come to assume in supporting such networks and, more broadly, in the economy of European overseas empires? Missionaries, just like merchants and other investors, sought the most profitable ventures, as illustrated by Claudio Ferlan's chapter on the Jesuits in Paraguay, who became a leading producer of the then highly popular yerba maté. The same Jesuits chose to acquire shares in the Macau silk trade, which, under the authority of the local Portuguese captain-major, drew considerable profits by bringing high quality Chinese silk to Japan—which was experiencing an unprecedented mining boom—and exchanging it for silver. While for their part not investing in such trade, the Jesuits' Franciscan rivals nevertheless actively strove to help Spanish merchants negotiate trading rights in Japan: the Philippine-based merchants were keen to resell for a profit the silk that Chinese junks brought to Manila and which was traded for American silver. The missionaries were thus involved, directly or indirectly, in the

---

7   See Pierre-Antoine Fabre and Catherine Maire, eds., *Les antijésuites. Discours, figures et lieux de l'antijésuitisme à l'époque moderne* (Rennes: Presses Universitaires de Rennes, 2010).

8   Luke Clossey, *Salvation and Globalization in the Early Jesuit Missions* (Cambridge: Cambridge University Press, 2008), 162–63. Also James S. Cummins, *A Question of Rites: Friar Domingo Navarrete and the Jesuits in China* (Aldershot, UK: Scolar Press, 1993), 27.

9   William Francis Rea, *The Economics of the Zambezi Missions, 1580–1759* (Rome: Institutum Historicum Societatis Iesu, 1976), 28–43.

world-wide circulation of two global commodities, silver and silk, the latter being sold not just in Japan, but also in Europe and New Spain.[10] In the process, they did not shy away from becoming involved in imperial rivalries, as Portuguese and Spanish interests collided in uncolonized Japan.

This example is but one of many illustrating how our understanding of the early modern missions might benefit from a wider, transnational perspective—one that is mindful of connections between the various colonies and outposts of European presence across the world—in contrast with historiographic traditions firmly grounded in national frameworks.[11] In the same way, while the conflicts that arose when imperial networks and their competing commercial and political interests came into contact are easily documented, these should not obscure the quieter relations of cooperation across supposedly antagonistic imperial and religious affiliations. As Luke Clossey, in particular, points out, the missions could not survive on their own, but did so because of the economic and financial relations they tied with various colonies and Europe.[12] "Connected history" thus invites us to put the missions firmly in the context of early modern globalization, in a comparative approach that seeks to understand how each mission managed to insert itself into regional and global economic and imperial networks, whether through competitive struggle or cooperation.

1.2   *Missionaries as Cross-cultural Agents*

The business acumen displayed by the missionaries could be put to various uses, and not just the pursuit of their own interests: other groups and institutions, whether European or local, were keen to mobilize their skills. While this undoubtedly enhanced the missionaries' social position and allowed them to build alliances, it also gave them a singular role in local societies, which could raise eyebrows and earn them enemies as well. That polymorphic and ambiguous social role is yet to be comprehensively assessed. Their work as interpreters in so-called "cross-cultural trade"[13]—lending their linguistic and cultural skills

---

10   Dennis O. Flynn, Arturo Giraldez, "Silk for Silver: Manila-Macao Trade in the 17th century," *Philippine Studies* 44, no. 1 (1996): 52–68.

11   Serge Gruzinski, "Les mondes mêlés de la Monarchie Catholique et autres *connected histories*," *Annales HSS* 56e année/1 (2001): 85–117, and *Les quatre parties du monde* (Paris: Editions de La Martinière, 2004); Sanjay Subrahmanyam, "Holding the World in Balance: The Connected Histories of the Iberian Overseas Empires, 1500–1640," *The American Historical Review* 112, no. 5 (2007): 1359–85.

12   Clossey, *Salvation and Globalization*, 162.

13   Philip D. Curtin, *Cross-Cultural Trade in World History* (Cambridge: Cambridge University Press, 1984). Francesca Trivellato defines intercultural trade as an extended credit or commercial cooperation relationship between merchants belonging to distinct communities.

to help European merchants and officials negotiate with local populations—
is well known, but offers an inaccurately passive image of their function. The
sources indeed reveal a wide berth of activities, such as those famously assumed by João Rodrigues Tçuzu (1561–1663), the Jesuits' most respected lin-
guist, and author of the first Japanese grammar, who served as Shogun Tokugawa Ieyasu's commercial representative in Nagasaki.[14] Missionaries should thus
be regarded as fully-fledged agents, rather than instruments (whether of their
order or of other parties), or maybe even as a specific merchant group, with its
own rules, practices and solidarities, which contributed to shaping economic networks across empires. How sizeable was their impact on world trade?
How strong were their affiliations with empires, and to what extent could they
escape the regulations applicable to ordinary merchants because of their religious status? How did they deal with such regulations when these ran counter
to the interests of the missionary enterprise? Paying attention to the missionaries' agency means identifying individual and collective strategies and understanding their rationale: what gains they were seeking through their involvement, but also what risks they were taking and what challenges they faced.
The so-called Lavalette affair, named after the Jesuit superior for Martinique,
is a telling example of how an individual could, within the bounds of official
regulations—albeit outside his Order's oversight—engage in financial speculation on a grand scale and leave his mission over six million pounds in debt
in 1762.[15] The missionaries' role in economic empire-building, meanwhile, is
probably best highlighted at the margins and frontiers of empires, where the
European presence was limited and vulnerable.[16] In early seventeenth century
Angola, plans were made for the erection of a fort to house the Jesuits, who
were meant to facilitate negotiations with local kingdoms so as to foster trade
in the region.[17] In the case of Japan (and arguably, Macau), the Portuguese
presence was rendered sustainable by the close alliance of merchants and
missionaries, under the auspices of the Goa authorities. The Jesuits were the

See *The Familiarity of Strangers: The Sephardic Diaspora, Livorno, and Cross-Cultural Trade in the Early Modern Period* (New Haven, CT: Yale University Press, 2009), 2.

14   Michael Cooper, *Rodrigues the Interpreter: An Early Jesuit in Japan and China* (New York; Tokyo: Weatherhill, 1974).

15   D. G. Thomson, "The Fate of the French Jesuits' Creditors under the Ancien Régime," *The English Historical Review* 91, no. 359 (1976): 255–77.

16   Malyn Newitt, "Formal and Informal Empire in the History of the Portuguese Expansion," *Portuguese Studies* 17 (2001): 1–21.

17   Diogo Ramada Curto, "Idéologies impériales en Afrique occidentale au début du XVIIᵉ siècle," in *L'Empire portugais face aux autres empires, XVIᵉ-XVIIᵉ siècles*, ed. Luiz Felipe de Alencastro and Francisco Bettencourt (Paris: Maisonneuve et Larose, 2007): 213.

only permanent European presence in Japan, and one of their first commercial endeavors was to arrange with local lords (*daimyō*) the visit of Portuguese merchant ships, in the hope of establishing stable trade routes in East Asia. It is thus necessary to give the missionaries' singular position in the developing world trade the attention it deserves.

2   From the Global to the Local and *Vice Versa*: Rethinking the Missionaries' Social Integration Overseas

2.1   *Funding the Missions*

Assessing the missionaries' involvement in global networks also entails examining their position at a local level, a necessary step, in fact, if one is to understand the economic foundations.[18] A "micro-historical" approach allows for an accurate portrayal of the diversity of the social and economic settings encountered by the missionaries, and of the relationships they built with other agents and groups, whether local or European. For this purpose, it is useful to address the question—which is yet to be systematically examined across the different religious orders—of how missionaries funded their activities.[19]

Historians have devoted much attention to royal patronage, in particular in the case of Iberian missions (*patronato/padroado*), as the major source of funding available to the missionary orders. Kings were assigned by the pope a set of privileges and duties in return for the right of conquest: they were to provide for the building of churches, for supporting the clergy and for funding the missions directed at the non-Christians, while earning the right to appoint bishops and collect tithes. For example, in the bull *Romanus Pontifex* (1455), Pope Nicholas V (1447–1455) confirmed the Crown of Portugal's dominion over lands south of Cape Bojador (present day Morocco). To the Papacy, the

---

18   Francesca Trivellato, "Is There a Future for Italian Microhistory in the Age of Global History?" *California Italian Studies* 2, no. 1 (2011), accessed January 14, 2019, https://escholarship.org/uc/item/0z94n9hq. See also the special issue on global history and microhistories, edited by John-Paul A. Ghobrial in *Past and Present* 242, Issue Supplement 14 (2019).

19   For an overview of the historiography of the Jesuit missions' financing, see Frederik Vermote, "Financing Jesuit Missions," in *Oxford Handbook of the Jesuits*, ed. Ines G. Županov (Oxford: Oxford University Press, 2018), accessed January 9, 2019, http://www.oxfordhandbooks.com/view/10.1093/oxfordhb/9780190639631.001.0001/oxfordhb-9780190639631-e-6. Studies devoted to other religious orders are less numerous. See for instance, on the Discalced Carmelites, Christian Windler, *Missionare in Persien. Kulturelle Diversität und Normenkonkurrenz im globalen Katholizismus (17.–18. Jahrhundert)* (Vienna; Cologne; Weimar: Böhlau, 2018).

Catholic kings' discoveries and conquests were an extraordinary opportunity to win converts and expand the Faith. In return for which rights and privileges, such as commercial monopolies, could be granted. As an arbitrator between Christian princes, the pope was also keen to forbid other European nations, Spain in particular, from infringing on the Portuguese' rights to subjugate the regions they were exploring.[20] In the 1493 bull *Inter coetera*, Pope Alexander VI (1492–1503) recognized Spain's claim to any discovered lands not already held by a Christian prince, while reasserting Portugal's previous rights. The decision's terms were later clarified by both parties through the treaties of Tordesillas (1494) and Zaragoza (1529).

Recent scholarly works have been more interested in exploring the diversity of resources mobilized by the missionaries and have highlighted the pivotal role played by the laity in supporting the missions. Indeed, as royal subsidies all too often proved insufficient or failed to make their way to the missionaries, the latter were left to look for other patrons. Ariane Boltanski's chapter demonstrates how critical French and Italian noble patronage was to the running of Jesuit educational institutions. Sponsorship by the European nobility was not restricted to the "Inner Indies": they were equally interested in overseas missions, with the Bavarian dukes, for instance, among the most prominent donors of the Jesuit Chinese mission.[21] Yet relying on this kind of support involved similar risks as royal patronage: the hazards of navigation and the corrupt practices of imperial agents all too often meant the funds never reached their destination.[22] Securing more reliable local benefactors was thus necessary for the long-term sustainability of the missions. Aliocha Maldavsky, for instance, has shown that the colonists' support was instrumental in the evangelization of Peru, through an analysis of donations and of the pious foundations

---

20   Charlotte de Castelnau-L'Estoile, "Une Église aux dimensions du monde: expansion du catholicisme et ecclésiologie à l'époque moderne," in *Les Clercs et les Princes: doctrines et pratiques de l'autorité ecclésiastique à l'époque moderne*, ed. Patrick Arabeyre and Brigitte Basdevant (Paris: Presses de l'École nationale des Chartes, 2013): 315–18. See also Giovanni Pizzorusso, "Il *Padroado régio* portoghese nella dimensione "globale" della Chiesa romana. Note storico-documentarie con particolare riferimento al Seicento," in *Gli archivi della Santa Sede come fonte per la storia del Portogallo in età moderna*, ed. Giovanni Pizzorusso, Gaetano Platania, Matteo Sanfilippo (Viterbo: Sette Città, 2012), 157–99.

21   Clossey, *Salvation and Globalization*, 174. See also Ronnie Po-Chia Hsia, *Noble Patronage and Jesuit Missions: Maria Theresa Von Fugger-Wellenburg (1690–1762) and Jesuit Missionaries in China and Vietnam* (Rome: Monumenta Historica Societatis Iesu, 2006).

22   See the case of the Japanese mission in Hélène Vu Thanh, "Un équilibre impossible: financer la mission jésuite du Japon, entre Europe et Asie (1579–1614)," *Revue d'Histoire Moderne et Contemporaine* 63, no. 3 (2016): 7–30.

known as *encomiendas*.[23] In uncolonized lands such as China, donations from converts could be a major source of funding, and in the case of Japan, non-Christian friends of the mission could make significant contributions both in silver and in kind.[24] Missions thus survived and grew, thanks to the ability of their members to secure resources at global as well as local levels.

Missionaries imagined solutions other than just reaching out to the laity for support. One which never quite materialized was for the different orders to pool the support and logistical means provided by the state, a strategy which could have improved the reliability and efficiency of royal patronage. One such notable plan was devised in the context of the Iberian Union (1580–1640), under which Portugal and Spain shared the same monarch, although the two empires remained administratively separate. In 1597, the Madrid-based Franciscan procurator for the Philippines, Francisco de Montilla, suggested a single, common supply chain for the various Japanese missions: the Jesuits and the mendicant orders, associated with the Portuguese and Spanish empires respectively, would both use the shorter Atlantic and Pacific sea routes for the shipment of men and supplies.[25] The Jesuit would thus enjoy the benefits of faster shipment, while the sending of missionaries would be less expensive for the Crown. Enduring Iberian rivalries meant the plan was politically unrealistic, however. It is also possible that differences in the way the orders were supported and managed would have made it impractical, but a comparative study would be needed to confirm this. Another solution would have been for the orders to reallocate resources globally, and make sure resource-rich provinces subsidized needier ones. The Franciscans in some cases managed to do just that: their Chinese mission relied on excess funds transferred from New Spain and transited through the Philippines.[26] The Jesuits, for their part, wrote this plan off as impossible, because one of the *Constitutions'* clauses forbade solidarity between missions: each was intended to be financially independent and not accountable for any financial mishaps outside its jurisdiction. In reality,

---

23   Aliocha Maldavsky, "Giving for the Mission: The *Encomenderos* and Christian Space in the Andes of the Late Sixteenth Century," in *Space and Conversion in Global Perspective*, ed. Wietse de Boer et al. (Leiden; Boston: Brill, 2014): 260–84.

24   Gail King, "Candida Xu and the Growth of Christianity in China in Seventeenth Century," *Monumenta Serica* 46 (1998): 49–66; Helena Rodrigues, "Local Source of Funding for the Japanese Mission," *Bulletin of Portuguese/Japanese Studies* 7 (2003): 115–37.

25   Hélène Vu Thanh, "Une désobéissance à l'échelle du monde? Les rapports conflictuels de la mission franciscaine du Japon et des autorités espagnoles (XVIᵉ-XVIIᵉ siècles)," in *Paradigmes rebelles. Pratiques et cultures de la désobéissance à l'époque moderne*, ed. Gregorio Salinero, Águeda García Garrido, and Radu Paun (Geneva: Peter Lang, 2018), 517.

26   Clossey, *Salvation and Globalization*, 187.

Jesuit missions had multiple financial ties with one another: such was the case with the Indian, Japanese and Chinese missions, which until 1611 were part of the same province. The Japanese mission, for instance, owned palm groves in Baçaim, to the north of Mumbai, and relied on the profits they generated. The Goa mission, for its part, accumulated debts towards the Japanese mission by withholding part of the money that was allocated to it by the Crown. By the same token, the Chinese mission was partly funded by the dividends earned from the Japanese mission on the silk trade. And when in 1614 the missionaries were expelled from the country and retreated to Macau, there were heated debates about what to do with the profits from the trade, which continued for a few decades. Should it remain the preserve of a mission which now existed only on paper, or should it be transferred to its then much more promising Chinese counterpart? The latter proposition incensed the Visitor to the East Indies, Sebastião Vieira, who claimed the Chinese mission "wanted to adorn itself with the jewels of others."[27] Studying the financial links between missions hence reveals relationships that involved cooperation and interdependence, but also conflict, rivalry and changing power equilibriums. It also invites us to have a closer look at regional and not just global interactions, as it is mostly at regional and local levels that alternativates to scarce and intermittent funding from Europe were sought. Participation in economic activities, and especially trade, however proved one of the most contentious issues.

2.2   Local Markets, Local Opportunities

Indeed, local donations did not always provide the resources to match the missionaries' ambitions. Seizing local economic opportunities was then the next option, sometimes done as a result of donations. A generous benefactor could bequeath productive land to the orders, such as the Santa Lucía hacienda in New Spain, which became Jesuit property in 1576 and which they turned into an economic powerhouse.[28] Jesuit involvement in this kind of economic activity is now well-documented as far as the Americas are concerned, but there are fewer studies concerned with Asia.[29] This imbalance

---

27   Liam Matthew Brockey, *The Visitor: André Palmeiro and the Jesuits in China* (Cambridge, MA: The Belknap Press of Harvard University Press, 2014), 390.

28   Herman Konrad, *A Jesuit Hacienda in Colonial Mexico: Santa Lucía, 1576–1767* (Mexico: Fondo de cultura económica, 1995), 4.

29   On America, see for instance Magnus Mörner, *The Political and Economic Activities of the Jesuits in the La Plata Region: the Hapsburg Era* (Stockholm: Petherson, 1953); Nicholas Cushner, *Lords of the Land: Sugar, Wine, and Jesuits Estates of Coastal Peru, 1600–1767* (Albany, NY: State University of New York Press, 1980); Sandra Negro, Manuel Marzal, ed., *Esclavitud, economía y evangelización: las haciendas jesuitas en la América*

can be explained by the unequal wealth of sources available, more often scarce and patchy in the case of Asia than in the Americas.[30] In any case, further research is needed on the way the missionaries considered the economic opportunities available to them, based on their understanding of the workings of local societies, which they helped shape. In the case of Japan, the search for local support pushed the Society of Jesus to rely on forms of servitude specific to Japanese society, as demonstrated in Rômulo da Silva Ehalt's chapter. The Jesuits, at the insistence of local lords (*daimyō*), accepted contributions in corvée labor, which provided them with various services and resources in kind. The Jesuits minutely studied the Japanese corvée (*kuyaku*) system, which became an indispensable source of supplies for the missionaries' everyday survival. Meanwhile, the Society's dependence on the income from the Macau silk trade, combined with the wish to create a safe haven for converts facing the persecutions of hostile *daimyō*, led the missionaries to accept the donation of the village of Nagasaki by the Ōmura daimyō in 1580. As the fishing village quickly grew into Japan's only Christian town and a major regional trading hub, the Jesuits came to oversee many aspects of its administration, and in particular the running of its thriving port. However, the missionaries' influence can also be witnessed in Middle East or American colonial societies. Felicita Tramontana examines how the Franciscans in Palestine became involved in the local economy. Not mere consumers of daily commodities, they took part in the production and trade of craftwork, contributing to the refinement of local skills, and also invested in rural property, which was managed by the local population.[31] In the case of Mexico, the

---

virreinal (Lima: Pontifica universidad católica del Perú, 2005). On Asia, see Charles Boxer, *Portuguese Merchants and Missionaries in Feudal Japan, 1543–1640* (London: Variorum reprints, 1986); Frederick Vermote, "The Role of Urban Real Estate in Jesuit Finances and Networks between Europe and China, 1612–1778" (PhD diss., University of British Columbia, 2013).

30   On sources about the Jesuit mission in China, see Noël Golvers, *François de Rougemont S. J., Missionary in Ch'ang-Shu (Chiang-Nan): A Study of the Account Book (1674–1676) and the Elogium* (Leuven: Leuven University Press, 1999). On America, see Julia J. S. Sarreal, *The Guaraní and Their Missions: A Socioeconomic History* (Stanford, CA: Stanford University Press, 2014). Sarreal studied the Jesuit mission in Paraguay from its birth in the sixteenth century to its dissolution in the eighteenth, but her quantitative analysis only covers the seventeenth to eighteenth century period, due to the lack of sources on the first part of the mission's history.

31   Felicita Tramontana, "Trading in Spiritual and Earthly Goods. Franciscans in Semi-rural Palestine," in *Catholic Missionaries in Early Modern Asia. Patterns of Localization*, ed. Nadine Amsler et al. (London; New York: Routledge, 2020), 130–32.

Jesuits' influence on local economic life, owing to their ownership of the Santa Lucía hacienda, on which hundreds of slaves and workers toiled, contributed to the stratification of local society in a distinctive manner. While social and labor status was usually coterminous with race and class origins in colonial society, Konrad shows that around Santa Lucía, work roles alone were more decisive in determining social position. The hacienda's administrators indeed organized work relations through an original system where retribution, food rations and obligations were assigned on an individual basis.[32] In passing, the case illustrates that the missionaries should not be seen as the mere instruments of colonial order, even when they contributed substantially to its economic life. By the same token, while the missionaries were keen to keep their business thriving, the indigenous population, including converts, should not be assumed to have been passive agents. On the contrary, they devised strategies to make the most of the special economic conditions created by the missionaries. The Jesuit reductions in Paraguay (*reducciones* or fixed villages) provide examples of such strategies. For the Guaraní, the reductions may have meant a brutal change in living conditions, including forced sedentism, but that does not mean the people were passive recipients of the Society's instructions. Julia S. Sarreal reveals the full berth of the Guaraní leaders' agency, as the latter were entrusted with key roles in running the reductions.[33] The Guaraní benefitted from the reductions economically and the Jesuits offered protection from slave hunters (*bandeirantes*) coming from Brazil. But things did not go as smoothly in other regions: the Society faced accusations of self-enrichment and their activities were deemed shamefully incompatible with their religious calling.

3   Business and Religion: Toward a Missionary-Specific Ethic?

3.1   *Poverty and the Circulation of Wealth*
As far as evangelical missions are concerned, there have been relatively few studies of the theological and moral aspects of religious involvement in economic activities. This may reflect the common assumption that the Catholic Church took an interest in wealth and trade only to denounce them, while quietly enriching itself at the expense of the faithful—in diametrical opposition to Protestant doctrines, which praised the accumulation of business wealth as

32   Konrad, *A Jesuit Hacienda in Colonial Mexico*, 232.

33   Sarreal, *The Guaraní and Their Missions*, 54.

a divine mandate, and which hence allowed for the emergence of capitalism.[34] While this dichotomy usefully highlights substantial doctrinal approaches to business and wealth among the Christian denominations, it also oversimplifies and exaggerates them. As the historiography of the medieval era has abundantly shown, theologians took a keen interest in economic realities as early as the thirteenth century, in the context of flourishing Italian merchant cities. The religious orders, in particular the mendicants, took a stance on a wide range of issues pertaining to wealth, its administration and its circulation, in ways that defy caricature.[35] Yet in the new world of economic exchanges that was emerging with the early modern globalization, how did the Church's view of economic activities, and of the pillar of religious life that was poverty, evolve? How did newer religious orders, such as the Society of Jesus, consider such issues, and how far did their position depart from those of the other orders? What is certain is that the missionaries' growing business activities became a frequent source of tension. Canon 142 of the *Codex Juris Canonici* indeed barred religious men from taking part in many business activities and from any kind of trading, but such prohibitions were often ignored, with few consequences. In this context, of particular interest are the debates and controversies that arose among the missionary orders—with all their accusations, defenses and rationalizations—on issues of commerce and religion.[36]

The missionary orders were far from settled on a unanimous position. The Jesuits defended a narrow interpretation of the proscription, which in their view only applied to goods bought and sold with the intent of making a profit. It could reasonably be assumed that such intent was foreign to the missionaries, dedicated as they were to the subsistence of their missionary project and to the promotion of Christian charity. Such was the argument put forward by the Visitor to the East Indies, Alessandro Valignano (1539–1606), in defense of the Society's investment in the silk trade between China and Japan. In contrast, the Franciscans in Japan ostensibly conformed to their order's rules and to the poverty ideal: they owned neither the land nor the buildings that housed them and subsisted only on alms given by the

---

34   The idea was famously put forward by Max Weber, *The Protestant Ethics and the Spirit of Capitalism*, trans. Stephen Kalberg (Oxford: Oxford University Press, 1964, 2010), and was in turn criticized by Fernand Braudel in *La dynamique du capitalisme* (Paris: Arthaud, 1985).

35   For an overview of the medieval historiography on those issues, see Valentina Toneatto, "La richesse des Franciscains. Autour du débat sur les rapports entre économie et religion au Moyen Âge," *Médiévales* 60 (2001), accessed January 11, 2019, doi: 10.4000/medievales.6220.

36   John P. Beal, *New Commentary on the Code of Cannon Law* (New York; Mahwah, NJ: Paulist Press, 2000), 378.

local population. Valignano's project was incompatible with the Franciscan principle of administrating the order's collective property in a completely disinterested manner, a situation which the Visitor recast as an opposition between Jesuit prudence and Franciscan insouciance: instead of planning for their subsistence, the latter left it all to divine Providence and the observance of the Gospel. Conversely, the Franciscans routinely made scathing attacks against the Jesuits, accusing them of having renounced their vow of poverty. It is true that the Japanese context particularly invited conflict, as the mendicant orders spent decades bitterly challenging the Jesuits' legal monopoly on the country. Yet Japan was no exception: the same kind of conflict can be observed in the case of Brazil, where Manuel de Nóbrega (1517–1570) also had to defend, against Franciscan attacks, the Society's decision to participate in trade so as to minimize its dependence on the Crown. Nóbrega advocated a pragmatic position, according to which one should do one's utmost to support evangelization, or, to put it in another way, that the ends justify the means.[37] Controversies also arose within the orders and not just between them.[38] In the case of the Society of Jesus in Japan, the superior, Francisco Cabral (1529–1609), was critical enough of the Visitor's choices to end up being removed from the country by the latter.[39] These controversies, whether internal or external to the orders, reached well outside missionary circles and in fact received worldwide publicity, owing to the abundant correspondence with Europe and the circulation of printed diatribes and defenses. Such debates on the proper relation between commerce and religion, which primarily involved the missionaries, their orders' leadership, as well as the papacy, are thus worthy of closer examination.

3.2   *Making Profit: Economic Exchanges and Apostolic Purposes*

At the heart of the discussions were a number of key notions, such as that of profit. Historians have often looked at the notion from the perspective of present economic realities. In this context, the missionaries, in particular the members of the Society of Jesus, have been portrayed as animated by a rational search for better returns on investment, and as such, as forerunners of

---

37   Luiz Fernando Conde Sangenis, "Controvérsias sobre a pobreza: franciscanos e jesuítas e as estratégias de financiamento das missões no Brasil colonial," *Estudos Históricos* 27, no. 53 (2014): 27–48.

38   Michela Catto, *La Compagnia divisa: il dissenso nell'Ordine gesuitico tra '500 e '600* (Brescia: Morcelliana, 2009).

39   Liam Matthew Brockey, "Authority, Poverty and Vanity: Jesuit Missionaries and the Use of Silk in Early Modern East Asia," *Anais de história de além-mar* 17 (2016): 179–222.

capitalism.[40] Charles Boxer presented the Society of Jesus as the "world's first multinational corporation." This point of view was later criticized by Dauril Alden in *The Making of an Enterprise*, his influential work on the financing of the Jesuit Portuguese assistance, which spanned the globe from Brazil to Asia.[41] Alden indeed highlights the Society's methodical search for means of supporting itself and the way its financial structures intertwined with those of the Portuguese Empire, but he also points out that Jesuits' trading operations never were on a scale comparable to that of the Dutch and English companies. Alden's model however sidelines the Jesuits' main purpose, conversion to Catholicism, to which the search for finance was always subordinate. The Jesuits' financial and administrative shrewdness has also been questioned recently: Julia Sarreal has demonstrated how the Jesuits' methods in Paraguay proved increasingly inefficient, particularly during the eighteenth century, while James Riley has stressed the need for a more dynamic understanding, considering the substantial changes that can be observed in the Jesuits' management of their property over time.[42] It is therefore necessary to move away from the birth-of-capitalism framework, or at least from the perception of the Jesuits as pioneers of economic rationality, and instead set the order's practices firmly within the missionary project. How did religious principles structure the missionaries' business practices?[43] Addressing this question calls for a comparison with the practices of other economic actors (state agents, private merchants and producers, trade companies), so as to reveal the missionaries' specificities in this domain. This is what Julia Sarreal began doing with her study of the Paraguay missions, as she compared the Jesuits' way of managing the mission's property with the methods later used by the agents of the Crown once it took over. Sarreal describes the shift from a collectivist-oriented organization, where profits serve the community, to a more individualist management of land—a shift that did not result in a dramatic improvement in productivity.[44] Meanwhile,

---

40   See for example Nicholas Cushner, *Farm and Factory: The Jesuits and the Development of Agrarian Capitalism in Colonial Quito 1600–1767* (Albany, NY: State University of New York Press, 1982).

41   Dauril Alden, *The Making of an Enterprise: The Society of Jesus in Portugal, its Empire and Beyond, 1540–1750* (Stanford, CA: Stanford University Press, 1996).

42   Sarreal, *The Guaraní and Their Missions*, 7. James D. Riley, "The Wealth of the Jesuits in Mexico, 1670–1767," *The Americas* 33, no. 2 (1976): 227–28.

43   A few works have studied the influence of Jesuit spirituality and of the *Spiritual Exercizes* of Ignatius of Loyola on their accounting pratices. See Paolo Quattrone, "Accounting for God: Accounting and Accountability Pratices in the Society of Jesus (Italy, XVI-XVII centuries)," *Accounting, Organizations and Society* 29 (2004): 647–83.

44   Sarreal, *The Guaraní and Their Missions*, 115.

it is equally important to take into account the way missionaries perceived economic exchanges and the ethical-normative frame that governed the religious administration of wealth. This can be carried out by examining theological categories and, more broadly, the vocabulary used by the missionaries, as exemplified by Giacomo Todeschini's works on the medieval era.[45] Todeschini analyzed the phrases ecclesiastics used to describe their everyday business, inviting us to pay attention to the construction of notions such as *avaritia*, *usura*, *caritas* or administration, and to the discursive systems they formed. In the case studies in this volume, a key object of analysis should thus be the missionaries' conceptualization of globalized economic exchanges, which needs to be approached in close relation to the missionaries' apostolic purpose. This in turn means examining not just accounting documents, but a wide range of administrative and theological sources. An example is provided by Charlotte de Castelnau and Carlos Zeron, who studied the Brazilian Jesuit mission's project to reform the *aldeias* (Indian groups settled in villages led by missionaries) at the beginning of the seventeenth century, and demonstrated how it was in part structured by a dual economic and spiritual logic.[46] The aldeias were meant to be supported by sugar-cane mills, then an expanding business. Work in the mills was intended to stimulate the Indians' spiritual progress, but also the missionaries' evangelical zeal: the notion of profit here took on a dual meaning, both material and spiritual.

Missionaries reflected not just on their own economic activities, but also took an interest in the wider context of economic exchange. That brings us to the question of how religious norms shaped everyday business practices, in particular in matters of trade, and what kind of influence the missionaries exerted on other economic actors. How did such norms, grounded as they were in scholastic and moral philosophy, evolve in the context of the early modern globalization? Several authors have thus underscored the influence that theologians wielded on trade in European empires. Carlos Zeron has highlighted the contribution made by Jesuits and other Portuguese theologians and canon law scholars to theories about, and the legal regulation of the pillar of the colonial

---

45   Giacomo Todeschini, *Richesse franciscaine. De la pauvreté volontaire à la société de marché* (Lagrasse: Verdier, 2008) and *Les Marchands et le Temple. La société chrétienne et le cercle vertueux de la richesse du Moyen Âge à l'époque moderne* (Paris: Albin Michel, 2017).

46   Charlotte de Castelnau-L'Estoile and Carlos Zeron, "Une mission glorieuse et profitable. Réforme missionnaire et économie sucrière dans la province jésuite du Brésil au début du XVIIe siècle," *Revue de synthèse* 2–3 (1999): 335–58.

economy that was slavery.[47] As Zeron demonstrates, the Jesuits were able to influence regulations so as to protect Indians from enslavement, advocating instead the exploitation of enslaved Africans. In fact, a specific Jesuit slave trade
was organised between the Brazilian province and the Angola mission towards
the end of the sixteenth century. Theologians were also concerned with the
spiritual aspects of trade with non-Christians, and especially Muslims, in Africa and around the Indian Ocean. While the rhetoric of the Crusade was still
pervasive and canon law in principle banned the selling of arms, horses, metal
and timber to Muslims, which might be used against Christians, diverse inter-
faith trade relations prospered. Giuseppe Marcocci has shown how the theologians' discourse was mobilized by the Portuguese Crown to tighten its control
over merchants in the context of rapidly expanding private trade. The church's
prescriptions hence became a political and economic tool used by the Crown
in its effort to keep overseas trade under its control.[48]

Finally, a study on economics and evangelization would not be complete
without an examination of the consequences of conversion on the new Christians' economic practices, and of the weight of the new prescriptions imposed
on them, in particular in the context of societies that were not ruled by Europeans. Missionaries there were confronted with economic practices that Christianity condemned, but that were both legal and commonplace. This was the
case with moneylending in Japan in particular, which in some contexts was
even considered a charitable act. Should converts be forbidden from lending
money with interest, and when they did so, should they be ordered to return
the interest money, as prescribed by canon law? This is the kind of question
that Jesuit missionaries submitted to the theologian, Francisco Rodrigues,
testing the limits of the Japanese mission's purported "exceptionalism."[49] The
"doubts" (dubia) in which missionaries described their dilemmas, as well as
the confession manuals, are therefore promising sources for identifying the
specific issues arising in the peculiar context of the missions. A distinctive

---

47   Carlos Zeron, *Ligne de foi. La Compagnie de Jésus et l'esclavage dans le processus de for-
      mation de la société coloniale en Amérique portugaise (XVIᵉ-XVIIᵉ siècles)* (Paris: Honoré
      Champion, 2009).

48   Giuseppe Marcocci, "Trading With the Muslims: Religious Limits and Proscriptions in
      the Portuguese Empire (ca. 1480–1570)," in *Religion and Trade: Cross-cultural Exchanges
      in World History, 1000–1900*, ed. Francesca Trivellato, Leor Halevi and Cátia Antunes
      (Oxford: Oxford University Press, 2014): 91–107.

49   Ana Fernandes Pinto and Silvana Remedio Pires, "The 'resposta que alguns padres de
      Japao mandaran preguntar': a Clash of Strategies," *Bulletin of Portuguese/Japanese Studies*
      11 (2005): 9–60.

missionary casuistry of exchanges was indeed emerging, owing to the circulation of questions and opinions across the four continents.[50]

4   Chapter Contributions: Lived and Imagined Order of Missionary Economy

The chapters in the volume are loosely grouped under four thematic nodes, but in fact relate on all levels and their sources and conclusions mostly propose similar arguments. There are no exceptions to the fact that missions and missionaries were deeply involved in the economic and financial lives of the places—as distant as Paraguay and Nagasaki—they came to inhabit and administer.

In the opening chapter of this volume—"The Cross and the Silk: Trading Activities by the Society of Jesus in Japan (1549–1650)"—Hélène Vu Thanh examines the evolving role of the Jesuit missionaries in Japan, from simple translators and commercial mediators between Portuguese and Japanese traders to commercial investors in their own right, and finally to administrators of the port town of Nagasaki from 1580s onwards. In a finely-grained analysis, she details the changing political circumstances in which Jesuits had to deal with multiple agents, all of them involved in one way or another in the profitable trade exchanging Chinese silk for Japanese silver.

The rise and fall of the Jesuit economic, administrative and utopian bubble in Nagasaki has been recently studied, the author points out, by historians interested in this exemplary urban Christian town in Asia, but a global approach to the aspect of the trade in which Jesuits directly participated is still undeveloped. The role of Jesuit procurators and the process of missionary integration into Nagasaki's political and social structure are especially addressed in this chapter, which focuses very closely on local aspects of commercial activities. As a result, she relies on the "global micro-history" approach to trace the multiple interests of the commercial agents in the city and their entangled relations. The fragility of intercultural trade has been studied in many other contexts in recent scholarship, but the Japanese case is important both because of its initial success and its ultimate failure.

---

50   Giuseppe Marcocci, "Conscience and Empire: Politics and Moral Theology in the Early Modern Portuguese World," *Journal of Early Modern History* 18 (2014): 487–88. See also Odd Langholm, *The Merchants in the Confessional: Trade and Price in the Pre-Reformation Penitential Handbooks* (Leiden: Brill, 2003).

In the first section, we are presented with the major actors in this mercantile fable turned tragedy: Portuguese merchant diaspora, Japanese lords or
daimyō, and Jesuits as cultural mediators and translators. The Jesuits thus imposed themselves as go-betweens, negotiators and deal makers with a view to
redirecting sufficient profit for the funding of their missions and churches, and
acquiring concessions for further Christianization of Kyushu, its islands and
the regions further north.

With the arrival of Alessandro Valignano, as is well known, the sedentariza-
tion of the missions received an additional impetus and his ambitious project
of establishing educational institutions and recruiting local Christians into the
Jesuit order proved very costly, stretching precarious Jesuit finances to the limits. Since the papal and royal subsidies trickled slowly and irregularly—some
were also captured in Goa, according to Valignano's complaints—the decision
was made to invest in China's silk trade (*nau do trato*). The initial sum came
from Luís de Almeida (c.1523–1583), a Jesuit who bequeathed his personal fortune (4,000 ducats) to be invested in the China trade. This arrangement was
successful for a while, before criticisms from other Jesuits and Franciscan
missionaries became louder and profits dwindled due to a changing political
situation.

One of the key Jesuit actors, according to the author, was a procurator of
Japan. This important Jesuit office, according Vu Thanh, reveals "the confusion
between the roles of mediator and participant in the commercial activities."
The procurator had the most difficult task of giving assurances to all parties
that the deal was trustworthy and thence consolidate the position of the Society of Jesus in the local political hierarchy. However, whatever schemes were
adopted, such as *respondência* bonds, the Jesuits ran a deficit and were chron-
ically short of money, unable to financially withstand events such as ship-
wrecks and other types of calamities. One way to strengthen their position in
the society, and preserve their reputation as trusted arbiters of intercultural
commerce, was to take up legislative and judicial authority in the city as bestowed on them by the daimyo Ōmura. However, the arbitration between Japanese and Portuguese merchants only undermined Jesuit reputation and trust-
worthiness, since the politically sensitive decisions they had to take were not
always impartial. They were thus accused of privileging Japanese merchants.

The breakdown of the Jesuit monopoly and grip over Nagasaki, precipitated
by the Franciscan arrival, is well known, as is its ending in persecution and
martyrdom in 1597. According to the author, the growth of Nagasaki and the
growing power of the shōgun and his interest in taking hold of administration
of the city, made the situation for the Jesuits unsustainable. The Jesuit economic utopia was about to end, but not without ugly internal strife within the

order in Japan and Macau and with other ecclesiastical actors (Franciscans and Dominicans).

The decrees of 1612 and 1614 prohibited Christianity, and from then on the Jesuits were only able to stay on clandestinely, although they continued their trade ventures for some time, as if hoping the political tide would change. By the 1620s, however, the Jesuit had reoriented the trade towards south-east Asia. The mission in Japan failed, but the Jesuits learnt an important lesson: the only way to survive and expand was by finding and maintaining a balance between local and global trade. Even more importantly, they realized that investing in land ownership rather than relying solely on maritime trade may be a better policy for the survival of their missions and settlements.

Across the oceans, on the other side of the planet in the Americas, a settler economy and colonial possession of land had been developing from the early sixteenth century. The Jesuits who arrived relatively late, after the mendicant orders, reproduced some of the same models of economic activity as in Asia. The story of the commercialization of yerba maté is not identical to the story of silver for silk trade in Japan, however. Claudio Ferlan, in his chapter—"*Yerba Maté* in the Jesuit Reductions: From Ritual Drink to Economic Resource (17th-18th Centuries)"—weaves a fascinating history of the plant (*Ilex paraquariensis*) discovered in the Upper Paraná region, today shared by Paraguay and southern Brazil, as early as 1554. Its cultivation and commercialization were closely connected to exploitation of the native Tupi-Guaraní population in the area, bringing both profit and disaster to local communities. Ferlan's rich fresco includes the ups and down of the cultivation and trade of the leaves of yerba mate, likened, in the beginning, to other demonic and superstition-ridden drinks and substances also discovered in the Americas, such as chocolate and tobacco. The profitability of trade overwrote the negative assessment of the plant and made it into an important commodity for the *encomenderos*—former *conquistadores*—and for the Jesuit reductions. After defining it as a "secular" product like Chinese tea, consumption of yerba maté, stimulated by its slightly addictive quality, spread widely within Spanish colonial America. From a staple food supplement with certain useful and thaumaturgic qualities, observed both by the Guaraní and the Spanish, the maté became a commercial success. The European settlers in America developed, according to Ferlan, "a material culture relating to this special plant: the bowl and the straw (*bombilla*) acquired an economic and symbolic meaning." The author argues that drinking maté turned into a marker of social status, with the utensils used for drinking even becoming artistic objects. Most importantly, it transformed a plant used for private consumption by indigenous people into a marketable commodity, and thus contributed, sadly, to the extreme exploitation of the Tupi-Guaraní.

The collection of the leaves in far away *yerbales*, a time-consuming and dangerous activity, and later on cultivation of the trees closer to inhabited localities, became a matter of rivalry between the settlers, *encomenderos* and the Jesuit reductions. The chapter follows various actors: Jesuit missionaries trying to gain profit for the sake of maintaining missions; *bandeirantes* raiding the villages producing yerba maté; and theologians and Spanish administrators trying to understand and apply canonical and colonial laws to maintain "justice" and order by curbing unnecessary exploitation of the native labor. As Ferlan shows, most of the important official decisions taken by ecclesiastical and colonial authorities—such as reminding priests and missionaries of the church interdiction against commerce—remained mostly dead letters. However, concessions were made to the religious orders, Jesuits included, such as tax-free export of a defined quota of the product. In 1667, the Buenos Aires *Audiencia* granted the Jesuits the right to export a quota (12,000 *arrobas*) to the Santa Fe market. It was such and similar concessions that got the missions going, since, as in Asia, the money promised by the royal treasury was too slow in trickling down if it came at all.

Of course, for Jesuits, the profits from this trade and other economic activities were only means to a higher end: creating new, perfect Christian communities among the former "pagan" nomads. Settling them down into reductions was seen as a means of educating them in civilized, land-bound life (or organized labor) and teaching them corporeal and social discipline as it was conceived and defined by Church legislation. In their effort at rational administration and toward the survival of their communities, the Jesuits engaged their resources in purchasing estates (*estancias*) and stimulating cereal and cattle production in addition to earning extra cash through yerba maté production.

As is well known, Jesuit-run enterprises hit the wall when the order was expelled from the Vice-royalty, perhaps precisely because the Christian "welfare" *avant la lettre*, for the Amerindians that the Jesuits tried to enforce and maintain, with ever more difficulty, clashed with the political/territorial/economic processes of consolidation taking place within Spanish and Portuguese colonies. While commercialization of yerba maté made the Jesuit fortune needed for the mission, it also proved perilous for the preservation of the way of life of their missionary charges.

The third chapter—"From Tenants to Landlords: Jesuits and Land Ownership in Japan (1552–1614)"—by Rômulo da Silva Ehalt takes up where Hélène Vu Thanh left off. It addresses in minute detail and from new archival materials the question of land donations and the subsequent Jesuit landownership in Japan. That the Japan Jesuits were also on the receiving end of land donations is a topic that has received little attention from historians. The donation of the small village of Nagasaki in 1580 has to be understood as the result of a particular political constellation amidst the conflict between minor and major warlords in the region. According to Japanese sources, studied by Ehalt, Jesuits also received other villages, ports and lands in addition to Nagasaki. Some of those forgotten donations appear in Jesuit documents as well, such as on the list compiled by Sebastião de Almeida. These under-studied texts provide a clue to the degree of Jesuit social, cultural and economic embeddedness in Japan. The author persuasively argues that the Jesuits were active and willing landlords, who understood that compared to trade, land ownership was a key to stable income, and that in attracting new donations they were in fact emulating local Buddhist organizations. Not only was land tenure profitable, it also denoted their political power, their "level of integration in local networks and their deep understanding of the social and political background of Japanese society." The problem was historical timing, since from 1587 Toyotomi Hideyoshi started to reform and change land policies and thus the Jesuits also became his political targets.

In 1552, the first real estate donation to the Jesuits was a Buddhist temple in Yamaguchi, bestowed on them by Ōuchi Yoshinaga (1532–1557) a leader of the Ōuchi clan, which was dependent on maritime trade. Other donations followed, connected also with the warlord's protection. Apart from temples, Jesuits also received donations of cities such as Hakata, and the revenues from these places provided a small but steady income, at least when they were not contested by other actors. From 1560, according to Ehalt, the Jesuits made more aggressive efforts in "amassing land and revenues," such as the important western city of Hakata and Yokoseura, a small port in the north of the Sonogi Peninsula. These acquisitions established a new pattern with wider administrative rights, and often included the stipulation that the inhabitants be exclusively Christian.

According to Ehalt, there was a discrepancy between the amount of revenue collected by the donator's clan and the much lesser sum paid to the Jesuits. On the other hand, the values were calculated in silver and thus probably reimbursed in cash. Of course, this was a dress-rehearsal for Nagasaki, but as the Jesuits learnt to their own cost, donations could both be given and taken away. Thus they lost many places, including Nagasaki in 1587 when Hideyoshi took over. Moreover, the strained relations and constant fighting between the clans made the flow of revenue income uncertain.

Some Jesuit landholdings were purchases rather than donations, but various Jesuits had scruples about this kind of monetary acquisition. Alessandro Valignano allowed the purchase of land under exceptional circumstances in regions under Christian warlords, in order to safeguard investments. He justified this

decision in a letter to Claudio Acquaviva (1543–1615), Superior General of the
Society of Jesus, in 1583 by citing problems with the *nau do trato*.

In 1592 the priests decided to invest massively in real estate. It was a rather
badly chosen moment, given that they were already under Hideyoshi's expulsion order, but it was also a decision that provoked conflict within the Society.

Besides urban revenue, Jesuits also acquired access to revenues from agricultural production, as well as labor and supplies obtained from locals. These
donations confirmed Jesuit political authority in the region. The term *chigyō*
used for this kind of land tenure—in which "the administration of the entire
villages was given to the donatory"—refers to both political power and the
land itself, but was explained as *possessio* in the Latin-Portuguese-Japanese
dictionary of 1595. One fascinating part of this chapter is Ehalt's effort at sys-
tematizing and showing the problems both the Jesuits and the author faced in
providing comparisons and analogies between Japanese and European land
tenure terminology and the legal authority such possession entailed.

The question of slavery, servitude and corvée labor is also addressed in the
chapter. Jesuit documents mention unpaid labor as *kuyaku*, and translate it as
"public service," while Japanese historians refer to it as a kind of corvée. According to Ehalt, the Jesuits nevertheless understood the way *kuyaku* worked
(resembling servitude and corvée labour) and made good use of it. Jesuits were
known for their creative and experimental solutions, but according to Ehalt, it
seems the model of land ownership and financial arrangements in the local
setting came from Buddhist monasteries.

Christian Windler, in his contribution—"Going Local, Becoming Global: The Connected Histories of Early Modern Missionary Economies in Persia and on the Persian Gulf"—sets out to answer questions relating to missionary integration into local societies by looking into the material resources
they had at hand at any given moment. How much did they receive as "seed
money" from Europe and how much were they able to generate *in loco*? The
main focus of his study is the case of the Italian congregation of the Discalced
Carmelites in Persia and in the Persian Gulf, where some of its members had
been sent by a Roman Curia desirous of converting Muslims to Christianity,
negotiating an alliance with the Safavids and convincing Eastern Christians
to enter into a union with the Church of Rome. In a parallel move, the Portuguese king dispatched Augustinians from Goa with the same task and thus in
the seventeenth century, these first missionary sentinels were joined by Jesuits,
Dominicans, Capuchins and the priests who belonged to the Société des Missions étrangères de Paris (MEP). The patchwork of European religious orders
was anything but harmonious. It was an effect of the power struggle between
the Roman Curia and its newly established missionary agency—Congregation

for the Propagation of the Faith (*Propaganda Fide*) founded in 1622—and the Portuguese padroado, and, from the end of the 1620s, the French Crown.

In the first part of his contribution, Windler takes a long look into the discrepancy in perspectives concerning the funding of the missions between Roman Discalced Carmelite headquarters and Propaganda Fide, and the missionaries in Persia. On the basis of archival documents still scarcely studied, he argues that the funding coming from Rome was insufficient for conducting missionary operations, which compelled the missionaries to raise funds locally. In their quest for financial security the missionaries engaged in activities perceived as scandalously "worldly" in Rome. Rules prohibiting trade by the regulars were applied to the Jesuits here, as in Japan and elsewhere, but as in those cases the fine points were constantly on the negotiating table. Among the negotiating chips were missionaries' assiduous and perpetual complaints and jeremiads of insufficient funds addressed to Rome. In Windler's words, these complaints had the symbolic value of legitimizing financial activities that frankly contravened papal orders. By looking into two Discalced Carmelite account books from Basra for the period between 1674 and 1727, and then from 1727 to 1772, the contours of the convent economy become less blurred, in spite of the admitted imprecision in account recording. For example, rose water and wine (from their local vineyard), as well as diamonds, appear as some of the traded items, but the most important contributor to their financial security was their hospitality service. They became famous for providing board and lodging to all Christian traders (Protestant and "schismatic" Eastern Christians included), travellers and other missionaries. Their medical and apothecary services were also important, but these do not appear in the account books because they were part of a "gift economy." Acquiring real estate was therefore crucial for the prosperity of the mission, while according to Windler, trade dealings may have been dissimulated in the accounts sent to Rome. Discalced Carmelite convents in Isfahan, New Julfa, and Shiraz had similar strategies for coping with financial insecurity and many of them went against the norms of proper conduct required of the religious order according to the papal prescriptions.

The convent economy in Isfahan, according to Windler, debuted with the concession of land and a house by the shah 'Abbās I on two occasions, and these remained in the missionaries' possession until the end of the mission in the 1750s. Cultivating "friendship" with Asian kings was a widespread missionary strategy throughout the period. Finally, it was the management and maintenance of a network of friends and allies—Catholic, Armenian, Protestant, Muslim and "pagan"—that sustained Discalced Carmelite businesses, some of which, like lending money at interest, would have been considered downright sinful by any respectable Catholic. Although in 1709 the Congregation for the

Propagation of the Faith sent a report to the Holy Office stating that missionaries in Persia had lent money to merchants, and claiming such action licit, no specific sanction against the missionaries had ever been enforced. Windler sums it up in the following statement: "Both the normative universalism and its relativization in lived practice were characteristic of a latent conflict that was experienced by missionaries all over the world." The process of confessionalization meant both the refusal to acknowledge local practices and their tacit toleration.

In his contribution, meteorologically entitled, "Monsoonal Missions: Asian Trade Diasporas in Spanish Missionary Strategies, 1570–1700," Ryan D. Crewe focuses on Spanish Asian missions outside the Philippines with an emphasis on indigenous agency, which "forced course-corrections, experimentation, and adaptations" upon the missionaries, whether they liked these or not. As announced in the title, the missionary agents he follows from Mexico to Philippines to the China Seas and back were embedded in trade networks in maritime Asia and dependent on biannual monsoons. The success of the maritime trading post was premised on conviviality, pluralism and religious tolerance. Ironically, missionaries were therefore taking advantage of the free movement of people and goods only to impose, in theory at least, Roman Catholicism on all Asian peoples. According to Crewe, the missionaries were "specialized intermediaries" with a bundle of political authority from the Spanish patronato, which had been important to the East Asian merchants, working generally on their own and in fact desiring some kind of overarching political framework. What merchants lacked, missionaries had in abundance. Hence the beginning of a useful collaboration in the "contact zones" of maritime Asia, frothing with "perils stemming from miscommunications and miscalibrations." The author sees two strategies at play: one outbound, depending on merchant networks and diplomacy, and the other inbound, working diligently in port cities. In both cases, the missionaries mostly played the role of intermediaries. The first target of their conversion efforts were Chinese Sangley merchants (or Hokkien) for whom the Spanish mendicant missionaries acted as interpreters and mediators with the intention of slowly transforming them into converts. This was a case of Spanish accommodation, so often attributed to missionary endeavors under the Portuguese padroado. The missionaries were so desirous and impatient to reach China that in an extreme secular gesture, and as part of their outbound strategy, they offered themselves to Hokkiens as slaves.

The mendicants' dreams of the conquest of China were based on theories developed from early Jesuit descriptions of the Chinese as highly civilized people, lacking only the Christian message. At the same time, since foreigners were banned from the Middle Kingdom, the Hokkien merchants were reluctant to admit these Christian hotheads on the junks loaded with American silver on their return journeys to the Chinese continent. Two Augustinians, Fray Martín de Rada and Fray Jerónimo Martín, did reach Fujian and their approach shifted from the outbound strategy of commerce to high diplomacy, but the Chinese authorities kept the Iberians at bay and not much came out of the projected spiritual conquest.

With China not responding to their enthusiasm, the outbound strategy took the mendicants to Japan in the 1580s and 1590s and led them to dream of amassing an army to physically conquer China. However, all mendicant diplomatic endeavors and successes were short-lived and ended in Japan in well-known and widely illustrated persecutions and gory crucifixions of Franciscans and Japanese Christians at Nagasaki in 1597.

The inbound strategy focused on the merchant diasporas in Manila became even more popular after the experience of outbound disasters. The Sangley community that married its fortunes with the Spanish was the primary target, but as Crewe shows, the religious orders (Dominicans, Discalced Franciscans and Augustinians) were divided over the methods of conversion imported from the Americas. In addition, their inherited mutual rivalry complicated the process. However, a small number of wealthy Sangley merchants converted, gaining considerable administrative authority in Manila and becoming willing collaborators with the Spanish. In the long run some of them became native clergy, although not until later in the colonial period. On the other hand, by the early seventeenth century, Japanese Christians affiliated with mendicants came to Manila to study for their ordination. Finally, after the expulsion of missionaries from Japan, many Japanese Christians settled in Manila and in Macau, imagined as future springboards for return. Of course, that idea had to be abandoned.

Not all was lost and Crewe ends his chapter with an unexpected lucky advance bringing Christianity and Dominicans to China and Cochinchina. All the earlier elaborate plans failed, and it took a bunch of dedicated local converts to open the door to the Glad Tidings. It was thus local structures and local cultural mores that prevailed in the long run and determined the success or failure of the Spanish missions.

Ariane Boltanski's contribution to the volume—"Funding the Propagation of the Faith: Noble Strategies and the Financial Support of Jesuit Colleges in France and Italy (c.1590–c.1650)"—brings us closer to the very seat of Jesuit power in Rome, a fact that did not make administration of Jesuit property and finances any easier than it was in Paraguay. She is interested in understanding the workings of the pious foundations of the nobility and their support of the missions within Europe, in particular within France and Italy,

from the end of the sixteenth to the middle of the seventeenth century. The
nature and extent of these lay capitalizations and their effects on the financial
assets of Jesuit establishments are at the heart of the analysis.

The nobles of the high and medium nobility of the sword (*noblesse d'épée*)
were important benefactors and patrons of the Jesuit colleges, which were
"epicentres" of various religious, devotional, missionary and pastoral projects.
Boltanski uses a comparative approach to highlight the entanglement of religious and worldly interests in the "charitable" investments of the nobility. The
question she poses concerns the impact of lay agency in funding Jesuit institutions and missionary endeavours.

Her detailed analysis is focused on missions in the Protestant regions in
France, such as the residences and colleges of the Gévaudan-Vivarais-Cévennes
group and the colleges of Charleville and Chambéry. Another type of foundation was developed in Christianized territories inhabited by "heterodox" Catholics and populations bordering on heresy. The colleges of Corsica, in the Kingdom of Naples, and especially in Apulia, were established for this purpose. To
these must also be added colleges in France (Nevers, Chaumont-en-Bassigny)
or in Mirandola in Italy, which targeted local urban and rural populations.

These Jesuit establishments were founded and maintained over time as *joint
ventures* with noble benefactors forming consortia. Managing property was for
the Jesuits a guarantee of the longevity of their educational institutions and
residences. The colleges studied by Boltanski were founded at the request of
the nobility in the first years of the seventeenth century. The Society of Jesus
proved rather cautious about accepting offers that might not last due to insufficient endowments and unstable assets and/or annuities, and thus reviewed
carefully any such request.

In all the cases studied, the foundation would start with an initial substantial donation by a noble founder, but local stakeholders—notables, members
of the urban oligarchy, bishops and similar—were also summoned to contribute their opinion on the project of opening a Jesuit college. "A foundation was,
in fact, the start of an intricate social network," remarks Boltanski, a network
through which the Jesuits rooted themselves into a locality, and ensured that
the college retained multiple sources of investment. Multiple donors were
part of a financial safety net ensuring the financial autonomy of the Jesuit institution, and were, in fact, long-term projects of capitalization. At the same
time, these foundations were considered worldly investments guaranteeing
the salvation of the benefactors and their descendants, and were designed to
last eternally. If nobles saw themselves as patrons, the Society of Jesus denied
both patronage and jurisdiction over these institutions to their founders and
principal donors, offering instead salvation and memory of the noble donor's

lineage. Services such as masses and funerals were granted as honorary privi-leges, as was the practice of inscribing donors' names on the walls.

In most cases, the initial donation required successive recapitalizations, which meant that over time some endowments rose while other declined, and there would appear a gap between the financial commitments of the founder and the actual resources of the college. It was also usual that financial prom-ises were only partly fulfilled and honored. Consequently, in the long run the Society of Jesus became embroiled in lawsuits, especially with the descendants of the benefactors. Various other factors, such as inflation, contributed to the state of permanent financial instability of most of the Jesuit colleges. In a word, Jesuit institutions were unable to become self-sufficient and autonomous and continued to depend on local noble or rich patrons. The capital and the sourc-es of income were thus fragmented and the Jesuit foundations needed ever more contributions and ecclesiastical benefices. Despite the diversification of revenues, more often than not the colleges experienced financial difficulties and accumulated debts. Noble patronage was therefore indispensable but it also embroiled Jesuit establishments in a web of financial constraints, making them dependent on local economy circuits.

Sébastien Malaprade's chapter—"The College of San Hermenegildo in Se-ville: The Centerpiece of a Global Financial Network"—paints the dark side, as far as Jesuit adversaries saw it, of disastrous and amoral Jesuit financial schemes. More notorious in historiography, and relatively better studied is Antoine Lavalette case a century later in 1761, although the scenario is sim-ilar to Malaparade's case study. The Jesuits overinvested, overstretched their indebtedness and as they went bankrupt, attracted the ire of their creditors and of just about everybody else, other Jesuits included. Malaprade's intention in casting new light on the case of the College of San Hermenegildo in Seville, which went bankrupt in 1645 and then slowly sank even lower in the public eye, creating scandal after scandal for another decade, is a felicitous one and his study is amazingly detailed.

The College of San Hermenegildo, founded in 1580, was an eminent Andalu-sian educational institution, which grew from five hundred students (exempt from fees) to a thousand in the beginning of the seventeenth century. It was also considered an exemplary and trustworthy financial power-house connect-ed to local and global economic networks. The goods and moneys that passed through its hands—specifically, the hands of the skillful procurators—came from the silver mines in the Americas and from local wine, wheat and olive production. The college was renowned for being a "bank" and "a trade hub" that expanded its landholdings and portfolios by borrowing and lending mon-ey. It also had, just as Arianne Bolanski showed in her chapter, a fair number of noble benefactors who both provided endowments and also became clients in financial schemes provided by the college procurators. During the long judicial process, the superior of the college tried to put the blame on the procurator, Andrés de Villar and his helpers, but the documentation reveals that the details of the transactions were known and approved by the rector and the provincial. In fact, and to the contrary, Andrés de Villar, with the backing of his creditors, accused his hierarchy—the rector, Pedro de Marmol, and the provincial of Andalusia, Pedro de Áviles—of having encouraged bankruptcy proceedings in order to evade their contractual obligations. Thus, while the college continued to grow richer and enrich its clients, merchants and creditors, all was well, but when a credit glitch (inevitable in the early modern period when financial uncertainty was endemic), the whole house of cards came crashing down.

In fact Malaprade shows that the college's financial and credit services were appreciated locally since they compensated for the lack of banking institutions. Its creditors called it "a private bank," in fact and the fact that it was in the hands of a religious institution enshrined in sumptuous buildings, perceived as rich, and also as the center of the "moral economy" of the region, allowed Jesuits to invest more in trade and in their landholdings, and receive more credit. What happened when things went downwards was in many ways the effect of various contingent events and uncertain global processes. In 1635 and 1643 poor harvests left college funds in the red and triggered a chain reaction of unpaid bills and losses. The fragility of early modern credit schemes was thus suddenly revealed, just as in the Lavalette case. The evidence of the college's insolvency appeared at the apex of the Spanish economic crisis when the annual shipment of silver failed to arrive to Seville in 1640, the year in which Spain and Portugal waged a war of separation. There was a revolt of Catalan peasants and various military fronts had to be financed from 1635 following the French intervention in the Thirty Years' War. Premised on a free flow of silver from America and exchange trade of goods from Spain, the disruption deeply affected the economic plans of the college.

The jittery credit market and, as Malaprade shows, the miscalculated response by the superiors to the first hints of crisis, brought down the "trust" and "reputation" of the college bank and as the legal process dragged on, the clients who supported it all joined together in tarnishing the college's moral standing.

In her contribution, "Missionaries as Merchants and Mercenaries: Religious Controversies over Commerce in Southeast Asia," Tara Alberts traces the multiple anxieties the missionaries faced in their quest for funding. One of them was the perception that to engage in financial dealings was, from the Christian point of view, morally ambivalent behavior or downright sin. By looking into debates about various methods of funding, she argues that a new rhetoric of missionary spirituality came into being. She thus proposes to measure "the impact of economic realities on the spiritual lives of missionaries." The missionary corporations at the center of her study are those belonging to the Société des Missions Etrangères (MEP) founded in Paris in 1658. Stationed in hubs of international maritime trade, a long way from their Parisian headquarters, missionaries were permanently on the lookout for patronage opportunities and along the way experimented with a variety of funding methods. Some of the primary sources Alberts uses are published missionary journals, such as the one by Jacques de Bourges, *Relation dv voyage de Monseigneur l'Evêque de Beryte, Vicaire Apostolique dv Royavme de la Cochinchine* (Paris: Denys Bechet, 1668). These published works were instrumental in educating missionaries and legitimizing funding strategies by alleviating tensions between the material and spiritual realms.

Indeed, de Bourges provides a very detailed analysis and description of his journey, not neglecting exchange rates, objects to hide from the inquisitive eyes of customs officers, material to bring or not, and the general assessment of the various local economic and social mores. One of his strategic advices is not to load oneself down with silver because European coins are not marketable. He also provides tips on how and where to conceal articles that would most certainly attract high tax duties.

Missionary awareness of the financial aspects of their expedition manifests also in their denunciation of other European missionaries they encountered in south-east Asia—those under the Portuguese padroado in particular. In Ayutthaya, according to de Bourges, the Jesuits, Dominicans and Franciscans as well as other secular priests in Siam had been shamelessly engaged in trade, being "avaricious" and "lacking in science." He and his companions therefore reported them to the Propaganda Fide. The Jesuits, who were "the worst" (or the most successful) cooperated openly with the Dutch East India Company and used their vessels for the transportation of commercial goods.

In fact, French MEP missionaries quickly adapted to the circumstances and the financial actions they decried in others, such as providing capital loans to both converts and non-Christians, became acceptable, according to the justification that the poor souls were saved from exorbitant rates of interest by other lenders who could also throw them into debt bondage.

The principal patron of the MEP missionaries was the French king, a structurally similar arrangement to the Iberian patronage system and similarly insufficient. Their resources were therefore supplemented by the financial support of various benefactors in Europe and in the mission territories. These arrangements were fine until a benefactor died or the situation changed and the whole plan had to be renegotiated. Royal patronage by non-Christian kings

was welcome, but it is clear that it was forthcoming only because the missionaries were perceived as agents of European commercial interests or because
they provided services based on their "sciences," such as mathematics and as-
tronomy, or their skills, such as medicine and engineering. Local small donors
in Cochinchina and Tonkin provided crucial support for the daily survival of
the missions. Even the alms and fines helped the church machine going.

Regarding land ownership—addressed also in all the other chapters in this
volume—the Iberian holdings in southeast and east Asia were relatively small.
In the Philippines this funding measure—a land grant with the right to extract
corvée and slave labor and tribute—would grow in time, but elsewhere, without colonial state backing, land developments remained important but mostly
ephemeral projects, bringing in limited and unreliable income. Moreover, ecclesiastical property was frowned upon by local colonial authorities, and used
as an argument against the sinful behaviour of the clerics and their greed for
secular enrichment.

Spiritual damage from dealing with money was a real issue, and a subject
of controversy, especially the revenues coming from trade. In principle, commerce was considered one of the grounds for Portuguese ecclesiastical patronage right, together with conquest and discovery. The MEP missionaries were
aware of their dependence on trade connections, in particular the Compagnie
des Indes Orientales, which in return expected them to share strategic knowledge and useful intelligence.

At the time the MEP missionaries arrived in Cochinchina, Tonkin and Siam,
they found that Jesuits had moved their important commercial hub to these
regions after expulsion from Japan. As a result, treatises were written, such as
the one by Lambert de la Motte and Pallu, with the collaboration of two French
Jesuits (*Religiosus Negotiator*), denouncing the "sordid and filthy commerce
which profanes the church of God." They reiterated the well-worn creed that
missionaries must put their faith in God first of all and rely on alms from Rome
and from pious benefactors. By way of these debates, the missionaries were
creating the image of an ideal evangelist. The hard line taken meant missionaries and merchants were diametrically opposed. Alberts brilliantly argues that
the criticism of commerce was also part of the performance of a particular sort
of spirituality, which found sympathetic ears among the French *dévots,* who
were the most natural and willing supporters of the missions. Thus the self-
fashioning of the French MEP missionaries had more to do with expectations
at home than the local missionary situation. Their seminary in Ayutthaya had
been in this respect, Alberts argues, "an outpost of continuing French spiritual
reform, where these varied but complementary strains of spirituality came together, transplanted into and reinvigorated by the Buddhist context."

As usual the missionaries were divided. The new-fangled spirituality of the diocesan priests who joined the MEP earned them scorn and accusations from their missionary rivals. Interestingly, the attack came from the Jesuits, although the method of accommodation practiced in China and India was somewhat similar to the French missionary project. Their "*alumbrado*" spiritual energy was seen as tipping into heterodoxy.

Were these missionary posturings simply investment prospectuses? Alberts asks. Perhaps, but in the long run these and similar reflections were responsible for shaping beliefs, attitudes, and moral understandings concerning trade, and they provided a particular missionary niche in the spiritual economy.

"Regulating the Forbidden: Local Rules and Debates on Missionary Economy in the Jesuit Province of Paraguay (17th–18th Centuries)," a chapter contributed by Fabian Fechner, is also concerned with the "gap between the monastic ideal of poverty and the concrete financial needs," to which the Jesuits in the Paraguayan missions, engaged in commerce and agriculture, had to attend and justify in light of their professed spiritual duties. Fechner's analysis is, therefore, focused on the way in which local Jesuit actors negotiated what was licit or illicit in economic activities and the debates around these issues involving the Roman Curia. He argues, with a tinge of irony, that "through collective decision-making processes, an illegal practice could become practically 'legal' for a certain local context." In order to understand this, he claims, we have to look into archives—correspondence and private memoirs—referring to local issues, rather than into general rules promulgated in printed Jesuit collections. The most useful sources for understanding local debates were letters from the Superior General to the Paraguayan missions and the yearly official responses coming from the provincial's discussions ("*consultas*") with his counsellors or the so-called "*consultors.*" The major source used in his study is summaries of all the consultations between 1731 and 1747 preserved in a special register, *Libro de consultas*. Other important sources are files of the Provincial Congregations, taking place every three, or in the case of overseas provinces, every six years. Less helpful, according to the author, are the normative sources such as the *Constitutions* and the printed decrees of the General Congregations that define rules but provide no indication whether or not these rules were ever put in practice. The correspondence of the temporary provincial procurators elected on this occasion and sent to Rome to participate in the Congregation of Procurators or a General Congregation are also informative concerning how the Jesuit decision-making networks operated. Another type of documentation, shipping lists or bills, indicates the volume of trade, but reveals nothing about economic relations and financial structures. In general, Fechner argues, in spite of the tension between economics and religion, as we have seen in other chapters in the volume, economic profit was tolerated when deemed absolutely necessary to secure solid funding of a given enterprise.

One of the invisible issues in the normative printed and codified texts is Jesuit involvement in slavery and the use of slave labor, which was a core element of colonial agriculture. The importance of slave labor is attested since there were approximately 17,275 slaves of African origin who worked on Jesuit farms in South America at the time of the suppression of the Society of Jesus in 1767. While in the local Paraguayan *estancias* (farms) Amerindians were used as forced labor, they were never slaves, as was the case with the indigenous Tupí-Guaraní in Jesuit *aldeias* (villages) in Brazil. Buying and selling slaves was the responsibility of the provincial and his consultors. However, it is hard to find detailed records elsewhere.

Fechner identifies three stages in the agricultural and preindustrial production practiced in the Paraguayan missions. In the first phase, the missionaries tried to persuade the Jesuit Curia in Rome to approve their various economic projects, such as cultivating wheat and corn for their own consumption while also selling the surplus on the market in Brazil. Muzio Vitelleschi, the then Superior General in Rome, rejected this proposal in his Latin postulate "*responsum ad postulatum*"). However, local Provincials usually did not wait for an answer before starting a business. Such was the case with the soap workshop in Salta, which is today in north-western Argentina, the revenue of which went into the foundation of the *colegio*, although the correspondence between Rome and Jesuits contains constant bickering about whether this was licit or illicit.

The second stage, from 1632 onwards, saw Rome more accepting of the Paraguayan demands for economic development of the missions. A formal framework for the administration of earnings was created and completed between 1637 and 1644, according to which only *colegios* were allowed to earn a surplus from agriculture and manufacturing. For a century, manifold economic activities in the missions—soap making, cattle farming, mule commerce, production of wool, cultivation of tobacco, cedar wood and the yerba maté trade, etc.—developed and thrived. With the extension and professionalization of economic networks, the office of a specialized procurator was established in Lima, which was directly responsible for all economic dealings, such as, for example, fixing the price in the transregional commerce of mules.

Profit related to differences in prices of the traded articles, brought to the Jesuit debate the problem of the just price (*precio justo*), which was determined by the Provincial through agreement at the consultation (*consulta*) meetings. Fechner shows that besides manufacture, commerce of goods and the slave trade were the basis of the Jesuit missionary economy and these involved non-Jesuit lay merchants and clients as well. For example, the Jesuits provided transcontinental money transfer services, which were mostly secret dealings since religious orders were exempt from royal taxation on these kinds of activities.

Fechner concludes that the financial and economic activities point to the fact that Society of Jesus was far less "monolithic" than its projected image, and that a fair amount of independent and autonomous economic decisions were made locally. Moreover, from the archival documentation, it is clear that the Jesuit Curia had no clear vision and was unable to enforce any kind of unified order on and in the missions.

Bibliography

Agmon, Dana. *A Colonial Affair: Commerce, Conversion, and Scandal in French India.* Ithaca, NY; London: Cornell University Press, 2017.

Alden, Dauril. *The Making of an Enterprise: The Society of Jesus in Portugal, its Empire and Beyond, 1540–1750.* Stanford, CA: Stanford University Press, 1996.

Beal, John P. *New Commentary on the Code of Canon Law.* New York; Mahwah, NJ: Paulist Press, 2000.

Bériou, Nicole, and Jacques Chiffoleau, eds. *Économie et religion. L'expérience des ordres mendiants (XIIIe-XVe siècles).* Lyon: Presses universitaires de Lyon, 2009.

Berman, Constance Hoffman. *Medieval Agriculture, The Southern French Countryside, and the Early Cistercians: A Study of Forty-Three Monasteries.* Philadelphia: The American Philosophical Society, 1986.

Boxer, Charles. *Portuguese Merchants and Missionaries in Feudal Japan, 1543–1640.* London: Variorum reprints, 1986.

Braudel, Fernand. *La dynamique du capitalisme.* Paris: Arthaud, 1985.

Brockey, Liam Matthew. "Authority, Poverty and Vanity: Jesuit Missionaries and the Use of Silk in Early Modern East Asia." *Anais de história de além-mar* 17 (2016): 179–222.

Brockey, Liam Matthew. *The Visitor. André Palmeiro and the Jesuits in China.* Cambridge, MA: The Belknap Press of Harvard University Press, 2014.

Broggio, Paolo. *La teologia e la politica: Controversie dottrinali, Curia romana e monarchia spagnola tra Cinque e Seicento.* Florence: Leo S. Olschki, 2009.

Brown, Peter. *Through the Eye of a Needle: Wealth, the Fall of Rome, and the Making of Christianity in the West, 350–550 AD.* Princeton, NJ: Princeton University Press, 2012.

Castelnau-L'Estoile, Charlotte de, and Carlos Zeron. "Une mission glorieuse et profitable. Réforme missionnaire et économie sucrière dans la province jésuite du Brésil au début du xviie siècle." *Revue de synthèse* 2–3 (1999): 335–58.

Castelnau-L'Estoile, Charlotte de, Marie-Lucie Copete, Aliocha Maldavsky, Ines G. Županov, eds. *Missions d'évangélisation et circulation des savoirs, XVIe-XVIIIe siècles.* Madrid: Casa de Velázquez, 2011.

Castelnau-L'Estoile, Charlotte de. "Une Église aux dimensions du monde: expansion du catholicisme et ecclésiologie à l'époque moderne." In *Les Clercs et les Princes: doctrines et pratiques de l'autorité ecclésiastique à l'époque moderne*, edited by Patrick Arabeyre and Brigitte Basdevant, 313–30. Paris: Presses de l'École nationale des Chartes, 2013.

Catto, Michela. *La Compagnia divisa: il dissenso nell'Ordine gesuitico tra '500 e '600*. Brescia: Morcelliana, 2009.

Clossey, Luke. *Salvation and Globalization in the Early Jesuit Missions*. Cambridge: Cambridge University Press, 2008.

Cooper, Michael. *Rodrigues the Interpreter: An Early Jesuit in Japan and China*. New York; Tokyo: Weatherhill, 1974.

Cummins, James S. *A Question of Rites: Friar Domingo Navarrete and the Jesuits in China*. Aldershot, UK: Scolar Press, 1993.

Curtin, Philip D. *Cross-Cultural Trade in World History*. Cambridge: Cambridge University Press, 1984.

Curto, Diogo Ramada. "Idéologies impériales en Afrique occidentale au début du XVIIe siècle." In *L'Empire portugais face aux autres empires, XVIe-XVIIe siècles*, edited by Luiz Felipe de Alencastro and Francisco Bettencourt, 203–47. Paris: Maisonneuve et Larose, 2007.

Cushner, Nicholas. *Farm and Factory: The Jesuits and the Development of Agrarian Capitalism in Colonial Quito 1600–1767*. Albany, NY: State University of New York Press, 1982.

Cushner, Nicholas. *Lords of the Land: Sugar, Wine, and Jesuits Estates of Coastal Peru, 1600–1767*. Albany, NY: State University of New York Press, 1980.

Fabre, Pierre-Antoine, and Catherine Maire, eds. *Les antijésuites. Discours, figures et lieux de l'antijésuitisme à l'époque moderne*. Rennes: Presses Universitaires de Rennes, 2010.

Flynn, Dennis O., and Arturo Giraldez. "Silk for Silver: Manila-Macao Trade in the 17th Century." *Philippine Studies* 44, no. 1 (1996): 52–68.

Gerritsen, Anne, and Giorgio Riello, eds. *The Global Lives of Things. The Material Culture of Connections in the Early Modern World*. London; New York: Routledge, 2015.

Ghobrial, John-Paul A., ed. "Global History and Microhistories." *Past and Present* 242, Issue Supplement 14 (2019).

Godinho, Vitorio Magalhães. *L'Économie de l'empire portugais aux XVe et XVIe siècles*. Paris: SEVPEN, 1969.

Golvers, Noël. François de Rougemont, S. J., *Missionary in Ch'ang-Shu (Chiang-Nan): A Study of the Account Book (1674–1676) and the Elogium*. Leuven: Leuven University Press, 1999.

Gruzinski, Serge. "Les mondes mêlés de la Monarchie Catholique et autres connected histories." *Annales HSS* 56e année/1 (2001): 85–117.

Hsia, Ronnie Po-Chia, ed. *A Companion to Early Modern Catholic Global Missions*. Leiden; Boston: Brill, 2018.

Hsia, Ronnie Po-Chia. *Noble Patronage and Jesuit Missions: Maria Theresa Von Fugger-Wellenburg (1690–1762) and Jesuit Missionaries in China and Vietnam*. Rome: Monumenta Historica Societatis Iesu, 2006.

King, Gail. "Candida Xu and the Growth of Christianity in China in Seventeenth Century." *Monumenta Serica* 46 (1998): 49–66.

Konrad, Herman. *A Jesuit Hacienda in Colonial Mexico: Santa Lucía, 1576–1767*. Mexico: Fondo de cultura económica, 1995.

Langholm, Odd. *The Merchants in the Confessional: Trade and Price in the Pre-Reformation Penitential Handbooks*. Leiden: Brill, 2003.

Le Goff, Jacques. *La Bourse et la vie: économie et religion au Moyen Âge*. Paris: Hachette, 1986.

Maldavsky, Aliocha. "Giving for the Mission: The Encomenderos and Christian Space in the Andes of the Late Sixteenth Century." In *Space and Conversion in Global Perspective*, edited by Wietse de Boer, Giuseppe Marcocci, Aliocha Maldavsky, and Ilaria Pavan, 260–84. Leiden; Boston: Brill, 2014.

Marcocci, Giuseppe. "Trading With the Muslims: Religious Limits and proscriptions in the Portuguese Empire (ca. 1480–1570)." In *Religion and Trade: Cross-cultural Exchanges in World History, 1000–1900*, edited by Francesca Trivellato, Leor Halevi and Cátia Antunes, 91–107. Oxford: Oxford University Press, 2014.

Marcocci, Giuseppe. "Conscience and Empire: Politics and Moral Theology in the Early Modern Portuguese World." *Journal of Early Modern History* 18 (2014): 473–94.

Marcocci, Giuseppe. *A consciência de um império. Portugal e o seu mundo (sécs. XV-XVII)*. Coimbra: Imprensa da Universidade de Coimbra, 2012.

Mörner, Magnus. *The Political and Economic Activities of the Jesuits in the La Plata Region: The Hapsburg Era*. Stockholm: Petherson, 1953.

Negro, Sandra, and Manuel Marzal, eds. *Esclavitud, economía y evangelización: las haciendas jesuitas en la América virreinal*. Lima: Pontifica universidad católica del Perú, 2005.

Newitt, Malyn. "Formal and Informal Empire in the History of the Portuguese Expansion." *Portuguese Studies* 17 (2001): 1–21.

Pinto, Ana Fernandes, and Silvana Remedio Pires. "The "resposta que alguns padres de Japao mandaran preguntar": a Clash of Strategies." *Bulletin of Portuguese/Japanese Studies* 11 (2005): 9–60.

Pizzorusso, Giovanni. "Il *Padroado régio* portoghese nella dimensione "globale" della Chiesa romana. Note storico-documentarie con particolare riferimento al Seicento." In *Gli archivi della Santa Sede come fonte per la storia del Portogallo in età moderna*, edited by Giovanni Pizzorusso, Gaetano Platania, Matteo Sanfilippo, 157–99. Viterbo: Sette Città, 2012.

Quattrone, Paolo. "Accounting for God: Accounting and Accountability Pratices in the Society of Jesus (Italy, XVI-XVII centuries)." *Accounting, Organizations and Society* 29 (2004): 647–83.

Rea, William Francis. *The Economics of the Zambezi Missions, 1580–1759*. Rome: Institutum Historicum Societatis Iesu, 1976.

Riello, Giorgio. *Cotton: The Fabric that Made the Modern World*. Leiden; Boston: Brill, 2003.

Riley, James D. "The Wealth of the Jesuits' in Mexico, 1670–1767." *The Americas* 33, no. 2 (1976): 226–66.

Rodrigues, Helena. "Local Source of Funding for the Japanese Mission." *Bulletin of Portuguese/Japanese Studies* 7 (2003): 115–37.

Sangenis, Luiz Fernando Conde. "Controvérsias sobre a pobreza: franciscanos e jesuítas e as estratégias de financiamento das missões no Brasil colonial." *Estudos Históricos* 27, no. 53 (2014): 27–48.

Sarreal, Julia J. S. *The Guaraní and Their Missions: A Socioeconomic History*. Stanford, CA: Stanford University Press, 2014.

Subrahmanyam, Sanjay. "Holding the World in Balance: The Connected Histories of the Iberian Overseas Empires, 1500–1640." *The American Historical Review* 112, no. 5 (2007): 1359–85.

Thomson, D. G. "The Fate of the French Jesuits' Creditors under the Ancien Régime." *The English Historical Review* 91, no. 359 (1976): 255–77.

Todeschini, Giacomo. *Richesse franciscaine. De la pauvreté volontaire à la société de marché*. Lagrasse: Verdier, 2008.

Todeschini, Giacomo. *Les Marchands et le Temple. La société chrétienne et le cercle vertueux de la richesse du Moyen Âge à l'époque moderne*. Paris: Albin Michel, 2017.

Toneatto, Valentina. "La richesse des Franciscains. Autour du débat sur les rapports entre économie et religion au Moyen Âge." *Médiévales* 60 (2001). Accessed January 11, 2019. doi: 10.4000/medievales.6220.

Tramontana, Felicita. "Trading in Spiritual and Earthly Goods. Franciscans in Semi-rural Palestine." In *Catholic Missionaries in Early Modern Asia. Patterns of Localization*, edited by Nadine Amsler, Andreea Badea, Bernard Heyberger, and Christian Windler, 126–41. London; New York: Routledge, 2020.

Trivellato, Francesca. *The Familiarity of Strangers: The Sephardic Diaspora, Livorno, and Cross-Cultural Trade in the Early Modern Period*. New Haven, CT: Yale University Press, 2009.

Trivellato, Francesca. "Is There a Future for Italian Microhistory in the Age of Global History?" *California Italian Studies* 2, no. 1 (2011). Accessed January 14, 2019. https://escholarship.org/uc/item/0z94n9hq.

Vermote, Frederik. "Financing Jesuit Missions." In *Oxford Handbook of the Jesuits*, edited by Ines G. Županov. Oxford: Oxford University Press, 2018. Accessed

January 9, 2019. http://www.oxfordhandbooks.com/view/10.1093/oxfordhb/9780190639631.001.0001/oxfordhb-9780190639631-e-6.

Vermote, Frederik. "The Role of Urban Real Estate in Jesuit Finances and Networks between Europe and China, 1612–1778." PhD diss., University of British Columbia, 2013.

Vu Thanh, Hélène. "Une désobéissance à l'échelle du monde? Les rapports conflictuels de la mission franciscaine du Japon et des autorités espagnoles (XVIe-XVIIe siècles)." In *Paradigmes rebelles. Pratiques et cultures de la désobéissance à l'époque moderne*, edited by Gregorio Salinero, Águeda García Garrido, and Radu Paun, 507–28. Geneva: Peter Lang, 2018.

Vu Thanh, Hélène. "Un équilibre impossible: financer la mission jésuite du Japon, entre Europe et Asie (1579–1614)." *Revue d'Histoire Moderne et Contemporaine* 63, no. 3 (2016): 7–30.

Weber, Max. *The Protestant Ethics and the Spirit of Capitalism*. Translated by Stephen Kalberg. Oxford: Oxford University Press, 2010 [1964].

Windler, Christian. *Missionare in Persien. Kulturelle Diversität und Normenkonkurrenz im globalen Katholizismus (17.–18. Jahrhundert)*. Vienna; Cologne; Weimar: Böhlau, 2018.

Zeron, Carlos. *Ligne de foi. La Compagnie de Jésus et l'esclavage dans le processus de formation de la société coloniale en Amérique portugaise (XVIe-XVIIe siècles)*. Paris: Honoré Champion, 2009.

Županov, Ines G., and Pierre-Antoine Fabre, eds. *The Rites Controversies in the Early Modern World*. Leiden; Boston: Brill, 2018.

PART 1

Missionaries as Traders: The Case of the Society of Jesus

∵

CHAPTER 3

The Cross and the Silk

Trading Activities by the Society of Jesus in Japan (1549–1650)

Hélène Vu Thanh

At the beginning of the seventeenth century, the bishop of Japan, Luís Cerqueira (1551–1614), described the essential role played by João Rodrigues (1561–1633), procurator of the Society of Jesus:[1] "He acted as an interpreter for the Portuguese before the Kubo [the shōgun Ieyasu Tokugawa], as he had for his predecessor the Taikō [Toyotomi Hideyoshi] and, for this reason, he was often in contact with the governors of Nagasaki."[2] Cerqueira stressed the procurator's role as an intermediary in the intercultural trading that built up between the Portuguese and the Japanese from the middle of the sixteenth century. Although the Jesuits were often considered as cultural mediators, particularly because of their language learning and their observations of local cultures and religions, in Asia and in America or Africa, they nevertheless put these talents to use for more mercantile purposes.[3] The Jesuits also appear as real commercial mediators, whose duties and aims have yet to be clarified. In the case of Japan, the Society of Jesus had a close relationship with Portuguese merchants from the beginnings of the evangelization of the Archipelago by Francis Xavier (1506–1552) in 1549.[4] The Jesuits facilitated their installation in the ports of certain *daimyō* (local lords), who wished to gain access to Chinese silk and to firearms, useful in times of civil war.[5] This role as simple intermediaries rapidly

---

1   Luís Cerqueira was also a member of the Society of Jesus. On Cerqueira, see João Paulo Oliveira e Costa, "O cristianismo no Japão e o episcopado of D. Luís Cerqueira" (PhD diss., New University of Lisbon, 1998).

2   "Certidão de D. Luís Cerqueira acerca da apostasia de Omura Yoshiaki," Nagasaki, March 6, 1606, in Archivum Romanum Societatis Iesu [hereafter ARSI], *JapSin* 21 I, fol. 95v.

3   See for Brazil, Charlotte de Castelnau-L'Estoile, *Les Ouvriers d'une vigne stérile, les Jésuites et la conversion des Indiens au Brésil 1580–1620* (Lisbon; Paris: Centre Calouste Gulbekian, 2000); for India, see Ines G. Županov, *Disputed Missions: Jesuit Experiments and Brahmanical Knowledge in Seventeenth Century India* (Oxford; New York: Oxford University Press, 1999).

4   On the beginnings of the evangelization of Japan, see Léon Bourdon, *La Compagnie de Jésus et le Japon* (Paris; Lisbon: Centre Calouste Gulbekian, 1993).

5   On Japan's political situation at this period, see John Whitney Hall, "The *Bakuhan* System," in *The Cambridge History of Japan, vol. 4, Early Modern Japan*, ed. John Whitney Hall (Cambridge: Cambridge University Press, 1991), 128–82.

changed, both because the Jesuits took part in exchanges by investing in the silk trade and because they made themselves into the masters of the port of Nagasaki, where exchanges were agreed between Portuguese and Japanese merchants from 1580 onwards. The aim of this chapter is to question the social and political role of the Jesuits in Nagasaki, through a study of their function as commercial mediators.

The economic role of the Society of Jesus has only been studied in a partial manner by historians, who concentrate more on the issues around the financing of the missions.[6] The participation of the Jesuits in commercial activities has been analyzed more for American lands than for Asian lands, due to the status of the Jesuit landowners there, or because of their involvement in the Atlantic slave trade.[7] In the case of Japan, a few studies have considered the involvement of the Jesuits in the silk trade between Macau and Nagasaki, stressing the global aspects of this trade.[8] Others have analyzed the role of Jesuit procurators, describing the functions they exercised, but not the way they integrated into Nagasaki's social and political environment.[9] On the other hand, although studies of the Christian town have proliferated in recent years, taking account of the economic role of the Jesuits to a certain extent, these

6 Studies on the subject remain rare, however. See Dauril Alden, *The Making of an Enterprise: The Society of Jesus in Portugal, its Empire and Beyond, 1540–1750* (Stanford, CA: Stanford University Press, 1996); Charles J. Borges, *The Economics of the Goa Jesuits, 1542–1759* (New Delhi: Concept Publishing Company, 1994); Frederik Vermote, "The Role of Urban Real Estate in Jesuit Finances and Networks between Europe and China, 1612–1778" (PhD diss., University of British Columbia, 2013).

7 Magnus Mörner, *The Political and Economic Activities of the Jesuits in the La Plata Region, the Hapsburg Era* (Stockholm: Petherson, 1953); Nicholas Cushner, *Lords of the Land: Sugar, Wine, and Jesuit Estates of Coastal Peru, 1600–1767* (Albany, NY State University of New York Press, 1980); Sandra Negro, Manuel Marzal, eds., *Esclavitud, economía y evangelización: las haciendas jesuitas en la América virreinal* (Lima: Pontifica universidad católica del Perú, 2005). On the Jesuits' involvement in the slave trade between Angola and Brazil, see Luiz Felipe de Alencastro, *O trato dos viventes: formação do Brasil no Atlântico Sul séculos XVI e XVII* (São Paulo: Companhia das letras, 2000) and Carlos Zeron, *Ligne de foi. La Compagnie de Jésus et l'esclavage dans le processus de formation de la société coloniale en Amérique portugaise (XVIe–XVIIe siècles)* (Paris: Honoré Champion, 2009).

8 Charles Boxer, *Portuguese Merchants and Missionaries in Feudal Japan, 1543–1640* (London: Variorum reprints, 1986); Michael Cooper, "The Mechanics of the Macao-Nagasaki Silk Trade," *Monumenta Nipponica* 27, no. 44 (1972): 423–43.

9 Michael Cooper, *Rodrigues the Interpreter, an Early Jesuit in Japan and China* (New York; Tokyo: Weatherhill, 1974); Daniele Frison, "The Office of Procurator through the Letters of Carlo Spinola SJ," *Bulletin of Portuguese/Japanese Studies* 20 (2010): 9–70; Mihoko Oka, "A Memorandum by Tçuzu Rodrigues: The Office of Procurador and Trade by the Jesuits in Japan," *Bulletin of Portuguese/Japanese Studies* 13 (2006): 81–102.

concentrate mainly on the local administration or the Portuguese influence on the urban landscape.[10]

This chapter therefore aims to complement these studies, putting the accent first of all on the local aspect of the commercial activities of the Society of Jesus in Japan. It builds on recent scholarship demonstrating that clerics working in the missions were "more than just missionaries of the Christian faith," since they performed various social roles in the field.[11] Without omitting the fact that this trade has global connections, the aim here is to analyze it in relation to the town of Nagasaki and to present the Jesuits as local agents.[12] This "global microhistory" approach enables us to understand the changes in the role of the Jesuits in the silk trade and to observe the way in which they adapted to the political and social context, managing it to serve their own religious and economic interests, while maintaining the link with the Portuguese merchants.[13] The Jesuits appear as real go-betweens, for the Portuguese and the Japanese merchants, as agents with detailed knowledge of both the regional silk market around the South China Sea and local Japanese market.[14] They were also well aware of the power relations within the town, of which they were an essential component. Yet the studies of the go-betweens often ignore the role of the religious players in commercial activities, particularly during the sixteenth and seventeenth

10   Cristina Castel-Branco, Margarida Paes, "Fusion Urban Planning in the 16th Century: Japanese and Portuguese Founding Nagasaki," *Bulletin of Portuguese/Japanese Studies* 18, no. 19 (2009): 67–103; Alexandra Curvelo, "Nagasaki. An European Artistic City in Early Modern Japan," *Bulletin of Portuguese/Japanese Studies* 2 (2001): 23–35; J. S. A Elisonas, "Nagasaki: The Early Years of an Early Modern Japanese City," in *Portuguese Colonial Cities in the Early Modern World*, ed. Liam Matthew Brockey (Farnham, UK: Ashgate, 2008): 63–102. The work of Reinier H. Hesselink, *The Dream of Christian Nagasaki: World Trade and the Clash of Cultures, 1560–1640* (Jefferson, NC: McFarland, 2015) stands out as an approach which gives more importance to commercial questions.

11   See Ronnie Po-Chia Hsia, "Translating Christianity: Counter-Reformation Europe and the Catholic Mission in China, 1580–1780," in *Conversion. Old Worlds and New*, ed. Kenneth Mills and Anthony Grafton (Rochester: University of Rochester Press, 2003), 87–108; and Christian Windler, *Missionare in Persien. Kulturelle Diversität und Normenkonkurrenz im globalen Katholizismus (17.–18. Jahrhundert)* (Cologne; Weimar; Vienna: Böhlau Verlag, 2018).

12   On missionaries as local agents in Asia, see Nadine Amsler and al., *Catholic Missionaries in Early Modern Asia. Patterns of Localization* (London; New York: Routledge, 2020).

13   Francesca Trivellato, "Is There a Future for Italian Microhistory in the Age of Global History?" *California Italian Studies* 2, no. 1 (2011), accessed September 4, 2018, https://escholarship.org/uc/item/0z94n9hq.

14   On the Jesuits' involvment in the global silk market in the South China Sea, see Geoffrey C. Gunn, *World Trade Systems of the East and West. Nagasaki and the Asian Bullion Trade Networks* (Leiden; Boston: Brill, 2018), chap. 3.

centuries, preferring to concentrate on their work as interpreters.[15] The Jesuits do appear to have acted as mediators in the intercultural trade that was created in Nagasaki. Studies of intercultural trade have proliferated in recent years, in the tradition of Philip Curtin's work, or more recently, that of Francesca Trivellato.[16] The latter defines intercultural trade as an extended credit or commercial cooperation relationship between merchants who belong to distinct communities.[17] In the case of Japan, the Society of Jesus played a part in bringing the Japanese merchants into contact with Portuguese merchants, who only landed on the coasts of the Archipelago once a year on average. But, on the one hand, the Jesuits also took part in the trade, which begs the question of their agency and of their objectives with respect to other economic players; on the other, this intercultural trade took place in Nagasaki, the only town in Japan where the Christian population was in the majority and where the influence of the Society also impacted the society or local politics. This particularity invites us to question the specific choices made by religious players in fulfilling this intermediary function between two merchant communities, but also the difficulties any such arrangement raises for the different players involved. The local rulers' political and economic interests were also at stake and a key factor in the missionaries' ability to lead their activities, in a volatile political setting. In the final analysis, we must understand why the foundation by the Jesuits of Nagasaki as a merchant and Christian city proved to be fragile at the turn of the seventeenth century and eventually harmed the Japanese-Christian order and community.

1 The Jesuits as Essential Intermediaries

The Portuguese are regularly portrayed as a merchant diaspora, establishing trading posts at strategic points on the Asian maritime routes, where they then

---

15 On this subject, see Alida C. Metcalf, *Go-betweens and the Colonization of Brazil, 1500–1600* (Austin, TX: University of Texas Press, 2005). Metcalf analyzes this role performed by the Jesuits especially in the cultural and political domains, paying little attention to the economic domain. See also Simon Schaffer et al., eds., *The Brokered World: Go-Between and Global Intelligence, 1770–1820* (Sagamore Beach, MA: Science History Publications, 2009), and Francesca Trivellato, Leor Halevi, Cátia Antunes, eds., *Religion and Trade: Cross-cultural Exchanges in World History, 1000–1900* (Oxford: Oxford University Press, 2014).

16 Philip D. Curtin, *Cross-Cultural Trade in World History* (Cambridge: Cambridge University Press, 1984).

17 Francesca Trivellato, *The Familiarity of Strangers: The Sephardic Diaspora, Livorno, and Cross-Cultural Trade in the Early Modern Period* (New Haven, CT: Yale University Press, 2009), 2.

settled.[18] Japan was an exception to this pattern: the Portuguese merchants landed on the coast of the Nippon Archipelago in 1542, but no community of *casados* settled there on a long-term basis. The merchants were content to make the trip between China and Japan once a year, taking advantage of the Chinese prohibition against coastal populations trading with Japan, due to the action of Japanese pirates (*wakō*) in the waters of the China Sea.[19] The Portuguese brought Chinese silk, purchased at half-yearly fairs in Canton, which they exchanged for Japanese money generated by the mining operations that were booming. In this context, the only continuous European presence in Japan was that of the Society of Jesus, installed in the south of the Archipelago from 1549.[20] The Society's members took advantage of their linguistic knowledge with the Portuguese merchants, and also their cultural knowledge of the country, in which they boasted expertize, regularly stressing the complexity, particularly of social conventions, such as the gifts exchanged during courtesy visits paid to the lords. Their evangelization strategy, founded on the principle of accommodation, gave them great capacities for observation of local customs, highlighting the benefits of those capacities that Portuguese merchants could take advantage of. The merchants therefore chose to rely on the Jesuits to act as go-betweens in the negotiations that were necessary with the daimyō so as to open trading relations and obtain favourable concessions in relation to taxes. This policy of leaving representatives in situ, who learned the language and the customs of the country, had been used in Africa and in Brazil, when the Portuguese made use of the services of prisoners (*degredados*) who had been sent into exile.[21] The particularity of Japan is rooted in the fact that this role was entrusted to a religious community, who settled deliberately in the Archipelago and followed their own objectives, without any thoughts of colonization.

---

18   Curtin, *Cross Cultural Trade in World History*, 137–38.

19   For a chronology of the arrival of the Portuguese merchants in Japan, see Charles Boxer, *O grande navio de Amacau* (Macau: Fundação Oriente, 1989). On the situation in the China Sea, see Sanjay Subrahmanyam, *L'Empire portugais d'Asie, 1500–1700* (Paris: Maisonneuve et Larose, 1999), 131–39.

20   I use the term "European presence" because, although it is linked to the interests of the Portuguese empire, the Society of Jesus in Japan was not solely made up of the Portuguese, but also of Spaniards, Italians and Japanese.

21   See Janaína Amado, "Viajantes involuntários: degredados portugueses para a Amazônia colonial," *História, Ciências, Saúde – Manguinhos* 6 (2000): 823–32; Maria Cândida D. M. Barros, "The Office of *Lingua*: A Portrait of the Religious Tupi Interpreter in Brazil in the Sixteenth Century," *Itinerario* 25, no. 2 (2001): 112–14.

However, the Jesuits were not content to simply play the role of mediators between the Portuguese merchants and the daimyō, which would have consisted in introducing the parties who were present and translating the words exchanged. They were keen to take full advantage of the situation, performing the function described by sociologist Georg Simmel as *"tertius gaudens"* (the third who enjoys).[22] This person benefits from lack of agreement between the two parties present, to make a gain that one of the two parties would not have granted in other circumstances. In the case of the Society of Jesus in Japan, the latter intended to obtain concessions, both on the part of Portuguese merchants and from the daimyōs, in order to further the evangelization of the country. On the one hand, the Society of Jesus wanted the Portuguese merchants to come to the Japanese coast regularly, as they were dependent upon them for the transport of gifts, objects necessary for the everyday running of the mission and of the missionary personnel. Francis Xavier was not wrong when he pointed out as soon as he arrived in the Land of the Rising Sun that it was necessary to demonstrate the significant profits made from the pepper trade with the Portuguese merchants.[23] Although the King of Portugal made a commitment to support evangelization and the missionaries, it is nevertheless the case that the Jesuits had to negotiate for the support of the Portuguese as time went on so as to reconcile the two objectives, religious and commercial. On the other hand, the Jesuits intended to obtain concessions from the daimyō on the openings of missions. In the course of discussions about Portuguese merchants coming to one port rather than another, Cosme de Torres (c.1510–1570), superior of the mission from 1551, thus set out instructions that were sent to captains-major coming from Japan, in which he drew up a list of ports to be visited exclusively, as they belonged to daimyō favorable to Christianity.[24] However, at this time, the Jesuits were non-partisan in the exchanges, in the sense that their aim was first and foremost to consolidate relations between the Portuguese and the Japanese: they were able to maintain their impartiality, as they had interests with both parties. The situation changed at

---

22   Georg Simmel, *The Sociology of Georg Simmel*, trans. Kurt H. Wolff (New York: Free Press, 1950), 154.

23   François Xavier to Antoine Gomes, Kagoshima, November 5, 1549, in Francis Xavier, *Epistolae S. Francisci Xaverii aliaque eius scripta / Nova editio ex integro refecta textibus, introductionibus, notis, appendicibus aucta, vol. 1*, ed. Georg Schurhammer and Joseph Wicki (Rome: Monumenta Historica Societatis Iesu, 1944–1945), 648–49.

24   Bourdon, *La Compagnie de Jésus et le Japon*, 257. The captain-major was the official representative of the Portuguese power in East Asia and had a licence authorizing him to carry out trade between China and Japan.

the beginning of the 1580s, when the Jesuits became involved in commercial activities.

2   From Intermediaries to Traders

The 1580s represented a turning point for the mission in Japan with the arrival of a Visitor to the East Indies, Alessandro Valignano (1539–1606).[25] Initially, Valignano appeared to favor acceptance of the donation of Nagasaki by the daimyō Ōmura Sumitada (1533–1587).[26] The latter granted the port to the Society of Jesus, who took over the administration of the town, even though the lord's sovereignty was preserved over the territory. In exchange, the Portuguese merchants undertook to land exclusively on the daimyō's land in the city of Ōmura. Also, the Visitor decided to reorganize the mission and encouraged the opening of schools in the Archipelago, in order to train Japanese recruits who had joined the Society of Jesus. This educational policy proved to be costly however, and forced the Jesuits to look for new sources of funding, as the royal and papal donations were now insufficient and irregularly paid. The Visitor was therefore looking for reliable sources of revenue, which led him to invest part of the Japan mission's capital in silk trading. This financing policy was not new: when he entered the Society of Jesus in 1556, Luís de Almeida (c.1523–1583) bequeathed his fortune (4,000 ducats) to the Order, which immediately invested it in the silk trade so as to procure annual dividends for the Japanese mission.[27] Yet it became systematic after Valignano, who bound the Jesuits of Japan to the Macau Senate contractually by signing an agreement, called *armação*. The terms of the agreement stipulated that the Society of Jesus could invest 50 piculs of silk (approximately three tonnes) per year in the ship which made the crossing between Macau and Japan. According to Valignano, the religious community made significant profits from

---

25   The Visitor was responsible for inspecting the missions in Asia and proposing new pastoral directions. On Valignano, see Adolfo Tamburello, M. Antoni Üçerler and Maria Di Russo, eds., *Alessandro Valignano, uomo del Rinascimento: ponte tra Oriente e Occidente* (Rome: Institutum Historicum Societatis Iesu, 2008).

26   George Elison, *Deus Destroyed: The Image of Christianity in Early Modern Japan* (Cambridge, MA: Harvard University Press, 1988): 85–106.

27   ARSI, *JapSin* 23, fol. 5v. The Jesuits in Japan were not the only ones trading in local products and commodities in Asia. The Jesuits in the Moluccas also invested in the clove trade. See the letter from Valignano to general Acquaviva, Cochin, December 20, 1586 in Joseph Wicki, ed., *Documenta Indica XIV (1585–1588)* (Rome: Institutum Historicum Societatis Iesu, 1979), 445.

this investment: "Indeed, to support this enterprise, at present we only have the trade from the China ship, upon which the Fathers usually import ten or twelve thousand ducats of silk, in connection with the merchants in the Chinese ports; they all sell together. The income that the Fathers made was five to six thousand ducats every year."[28]

When the contract was signed it marked a significant breakthrough, as it changed the Jesuits' status from that of intermediaries between the Portuguese and the Japanese to that of silk traders. The Society of Jesus was now directly involved in commercial transactions, and particularly in the silk sale price in Japan, even though the Portuguese carried out most of the financial operations. This was all the more apparent after 1604, the year when the *pancada* system (*itowappu* in Japanese) was brought in by the Tokugawa shōgun, which advocated bulk silk sales, at a set price negotiated between Portuguese and Japanese merchants.[29] Despite the fact that Jesuit silk was exempt from the pancada, experience showed that the prices set in negotiations were generally the best prices sellers could obtain, which obliged the Society of Jesus to align their prices with those negotiated by the Portuguese merchants.[30] The Order had a vested interest in keeping them as high as possible. The financial affairs of the Society of Jesus in Japan were henceforth closely linked to those of the Portuguese merchants, which did not stop them continuing to play the role of intermediaries between the Portuguese and the Japanese. The neutrality of the Jesuits in the negotiations was called into question, due to multiple risks of conflict of interest, and this was perceived by Bishop Cerqueira, who warned other members of the Order against too much involvement in commercial activities.[31] While trading had facilitated the Jesuit settlement in Japan, it proved to be a source of conflict within the Society and outside of it. This did not stop the Jesuits continuing their double role as principal agents in trade and as intermediaries in Nagasaki, up to the point where they occupied a central position in the local society.

---

28 Alessandro Valignano, *Les Jésuites au Japon*, trans. Jacques Bésineau (Paris: Desclée de Brouwer, 1990), 227. Valignano uses the word *ducat* as a synonym for *cruzado*, the gold unit used in the Portuguese Empire. One Spanish ducat was equivalent to 1.1 cruzado. See James C. Boyajian, *Portuguese Trade in Asia under the Habsburgs, 1580–1640* (Baltimore; London: The John Hopkins University Press, 1993), 322.

29 Oka, "A Memorandum by Tçuzu Rodrigues," 94–95.

30 "Couzas que podem servir para os Procuradores da Vice-Provincia do Japão (1629)," Biblioteca da Ajuda, *Jesuítas na Ásia* [hereafter BA/JA], 49–V-8, fol. 338–8v.

31 Letter from Cerqueira to general Acquaviva, Nagasaki, March 23, 1603 in ARSI, *JapSin* 20 I, 167.

3   Mediators and Arbitrators: The Central Position of the Jesuits in
         Nagasaki

The person who best embodied the confusion between the roles of mediator and participant in commercial activities was the procurator of Japan.
Considered the second most important person in the mission, the procurator was responsible for managing the finances at a local level, collecting gifts
and donations from Europe, and distributing the resources between the different residences.[32] He was also responsible for the sale of the silk brought
every year by the *Nau do trato* (the Portuguese ship coming from Macau), and
which belonged to the Society. For this reason, he worked in close collaboration with the procurator of Macau, who was responsible for purchasing the
Chinese silks then sent to Japan on behalf of the Society, and for managing
the financial affairs of the mission in this Portuguese colony.[33] However, the
duties of the procurator in Nagasaki were not limited to managing the internal
finances and commercial affairs of the order. He carried out a double function
as a mediator between the Portuguese and the Japanese, and as a trader. This
delicate position justified the particular attention paid to the choice of candi-
date. For Macau, a Jesuit was recruited who was capable of creating a climate
of trust with the Portuguese merchants: the Italian Carlo Spinola (1565–1622),
for example, was chosen in 1601 for his interpersonal qualities.[34] The Nagasaki
post was preferably entrusted to a Portuguese national with good knowledge
of Japan: the person who held this post for some time (1598–1607) was one of
the mission's most eminent figures, João Rodrigues, known as "the Interpreter,"
and one of the best speakers of the local language.

Indeed, the mediation duties of the procurator consisted in interpreting for
the merchants during negotiations that took place for the annual sale of silk
within the framework of the pancada; the procurator was there to facilitate
the process leading up to the price agreement, although he did not intervene
in the final decision. The discussions, which lasted approximately one week
according to Valignano, were held in a building near the Society's school in

---

32   On the role of the procurators, see J. Gabriel Martinez-Serna, "Procurators and the Making
      of Jesuits'Atlantic Network," in *Soundings in Atlantic History: Latent Structures and
      Intellectual Currents 1500–1830*, ed. Bernard Bailyn and Patricia L. Denault (Cambridge,
      MA; London: Harvard University Press, 2005), 181–209.

33   See the rules of the procurator of Macao, drawn up by the visitor Francisco Pasio in 1617,
      in BA/JA, 49–IV–66, fol. 10–13.

34   Letter from Carlo Spinola to the Assistant of Portugal, João Alvares, Macao, January 27,
      1602, in ARSI, *JapSin* 36, fol. 149.

Nagasaki.[35] The Jesuits therefore provided neutral ground to ensure the negotiations between the parties ran smoothly. The procurator of Nagasaki also performed the role of gold broker on behalf of the daimyō or the shōgun, for whom he was the personal sales assistant.[36] The daimyō or the shōgun entrusted a quantity of money (silver coins) to the Society, and it was their responsibility to exchange it for gold or silk in China.[37] As silver had greater value than gold in China, the Japanese lords thus made substantial profits. Although the Jesuits made no financial gain from the exchange, this activity was authorized and even encouraged by Valignano, so as to garner the goodwill of the Japanese leaders. Valignano did however demand that the procurator should possess specific skills, as he had to give assurances on the quality of the money and recruit a person who was competent to do so.[38] The post of mediator was seen as a means of reinforcing the Society's ties with the local society and consolidating its position in the eyes of the Japanese authorities, which were wary of the Christians.

It was without doubt the financial affairs carried out by the procurator that added to the confusion between the roles of mediator and trader. On the one hand, the Society ran up considerable debts, in particular in order to finance their participation in the silk trade, which was not without risks. The sea route between Macau and Japan was indeed a treacherous one and ships were lost on the way to Japan on several occasions, causing serious losses to the mission.[39] At the beginning of the seventeenth century, the procurator Carlo Spinola pointed out that the Japanese Jesuits had to borrow five thousand cruzados from two Japanese and one Portuguese lord.[40] In return, the Jesuits also acted as money lenders, both to the Portuguese and to the Japanese.[41] Finally, the Society invested certain sums that belonged to the order in *respondência* bonds, while agreeing to act as intermediaries for Japanese people who wanted

---

35 Valentim Carvalho, *Apologia*, ed. José Eduardo Franco (Lisbon: Centro cientifico e cultural de Macau, 2007), 97.

36 See the analysis of the criticism of the bishop of Japan, Luís Cerqueira, by Cooper, *Rodrigues the Interpreter,* 252–56.

37 BA/JA, 49–IV–66, fol. 38v.

38 "Couzas que podem servir para os Procuradores da Vice-Provincia do Japão (1629)," BA/JA, 49–V–8, n°16.

39 On the Macau ship's visits to Japan, see the table in George Bryan Souza, *The Survival of Empire: Portuguese Trade and Society in China and the South China Sea, 1630–1754* (Cambridge: Cambridge University Press, 1986), 55. They become less regular by the 1590s, at which point years without visits are not uncommon.

40 Letter from Carlo Spinola to general Acquaviva, Nagasaki, March 21, 1613, ARSI, *JapSin* 36, fol. 159v.

41 "Regimento do procurador que està em Japão," BA/JA, 49–IV–66, fol. 39.

to invest their money in this same type of contract.[42] The respondência was a system of debit/credit between two partners, used as a means of maritime insurance in trading transactions between the Portuguese and the Japanese.[43] The Society was therefore aware that its financial interests depended on both the Portuguese and Japanese merchants. This became a source of problems at a time when the power dynamic was still under construction in Nagasaki, and where the Jesuits were seeking to strengthen their position within urban society.

4 The Jesuits as Arbiters in Urban Society

The balance in the relations between the Japanese and the Portuguese was all the more difficult to maintain given the Jesuits had taken a prominent position in Nagasaki, wielding influence that extended far beyond the economic domain. The Society of Jesus thus played an important political role within the town. The donation of Nagasaki by the daimyō gave them explicit legislative and judicial authority over the town. Although the Jesuits called upon local personnel to render justice, the missionaries took part in the development of a special local law, taking inspiration from Christian principles of positive and natural law: the death penalty was thus forbidden, which was an exception in Japan.[44] Although the town was taken back in 1587 by Toyotomi Hideyoshi (1537–1598), then at the head of Japan, with a representative of the central power (*bugyō*) taking up residence, the Society of Jesus continued to have particular prestige in the town. Their support proved necessary to enter posts in the local administration, such as that of *daikan*, responsible for collecting taxes.[45] This political weight also brought with it considerable social and religious influence. Nagasaki had become the only town in Japan where the population was mainly Christian and where the bishop lived. The Jesuits also contributed to the foundation of charitable institutions, such as the brotherhoods (*confrarias*): the Nagasaki brotherhood was one of the richest and most powerful in

---

42 "Carregaçam de Macao para Japam no anno de 617," BA/JA, 49-V-7, fol. 109–109v; rules of the procurator, BA/JA, 49-IV-66, fol. 15.

43 Mihoko Oka, and François Gipouloux, "Pooling Capital and Spreading Risk: Maritime Investment in East Asia at the Beginning of the Seventeenth Century," *Itinerario* 37, no. 3 (2013): 78.

44 Valignano, *Les Jésuites au Japon*, 93.

45 Murayama Toan, a friend of João Rodrigues, was appointed to this post in 1603 by Tokugawa Ieyasu. See the letter from Francisco Pasio to the general, Nagasaki, October 3, 1603, ARSI, *JapSin* 14 I, fol. 129.

Japan. It helped fund the hospital, opened by the Jesuits, and added to their sphere of influence.[46]

All these elements made the Society of Jesus an essential institution in Nagasaki, to which merchants addressed their requests for arbitration when conflict arose between them (see illustration 3.1). Such was the "reputation" and "trust" of the Jesuits.[47] Their in-depth knowledge of the rules of commerce and their business methods, which operated within judicial mechanisms at a time when bribery was widespread, made them sought-after arbiters, even though they were not official judges.[48] Moreover, for the Portuguese, the establishment of the Jesuits in the town and their detailed knowledge of the local institutions guaranteed them support, or at least advice, in the conflicts that arose between them and the Japanese merchants. This explains why the Jesuits were sought after as interpreters, although the Portuguese could have used *mestiços* interpreters from unions between Portuguese and Japanese women, who knew the language and the local customs.[49] In the same way, for Japanese merchants, the presence of the Jesuits provided a sort of guarantee for the loans: they could always turn to the missionaries to ask them to put pressure on the Portuguese, given their influence over them. Trust between the merchants was therefore built up partly thanks to the Society of Jesus, and this was probably what explained the maintenance of credit relations between the two parties following the persecutions.[50] This being the case, the Jesuits were indirectly involved in the development of trading rules via the arbitration process.

Recourse to the Society of Jesus as arbiter did not guarantee the impartiality of decisions, however. The Portuguese regularly accused the Jesuits of favouring the Japanese in negotiations, to maintain their position in the town.[51] These criticisms must be put into perspective, however. On the one hand, the

---

46   On the brotherhoods, see João Paulo Oliveira e Costa, "The *Misericórdias* among Japanese Communities in the 16th and 17th Centuries," *Bulletin of Portuguese/Japanese Studies* 5 (2003): 67–79.

47   Carvalho refers here to *Apologia* by Valignano, see Carvalho, *Apologia*, 95.

48   See the case of moneylenders in Kyōto in the fifteenth century, regularly subject to bribes by various political or religious institutions, in Suzanne Gay, *The Moneylenders of Late Medieval Kyoto* (Honolulu: University of Hawai'i Press, 2001), 110.

49   Luís Fróis, *Historia de Japam*, ed. Anabela Mourato, Nuno Camarinhas, and Tiago C. P. dos Reis Miranda (Lisbon: Biblioteca virtual dos descobrimentos portugueses n°10, 2002), vol. II, Part 1, chap. 100, fol. 363v and Francesco Carletti, *Voyage autour du monde (1594–1606)*, trans. Frédérique Verrier (Paris: Chandeigne, 1999), 175–76.

50   Tristão Tavares or Pero Fernandes de Carvalho signed bonds of respondência in 1637 and 1638, recognising their debts to Suetsugu Heizō, a Nagasaki merchant who apostatized around 1620. See Boxer, *O grande navio de Amacau*, 284–87.

51   BA/JA, 49–IV–66, fol. 39.

ILLUSTRATION 3.1 Jesuits as mediators between Portuguese and Japanese in Nagasaki,
Namban folding screen by Kano Naizen (1570–1616) (detail)
REPRODUCED WITH PERMISSION OF THE MUSEU NACIONAL DE ARTE
ANTIGA (LISBON)

Jesuits, and particularly João Rodrigues, shared a negative opinion of the Japanese merchants, considering them somewhat unreliable business partners.[52] On the other hand, the Jesuits and the bishop took part in proceedings opposing Japanese and Portuguese merchants, at the request of the bugyō, to whom the central power had entrusted the law of the town.[53] This was particularly the case in 1610, in a conflict between Vicente Roiz and Bernard Funamoto, who had invested in the Portuguese trader's ship, a claim disputed by the former.[54] The Japanese, on Funamoto's orders, set fire to the Portuguese trader's ship, and he lost its precious cargo of silver and silk. The matter was brought before the bugyō of Nagasaki, Safioye, who ruled in favour of the Japanese merchant, because he owed him money and hoped that a favourable ruling would mean erasure of his debt. According to Valentim Carvalho (1560–1631), the Jesuits refused to make a decision. But Francisco Pasio (1551–1612) points out that the Jesuits were forced by the bugyō to give an opinion in civil matters between Portuguese and Japanese parties in Nagasaki. They therefore handed down a verdict in favour of Roiz, to the dismay of Safioye.[55] This case highlights the delicate position of the Society of Jesus in Nagasaki: although it was a powerful institution, there was increasing competition from a central power that sought to reduce the Society's influence in all areas.

5   The Post-expulsion Economic Role of the Jesuits

The turn of the seventeenth century marked the beginning of protests by different players over the multiple roles taken on by the Society of Jesus in commercial activities, protests that gradually undermined the position of the Jesuits in Nagasaki. Criticisms were expressed first inside the urban community, following the installation of the mendicant order in Japan at the beginning of the seventeenth century (whose presence created competition for the Jesuits). It was not novel to see mendicant orders settle in Japan: from the 1580s, the Franciscans, who arrived from the Spanish Philippines, had been trying to set up a mission.[56]

---

52   João Rodrigues, "Couzas que podem servir para os procuradores" (1629), BA/JA, 49–V–8, fol. 641.
53   If a conflict broke out between the Portuguese, it was the captain-major who was charged with arbitrating the dispute.
54   Carvalho, *Apologia*, 79–80.
55   Cooper, *Rodrigues the Interpreter*, 263.
56   On the arrival of the Franciscans in Japan, see Hélène Vu Thanh, "The Role of the Franciscans in the Establishment of Diplomatic Relations between the Philippines and Japan: Trans-Pacific Geopolitics? (16th-17th centuries)," *Itinerario* 40, no. 2 (2016): 239–56.

The initiation by Toyotomi Hideyoshi of a period of persecution in 1597, which led to the martyrdom of Franciscans on the hills of Nagasaki, marked the abrupt end of this first attempt.[57] It was not until 1607 that the Franciscans managed to obtain an authorization from the Japanese authorities to settle once again in the town. The arrival of the Franciscans broke the monopoly and limited the influence that the Society of Jesus had thus far enjoyed in Nagasaki. The mendicant orders were highly critical of the Jesuits' participation in commercial activities, which they saw as incompatible with membership of a religious order.[58] Yet the Franciscans were also in competition for the Jesuits' role as arbiters, as some Japanese merchants were developing closer relationships with the mendicant orders. This was the case in particular for the daikan, Murayama Toan, a powerful merchant and former acquaintance of the Society of Jesus, who did not hesitate to finance the Franciscans' convent, against the advice of the Jesuits.[59] This episode highlights the fact that part of the local merchant community was distancing itself from the Society, although Toan's defection appears to have been isolated and triggered by strictly personal grievances.[60] It is nevertheless true that some inhabitants now supported orders other than the Society and joined brotherhoods in the sphere of influence of the Franciscans or the Dominicans, who settled in turn in Nagasaki in 1610, exacerbating the divisions in the Christian community.[61]

To these internal divisions in Nagasaki's urban society was added the challenge to the Jesuits' role as mediators from the daimyō from Ōmura in 1606, a date at which tensions surfaced between the Society and a person who had long been an active supporter of the Christians. The break with the Jesuits was a consequence of both the growth of Nagasaki at the start of the seventeenth century and the growing hold of the shōgun administration on the town's

---

57   Clotilde Jacquelard, "Une catastrophe glorieuse: le martyre des premiers chrétiens du Japon, Nagasaki, 1597," *e-Spania* 12 (2011), accessed September 11, 2018, doi: 10.4000/e-spania.20808.

58   The Jesuits voiced these criticisms which reached Europe in "Respuesta que se dio en esta Corte en Noviembre de 609 a una carta que se escrivio de Japon, en 14 de Henero de 607 contra los de la Compañía de aquellas partes," Real Academia de la Historia, *Cortes* 2665, fol. 309–10v.

59   Carla Tronu, "Sacred Space and Ritual in Early Modern Japan: The Christian Community of Nagasaki (1569–1643)" (PhD diss., School of Oriental and African Studies, London, 2012), 187.

60   Toan accused Rodrigues of making advances to his wife. See Dias' letter, Macao, December 6, 1615, in ARSI, *JapSin* 16 II, fol. 252v.

61   Jacinto Orfanel, *Historia ecclesiastica de los sucessos de la christandad de Japon desde el año de 1602 que entro en el la Orden de Predicadores hasta el de 1620* (Madrid: Alonso Martin, 1633), fol. 8v.

affairs.[62] Nagasaki was experiencing a steep demographic increase at this time, which resulted in the construction of new housing on Ōmura land, adjoining Nagasaki, as building land was saturated inside the town. The daimyō approved of this situation, as taxes were levied on these housing units, but shōgun representatives were less enthusiastic, due to the high number of jurisdictional conflicts with the daimyō administration. The shōgun sent an inspector to assess the situation and he recommended a merger of the two towns in 1605; as compensation, the daimyō from Ōmura received the land of Urakami. He felt wronged, however, as this land was much less profitable than the land he had relinquished. Accusing the Jesuits, and particularly João Rodrigues, of having suggested this solution to the central power, and therefore of overstepping their role as mediators by taking the side of the shōgun, the daimyō decided to break off relations with the Society: he apostatized and chased the missionaries from his land. This episode weakened the Jesuits and constituted the first official challenge to the role of the procurator Rodrigues.

More generally, the position of the Society of Jesus in Nagasaki was undermined by the internal divisions that were spreading through the order. The Jesuits were not just simple intermediaries between two distinct communities, the Portuguese and the Japanese; they belonged to both these groups entirely, and all the more so since the Society had recruited many Japanese brothers.[63] While the latter made up the majority of the orders' brothers and were indispensable in the work of evangelization and of the Society's economic affairs, they held no posts of responsibility within the mission. The European Jesuits held on to power and were wary of the local recruits. João Rodrigues thought they had to be kept away from commercial negotiations, as they might try to favor the Japanese merchants.[64] The Society of Jesus did not therefore manage to gain full recognition as a local institution, or at least as a neutral party between the communities. On the contrary, they were always perceived as linked to the Portuguese. These divisions fed the resentment of the Japanese brothers who, instead of protecting the Society when it was attacked by the central authority, were careful not to inform the European Jesuits, as in the Pessoa case.

---

62   The case was reported by Bishop Cerqueira in "Certidão de D. Luís Cerqueira acerca da apostasia de Omura Yoshiaki," Nagasaki, 6 mars 1606, in ARSI, *JapSin* 21 I, fol. 95–96v.

63   Natalie Rothman, *Brokering Empire: Trans-Imperial Subjects between Venice and Istanbul* (Ithaca, NY: Cornell University Press, 2011), 7.

64   On the difficult relations between the Europeans and the Japanese inside the Society of Jesus in Japan, see Hélène Vu Thanh, *Devenir japonais. La mission jésuite au Japon, 1549–1614* (Paris: PUPS, 2016), 125–48.

The dispute began in 1609–1610 and gave the central authority an excuse to challenge the Society's influence in Nagasaki, and particularly its role as a mediator. It started as a simple brawl between the Portuguese and the Japanese in Macau, leading to the death of forty Japanese on the orders of the captain-major, André Pessoa. When the latter arrived in Japan, he was greeted with an icy welcome by the bugyō of Nagasaki, who imposed restrictions on trading in silk.[65] The matter was also brought before the shōgun Ieyasu (1543–1616), who ordered the daimyō of Arima to seize the Portuguese carrack. Pessoa preferred to blow up the ship rather than be captured.[66] In retaliation, the shōgun demanded the expulsion of all the Jesuits, but then changed his mind and called only for the expulsion of João Rodrigues, on the advice of the governor of Nagasaki. The procurator was replaced in his post as interpreter for Ieyasu by the Briton Will Adams (1564–1620). On the one hand, the choice of Rodrigues as a scapegoat was no accident: as a privileged intermediary between Portuguese and Japanese merchants and official translator for the central authority, his expulsion appeared to be an indictment of the role played by the Society of Jesus in commercial affairs and of their proximity to the Portuguese. On the other hand, his replacement by Will Adams highlighted the diminishing Portuguese influence on the shōgun and the increase in European competition in Japan.

The departure of João Rodrigues was only a prelude to the wholesale expulsion of the missionaries and the prohibition of Christianity. Indeed, the Tokugawa followed a religious policy aimed at redefining the relations between the state and the religions. This policy also applied to Buddhism: forty-four measures were enacted in 1615 to control the temples, which henceforth came under the aegis of the state.[67] It was in this general context that the decrees of 1612 and 1614 prohibiting Christianity and ordering the expulsion of the missionaries from Japan must be understood. The independence of the missionaries in Nagasaki (in spite of the close monitoring of the bugyō), and their privileged links with foreign powers (the Iberians, and also the papacy), were considered potentially subversive by the *bakufu*.[68] Although Christianity was not immediately eliminated from Nagasaki, nor even from Japan, it

---

65   For a summary of the case, see Cooper, *Rodrigues the Interpreter*, 262–67.

66   João Rodriguez Giram, *Lettera annua del Giappone del 1609 e 1610* (Milan: Pacifico Pontio/ Giovanni Battista Piccaglia, 1615), 136–40.

67   Peter Nosco, "Early Modernity and the State's Policies towards Christianity 16th-17th Century Japan," *Bulletin of Portuguese/Japanese Studies* 7 (2003): 11.

68   Nathalie Kouamé, "L'État des Tokugawa et la religion. Intransigeance et tolérance religieuses dans le Japon moderne (XVIe-XIXe siècles)," *Archives de sciences sociales des religions* 137 (2007): 110–11. The term *bakufu* (literally "government in the tent") refers to the shogunate.

was nevertheless the case that the missionaries were obliged to exercise their ministry clandestinely, while the Japanese converts were subjected to persecution.[69] The Tokugawa also wanted to control maritime trade between Japan and the other European or Asian powers more closely. In the case of foreign merchants, the bakufu was not able to dispense with their services, but it was set on redefining the rules of trade for its own benefit and controlling its outer frontiers more effectively.[70] At first, the bakufu could not do without the Portuguese in silk trading due to the financial interests that bound many Japanese merchants to the Portuguese in Macau.[71] But the shōgun was keen on diversifying its commercial partners by encouraging English and Dutch merchants to intensify their exchanges with Japan.[72]

Following the persecutions, the Jesuits in Japan were forced to withdraw to Macau, which did not prevent them from continuing the trade. Apart from their in-depth knowledge of the local market, the missionaries thought that persecution would only be temporary, as was the case in the previous persecution suffered by the Society in 1587. It did not seem necessary to curtail their business relations with Japan. However, due to the persecutions, the Jesuits now had to have recourse to both Portuguese and Japanese intermediaries, abandoning a role they had performed until then. The Society continued investing in the Nau do trato, and also in junks or small vessels operating the sea link with Japan. A list, dating from 1617, sets out the different types of silk and cloth to be loaded on the boat belonging to captain Lopo Sarmento do Carvalho, who held the licence in that year, and also on the vessel owned by Antonio Terreira.[73] Also, the Jesuits were still linked to the Japanese by bonds of respondência, as revealed by the regulations of the Visitor Antonio Vieira for the procurator in 1617: the Visitor advises this procurator only to entrust money to trustworthy people, friends of the Society.[74] Finally, the Society continued to send gold to Japan on "Toan's son's" ship, Toan being one of the main merchants in Nagasaki, although we do not know if this money was destined for the maintenance of the missionaries who had secretly remained in Japan

---

69   João Paulo Oliveira e Costa, "Le jésuite Juan Baeza et la communauté chrétienne de Nagasaki pendant la persécution des shoguns Tokugawa," *Histoire, monde et cultures religieuses* 11, no. 3 (2009): 109–30; Hubert Cieslik, "The Great Martyrdom in Edo 1623: Its Causes, Course, Consequences," *Monumenta Nipponica* 10, nos. 1–2 (1954): 13.

70   Michael S. Laver, *The Sakoku Edicts and the Politics of Tokugawa Hegemony* (Amherst, NY: Cambria Press, 2011), 3–5.

71   Boxer, *Fidalgos in the Far East*, 119–20.

72   Souza, *The Survival of Empire*, 53.

73   BA/JA, 49–V–7, fol. 108v.

74   BA/JA, 49–IV–66, fol. 15v.

or whether the latter were supposed to invest it locally.[75] The prosperity of the Society of Jesus in Japan appears to have become increasingly dependent on that of Macau. This explains the Jesuits' desire to find other resources, and all the more so since the trade with Japan was dwindling as a result of offensives by the Dutch, who managed to secure their silk supplies in the 1620s.[76] The increasing repression of Christians and the ever stricter control exercised on international trade by the Tokugawa shōgun also pushed the Society to invest in new commercial routes. The Visitor André Palmeiro (1569–1635) therefore decided to redirect investments to trade with south-east Asia and to purchase a ship in the name of the Society of Jesus: the Jesuits thus acquired three or four ships before his death in 1635.[77] They left bound for Tonkin, loaded with silk purchased in Canton through the offices of brokers, and returned with a cargo made up of various textiles, and also benzoin or resin.[78] These new investments were also destined to finance the mission in China, which was then booming and which was under the aegis of the Japan mission. Taking advantage of its Japanese experience, from then on the Society of Jesus made the choice to reinforce its role as a commercial player in the China Sea and to limit its dependence on the Portuguese in Macau.

6   Conclusion

The Jesuits were definitely not just acting as interpreters between the Portuguese and the Japanese. They relied upon their linguistic and cultural prowess to gain a foothold as essential agents mediating between the merchants in the two communities, while investing themselves in the commercial activities which bound the Portuguese and the Japanese. On this basis, they took part in the development of the rules of commerce and the reinforcement of economic ties between Macau and the Land of the Rising Sun. The particularity of the Jesuits in Japan lay in the superposition of their duties as players and mediators in trade transactions: this situation resulted in them not being in competition with the other economic agents, but forced them to maintain a

---

75   BA/JA, 49–V–7, fol. 109.

76   Ernst van Veen, "VOC Strategies in the Far East (1605–1640)," *Bulletin of Portuguese/ Japanese Studies* 3 (2001): 101.

77   Letter from André Palmeiro to Muzio Vitelleschi, Macao, April 28, 1633, ARSI, *JapSin* 161 II, fol. 146.

78   Liam Matthew Brockey, *The Visitor: André Palmeiro and the Jesuits in China* (Cambridge, MA: The Belknap Press of Harvard University Press, 2014), 332.

complex balance between the local and the global, between the Portuguese and the Japanese. However, the Society of Jesus chose instead to use this double function to build their power and influence on a local level, in Nagasaki. It was then impossible to maintain any form of impartiality between the merchant groups while remaining a powerful urban institution. In parallel, the Jesuits were careful to maintain a wide range of links with the Portuguese. The Society of Jesus in Japan thus hesitated between becoming a fully-fledged local institution and remaining a group whose interests were partly linked to foreign merchants. This situation was all the more difficult because the Jesuits also had to deal with a central power that was in the process of strengthening its control, and that considered all external company as a threat to its stability. It was the combination of these two elements that helped trigger the persecutions at the start of the seventeenth century: the Society of Jesus was definitively put back in its place as a foreign religious order, while it lost its role as a mediator. The Jesuits in Japan then preferred to concentrate on their activities as participants in trading transactions and increase their influence within Macau's urban society. In the final analysis, the Jesuits in Asia learned lessons from the Japanese experience, because they chose to purchase land, rather than rely on maritime trade, to finance the Chinese mission, allowing this mission to grow and endure into the seventeenth and eighteenth centuries.[79]

Bibliography

Primary Sources

Archivum Romanum Societatis Iesu [ARSI]: *JapSin* 14 I; 16 II; 20 I; 21 I; 23; 36; 161 II.
Biblioteca da Ajuda: *Jesuítas na Ásia* [BA/JA], 49–IV–66; 49–V–7; 49–V–8.
Real Academia de la Historia: *Cortes* 2665.
Carletti, Francesco. *Voyage autour du monde (1594–1606)*. Translated by Frédérique Verrier. Paris: Chandeigne, 1999.
Carvalho, Valentim. *Apologia*. Edited by José Eduardo Franco. Lisbon: Centro cientifico e cultural de Macau, 2007.
Fróis, Luís. *Historia de Japam*. Edited by Anabela Mourato, Nuno Camarinhas, and Tiago C. P. dos Reis Miranda. Lisbon: Biblioteca virtual dos descobrimentos portugueses n°10, 2002.
Orfanel, Jacinto. *Historia ecclesiastica de los sucessos de la christandad de Japon desde el año de 1602 que entro en el la Orden de Predicadores hasta el de 1620*. Madrid: Alonso Martin, 1633.

---

79   The Jesuits also purchased land in Japan. See Rômulo Ehalt's chapter in this volume.

Rodriguez Giram, João. *Lettera annua del Giappone del 1609 e 1610*. Milan: Pacifico Pontio/Giovanni Battista Piccaglia, 1615.

Valignano, Alessandro. *Les Jésuites au Japon*. Translated by Jacques Bésineau. Paris: Desclée de Brouwer, 1990.

Xavier, Francis. *Epistolae S. Francisci Xaverii aliaque eius scripta / Nova editio ex integro refecta textibus, introductionibus, notis, appendicibus aucta, vol. 1*. Edited by Georg Schurhammer and Joseph Wicki. Rome: Monumenta Historica Societatis Iesu, 1944–1945.

Wicki, Joseph, ed. *Documenta Indica XIV (1585–1588)*. Rome: Institutum Historicum Societatis Iesu, 1979.

Secondary Sources

Alden, Dauril. *The Making of an Enterprise: The Society of Jesus in Portugal, its Empire and Beyond, 1540–1750*. Stanford, CA: Stanford University Press, 1996.

Alencastro, Luiz Felipe de. *O trato dos viventes: formação do Brasil no Atlântico Sul séculos XVI e XVII*. São Paulo: Companhia das letras, 2000.

Amado, Janaína. "Viajantes involuntários: degredados portugueses para a Amazônia colonial." *História, Ciências, Saúde – Manguinhos* 6 (2000): 823–32.

Amsler, Nadine, Andreea Badea, Bernard Heyberger, and Christian Windler, eds. *Catholic Missionaries in Early Modern Asia. Patterns of Localization*. London; New York: Routledge, 2020.

Barros, Maria Cândida D. M. "The Office of Lingua: A Portrait of the Religious Tupi Interpreter in Brazil in the Sixteenth Century." *Itinerario* 25, no. 2 (2001): 110–27.

Borges, Charles J. *The Economics of the Goa Jesuits, 1542–1759*. New Delhi: Concept Publishing Company, 1994.

Bourdon, Léon. *La Compagnie de Jésus et le Japon*. Paris; Lisbon: Centre Calouste Gulbekian, 1993.

Castelnau-L'Estoile, Charlotte de. *Les Ouvriers d'une vigne stérile, les Jésuites et la conversion des Indiens au Brésil 1580–1620*. Lisbon; Paris: Centre Calouste Gulbekian, 2000.

Boyajian, James C. *Portuguese Trade in Asia under the Habsburgs, 1580–1640*. Baltimore, MD; London: The John Hopkins University Press, 1993.

Boxer, Charles. *Portuguese Merchants and Missionaries in Feudal Japan, 1543–1640*. London: Variorum reprints, 1986.

Boxer, Charles. *O grande navio de Amacau*. Macau: Fundação Oriente, 1989.

Brockey, Liam Matthew. *The Visitor: André Palmeiro and the Jesuits in China*. Cambridge MA: The Belknap Press of Harvard University Press, 2014.

Castel-Branco, Cristina, and Margarida Paes. "Fusion Urban Planning in the 16th Century: Japanese and Portuguese Founding Nagasaki." *Bulletin of Portuguese/Japanese Studies* 18–19 (2009): 67–103.

Cieslik, Hubert. "The Great Martyrdom in Edo 1623: Its Causes, Course, Consequences." *Monumenta Nipponica* 10, nos. 1–2 (1954): 1–44.

Costa, João Paulo Oliveira e. "O cristianismo no Japão e o episcopado de D. Luís Cerqueira." PhD diss., New University of Lisbon, 1998.

Costa, João Paulo Oliveira e. "The Misericórdias among Japanese Communities in the 16th and 17th Centuries." *Bulletin of Portuguese/Japanese Studies* 5 (2003): 67–79.

Costa, João Paulo Oliveira e. "Le jésuite Juan Baeza et la communauté chrétienne de Nagasaki pendant la persécution des shoguns Tokugawa." *Histoire, monde et cultures religieuses* 11, no. 3 (2009): 109–30.

Cooper, Michael. "The Mechanics of the Macao-Nagasaki Silk Trade." *Monumenta Nipponica* 27, no. 44 (1972): 423–33.

Cooper, Michael. *Rodrigues the Interpreter, an Early Jesuit in Japan and China.* New York; Tokyo: Weatherhill, 1974.

Curtin, Philip D. *Cross-Cultural Trade in World History.* Cambridge: Cambridge University Press, 1984.

Curvelo, Alexandra. "Nagasaki: An European Artistic City in Early Modern Japan." *Bulletin of Portuguese/Japanese Studies* 2 (2001): 23–35.

Cushner, Nicholas. *Lords of the Land: Sugar, Wine, and Jesuit Estates of Coastal Peru, 1600–1767.* Albany, NY: State University of New York Press, 1980.

Elison, George. *Deus Destroyed: The Image of Christianity in Early Modern Japan.* Cambridge, MA: Harvard University Press, 1988.

Elisonas, J. S. A. "Nagasaki: the Early Years of an Early Modern Japanese City." In *Portuguese Colonial Cities in the Early Modern World,* edited by Liam Matthew Brockey, 63–102. Farnham, UK: Ashgate, 2008.

Frison, Daniele. "The Office of Procurator through the Letters of Carlo Spinola SJ." *Bulletin of Portuguese/Japanese Studies* 20 (2010): 9–70.

Gay, Suzanne. *The Moneylenders of Late Medieval Kyoto.* Honolulu: University of Hawai'i Press, 2001.

Gunn, Geoffrey C. *World Trade Systems of the East and West. Nagasaki and the Asian Bullion Trade Networks.* Leiden; Boston: Brill, 2018.

Hall, John Whitney. "The Bakuhan System." In *The Cambridge History of Japan, vol. 4, Early Modern Japan,* edited by John Whitney Hall, 128–82. Cambridge: Cambridge University Press, 1991.

Hesselink, Reinier H. *The Dream of Christian Nagasaki: World Trade and the Clash of Cultures, 1560–1640.* Jefferson, NC: McFarland, 2015.

Hsia, Ronnie Po-Chia. "Translating Christianity: Counter-Reformation Europe and the Catholic Mission in China, 1580–1780." In *Conversion. Old Worlds and New,* edited by Kenneth Mills and Anthony Grafton, 87–108. Rochester: University of Rochester Press, 2003.

Jacquelard, Clotilde. "Une catastrophe glorieuse: le martyre des premiers chrétiens du Japon, Nagasaki, 1597." *e-Spania* 12 (2011). Accessed September 11, 2018. doi: 10.4000/e-spania.20808.

Kouamé, Nathalie. "L'État des Tokugawa et la religion. Intransigeance et tolérance religieuses dans le Japon moderne (XVIe-XIXe siècles)." *Archives de sciences sociales des religions* 137 (2007): 107–123.

Laver, Michael S. *The Sakoku Edicts and the Politics of Tokugawa Hegemony*. Amherst, NY: Cambria Press, 2011.

Martinez-Serna, J. Gabriel. "Procurators and the Making of Jesuits'Atlantic Network." In *Soundings in Atlantic History: Latent Structures and Intellectual Currents 1500–1830*, edited by Bernard Bailyn and Patricia L. Denault, 181–209. Cambridge, MA; London: Harvard University Press, 2005.

Metcalf, Alida C. *Go-betweens and the Colonization of Brazil, 1500–1600*. Austin, TX: University of Texas Press, 2005.

Mörner, Magnus. *The Political and Economic Activities of the Jesuits in the La Plata Region, the Hapsburg Era*. Stockholm: Petherson, 1953.

Negro, Sandra, and Manuel Marzal, eds. *Esclavitud, economía y evangelización: las haciendas jesuitas en la América virreinal*. Lima: Pontifica universidad católica del Perú, 2005.

Nosco, Peter. "Early Modernity and the State's Policies towards Christianity 16th-17th Century Japan." *Bulletin of Portuguese/Japanese Studies* 7 (2003): 7–21.

Oka, Mihoko. "A Memorandum by Tçuzu Rodrigues: The Office of Procurador and Trade by the Jesuits in Japan." *Bulletin of Portuguese/Japanese Studies* 13 (2006): 81–102.

Oka, Mihoko, and François Gipoulous. "Pooling Capital and Spreading Risk: Maritime Investment in East Asia at the Beginning of the Seventeenth Century." *Itinerario* 37, no. 3 (2013): 75–91.

Rothman, Natalie. *Brokering Empire. Trans-Imperial Subjects between Venice and Istanbul*. Ithaca, NY: Cornell University Press, 2011.

Schaffer, Simon, Lissa Roberts, Kapil Raj, and James Delbourgo, eds. *The Brokered World: Go-Between and Global Intelligence, 1770–1820*. Sagamore Beach, MA: Science History Publications, 2009.

Simmel, Georg. *The Sociology of Georg Simmel*, translated by Kurt H. Wolff. New York: Free Press, 1950.

Souza, George Bryan. *The Survival of Empire: Portuguese Trade and Society in China and the South China Sea, 1630–1754*. Cambridge: Cambridge University Press, 1986.

Subrahmanyam, Sanjay. *L'Empire portugais d'Asie, 1500–1700*. Paris: Maisonneuve et Larose, 1999.

Tamburello, Adolfo, M. Antoni Üçerler and Maria Di Russo, eds. *Alessandro Valignano, uomo del Rinascimento: ponte tra Oriente e Occidente*. Rome: Institutum Historicum Societatis Iesu, 2008.

Trivellato, Francesca. *The Familiarity of Strangers: The Sephardic Diaspora, Livorno, and Cross-Cultural Trade in the Early Modern Period.* New Haven, CT: Yale University Press, 2009.

Trivellato, Francesca. "Is There a Future for Italian Microhistory in the Age of Global History ?" *California Italian Studies* 2, no. 1 (2011). Accessed September 4, 2018, https://escholarship.org/uc/item/0z94n9hq.

Trivellato, Francesca, Leor Halevi, Cátia Antunes, ed. *Religion and Trade: Cross-cultural Exchanges in World History, 1000–1900.* Oxford: Oxford University Press, 2014.

Tronu, Carla. "Sacred Space and Ritual in Early Modern Japan: The Christian Community of Nagasaki (1569–1643)." PhD diss., School of Oriental and African Studies, London, 2012.

Veen, Ernst van. "VOC Strategies in the Far East (1605–1640)." *Bulletin of Portuguese/Japanese Studies* 3 (2001): 85–105.

Vermote, Frederik. "The Role of Urban Real Estate in Jesuit Finances and Networks between Europe and China, 1612–1778." PhD diss., University of British Columbia, 2013.

Vu Thanh, Hélène. *Devenir japonais. La mission jésuite au Japon, 1549–1614.* Paris: PUPS, 2016.

Vu Thanh, Hélène. "The Role of the Franciscans in the Establishment of Diplomatic Relations Between the Philippines and Japan: Trans-Pacific Geopolitics? (16th-17th centuries)." *Itinerario* 40, no. 2 (2016): 239–56.

Windler, Christian. *Missionare in Persien. Kulturelle Diversität und Normenkonkurrenz im globalen Katholizismus (17.–18. Jahrhundert).* Cologne; Weimar; Vienna: Böhlau Verlag, 2018.

Zeron, Carlos. *Ligne de foi. La Compagnie de Jésus et l'esclavage dans le processus de formation de la société coloniale en Amérique portugaise (XVIe-XVIIe siècles).* Paris: Honoré Champion, 2009.

Županov, Ines G. *Disputed Missions: Jesuit Experiments and Brahmanical Knowledge in Seventeenth Century India.* Oxford; New York: Oxford University Press, 1999.

CHAPTER 4

Yerba Maté in the Jesuit Reductions

From Ritual Drink to Economic Resource (17th–18th Centuries)

Claudio Ferlan

1 Europeans Encounter Maté

The first European encounter with yerba maté dates from 1554, when an expedition led by the Basque conquistador, Domingo Martínez de Irala, began exploring the region of the Upper Paraná. Martínez de Irala was the self-proclaimed commandant of the town of Nuestra Señora de Asunción, which had been founded by a group of men fleeing from Santa María de los Buenos Aires when the latter succumbed to a lengthy siege laid by the *querandíes* natives and their allies. When patrolling the area the explorers noticed the Guaraní drinking in a strange way: they used a straw to suck a liquid flavored with certain finely chopped herbs from a gourd. The Spaniards tried the drink and found the sharp flavor to their taste; they noted it had a stimulating effect, and thinking it the secret to the natives' good humor and excellent health, soon added it to their own routines. On returning to Asunción the *conquistadores* brought a supply of crushed and toasted leaves ready for consumption. As far as we know, that region and that troop of men launched the European craze for yerba maté.[1]

Yerba maté is not a herb or weed but the leaf of a tree (*Ilex paraquariensis*), commonly found in the Uruguay and Paraná river basin, especially in the regions of Mbaracayú and Guairá, which are both in the Upper Paraná, the former on the right bank in the eastern part of present-day Paraguay, the second on the left bank, nowadays straddling eastern Paraguay and southern Brazil.

When the Guaraní met the Europeans, there was something over two million people living in the region bounded by the rivers Uruguay, Paraguay and Paraná and lying between the Dos Patos Lagoon and the Atlantic Ocean.[2] They

---

1   Javier Ricca, *El mate* (Buenos Aires: Penguin, 2012), 26; Juan Carlos Garavaglia, *Mercado interno y economía colonial. Tres siglos de historia de la yerba mate, Edición 25° Aniversario* (Rosario: Prohistoria, 2008), 38.
2   Francisco Silva Noelli, "La distribución geográfica de las evidencias arquelógicas guaraní," *Revista de Indias* 44, no. 230 (2004): 17–34.

were a semi-nomadic, semi-settled people. They grew wheat, manioc, puls-
es, peanuts, sweet potato and gourds, and they hunted and fished. They also
cultivated a small amount of tobacco for ritual purposes. Every two years or
so they moved on when their cultivable land was exhausted. Yerba had a key
role in their diet and a distinct cultural significance. As they explained to the
early missionaries, maté increased their capacity for work, kept them going
when food was short, purged the stomach, kept the senses alert and warded off
somnolence.[3] The Tupi-Guaraní *indios* had used it aeons before the Spanish
arrived, as archaeologists have shown, and were well aware of its energizing
and stimulating properties; but they also employed it to heal wounds, treat
some forms of intoxication and sunstroke, and as an emetic and a purge.[4] They
would toast the leaves over the fire, then pound them and chew them. Alternatively, after toasting, they would place the leaves inside a half gourd (or a cow's
horn), soak them in water and drink the infusion. In the early days they would
quite cheerfully swallow the occasional fragment of leaf; later on they used a
straw (known as *tacuapí* in Guaraní, *bombilla* in Spanish) to filter the drink,
which the locals gave the simple name of *caá*, meaning grass or weed in their
language. But the Guaraní only used maté for their own consumption, and not
for commercial purposes.

    The Spaniards showed an immediate interest in maté, as they did with other
American plants, in order to control the newly-discovered territories through
knowledge.[5] They were struck by the curious way of drinking the infusion
which they came to call "maté," the word for gourd in Quechua dialect—a sign
of their scant attention to local parlance, and also of the success of yerba on
the Peruvian market. In proper Spanish, it was known as Paraguayan weed,
"yerba del Paraguay." In his 1747 report, José Cardiel, a Jesuit who had worked
in the reductions for over thirty years, confirmed that the plant was indeed
not an herb and there was no telling why the natives called it *caá*, which was
unsuitable for a tall sturdy tree like an orange.[6] The right explanation might be

---

3   Julia J. S. Sarreal, *The Guaraní and Their Missions. A Socioeconomic History* (Stanford, CA: Stan-
    ford University Press, 2014), 17, 82–83.
4   Christine Folch, "Stimulating Consumption: Yerba Mate Myths, Markets and Meanings from
    Conquest to Present," *Comparative Studies in Society and History* 51, no. 1 (2010): 11; P. Pablo
    Hernández, *Organización social de las doctrinas guaraníes de la Compañía de Jesús* (Barcelo-
    na: Gustavo Gil Editor, 1913), 198–99.
5   Samir Boumediene, *La colonisation du savoir. Une histoire des plantes médicinales du "Nou-
    veau monde" (1492–1750)* (Vaulx-en-Velin: Editions des Mondes à faire, 2016), 91–93.
6   Guillermo Furlong, *José Cardiel SJ y su Carta-relación (1747)* (Buenos Aires: El Ateneo,
    1953), 148.

that proposed by Julio Juan de Mata Santiago Storni in his *Hortus Guaranensis* (1944), a fully-documented treatise on Guaraní etymology. Storni diverges from the common opinion that the Guaraní simply called maté *caá*. When picking up the native tongue, he argued, the conquistadores and Jesuits left off the attribute *cogoí* that served to distinguish the plant: *caá cogoí* really means "weed to pick." Other sources mention the Guaraní expression *caá guazú*, the great or splendid weed par excellence.[7]

As maté began to catch on with European settlers in America, a material culture relating to this special plant developed: the bowl and straw acquired an economic and symbolic meaning. Besides the gourd, Europeans took to using a wooden receptacle of bamboo (or the highly scented *palo santo*), or one made of baser or nobler metal; precious metal would be used for the bombilla. Thus the utensils for drinking maté turned into social status symbols and sometimes even artistic objects. With its awareness of social nuances, European culture was thus grafted onto a traditional egalitarian native custom.[8] Moreover, the Spanish quickly understood the economic potential of maté. The fashion for this Guaraní infusion among colonial society became entangled in the dietary habits of Europeans of the day: the seventeenth century saw a growing taste for stimulating beverages such as coffee, tea and chocolate. While maté-drinking spread among the Spanish expatriates, the dream of finding gold and silver mines in the Guaraní area began to evaporate. Other sources of wealth were sought, and yerba was one of them. The *encomenderos*—former conquistadores who had become wealthy settlers by extracting tributes and labor—latched on to it as a marketable commodity at the end of the sixteenth century, but in their management of the harvest, they brought hardship to the Guaraní, who were soon pressed with unsustainable demands on their labor. What blighted the natives' lives, apart from sheer overwork, was a style of labor foreign to their culture. The relationship between human beings and nature had changed, on grounds beyond their understanding: producing more than could be consumed. The Jesuit Antonio Ruiz de Montoya (1585–1662) reported disconsolately that the maté harvest had been the ruin of thousands of natives. With his own eyes he had seen "great chests of Indio bones," when shipping the produce. Historical and demographic analyses confirm the Jesuit missionary's tale, revealing a sharp difference in trends between the population working in

---

7 Ramón Pardal, *Medicina aborigen americana*, 2ª edición (Buenos Aires: Editorial Renacimiento, 1998), 274; Héctor Sainz Ollero, *José Sánchez Labrador y los naturalistas jesuitas del Rio de la Plata* (Madrid: Ministerio de obras públicas y urbanismo, 1989), 259.

8 Amaro Villanueva, *El mate. Arte de cebar* (Buenos Aires: Fabril, 1960), 26–27.

the *encomienda* and those in the Jesuit settlements.[9] The Society of Jesuit indeed went into maté production through the reductions (*reducciones*), where they gathered and ruled over native Paraguayan tribes. The Jesuits hoped not only to generate financial resources, but to create a durable socioeconomic system that would protect native converts from colonial exploitation and abuse. The choice of maté production was not an obvious one and had its opponents among the Society. Moreover, I argue, one of its consequences was that it put the Jesuits in competition with the encomenderos on the regional maté market. The Jesuit maté venture's development is thus revealing of the tensions that marred colonial Paraguay's society.

In this first period of commercial exploitation—during the last thirty years of the sixteenth century—yerba maté was gathered from December to August, forcing the natives into perilous expeditions in unhealthy regions like Mbaracayú. On the journey to the *yerbales* (as the lands where the Ilex flourished were known), the workers had an armed escort to defend them from wild animals and raids by hostile Indians. The group would halt in the densest woodland areas and proceed first to select the trees for harvesting. Then the branches of the best trees would be hacked off by axe, leaving a bare trunk. The branches were then rendered into small pieces and given a brief initial drying by the fire. Packed in special containers, they were ranged on reed supports (*tuwatas*) stretched four or five metres off the ground. Underneath, a fire was kept burning for twenty-four hours, the smoke toasting the leaves. These were then separated from the branches by beating over leather hides. In the end the leaves were crushed to powder, which was then wrapped in leather to protect it from humidity. The finishing process to achieve top quality might take months. One commonly-employed method was to pack the powder in leather bags which would be wetted and tightly sewn. As they dried, the bags would shrink, compressing the powder. Each bag weighed from five to ten *arrobas* (in Spanish measurements of the time, one *arroba* corresponded to about 11.5 kilos). After gathering ten or twenty thousand kilos, the natives headed for the river, sometimes a march of dozens of miles, and to the trading centre.[10]

As mentioned, maté began to be marketed, but it was still a niche product. Early mention of it in documents from the last decades of the sixteenth

---

9   Antonio Ruiz de Montoya, *Conquista espiritual hecha por los religiosos de la Compañía de Jesús, en las Provincias de Paraguay, Uruguay y Tape* (Madrid: Imprenta del Reyno, 1639), 8; Garavaglia, *Mercado interno y economía colonial,* 174–201.

10   Lizete Dias de Oliviera, *Les Réductions Guarani de la Province Jésuite du Paraguay. (Étude historique et sémiotique)* (Villeneuve d'Ascq: Presses Universitaires du Septentrion, 1997), 286–88.

century place it below wine and sugar among transported goods.[11] Wine
played a leading role in colonial trade, especially that from the vineyards of
Chile and Peru. So large was the slice of the market that traders and producers
back home sought to obtain a restriction on the American quota to protect
the Spanish production. Some steps were taken, but with little impact on the
growth of Latin American vineyards. In Paraguay, it was a different story: the
middle decades of the seventeenth century saw a crisis in local wine production.[12] The encomenderos saw maté production as an alternative, but soon
faced opposition from local authorities, with the backing of the Jesuits. Her-
nando Arias de Saavedra (Hernandarias, 1561–1634), who had three terms as
governor of Río de La Plata, was firmly opposed to yerba maté and wanted to
curb its consumption, just as he wanted to do with alcohol. But he also wanted to protect the natives from bad treatment by the encomenderos. In 1596,
he passed an ordinance making it illegal to send indigenous people to harvest
maté, and likewise to trade in it. Penalties for infringement were to be exemplary, including burning confiscated leaves in the public square. The governor
set a personal example by lighting himself the first fire.[13] Despite all such steps,
exploitation of natives in the yerbales worsened in the years that followed. On
December 29, 1603, Hernandarias was forced to modify his ordinances in a
repeated attempt to improve yerba maté workers' conditions. His successor,
Diego Martín de Negrón (c.1569–1613), followed the same policy. But, though
the new governor redoubled his efforts, savage exploitation of native workers
in the yerbales continued, leading Philip III (1598–1621) to appoint an official
Visitor to curb the excesses of the encomienda: Francisco de Alfaro (c.1551–
1664), a highly esteemed official presiding over the Charcas Audiencia. Before
journeying to Asunción, Alfaro researched the issue and conducted numerous
personal interviews in Córdoba, especially with Church authorities. The up-
shot was a series of ordinances (October 11, 1611), in which he was influenced
by the Jesuit Diego de Torres Bollo (1551–1638) and supported by Hernandarias.
The drift of these debates was to put an end to the encomienda system and
set up a mission organization eschewing the typical exploitation of native labor and disrupted residential patterns. The Jesuit reductions were part of this
project which proved decisive in consolidating Jesuit autonomy in the Spanish

---

11   Garavaglia, *Mercado interno y economía colonial,* 65–66.
12   Garavaglia, 234–36.
13   José Guevara, *Historia de la conquista del Paraguay, en Colección de obras y documentos
        Pedro de Angelis, reimp. de la edición de 1836* (Buenos Aires: Plus Ultra, 1936), 75; Juan
        Francisco Aguirre, "Diario del capitán Juan Francisco Aguirre," *Revista de la Biblioteca
        Nacional de Buenos Aires* 19, 47–48 (1948): 360–61.

colonial world.[14] In the plans of Alfaro and his illustrious backers, village economy in the Jesuit missions should not involve wine, *chicha* (a fermented beverage derived from maize), honey or maté. Work in the yerbales was likewise banned from December to March, the months when sickness was rife. But such rules were none too scrupulously applied. In the late 1620s, they clashed with the policy of the governor Cespedes Xeria, who was bent on building up maté production, raising protests from the Jesuits who opposed his measures. Their protest was set at naught, however: Cespedes Xeria's term of office may justly be seen as the moment when yerba production took off.[15]

2   From Suspicion to Recognition: Yerba Maté in the Jesuit Reductions

In 1607, Diego de Torres Bollo became the first provincial of the newly-fledged Jesuit province of Paraguay and initiated the reduction policy in order to protect the natives from the encomenderos' abuse. The Society's enormous territory stretched across present-day Paraguay, Uruguay, Argentina and parts of Bolivia, Chile and Brazil, and the center was established at Córdoba. Torres negotiated successfully with the Spanish Crown to gain a ten-year exemption from work in the encomiendas for any native who converted to Christianity and opted for loyalty to the King of Spain. This made Society of Jesus villages a focus of attraction. The first reduction on Guaraní territory was established on December 29, 1609 in the region of the Paraná, and the village was named San Ignacio Guazú. The foundation aimed to include natives in the process of colonization, whilst protecting them from harassment by conquistadores. Unlike those in other areas of Spanish-Portuguese America, the Jesuit reductions in the province of Paraguay gave the fathers not just spiritual authority, but responsibility for justice and administration of agriculture and animal husbandry. On the heels of San Ignacio Guazú there followed the missions of Loreto and San Ignacio Miní in the Guairá region, which was particularly plagued with raids by *bandeirantes* who were nothing short of slave-traders. Over the years, the Jesuits were forced to close down some missions and harbor fugitives in others.[16]

From the outset, the Spanish Jesuits were outspoken opponents of the massive yerba maté consumption that they noticed among the natives. They

---

14   Guillermo Wilde, *Religión y poder en las misiones de guaraníes* (Buenos Aires: SB, 2009), 89–90.

15   Garavaglia, *Mercado interno y economía colonial*, 67–71.

16   Sarreal, *The Guaraní and Their Missions*, 28–34.

compared maté to the fermented alcoholic beverages and stimulants known in other areas of the Americas, such as *pulque, chicha, chocolate, tobacco* or *coca*. In mid-American regions nearly all these substances had a recognized religious role, bringing the faithful closer to the realm of the gods and into competition with Catholic beliefs and practices. It followed that maté, too, would be branded by the missionaries as a pagan vice. What occurred with Paraguayan yerba had also befallen chocolate, the aphrodisiacal properties of which are mentioned by the chronicler Díaz del Castillo in describing the customs of Montezuma.[17]

The Guaraní traced maté back to an act of the gods, as found in various versions of their creation myth. One of the most widespread of these had it that the Ilex tree was a gift from Yací the moon and Araí the cloud, made to an old hunter in gratitude for saving them from a jaguar that attacked them when they were on a trip to earth.[18] Maté was thought to have curative properties and was used by Guaraní shamans to predict the future. In their culture sickness and death were not seen as natural phenomena. If you became ill, you were a victim: someone had stolen your soul, or had infected your body with some disruptive factor. By taking maté, communing with spirits, interpreting dreams, or harnessing the power of spells, the shaman could winkle out the malignant spirit, recover the soul and restore it to the patient. He could also identify the source of the trouble, usually by sucking the afflicted part of the body and making an object come of out his own mouth: a stone, a hair, or an insect.[19] One noteworthy source of such beliefs is Pedro Lozano (1696–1752). In his historical treatise he wrote that "witch doctors" (*hechiceros*) used the Paraguayan weed to hear the oracles of the devil, the "father of lies"; they would report what was said, prefacing their remarks with "the weed told me this or that."[20] Finally, consuming maté could lead to un-Christian behaviour according to the missionaries. Diego de Torres Bollo remarked that the natives admitted in confession their inability to attend Mass, due to the diuretic properties of maté. The constant to-ing and fro-ing was unworthy of a holy

---

17   Bernal Díaz del Castillo, *Historia verdadera de la conquista de la Nueva España* (Madrid: Historia 16, 1984 [1568]), 324.

18   Claudio Ferlan, " 'Yerba mate.' Storia di una bevanda che si beve in compagnia," in *Chi porta da mangiare? Il cibo tra eccessi e scarsità*, ed. Paolo Costa, Claudio Ferlan and Adolfo Villafiorita (Trento: FBK Press, 2013), 57–66.

19   Maxime Haubert, *La vie quotidienne des indiens et des jésuites du Paraguay au temps des missions* (Paris: Hachette, 1967), 15–16.

20   Pedro Lozano, *Historia de la conquista del Paraguay Río de la Plata y Tucumán, 3 vol.* (Buenos Aires: Imprenta Popular, 1873), 427.

place.[21] All these negative perceptions of maté led the missionaries to seek the opinions of European theologians on the use of this plant, in a way that is revealing of the difficulty of explaining native cultural practices to a European public, but also of the challenges in adapting Catholic norms to a markedly different human and material environment. Chocolate already puzzled Old World theologians. Some deemed it dangerous while others considered it an excellent and innocuous nutriment. At the fringe of the long debate as to whether chocolate was permissible on days of ecclesiastical fasting, maté became an issue of its own: the majority concluded that yerba, unlike cocoa, was a drink and as such no impediment to fasting. This was the line taken by Antonio de Leon Pinelo in his famous treatise of canon law, which would long influence thinking about religious fasting.[22] Yet many Jesuits, such as Diego de Torres Bollo, believed that Ilex leaves led to vice and addiction. He consulted Cardinal Federico Borromeo (1564–1631) as to the rights and wrongs of the Guaraní drink. Borromeo took advice from a Milanese doctor, Jacobus Antonius, and gave his answer: active steps should be taken to forbid consumption of a substance that so harmed body and soul. In 1619 the Cardinal sent the bishop of Asunción, Lorenzo de Grado (died 1627), an order to root out the use of the weed, and thus it was a doctor practicing in northern Italy whose advice decided the consumer regulation of a beverage in America.

If the Jesuit provincial's ruling reflected this statement, it was not enforced, and some Jesuits were actively promoting Ilex cultivation in the new reductions and speculating on its commercial potential.[23] Some, such as José de Arce (1651–1715) or Nicolás del Techo (1611–1680), sang the praises of maté, since heavy use kept the natives from drunkenness and alcohol abuse in general. For Techo, yerba maté held many advantages: it prompted unbroken sleep, lessened hunger, helped the digestion and cured a number of illnesses. The counter-indication was that, like wine, it inebriated people.[24] It would appear that Techo's opinion was not so wide of the mark: during his time yerba maté was used in some villages without prior toasting and would give whoever drank

21   Pablo Pastells, *Historia de la Compañía de Jesús en la Provincia del Paraguay. Tomo I* (Madrid: Victoriano Suárez, 1912), 385.

22   Antonio Leon Pinelo, *Cuestión moral si el chocolate quebranta el ayuno eclesiástico* (Madrid: Juan González, 1636), 64–65.

23   Archivum Romanum Societatis Iesu [hereafter ARSI], Paraquaria, Historiae II, 12, c. 60; Claudio Ferlan, "Ivresse et gourmandise dans la culture missionnaire jésuite. Entre bière et *maté* (XVIᵉ-XVIIIᵉ siècles)," *Archives de sciences sociales des religions* 178, 72 (2017): 269–70.

24   Guillermo Furlong, *Naturalistas argentinos durante la dominación española* (Buenos Aires: Huarpes, 1948), 80.

too much a headache and giddiness not unlike drunkenness.[25] Appreciation of the qualities of maté led to a change in perception. For the first Jesuits, as in the case of Antonio Ruiz de Montoya, maté was an instrument of evil, but it soon turned into a divine gift. The metamorphosis was first recorded by Diego de Zaballos in his *Tratado del recto uso de la yerba del Paraguay* (an elusive manuscript Juan Carlos Garavaglia thinks may never have existed) and later by Pedro Lozano in his *Historia*.[26] The latter wrote that St. Thomas procured the weed for the Guaraní. After visiting Brazil, the apostle was alleged to have come as far as the Paraná. Seeing the broad expanses of woodland there, he supposedly realized that the leaves of such trees were toxic. The saint toasted them and turned them into an excellent drink full of healing properties. Lozano's text fits neatly into the Catholic reconstruction, according to which the Tupi-Guaraní had for a long time kept up a tradition from St. Thomas' apostolate. And indeed, Jesuit records report the native story of a great sage and miracle-worker who visited their land long before the Spaniards. The Tupi called him Sumé, the Guaraní Pay Zumé; both of which the missionaries considered a corruption of the name Tomé, or Thomas.

As Jesuits became interested in the production and consumption of maté, they were increasingly alarmed by the exploitation of the natives by the encomenderos. Under the governorship of Marín de Negrón (c.1569–1613) especially, they began to press for abolition of the encomiendas in areas adjacent to their settlements, such as Loreto, San Ignacio-Mini, Santa María de Fe and Santiago. As a favor to the priests, the governor obtained a Crown decree that released natives from the encomiendas, provided they agreed to be incorporated into the Jesuit reduction population.[27] So that they would feel more at home in the missions and as an inducement, the Jesuit fathers provided the Guaraní with board and lodging, as well as the usufruct on a range of material possessions, including tools, maté and tobacco. Yerba became an important part of daily life and was cultivated in the reductions. Quite apart from its addictive properties, yerba drinking had powerful cultural significance, and indeed some missionaries were concerned at the way it kept alive a link with tradition. To give his readers an idea how important yerba was in Guaraní culture and diet, Cardiel likened its use to the Spanish penchant for bread and the

---

25   Leticia María Stoffel, *Los extranjeros y el mate. El llegado guaraní al mundo en apuntes para una folklo-historia de cuatro siglos* (Santa Fe: Colección Folklore y Antropología, Subsecretaria de Cultura de la Provincia de Santa Fe, 1999), 28.

26   Garavaglia, *Mercado interno y economía colonial*, 57–58; Lozano, *Historia de la conquista del Paraguay*, 203.

27   Ricca, *El mate*, 29.

Chinese fondness for tea.[28] As a token of respect for native culture—modest in the overall organization of the reduction—an attempt was also made to preserve tribal hierarchies in the form of pyramids of authority, at the apex of which were the Jesuits themselves.[29] The objective was undoubtedly attained, since from their foundation in 1609 with a few hundred initial native guests, the missions grew in size and number until there were thirty of them, totaling 140,000 persons. This was the peak year of 1732 when each mission had on average just over 4,500.[30] The growth of the Jesuit reductions led to the development of economic activities such as cattle breeding in order to sustain the indigenous people and the missionaries. Yet these economic activities soon competed with those of the encomenderos. The two systems—encomienda and reduction—could hardly coexist and Jesuit denunciations came thick and fast. Thus, in 1628, a letter from Father Duran protested against the encomenderos' exploitation of the native labor; they were forcing the Guaraní far from home for long spells in unhealthy regions, giving them nothing more than a piece of cloth in return for their hard labor.[31] Protests became increasingly numerous, as Jesuits themselves began to trade in maté.

3   Jesuit Maté Commerce

3.1   *An Economic Strategy Shaped by the Local Context*
To develop and finance the missions, the Society of Jesus needed to create an economic strategy embedded in its immediate environment, and which included material and human resources, and opportunities for progress and development, economic and otherwise. In the case of Paraguay, the Jesuits indeed chose to rely on a product that was local both in terms of production and consumption, as maté failed to appeal to European consumers in the way tobacco or cocoa did.

Most of the early written reports provide a comprehensive inventory of the mission area: its flora, fauna, and demographic, economic and political details. Such information would be larded with advice on ways of improving lifestyles

28   Sarreal, *The Guaraní and Their Missions*, 82–83.
29   Fernando Assunçao, *El mate. The mate* (Punta del Este: Mar y Sol Ediciones, 2001), 31; Wilde, *Religión y poder*, 147.
30   Sarreal, *The Guaraní and Their Missions*, 1.
31   *Documentos para la Historia Argentina. Iglesia, cartas anuas de la provincia del Paraguay, Chile y Tucumán de la CDJ (1609–1614)*, intro. Emilio Ravignani (Buenos Aires: Instituto de Investigaciones Históricas, Facultad de Filosofía y Letras, Pesuer t° xx, 1929), 307.

and harnessing natural resources in line with the European cultural model. Organization in the reductions thus reflected detailed knowledge of the conditions to be expected, complete with risks and latent potential. It was soon realized that yerba maté promised a financial contribution without equal. Information on the wealth of the land included mention of the ample supply of maté, a constant feature of annual letters, one example of which dates from the late 1630s. Concerning the reduction of San Ignacio Caaguazú we learn that: 1) The reduction system, which was used to Christianize all the indigenous people of Paraguay, was considered the best way of getting people accustomed to civilized life, by first of all persuading them to devote themselves to agriculture as a safe livelihood; 2) Around the reduction there was copious Paraguay weed, beloved of the Guaraní, while the land offered generous hunting and fishing, and, even more basic, had abundant salt resources, an indispensable condiment at mealtime and highly prized by natives and Europeans;[32] 3) Other local sources of wealth included fields capable of bearing rich crops of various cereals and cotton, and sustaining sheep, goats, mules and cows; 4) Rivers and streams also ensured plentiful irrigation and fishing resources.[33]

Jesuit internal documents and reports show that, as early as the late 1620s, maté had found its place in trade. At several points in time, various Jesuits were appointed as commissars in the trade run by bishops and governors of Asunción, confirming the Society's expertise in economic matters in Paraguay.[34] The new development was irksome to traders and encomenderos who were alarmed by this emerging contest. With hindsight one can only say they were right. The fluctuating attitude to yerba maté, typical during the early period of the reductions, persisted within the Society of Jesus, as is clear from the resolution of the provincial assemblies. The proceedings of the Sixth Provincial Congregation of 1637 approved maté production in the reductions, not only for inside consumption, but also for export, "despite opposition from important persons."[35] Meeting in 1677, the fathers in Paraguay took the opposite line from half a century earlier: they voted to ban yerba maté along with tobacco and chocolate. General Oliva (1600–1681) confirmed the measure and praised the zeal of the assembled fathers in trying to preserve morality.[36] The resolution

32 *Cartas anuas de la provincia del Paraguay, 1637–1639*, ed. Ernesto J. A. Maeder (Buenos Aires: Fundación para la Educación, la Ciencia y la Cultura, 1984), 167–68.

33 *Documentos para la Historia Argentina*, 726.

34 See Fabian Fechner's chapter in this volume.

35 José Luis Rouillon Arróspide, *Antonio Ruiz de Montoya y las reducciones del Paraguay* (Asunción: CEPAG, 1997), 224.

36 ARSI, Congregationes Generales et Provinciales, 80, cc. 118 and 122.

was nevertheless doomed to be a dead letter, however much it might be reiterated right into the eighteenth century.[37]

Thus, the Jesuits' commerce followed two different courses: it was geared to internal consumption in the reductions, and to external trade, for which specially appointed representatives of the Society of Jesus were responsible. From the beginning, such trade—internal especially—employed the so-called *moneda de la tierra* (currency of the soil): cotton, yerba maté, sugar, tobacco, sheep and other livestock. In the years when the colonial market in Paraguay and Peru began to be penetrated by the Society of Jesus, it was also going through a pronounced monetary crisis, connected with a drastic shortfall in precious metals, and one that was destined to last a long time. The crisis prompted not only barter, but a whole system of alternative circulation in which yerba mate was a precious enough commodity to be a negotiable tender, and thus contribute to the turnover of trade. It was preferred over other goods, especially tobacco, as less prone to deterioration. It was widely used to pay traders and taxes, especially tithes.[38] As for extra-reduction exchanges, these began to depend on the missions' *procuradurías* or *oficios* as of 1665, when what one might call Jesuit commercial offices were set up to oversee transactions and financial operations. These offices were directed by the procuradores and were in charge of marketing mission produce (yerba, cotton, tobacco, sugar, as well as hides and textiles). One part of the proceeds went to pay annual tribute to the Crown (in 1679, this was set at one silver *peso* per man aged between eighteen and fifty); another part was used to purchase objects that could not be generated within the missions (metal utensils, clothes, church ornaments); a third part was sent to the Society's mother house.[39] Soon the Jesuits' production began to represent a significant part of the global output in the region. In his seminal study of the maté market, Juan Carlos Garavaglia carefully analyzed sources of income and reckoned that, between 1667 and 1719, the Society of Jesus occupied a slice of trade oscillating between 40 and 30 percent.[40] Choosing 1667 as the *terminus a quo* for such book-keeping is no accident. That was the year when the Buenos Aires *Audiencia* granted the Jesuits the right to export a quota of maté (12,000 arrobas) to the Santa Fe market. That concession marked the order's definitive entry into the yerba market.

---

37   Garavaglia, *Mercado interno y economía colonial*, 53–54.
38   Garavaglia, 381–96.
39   Luis Alejandro Alvero, *Los jesuitas y la economía en el Río de la Plata. Notas de pensamiento económico Latinoamericano* (Catamarca: Universidad Nacional de Catamarca, 2002), 404; Pardal, *Medicina aborigen americana*, 279.
40   Garavaglia, *Mercado interno y economía colonial*, 71–78.

3.2   *A Society-Building Project*

For the reduction fathers, the development of yerba maté production was not only for economic purposes, it was also a key to their project for educating the natives. It was a consolidated Jesuit belief at the time that the only true wealth was labor, especially tilling the soil, which was seen as a social responsibility. An enormous effort was made to turn the natives from nomads into settled farmers. Organization of daily life hinged on this notion, and only when local output managed to make a surplus did the fathers begin to trade in the goods produced.[41] In early years, they showed constant concern for the survival of the reduction: though the local wealth was constantly affirmed, they were patently afraid this might not suffice to make their villages self-sufficient. The fathers faced this difficulty with rational administration through which they sought to augment their store of material goods, purchasing estates (*estancias*) and boosting cereal and cattle production to pay off debts before due and meanwhile achieve a hefty profit. Organized labor was thus a complete novelty to the Guaraní, based as it was on a collective effort by the community under the supervision of Jesuit administrators. In general, the plan met with success and agricultural investments enabled the missionaries to swiftly enter the colonial commercial round.[42] The other objective of the Jesuits was to put the Guaraní to work. A widespread belief among the colonists, whether clergy or lay, was that the natives were incorrigibly idle and unconcerned about self-improvement via work; so one of the missionaries' tasks was to correct that state of affairs. This mentality is evidenced in the annual letters, which contain complaints about indolence and insistently criticize the primitive nature of the native mind. It was not just innate lethargy: the Guaraní had habits that made them unsuited to working, such as drinking or smoking tobacco.[43] Such habits were ingrained from birth and were very hard to eradicate, despite all the fathers' efforts, and were considered detrimental to health and productivity.

Cultivation of yerba maté was no easy matter. In the early years of the reductions, it was picked in the yerbales, in the same way as in the system of encomiendas. Most of these picking grounds were a long way from the home base. Seven reductions had to take boats up the Uruguay river, and then

---

41   Alvero, *Los jesuitas y la economía en el Río de la Plata*, 398–99, 402–404.

42   Ernesto J. A. Maeder, *Misiones del Paraguay. Conflictos y disolución de la sociedad guaraní (1768–1850)* (Madrid: Mapfre, 1992), 160; Alvero, *Los jesuitas y la economía en el Río de la Plata*, 129–40; Sarreal, *The Guaraní and Their Missions*, 3–4.

43   ARSI, Paraquaria, Litt. Ann. I, 8, fol. 18v; cc. 18–18v; Pardal, *Medicina aborigen americana*, 208.

continue over land by cart, driving herds of cattle for the workers' food supply. The location of the other twenty-three missions meant that the natives had an exhausting and complicated march over land in order to gain the rivers.[44] Mules were the main means of locomotion, entailing enormous trains of animals since so much had to be transported: the cattle for food, the tools, yerba maté itself for ready consumption, and oxen and carts on which to load the leaves. When they reached a navigable waterway they would transfer to boats or canoes; though the last stretch would again be overland, given the location of the yerbales, and the final crop would need to be carried back to the boats on the men's shoulders. When the Guaraní reached the picking grounds, they were divided according to their tasks: some went reconnoitring and picking, some readied the drying facilities; others worked the product and bagged it for transport. All these tasks called for on-site preparation of materials (drying racks, toasting fireplaces, mortars). If the weather turned bad—since rainstorms were common—picking operations would come to a halt. Not that people could then be idle: they filled the time busily making ready for the return journey. Once they got back home to the *pueblo* and unloaded the harvest, the workers were summoned by the Jesuits to a mass of thanksgiving.[45]

Collecting yerba maté was thus a tiring ordeal. It entailed journeys of ninety miles or more. The Jesuits could hardly welcome this state of affairs, requiring as it did such annual decamping from the mission and absence for months on end. In the missionaries' opinion, this was detrimental to the Christian education of the menfolk and their families, and a serious test of monogamy. Thus the fathers set about planting *Ilex paraquariensis* inside the reductions—a far from simple task. In its native terrain, the tree grew vigorously with no problems; elsewhere it needed careful tending and was inclined to wither away. Planting from seed proved in vain, but they managed to take cuttings (bedded out or raised in water until the new plant formed). Trees for this process needed to be carried to the chosen site a year in advance, the roots earthed up and protected by leather wraps. Two months prior to planting out (in the winter season from June to August), they would pare off the branches, bed them in earth and await the appointed time. The saplings needed planting out following copious rainfall in one-meter square and one-meter-deep holes at distances of four meters. After that operation the soil around the new plants needed

44   Sarreal, *The Guaraní and Their Missions*, 83.
45   José Sánchez Labrador, *El Paraguay católico* [*1770*], *vol.* 2 (Buenos Aires: Coni Hermanos, 1910), 210–12; Hernández, *Organización social de las doctrinas guaraníes*, 200–203; Aguirre, "Diario del capitán Juan Francisco Aguirre," 254–73.

tamping down; then only time would tell if things had gone as they should.[46] It all took time and effort, but their labors were rewarded. By 1704, Jesuit sources record that every mission had its own yerbal. That proved a somewhat optimistic account. If one reads the inventory made at the time the Jesuits were expelled from Spanish overseas dominions (1767), it transpires that each reduction did have its own yerbal, but not all contained cultivated or home-grown Ilexes or were close to the village in question.[47] That meant that the Jesuits did not altogether abandon the *yerbales silvestres*, and some villages (for example Corpus in the Paraná and San Francisco Javier in the region of Uruguay) went on working those for the maté trade.[48] The province of Paraguay produced two kinds of yerba: *caaminí* and *de palo*. The first was more refined, of better quality, and more time-consuming and labor-intensive to process. It required pure maté leaves: the natives sieved these and removed the tiny stalks, impurities and all foreign bodies acquired in storage under earth or during canoe transport. That was not done for yerba de palo, where only the grosser impurities were removed. Both were then commercialized by the Jesuits.

4   Highways and Taxes: Commercialization of Maté

4.1   *A Continental Trade*

Maté needed to be transported long distances to be sold on the colonial market. A well-marked road grid enabled goods to move about the market, especially those produced in the reductions. Much of the communications network depended on compulsory native labor imposed by the Spanish state, usually at the behest of the encomenderos who informed the colonial authorities of their needs and the work required if goods were to be transported. Perhaps the most important route for Jesuit-produced yerba maté was the one linking Asunción to the Mbaracayú region. In the early decades of the reductions, transportation was mainly by river along the Rio Jejuy. Things changed dramatically in the 1670s, especially in 1676, when the bandeirantes' invasion compelled some missions to close down. For the ensuing forty years, the Jesuits were forced to make the journey by mule along treacherous tracks. One might reflect that the need for a constant chain of mules meant that maté producers, including the

---

46   Lizete Dias de Oliveira, *Les réductions Guarani de la province Jésuite du Paraguay—Étude historique et sémiotique* (Villeneuve d'Ascq: Presses Universitaires du Septentrion, 1997), 288–89.

47   Sarreal, *The Guaraní and Their Missions*, 83–84.

48   Maeder, *Misiones del Paraguay*, 160.

Jesuits, had to leave a substantial part of their wares in the hands of the cattle merchants.[49]

The main highway for driving cattle linked the towns of Salta and Córdoba, an important centre of the maté trade bound for Peru. Much of it went to the mining town of Potosí, where maté had a special use of its own, as reported in the mid-eighteenth century by Acarete du Biscay (1658), a French author of probable Basque origin, who described a journey from the Argentinian pampas to Potosí. By his account, the fumes from extraction works caused grave impairment of the miners' lungs; their only remedy lay in the "beverage made from Paraguayan weed."[50] At the time of Acarete du Biscay's journey, the Peruvian market had already entered upon the slow decline that would cause it to lose its central position in the yerba, as in other businesses.[51] For a number of decades, till 1715, the chief hub for maté distribution was the town of Santa Fe, with its strategic position on the Paraná river, when the Chaco inhabitants stepped up their raiding and Santa Fe began to lose importance. Where maté was concerned, the local authorities applied successfully to the Spanish Crown for a ruling, though it would count for little. The deliberation ruled that boats transporting the leaves down the Paraná from Asunción should stop at Santa Fe. The goods were to be unloaded and taken on towards Buenos Aires, the flourishing new hub for Rio Plata trade, or towards the hinterland. For all the attempt to ensure Santa Fe's commercial survival, between 1720 and 1770 Buenos Aires became the principal point of the distribution towards the markets of the Pacific coast.

The rise of this city was due not only to Jesuit merchandise, but to the adoption of the port of Buenos Aires for other merchant routes. For example, Córdoba stepped up the supplies of cattle and hides to the Atlantic port where they were loaded for distribution by sea.[52] River routes were quicker and cheaper than land routes, but often dangerous, as frequent capsizing shows. Navigation by river was tricky and called for skilled helmsmen, pilots and the canoe and small-craft services of *baqueanos* (experts at reading weather signs, river lore and obstacles, especially sandbanks). Overland caravans might be led by the Jesuits, or by professional merchants who normally hired carters and muleteers. Transport by river, on the other hand, would be left to natives

---

49   Sánchez Labrador, *El Paraguay católico*, vol. 2, 210–11; Garavaglia, *Mercado interno y economía colonial*, 446–51.
50   Acarete du Biscay, *Relación de un viaje al Rio de la Plata y de allí por tierra al Perú* [1657–1659] (Buenos Aires: Alfer & Vays, 1943), 77.
51   Garavaglia, *Mercado interno y economía colonial*, 409–16.
52   Garavaglia, 416–20.

under the occasional Jesuit; though as time passed, crews tended to be comprised of Spaniards and *mestizos* instead of natives from the reductions. At regular intervals of about thirty miles along merchant routes proper staging posts were established where carts might also be repaired. At the important town of Santiago del Estero, on the trail towards Peru and Chile, the Jesuits built workshops in which carts could be made or repaired. Their colleges functioned as dormitories and refreshment stations, and where there were no Jesuits present these facilities were administered by lay management. Such widespread organization naturally took time to set up and was not operational before the early years of the eighteenth century. At various hubs (Misiones, Santa Fe, Potosí, Buenos Aires, Salta), the Society had offices to keep track of business operations. The college of Córdoba had a secondary function as a kind of trading company; keeping constant tabs on the maté-producing reductions, it was capable of organizing shipments of yerba (or other merchandise). The Jesuits were meticulous organizers, insisting on detailed feedback from trading outposts. Thus Potosí sent back general news of price trends on the Peruvian market. The college there was an important sorting pool for wares arriving from the reductions.[53]

4.2   *Regulating the Jesuits' Commercial Activities*

The commercialization of maté implied knowledge of the trading routes, but also of the regulations of commercial activities by religious orders. The regulations drawn up for the New World, a few years after the arrival of the Spanish, required the Church to deliver tithes to the Catholic monarchs, who undertook in return to facilitate evangelization and Church organization in the Americas. Pope Alexander VI established this concession as per papal Bull *Eximiae Devotionis* of November 16, 1501.[54] Pius V's constitution *Dum ad uberes* later awarded the mendicant religious orders exemption from payment of taxation.[55] Subsequent bulls would both defend the clergy's privileges and remind them (even the non-mendicant orders) of their duty to abstain from business trafficking, a ban that was extended to the Peruvian province by the Third Council of Lima (1582–1583). This last merely confirmed a rule that had been reiterated in the provisions of canon law. Infringement was a grave

---

53   Nicholas Cushner, *Jesuit Ranches and the Agrarian Development of Colonial Argentina, 1650–1767* (Albany, NY: State University of New York Press, 1983), 80–82; Garavaglia, *Mercado interno y economía colonial*, 439–44.

54   Francisco Javier Hernáez, ed., *Colección de bulas, breves y otros documentos relativos a la Iglesia de América y Filipinas, vol. 1* (Kraus: Vaduz, 1964), 89–91.

55   Hernáez, *Colección de bulas*, 20–21.

transgression, carrying the penalty of excommunication.[56] But evidently the rubric was not always followed: the Council's renewed veto came after news of certain churches that could only be likened to marketplaces. Paul v felt obliged to spell out the point on May 7, 1607 (*Cum sicut accepimus*), though he altered excommunication to penalties under Church law. The pope Borghese's reasoning was twofold: priests were continuing to run illicit commercial transactions, regardless of excommunication, while they went on blithely administering the sacraments. Two years later he changed his mind again, however, and reintroduced the penalty of excommunication in the papal brief *Alias per nos* (June 6, 1608). Behind Paul v's injunctions it seems likely there was a petition from the Jesuits, who were fiercely critical of how the secular clergy were behaving.[57]

As for the norms of the Spanish crown, the Church privileges dated back to royal *cedulas* in 1531 and 1591: the first ruled that members of the clergy need not pay customs dues (*almojarifazgo*) on what they took with them for their personal upkeep when going out to the Indies; the second decreed that they were exempt from tax on goods purchased or sold, provided the transaction was free from commercial intent.[58] When the first reductions were founded, a royal cedula (January 30, 1607) was passed governing fiscal obligations: all menfolk incorporated in the reductions were granted a ten-year deferment on tax payments, dating from the moment the cedula arrived in the province of Paraguay. The material document was handed to the Jesuit Antonio Ruiz de Montoya.[59] Under the colonial fiscal system, tax was levied on all men between eighteen and fifty years of age, except village chieftains (*cacique*), their firstborns and members of the native council (*cabildo*). The Crown did not receive the whole sum levied from the mission villages: clergy stipends were deducted from the total and left *in loco*.[60]

56   Francesco Leonardo Lisi, *El Tercer Concilio Limense y la aculturación de los indígenas sudamericanos* (Salamanca: Ediciones Universidad de Salamanca, 1990), 166.

57   Hernáez, *Colección de bulas, vol. 2*, 368–69; America Pontificia, *Documenti pontifici nell'Archivio Segreto Vaticano rigurdanti l'evangelizzazione dell'America: 1592–1644, t. III*, ed. Josef Metzler (Vatican City: Libreria Editrice Vaticana, 1995), 249–69.

58   Celia López, *Con la cruz y con el dinero: los Jesuitas el San Juan colonial* (San Juan: Editorial Fundación Universidad Nacional de San Juan, 2001), 121–22.

59   María Cecilia Gallero, "El Tributo, la Yerba y las gestiones del Padre Antonio Ruíz de Montoya," in *Jesuitas, 400 años en Córdoba* (Córdoba: Universidad Nacional de Córdoba, Universidad Católica de Córdoba y Junta Provincial de Historia de Córdoba, 2000), 267.

60   Magnus Mörner, *The Political and Economic Activities of the Jesuits in the La Plata Region. The Hapsburg Era* (Stockholm: Library and Institute of Ibero-American Studies, 1953), 96–97.

In 1667, tax negotiations between the Society of Jesus and the Buenos Aires Audiencia reached the already-mentioned agreement that the reductions might export 12,000 arrobas of yerba maté. After that date, the amount destined for sale grew considerably. It is estimated that the reductions exported an average 8-9,000 arrobas annually. The amount thus fell within the Crown limit, but its sale came in extremely handy, especially to pay the bulk of the taxation.[61] The Paraguay merchants blamed the influx of maté from the reductions for the drop in prices that occurred in the late 1660s, especially on the Santa Fe market. That was undoubtedly one reason, but another was the better quality of maté from the Jesuit-run yerbales. The Society largely sold yerba caaminí, whereas other producers were almost exclusively putting yerba de palo on the market. Such a policy—over-production at the expense of quality—struck the Jesuit fathers as short-sighted. The fall in prices may also be attributed to the price of the early 1660s being objectively too high. However that may be, the price imbalance between the Asunción and the Santa Fe markets would not prove long-lasting, and by the early 1670s the differences had evened out. In 1676, Andrés de Robles, governor of Rio de la Plata, lodged a complaint with the Indies Council about the Jesuits' trading practices: he suspected that their trade on the Santa Fe market was in excess of the 12,000 arrobas allowance. Such trafficking, he added, was in flagrant breach of the well-known canonical norm (reiterated only a few years earlier by Clement IX) forbidding men of the Church to engage in trade. In their defense, the Jesuits called to witness the Santa Fe authorities, who vouched for the correctness of their behavior. Exportation duly went ahead, but when the Mbaracayú region fell into the hands of bandeirantes in 1676, the Spanish colonial authorities took fright: maté from the region might escape their control and play into the hands of the Portuguese, to the detriment of the Spanish and the inhabitants of the reductions alike. Thus, in 1677, Governor Corvalán applied to the Indies Council to radically reduce the reductions' yerbal export quota. To fill the gap, the reductions might trade in other commodities—tobacco, cotton—on the markets of Santa Fe and Buenos Aires. The Crown upheld neither the complaint nor the proposal, and no change was made to the maté trading allowance. Quite the reverse: in the following decade the reductions' share of the yerba maté market grew still further, though still keeping within the agreed terms.[62]

As the seventeenth shaded into the eighteenth century, the rulings from the Holy See focused largely on forbidding contracts and agreements between

61   Dias de Oliveira, *Les réductions Guarani*, 291.
62   Mörner, *The Political and Economic Activities of the Jesuits in the La Plata Region*, 150–51; 158.

laymen and clergy: agreements designed to pass off property as ecclesiastical when it was not, chiefly with a view to dodging tax obligations. But the Bourbon monarchy would not hear of Church legislation invading its own ambit, and stepped in to regulate commerce by the clergy via the already-mentioned *cedulas reales*. In 1684 (July 4) one of these ruled that yerba maté from the reductions or Indio *doctrinas* was not subject to tax (*sisa*). The same rule applied to all the Jesuit-run enterprises. Another cedula in 1708 exempted Jesuit goods destined for the Paraguay missions from taxation. A change would occur with Ferdinando VI (1746–1759) and above all with Carlos III (1759–1788). Both monarchs were bent on increasing state power by reforming the state apparatus, intervening in the economy and strengthening royal power in matters ecclesiastical. There was an attempt to curb the privileges enjoyed by various subjects, one of which was the Church, in Spain and in America. Within the Church set-up, the Society of Jesus played a leading role, especially overseas. The trend would culminate with a cedula in 1785 completely suppressing privileges and compelling the clergy to pay *almojarifazgo y alcabala*.[63] By that time, the Society of Jesus was out of the game.

Information handed down by Anton Sepp (1655–1733) enabled scholar Lizete Dias de Oliveira to calculate that, at the time when the Society of Jesus was expelled from Spanish overseas dominions (1767), the reduction of San Nicolás boasted two big yerbales, covering a surface area of roughly 132 hectares.[64] The study by Pedro Pablo Hernández concluded that, in the same period, the Jesuits made a plea that their hard-won yerbales beside their villages be kept up—and indeed others planted where they were missing—so as to spare the workers toil and journeying. But this was not to be: the missionary plantations fell into neglect, and the maté harvest depended once more on laborious trips to the Upper Paraná and Upper Paraguay.[65] It was previously noted that the inventories made after the Society of Jesus had been expelled show most villages had their own cultivated yerbal, some actually inside, others in the vicinity. Though many were indeed let go, one prime exception was the department area of Santiago where a good yield was still recorded in 1785.[66] Curiously, if one goes by the data on merchandise flowing towards Buenos Aires, it transpires that the total yerba production went up in the post-Jesuit years and even the share corresponding to the former missions grew: about 30,000 arrobas per year, nearly three time the famous limit of 12,000. The figures may be misleading since

63   López, *Con la cruz y con el dinero*, 119–24.
64   Dias de Oliveira, *Les réductions Guarani*, 289.
65   Hernández, *Organización social de las doctrinas guaraníes*, 203.
66   Maeder, *Misiones del Paraguay*, 161–63.

they refer chiefly to the low-grade yerba de palos which almost entirely ousted caaminí once the missionaries were forced to leave. The data suggestive of a rise in production in the post-expulsion period amount to very little, in short: the production model changed, and they refer almost uniquely to Buenos Aires. Although that city did become the main center for the harvest, as noted, prior to 1767 the pattern was quite different: the maté was distributed in a radically different way, first of all because of domestic consumption and inter-reduction exchange, with the Buenos Aires factor figuring last on the list.[67] What is certain is that, fifty years on from the Jesuit expulsion, visitors to the ex-missions reported the yerba maté plantations were almost entirely destroyed.[68]

Translated by Ralph Nisbet

Bibliography

Primary Sources

Archivum Romanum Societatis Iesu [ARSI]: Paraquaria, Historiae II, Litterae Annuae I; Congregationes Generales et Provinciales, 80.

Aguirre, Juan Francisco. "Diario del capitán Juan Francisco Aguirre." *Revista de la Biblioteca Nacional de Buenos Aires* 19, nos. 47–48 (1948): 9–602.

America Pontificia. *Documenti pontifici nell'Archivio Segreto Vaticano riguardanti l'evangelizzazione dell'America: 1592–1644, t. III.* Edited by Josef Metzler. Vatican City: Libreria Editrice Vaticana, 1995.

Biscay, Acarete du. *Relación de un viaje al Rio de la Plata y de allí por tierra al Perú* [1657–1659]. Buenos Aires: Alfer & Vays, 1943 [first French edition 1672].

Cartas anuas de la Provincia del Paraguay, 1637–1639. Edited by Ernesto J. A. Maeder. Buenos Aires: Fundación para la Educación, la Ciencia y la Cultura, 1984.

Díaz del Castillo, Bernal. *Historia verdadera de la conquista de la Nueva España.* Madrid: Historia 16, 1984 [1568].

Documentos para la Historia Argentina. Iglesia, cartas anuas de la Provincia del Paraguay, Chile y Tucumán de la CDJ (1609–1614). Introduced by Emilio Ravignani. Buenos Aires: Instituto de Investigaciones Históricas, Facultad de Filosofía y Letras, Pesuer t° XX, 1929.

Hernáez, Francisco Javier, ed., *Colección de bulas, breves y otros documentos relativos a la Iglesia de América y Filipinas, 2 vols.* Kraus: Vaduz, 1964.

---

67   Garavaglia, *Mercado interno y economía colonial*, 71–85.
68   Dias de Oliveira, *Les réductions Guarani*, 291; "Stimulating Consumption," 14–17.

Leon Pinelo, Antonio. *Cuestión moral si el chocholate quebranta el ayuno eclesiástico.* Madrid: Juan González, 1636.

Ruiz de Montoya, Antonio. *Conquista espiritual hecha por los religiosos de la Compañía de Jesús, en las Provincias de Paraguay, Uruguay y Tape.* Madrid: Imprenta del Reyno, 1639.

Secondary Sources

Assunçao, Fernando. *El mate. The mate.* Punta del Este: Mar y Sol Ediciones, 2001.

Alvero, Luis Alejandro. *Los jesuitas y la economía en el Río de la Plata. Notas de pensamiento económico Latinoamericano.* Catamarca: Universidad Nacional de Catamarca, 2002.

Alvero, Luis Alejandro. "Realidad Social y pensamiento económico en el Río de la Plata colonial." In *Esclavitud, economía y evangelización. Las haciendas jesuitas en la América virreinal*, edited by Sandra Negro and Manuel M. Marzal, 395–413. Lima: Pontificia Universidad Católica del Perú Fondo Editorial, 2005.

Boumediene, Samir. *La colonisation du savoir. Une histoire des plantes médicinales du "Nouveau monde" (1492–1750).* Vaulx-en-Velin: Editions des Mondes à faire, 2016.

Cushner, Nicholas. *Jesuit Ranches and the Agrarian Development of Colonial Argentina, 1650–1767.* Albany, NY: State University of New York Press, 1983.

Dias de Oliveira, Lizete. *Les Réductions Guarani de la Province Jésuite du Paraguay. (Étude historique et sémiotique).* Villeneuve d'Ascq: Presses Universitaires du Septentrion, 1997.

Ferlan, Claudio. " 'Yerba mate.' Storia di una bevanda che si beve in compagnia." In *Chi porta da mangiare? Il cibo tra eccessi e scarsità*, edited by Paolo Costa, Claudio Ferlan and Adolfo Villafiorita, 57–66. Trento: FBK Press, 2013.

Ferlan, Claudio. "Ivresse et gourmandise dans la culture missionnaire jésuite. Entre bière et *maté* (XVIe-XVIIIe siècles)." *Archives de sciences sociales des religions* 178, no. 72 (2017): 257–78.

Folch, Christine. "Stimulating Consumption: Yerba Mate Myths, Markets and Meanings from Conquest to Present." *Comparative Studies in Society and History* 51, no. 1 (2010): 6–36.

Furlong, Guillermo. *Naturalistas argentinos durante la dominación española.* Buenos Aires: Huarpes, 1948.

Furlong, Guillermo. *José Cardiel SJ y su Carta-relación (1747).* Buenos Aires: El Ateneo, 1953.

Gallero, María Cecilia. "El Tributo, la Yerba y las gestiones del Padre Antonio Ruíz de Montoya." In *Jesuitas, 400 años en Córdoba*, 259–74. Córdoba: Universidad Nacional de Córdoba, Universidad Católica de Córdoba y Junta Provincial de Historia de Córdoba, 2000.

Garavaglia, Juan Carlos. *Mercado interno y economía colonial. Tres siglos de historia de la yerba mate, Edición 25° Aniversario*. Rosario: Prohistoria, 2008.

Guevara, José. *Historia de la conquista del Paraguay, en Colección de obras y documentos Pedro de Angelis, reimp. de la edición de 1836*. Buenos Aires: Plus Ultra, 1936.

Haubert, Maxime. *La vie quotidienne des indiens et des jésuites du Paraguay au temps des missions*. Paris: Hachette, 1967.

Hernández, P. Pablo. *Organización social de las doctrinas guaraníes de la Compañía de Jesús*. Barcelona: Gustavo Gil Editor, 1913.

Lisi, Francesco Leonardo. *El Tercer Concilio Limense y la aculturación de los indígenas sudamericanos*. Salamanca: Ediciones Universidad de Salamanca, 1990.

López, Celia. *Con la cruz y con el dinero: los Jesuitas el San Juan colonial*. San Juan: Editorial Fundación Universidad Nacional de San Juan, 2001.

Lozano, Pedro. *Historia de la conquista del Paraguay Río de la Plata y Tucumán, 3 vols*. Buenos Aires: Imprenta Popular, 1873.

Maeder, Ernesto J. A. *Misiones del Paraguay. Conflictos y disolución de la sociedad guaraní (1768–1850)*. Madrid: Mapfre, 1992.

Mörner, Magnus. *The Political and Economic Activities of the Jesuits in the La Plata Region. The Hapsburg Era*. Stockholm: Library and Institute of Ibero-American Studies, 1953.

Ricca, Javier. *El mate*. Buenos Aires: Penguin, 2012.

Pardal, Ramón. *Medicina aborigen americana, 2ª edición*. Buenos Aires: Editorial Renacimiento, 1998.

Pastells, Pablo. *Historia de la Compania de Jesus en la provincia del Paraguay. Tomo I*. Madrid: Victoriano Suárez, 1912.

Rouillon Arróspide, José Luis. *Antonio Ruiz de Montoya y las reducciones del Paraguay*. Asunción: CEPAG, 1997.

Sainz Ollero, Héctor. *José Sánchez Labrador y los naturalistas jesuitas del Rio de la Plata*. Madrid: Ministerio de obras públicas y urbanismo, 1989.

Sánchez Labrador, José. *El Paraguay católico* [1770], *2 vols*. Buenos Aires: Coni Hermanos, 1910.

Sarreal, Julia J. S. *The Guaraní and Their Missions. A Socioeconomic History*. Stanford, CA: Stanford University Press, 2014.

Silva Noelli, Francisco. "La distribución geográfica de las evidencias arquelógicas guaraní." *Revista de Indias* 44, no. 230 (2004): 17–34.

Stoffel, Leticia María. *Los extranjeros y el mate. El llegado guaraní al mundo en apuntes para una folklo-historia de cuatro siglos*. Santa Fe: Colección Folklore y Antropología, Subsecretaria de Cultura de la Provincia de Santa Fe, 1999.

Villanueva, Amaro. *El mate. Arte de cebar*. Buenos Aires: Fabril, 1960.

Wilde, Guillermo. *Religión y poder en las misiones de guaraníes*. Buenos Aires: SB, 2009.

PART 2

The Integration of Religious Orders
into Global/Local Economic Networks

∵

CHAPTER 5

From Tenants to Landlords
Jesuits and Land Ownership in Japan (1552–1614)

Rômulo da Silva Ehalt

In 1677, the Jesuit Sebastião de Almeida (1622–1683) arrived in Macau. Among his many duties, the new Visitor to the Chinese mission was in charge of re-organizing the finances of the Society of Jesus in the country. He closely examined records of the Province of Japan, which still existed in exile long after the Jesuits had been expelled from the archipelago, and of the Vice-Province of China. Both factions experienced strained relations, especially after 1658, when the Japan Jesuits received the southern regions of Guangdong, Guangxi and Hainan Island in China as mission territories.[1] Scrutinizing the financial history of the Province of Japan, Almeida drew up a list of donations made to the missionaries roughly a century earlier.[2]

Yet, decades before Almeida took up his pen, a different Jesuit Visitor also struggled with the financial difficulties of the then-Vice-Province of Japan. In 1592, the Italian Alessandro Valignano (1539–1606), reporting to Rome the challenges faced by the mission, complained that missionaries in Japan had to

---

1 A number of people were fundamental in the elaboration of this chapter: Renato Brandão (Keiō University), James Fujitani (Azusa Pacific University), Eduardo Mesquita Kobayashi (University of Tokyo), Célia Tavares (Universidade Estadual do Rio de Janeiro), and Carlos Zeron (Universidade de São Paulo). For particularly helpful advice and suggestions, my gratitude goes to Liam Matthew Brockey (Michigan State University), Hélène Vu Thanh (Université de Bretagne-Sud/IUF), and Ines G. Županov (CEIAS-EHESS). Part of this chapter was discussed in early 2019 during a workshop at the Universidade Federal do Paraná, in Curitiba, thanks to a kind invitation by Andréa Doré and Márcia Namekata. Japanese names are listed in the traditional order of family name followed by first name, including in the bibliography. See Liam Matthew Brockey, *Journey to the East: The Jesuit Mission to China 1579–1724* (Cambridge, MA: The Belknap Press of Harvard University Press, 2007), 113–14, 124, and 149; Liam Matthew Brockey, *The Visitor: André Palmeiro and the Jesuits in Asia* (Cambridge, MA: Harvard University Press, 2014), 439.

2 There are three versions of the list: one is in Biblioteca da Ajuda (hereafter BA/JA), 49–IV–66, fol. 98–99v, while the other two are in the Society of Jesus Historical Archives (ARSI), *Japonica-Sinica* (hereafter *JapSin*) 23, fol. 1v–2v, and 5–6. Without analyzing its context, Japanese historian Takase Kōichirō has disputed the credibility of this source, claiming there are not enough documents on land ownership. Takase Kōichirō, *Kirishitan Jidai no Kenkyū* (Tokyo: Iwanami Shoten, 1977), 438.

pay for everything in cash. According to his report, the priests were known as rich men who disbursed when building their facilities, hired servants, bought gifts and made donations.[3] Most of their finances came from their participation in the Nagasaki-Macau trade, but the missionaries' money did not derive solely from the proceeds of their trading activities. As Charles Boxer noted, they also accepted donations from wealthy Japanese and Portuguese, although assistance from private patrons overseas, the Portuguese crown and the Pope rarely arrived.[4]

Jesuits in Japan were also at the receiving end of land donations, however, an aspect that has received little scholarly attention. Those familiar with the history of early modern European-Japanese relations know the case of the small village of Nagasaki, donated to the mission in 1580. The donation was a major event in the history of Kyūshū, an area scarred by clashes between Japanese warlords such as the Ryūzōji clan of Hizen, in the western part of the island, the Ōtomo of Bungo, in the east, and the Shimazu of Satsuma, in the south. After succeeding Oda Nobunaga (1534–1582) ahead of the increasingly centralizing administration, Toyotomi Hideyoshi (1537–1598) arrived in Kyūshū in 1586 and started his military campaign to conquer the island. Amidst all the conflict between major powers, smaller lords such as the Ōmura and the Arima struggled to maintain their domains. In this scenario, the support offered by Jesuit missionaries, both military and commercial, was crucial for these lords. Despite being the most famous donation, Nagasaki was not the only village bequeathed to the mission. Effectively, missionaries received land, villages, and ports in various areas, a fact confirmed by Jesuit and Japanese sources. Yet there has been no thorough consideration given to land donations received by the Society of Jesus in Japan.[5]

---

3 Alessandro Valignano, *Adiciones del Sumario de Japon,* ed. José Luiz Alvarez-Taladriz (Osaka: private edition, undated), 462.

4 Charles R. Boxer, *The Affair of the Madre de Deus: A Chapter in the History of the Portuguese in Japan* (London/New York: Routledge, 2011), 24–25. See also Hélène Vu Thanh, "Investir dans une Nouvelle Religion. Le Cas de la Mission du Japon (XVIe-XVIIe siècles)," in *L'Église des laïcs. Le sacré en partage (XVIe–XXe siècles),* ed. Ariane Boltanski, and Marie-Lucie Copete (Madrid: Casa de Velázquez, forthcoming).

5 A small number of researchers have analyzed the finances of the Japanese mission. See Takase Kōichirō, *Kirishitan Jidai no Kenkyū* (Tokyo: Iwanami Shoten, 1977), 175–661; Helena Rodrigues, "Local Source of Funding for the Japanese Mission," *Bulletin of Portuguese/Japanese Studies* 7 (2003): 115–37; Hélène Vu Thanh, "Un équilibre impossible: financer la mission jésuite du Japon, entre Europe et Asie (1579–1614)," *Revue d'Histoire Moderne et Contemporaine* 63, no. 3 (2016): 7–30; and Vu Thanh, " *L'Église des laïcs.*"

Inspecting Jesuit records kept in Macau at the time, Almeida compiled a list of donations made by major Japanese converts, such as members of the Ōtomo, the Ōmura and the Arima clans. His list documents not only the extension of Jesuit influence in Japan, but also the numerous benefits they enjoyed as landlords. By looking closely into Almeida's list and other European and Japanese sources from a local point of view, my intention is to show that the Jesuit mission of Japan—the Vice-Province of Japan from 1582 onwards—actively sought land ownership as a means of securing stable sources of income. By design or not, they were becoming increasingly like local Buddhist organizations, amassing a considerable amount of political power by owning land and obtaining regular donations from local lords. This suffices to show their level of integration in local politics and their deep understanding of the social and political background of Japanese society.[6] Land ownership represented not only stable sources of revenue, but also political and administrative power over certain areas. However, the strategy led missionaries in unforeseen directions, as they eventually became one of the many targets of land policies implemented by Toyotomi Hideyoshi in 1587.

1   Temples and Plots of Land

Since disembarking in 1549 in Kagoshima, Francis Xavier (1506–1552) established relations with numerous *daimyō* or Japanese warlords, including the Ōuchi clan, the powerful rulers of Suō and Nagato, on the southernmost tip of the main island of the Japanese archipelago. Being a clan dependent on its maritime trade, it is not surprising to learn that their interest in the missionaries, and whatever commercial advantages that could bring, led Ōuchi Yoshinaga (1532–1557), leader of the clan, to offer Cosme de Torres (1510–1570)—then superior of the Jesuits—the Daidōji, a Buddhist temple in Yamaguchi, his political capital. The donation in 1552 guaranteed the missionaries a building to use as a church and the ruler's protection.[7] This was the first time Jesuit missionaries received a real estate donation in Japan.

---

6   On a global scale, though, Japan Jesuits were following the pattern described by Vermote in his chapter on mission finances, which argues Jesuit missions combining four sources of income—state patronage, private benefactors, trade, and lands/properties. See Frederik Vermote, "Financing Jesuit Missions," in *Oxford Handbook of the Jesuits*, ed. Ines G. Županov (New York: Oxford University Press, 2019), 129.

7   Renzo de Luca, "Daidōji Saikyojō to Iezusukai Shiryō no Hikaku Kenkyū," *Kyūshū Shigaku* 135 (2003): 40–41.

The following year, the Ōtomo clan followed suit. Ōtomo Yoshishige (1530–1587)—later Ōtomo Sōrin—gave a property to the mission in Bungo, one of his fiefs, which abided by the same terms determined by the previous concession made by the Ōuchi clan: the daimyō donated land for the Jesuits to build their churches and living quarters. And just as in the Daidōji donation, the lord also compromised himself into protecting the missionaries by giving them a *kinzei*—a three-article edict promising to protect the receiving party from general harm.[8]

Yoshishige became the first to break this pattern in 1558. Almeida lists the city of Hakata, one of the main ports of Southern Japan, as donated by Yoshishige to the missionaries. In his *Historia de Japam*, written in the later decades of the sixteenth century, Luís Fróis (1532–1597) explains that the donation of Hakata gave the priests a small annual revenue—Almeida listed it as worth 400 *taels*, or 264,000 *réis*.[9] Gaspar Vilela (1525–1572) wrote that the daimyō gave the lot in Hakata to support their hospital in Funai, founded in 1556.[10] It was not the whole city that was donated to the mission, in fact, but rather a street ward. Miyazaki Katsunori explains the area handed over to the mission was in the Myōrakuji ward, an area that included the beach of Ikinohama. According to Miyazaki, the location suggests Yoshishige's plan to attract Portuguese ships to the port, although no such trading vessel ever docked in Hakata.[11] And, differently from what happened in Yamaguchi and in Bungo, that was the first time Jesuits received a donation that entitled them to an income, obtained from taxes collected from the citizens of the area.

In the following year, Cosme de Torres sent the priest Baltasar Gago (1515–1583) to Hakata in order to take over the donated area. The events following his arrival became one of the most traumatic episodes for the missionaries in

---

8   The *kinzei* was a specific type of protection that was usually negotiated between commoners and warlords. For the Daidōji kinzei, see de Luca, "Daidōji Saikyojō," 40. For more on kinzei and its negotiation, see Fujiki Hisashi, *Zōhyōtachi no Senjō—Chūsei no Yōhei to Doreigari* (Tokyo: Asahi Shinbunsha, 2005), 188–89.

9   *JapSin* 23, fol. 1v, 5v; BA/JA, 49–IV–66, fol. 98–98v; Luís Fróis, *Historia de Japam*, 1 (hereafter HJ followed by volume number), ed. Josef Wicki (Lisbon: Biblioteca Nacional de Lisboa, 1976), 127. Tael was the unit used to count silver in early modern East Asia. In 1598, Valignano explained that one tael was worth 660 réis. See *JapSin* 13 1, fol. 135v. Sebastião de Almeida considers one tael worth the same as one *koku* of rice.

10   *Cartas que los padres y hermanos de la Compañia de Iesus, que andan en los Reynos de Iapon escriuieron a los de la misma Compañia, desde el año de mil y quinientos y quarenta y nueue, hasta el mil y quinientos y setenta y uno* (Alcalá: en casa de Juan Iniguez de Lequerica, 1575), fol. 80v, and 87v; Vu Thanh, "L'Église des laïcs," 8.

11   Miyazaki Katsunori and Fukuoka Archive Kenkyūkai, *Kenperu ya Shiiboruto tachi ga mita Kyūshū, soshite Nippon* (Fukuoka: Kaichōsha, 2009), 18.

their first decades in the country: the city was attacked and the priest ended up being captured by Japanese *zōhyō*—low-ranking warriors and mercenaries who obtained revenues from spoils of war and captives—only to be rescued by local Christians. The plot where the residence and the church were being built was burnt to the ground, and the well they had was filled with trash. Gago and his companions had to leave the city wearing women's clothes. As a result, missionaries avoided Hakata, and no Jesuits entered the city after 1561.[12] Ten years after the donation, Yoshishige lost Hakata to rebels, which meant the end of Jesuit revenues.[13] Sebastião de Almeida wrote that the plot was donated to the Jesuits for ten years, which may be a reference to this period between 1557 and 1567. However, after Yoshishige regained control of Hakata in 1569, he made a new donation to the mission, although the date of this second donation remains uncertain.

Fróis explains that Jesuit priest Belchior de Figueiredo (?-1597) was sent to the city in 1575 by then superior Francisco Cabral (1528–1609), accompanied by former merchant and Jesuit brother Luís de Almeida (1525–1583), to retake the former church. Upon their arrival, young representatives of various wards approached the priest and demanded to use the building to store wood and other materials used in the local Gion festival.[14] Their plea was met with contempt by the Jesuits, who refused to concede. The quarrel continued for a month, until the church was eventually invaded by an angry mob demanding to use it. Older locals, or *toshiyori*—effectively, administrators of the ward—had to intervene to put an end to the dispute.[15]

In 1580, Ryūzōji Takanobu (1529–1584) attacked Hakata. The city was once again burned to the ground and sacked. Although the priests had managed to leave the area prior to the attack, they lost their church and residence in the process. According to Fróis, Jesuits enjoyed an annual revenue of 230 or 330 *cruzados* from the ward at the time.[16] It is uncertain whether they kept their lot in Hakata after this attack, however.

Ōtomo Yoshishige's donations also involved a plot of land in the village of Ohama, where Jesuits built a college for novices and had some crops, although

---

12   HJ I, 131, and HJ II, 445.

13   Yoshinaga Masaharu, *Kyūshū Sengokushi* (Tokyo: Ashishobō, 1981), 250.

14   For more on temples as storage for locals, see chapter eight in Fujiki Hisashi, *Mura to Ryōshu no Sengoku Sekai* (Tokyo: Tōkyō Daigaku Shuppankai, 1997). The Gion festival is an annual summer festival where floats are paraded on the streets of Japanese cities.

15   Miyazaki and Fukuoka, *Kenperu ya Shiiboruto tachi*, 18–19; HJ II, 446–47.

16   HJ III, 185–86; Josef Franz Schütte, *Introductio ad Historiam Societatis Jesu in Japonia, 1549–1650* (Rome: Institutum Historicum Societatis Jesu, 1968; hereafter MHJ), 589.

their revenue was minimal. In 1582, Yoshishige gave three temples in Tsukumi, the place he had chosen to live after retiring. According to Almeida, the revenue from these temples was enough to maintain the local Jesuit residence. Both Ohama and the temples in Tsukumi were lost when Hideyoshi redistributed the domains of the Ōtomo clan between 1587 and 1588.[17]

These early experiences with land and revenues donated by warlords cemented the notion among missionaries that they needed to be recognized as a religious organization similar to Buddhist sects in order to get access to this kind of income. Their understanding of the system is clear in the Japanese-Portuguese dictionary of 1603, where they included the entry *kishin* 寄進—"esmola, ou renda que se dá às varelas, ou mosteiros"—, tithes or revenues one gives to pagodas or monasteries. The kishin was a specific type of donation offered to religious organizations which included not only rice, silver, wood, and other materials, but also stable sources of income. Aware of this from the first decades of their presence in Japan, starting from the 1560s, Jesuits sought a new, more aggressive strategy of amassing land and revenues.

2   Expanding Their Reach

In the 1560s, Jesuits moved closer to the main trading center of Kyūshū: the western city of Hirado. They had allies in the region, such as the Koteda clan, vassals of the Matsura clan, lords of Hirado, but failed in their attempts to establish themselves in the city. In 1561, though, a dispute over the silk price in Hirado resulted in the deaths of fourteen Portuguese—including that year's captain-major, Fernão de Sousa. The Jesuits quickly seized their opportunity. The plan, which was executed by brother Luís de Almeida, was to convert a local ruler and secure a port for shipping from Macau.[18]

In the following year, missionaries successfully obtained the donation of Yokoseura, a small port on the northern part of the Sonogi Peninsula. The donation was made by Ōmura Sumitada (1533–1587), a small warlord interested in attracting Portuguese merchants and obstructing Hirado. The act included an area of two Portuguese miles—about eight kilometres—around the harbour.[19]

---

17   *JapSin* 23, fol. 1v, 5v; BA/JA, 49-IV-66, 98v; HJ II, 90; HJ IV, 16–17; Ōmura-shi Hensan
       Iinkai, *Shin'hen Ōmura-shi Shi, Dainikan Chūseihen* (Ōmura: Ōmura City, 2014; hereafter
       Chūseihen), 415.

18   Reinier H. Hesselink, *Dream of a Christian Nagasaki: World Trade and the Clash of Cultures
       1560–1640* (Jefferson, USA: McFarland & Company, 2016) 19–20.

19   Hesselink, *Dream*, 21.

Furthermore, the donation came with the specification that the port would have only Christian residents, unless otherwise allowed by the priests. Also, Japanese and Portuguese merchants would be exempt from any taxes for ten years whenever they chose Yokoseura for trade.[20] This new donation marked the beginning of a new pattern, as it included wider administrative rights over the donated village.

In the summer of 1562, the superior of the mission, Cosme de Torres, moved to the newly-established Christian port, while the priests and their Japanese converts spent their first months in the village building a new "church and a residence on the spot where formerly a Buddhist temple had stood."[21] Moreover, as Sumitada had agreed to make Yokoseura a Christian port, it became the first of a series of Jesuit domains in Japan exclusively inhabited by converted indigenous people. Villages and ports donated to the Japanese mission also became privileged spaces for Jesuits, where missionaries had the monopoly of both secular and spiritual authority and could closely monitor the religious development of Japanese converts.[22] In the end, Yokoseura was the blueprint for what would become the most important port in the lands of the Ōmura: Nagasaki.[23]

Nagasaki's donation in 1580 has been studied by numerous scholars.[24] Almeida's list considers Nagasaki generated a yearly revenue of 700 taels or 462,000 réis for the priests.[25] However, the income obtained from the port and its surrounding areas seems to vary according to the source. Some confirm Almeida, but others indicate annual revenues of 300 cruzados, 700 ducados, 1000 cruzados or 1000 ducados.[26] Nonetheless, while these values refer to taxes

---

20 Anno Masaki, *Kyōkairyō Nagasaki—Iezusukai to Nihon* (Tokyo: Kōdansha, 2014), 6, 41, and 81; *Cartas que os padres e irmãos da Companhia de Iesus escreuerão dos Reynos de Iapão & China aos da mesma Companhia da India, & Europa des do anno de 1549 até o de 1580*, I (Évora: por Manoel de Lyra, 1598; hereafter Cartas 1598 followed by volume number), fol. 109.

21 Hesselink, *Dream*, 21.

22 This followed a pattern similar to the Brazilian *aldeamentos*—villages established by the Portuguese, where Indigenous peoples from various nations could be found. See Carlos Alberto de Moura Ribeiro Zeron, *Linha de Fé: A Companhia de Jesus e a Escravidão no Processo de Formação da Sociedade Colonial (Brasil, Séculos XVI e XVII)* (São Paulo: Edusp, 2011), 42–43, 82–83.

23 Shimizu Hirokazu, *Shokuhō Seiken to Kirishitan—Nichiō Kōshō no Kigen to Tenkai* (Tokyo: Iwata Shoin, 2001), 240.

24 See the comprehensive list compiled in Hesselink, *Dream*, 260–72.

25 *JapSin* 23, fol. 1v, 5v, BA/JA, 49–IV–66, fol. 98v.

26 Anno Masaki, *Kyōkairyō Nagasaki*, 102. However, these differences can also be attributed to mistaken conversions made by different writers. In a letter written in January 1598, Valignano explained that mistakes like these were common in translations. According to

related to trading activities in the port, missionaries also enjoyed the benefits from the production of foodstuffs and other goods around the port.

Further donations by Sumitada were recorded by Afonso de Lucena (1551–1623), a missionary who lived for thirty-seven years in Ōmura: "He built some churches at his expense and gave the Society [of Jesus] some small places and revenues which somehow maintained us."[27] In his list, Sebastião de Almeida noted the following villages: "Iquinoura," "Toquitex," "Maxama" and "Fuxoins." By comparing these with Japanese sources such as the *Ōmura Keki* and the *Ōmura Gōsonki*, it is possible to identify most of the donated areas.[28] Iquinoura, for instance, is most definitely the village of Yukinoura. Located on the Sonogi Peninsula, it provided the mission an income of 120 taels or 79,200 réis every year.[29] Next is Tokitsu, a small port facing Ōmura Bay that also gave the mission 120 taels per year. The same revenue was obtained from "Maxama," although no Japanese source mentions any village or port with such a name. The last item is the Hōshōji, a temple referred by Lucena as "Fuxonji" and described in his journal as "our old place in Ōmura." According to Almeida, it represented an annual income of 100 taels or 66,000 réis. Located on the left margin of the Daijōgo River, the temple was an important centre for Buddhist believers in the fourteenth century; thus the income could be from taxes collected from residents of the village surrounding the complex. Sumitada donated it to the church and allowed the temple to become a language school and dormitory for the missionaries.[30] The Hōshōji also became Sumitada's final resting place until his remains were moved to a different area in 1599.[31]

Almeida also lists donations by Sumitada's son, Yoshiaki (1568–1615). According to the Jesuit, three places were donated by Yoshiaki: "Terai," "Canje"

---

him, one tael was actually worth 660 réis, while "one Spanish ducado was not worth more than 434 réis" (*JapSin* 13 I, fol. 135v).

27   Lucena, Afonso de, "De algumas cousas que ainda se alembra o Pe. Afonso de Lucena que pertencem à Christandade de Omura," in *Erinnerungen aus der Christenheit von Omura: 1578–1614*, ed. Josef Franz Schütte (Rome: Institutum Historicum Societatis Iesu, 1972), 142.

28   Compiled in 1703, the manuscript chronicle of the Ōmura clan, *Ōmura Keki*, is a major source on the clan's history, while the *Ōmura Gōsonki* is a detailed record of villages of the fief. See *Ōmura Keki*, volume 2, 10–12; also, Fujino Tamotsu, ed. *Ōmura Gōsonki*, 1 (Tokyo: Kokusho Kankōkai, 1982); Lucena, "De algumas coisas," 186; *JapSin* 23, fol. 1v–2, 5v; and BA/JA, 49–IV–66, fol. 98v.

29   *JapSin* 23, fol. 1v–2, 5v, BA/JA, 49–IV–66, fol. 98v.

30   Ōmura-shi, *Chūseihen*, 427–428, and 436.

31   Ōmura-shi Hensan Iinkai, *Shin'hen Ōmura-shi Shi, Daigokan Furoku* (Ōmura: Ōmura City, 2014), 526; Fujino Tamotsu, ed, *Ōmura Gōsonki*, 1 (Tokyo: Kokusho Kankōkai, 1982), 114–15, 232–33.

and "Finami." The first two, identified as the villages of Taira and Kanze, represented an annual revenue of seventy taels or 46,200 réis, while the last one—
the village of Hinami—was worth 180 taels or 118,800 réis. All these sources of
revenue in the lands of the Ōmura clan—with the exception of those taken
over by Hideyoshi in 1587—were kept until the missionaries were eventually
expelled by Yoshiaki in 1606.[32] According to Almeida, revenues from wood and
other supplies obtained from all villages donated by Sumitada and Yoshiaki
amounted to almost the same value in taels, although the calculation probably
did not include Nagasaki.[33]

Still, it seems there was a large discrepancy between the income obtained
from each village in silver and their production capacities. The chronicle *Ōmura Keki* lists the *kokudaka*—or the expected production value—for each village
during the Edo Period, when the land value for the whole Ōmura domain was
calculated as almost 28,000 *koku* after Tokugawa Hidetada (1579–1632) coordi-
nated the land survey of 1617. Before that, the total production expected from
the lands of the Ōmura during Yoshiaki's rule was a little over 26,000 koku, so
there was not much difference overall.[34]

The three villages donated by Yoshiaki to the mission clearly show this discrepancy. While both villages of Kanze and Taira are listed by Almeida as generating a yearly income of 70 taels to the missionaries, the former appears in
Japanese sources with an estimated yield value of 316 koku and the latter, 218
koku. Meanwhile, Hinami, the third village donated by Yoshiaki with a revenue of 180 taels, had an estimated value of 111 koku. There is no doubt that the
amounts registered by Almeida were rounded, but the difference between the
income obtained by Jesuits and the yield value of the first two villages is too
large. It appears there is no direct correspondence between land production
capacity and the revenue Jesuits obtained from each village. The most likely
scenario was that the Ōmura clan donated fixed amounts of revenue, based
not on the yield value of the land, but on an arbitrary amount. The clan did
not submit entire portions of its revenue to the mission, but rather donated
the right to a portion of the collected taxes. Also, considering villagers paid
their taxes through local village authorities, it is possible total revenues were
centralized in the hands of the clan before the promised amounts were passed
to the mission. Almeida writes down all these values, noting they were calculated in silver; thus it is highly probable that all income obtained from these
areas was paid in cash. The same process happened in Nagasaki: Anno Masaki

---

32   Lucena, "De algumas coisas," 160.
33   *JapSin* 23, fol. 1V–2, 5V–6, BA/JA, 49–IV–66, fol. 98v–99.
34   *Ōmura Keki*, 2, 38.

explains that the donation of Nagasaki consisted mainly of the concession of a fixed amount of land tax or *jishi* paid annually to the mission.[35] Thus, most donations in the domains of the Ōmura clan replicated the model of Nagasaki, and previously the model of Yokoseura, as the mission acquired the right to a certain fixed income from each village.

3   Becoming Landlords

It was in the lands of the Arima that the Jesuits were most successful in amassing territorial control and revenues. According to Valignano, when the mission established itself in Yokoseura, in the early 1560s, other local lords began looking for the priests. At that time, the priests were approached by a lord from Shimabara, who had sent one of his magistrates, the *jitō* of the port of Kuchinotsu, with a gift and an offer of a field where the missionaries could build their church. Jesuits gladly took the offer, and Luís de Almeida was dispatched to Shimabara. Soon, the region became part of the route used by missionaries between Nagasaki and Bungo.[36] In 1567, two Portuguese ships entered Kuchinotsu, followed by another in 1576, when Arima Yoshisada (1521–1577) was baptized and became Dom André, at least in Portuguese sources.[37]

Yoshisada died the following year, leaving his son Harunobu (1567–1612) in command of the Arima clan. In 1579, a Portuguese ship entered the port of Kuchinotsu—that year, while Ōmura Sumitada negotiated the donation of Nagasaki to the mission, Harunobu faced constant attacks from the Ryūzōji clan.[38] Through Sumitada, the priests suggested the lord of Arima to donate the port of Mogi, situated on Tachibana Bay, in exchange for military support. Mogi would give Jesuits easy access to the Shimabara Peninsula, the Amakusa Islands and Higo.[39] Harunobu accepted the offer and made the donation to the mission, which was confirmed by Ōmura Sumitada in 1580 along with Nagasaki. Reinier Hesselink also indicates that the donation favoured Sumitada as

35   Anno, *Kyōkairyō Nagasaki*, 95–96.

36   Alessandro Valignano, *Historia del Principio y Progresso de la Compañia de Jesús en las Indias Orientales (1542–1564)*, ed. Josef Wicki (Rome: Institutum Historicum Societatis Jesu), 448; Hesselink, *Dream*, 24.

37   Shimizu Hirokazu, "Arima Harunobu," in *Kirishitan Daimyō—Fukyō, Seisaku, Shinkō no Jissō*, ed. Gonoi Takashi (Tokyo: Miyaobi Shuppansha, 2017), 194–95.

38   Kudamatsu Kazunori, "Ōmura Sumitada," in *Kirishitan Daimyō—Fukyō, Seisaku, Shinkō no Jissō*, ed. Gonoi Takashi (Tokyo: Miyaobi Shuppansha, 2017), 175.

39   For more on the military support offered by the Jesuits, see Takase, *Kirishitan Jidai*, 120–25.

well, since the lord of Ōmura now had an escape route if the Ryūzōji attacked from the north.[40]

The village of Mogi was described in 1588 by Vice-Provincial of Japan Gaspar Coelho (1529–1590) as the source of about 300 cruzados or 120,000 réis of annual revenue to the mission, enough to maintain the residence and all the churches of Ōmura or Nagasaki.[41] However, according to Almeida's list, Harunobu donated rice paddies in Mogi that represented an annual revenue of 500 koku, which the author calculates to be equivalent to 500 silver taels or 330,000 réis. The value in koku on the list must not be understood as equivalent to the yield value of the land, though. Rather, since Almeida equates it to the amount collected in silver, it seems the listed income was obtained from the collection of taxes. The donation included wheat and barley fields, as well as wood and bamboo forests that also yielded the mission 500 taels every year. Furthermore, the priests obtained about 150 taels or 99,000 réis of salt, fish, vegetables and construction wood, which locals were obligated to deliver yearly to the mission.[42]

Takase considers the large disparity between the amount Coelho describes in his letter and what the list indicates for Mogi sufficient reason to discredit Almeida's source.[43] Still, the two seem to be referring to different incomes: while the priest describes revenues obtained from the village itself, Almeida's list refers to the income from its surrounding fields. Furthermore, this difference could be attributed to the disparity between Jesuit expectations and what they actually received from their landholdings. For instance, Valignano admitted in 1580 that, since Jesuits were not as cruel as Japanese warlords in punishing farmers, the latter did not work as hard as they could, and the missionaries did not earn as much as they could from their lands in Nagasaki and Mogi.[44] These values should thus not be taken as indicative of actual mission's economics. Instead, they point to the political power and influence Jesuits had in the region, which was sufficient to obtain those large donations.

Both Nagasaki and Mogi were taken over by Hideyoshi in 1587, whereupon he installed a new government in the following year.[45] Using Japanese sources,

---

40   Anno, *Kyōkairyō Nagasaki*, 98–99, Hesselink, *Dream*, 66–67.

41   Takase, *Kirishitan Jidai*, 431; Josef Franz Shchütte, ed., *Monumenta Historica Japoniae 1553–1654* (Rome: Institutum Historicum Societatis Jesu, 1975), 192.

42   *JapSin* 23, fol. 2, 6, BA/JA, 49–IV–66, fol. 99.

43   Takase, *Kirishitan Jidai*.

44   Alessandro Valignano, *Sumario de las Cosas de Japón (1583)*, ed. José Luís Alvarez-Taladriz (Tokyo: Sophia University, 1954), 78–79. Quoted by Takase, *idem*.

45   Nagasaki, Urakami and Mogi were taken by Hideyoshi in 1587. See HJ IV, 418.

Shimizu Hirokazu shows that the takeover involved Mogi, the inner town of Nagasaki (that is to say, its original six wards), part of the area of Urakami, the village of Ieno, and Sotome, as the group of villages of Azekari, Kurosaki, and part of Yukinoura was known. As these last three villages were located on the western coast of the Sonogi Peninsula, they were strategic ports for Portuguese ships navigating between Hirado, Nagasaki and Kuchinotsu.[46] In 1587, Francisco Pasio (1554–1612) wrote that Sumitada and Harunobu had complained that the villages taken by Hideyoshi were theirs to begin with, and both lords managed to collect taxes that year. For that reason, the mission did not immediately consider these villages lost, as both warlords had agreed to act on their behalf and keep the flow of monies to the Jesuits.[47] Nevertheless, beginning with the appointment of the first *daikan* of Nagasaki in the following year, Jesuits effectively lost all revenues from those areas taken by Hideyoshi.[48]

The donation of the region of Urakami, to the north of Nagasaki, was described by Luís Fróis as the result of a vow Harunobu made to the Church: if God gave him victory in the battle against Ryūzōji Takanobu, Harunobu would give the mission all the revenue from a famous monastery of the region. Japanese sources tell us that was the temple Manmyōji, located in Mount Onsen, now Mount Unzen. According to Fróis, Jesuits suggested Harunobu change his offer because, as the temple's revenue was split among many Christians and non-Christians, donating it to the mission could be problematic. Yet, the diary of Uwai Kakken (1545–1589), a warrior serving the forces of Satsuma, shows that the Shimazu had promised to rebuild the Manmyōji, which had been destroyed during the previous conflict with the Ryūzōji. Shimizu also explains that strained relations with neighbouring clans, such as the Fukahori, and the fact that monks from the Manmyōji had survived the battle, made it difficult for Harunobu to donate the temple. The daimyō decided to donate instead the villages of Urakami. In May of 1584, men led by Arima Harunobu, aided by a force sent by the Shimazu, defeated the army of Ryūzōji Takanobu in the Battle of Okita-Nawate. Takanobu died in battle, and Urakami's revenue was given to the Jesuits.[49]

The Jesuit possession of Urakami was not free from trouble. Lucena wrote that after defeating allies of the Satsuma and Arima and expelling them from

---

46   Shimizu Hirokazu, "Hizen Urakami no Bungō Katei," *Kirisutokyō Shigaku* 47 (1993): 40–42.

47   Cartas 1598 II, fol. 214v–215.

48   Shimizu considers the idea that Sumitada and Harunobu temporarily took back control of Nagasaki and Urakami a fabrication of later Japanese sources. Shimizu, *Shokuhō Seiken to Kirishitan*, 340.

49   MHJ, 396, and 431; HJ IV, 73; Shimizu, "Hizen Urakami," 36.

Hokame and Uchime—the outer and inner coasts of the Sonogi Peninsula near Nagasaki—Ōmura Sumitada took control over the region in 1586. According to Lucena, Jesuit superiors grew irate with Sumitada, demanding the priest intervened with the lord of Ōmura in order to restore Urakami to the mission. The Japanese warlord agreed and donated Urakami back to the church, letting the missionaries controll the area one more year until Hideyoshi took over Nagasaki. Lucena wrote that, if properly administered, the villages of Urakami could generate a yearly revenue of 3,000 taels, or 1,980,000 réis.[50] Furthermore, Shimizu believes that, as the group of villages of Sotome was taken by the Ōmura clan from the Arima in 1586, it is reasonable to suppose that these villages were also donated with Urakami this second time.[51] Although it is impossible to know whether he refers to the first or second donation, Almeida puts Urakami's rice paddies's annual income at 1500 koku, which he explains was the equivalent to 1500 taels or 990,000 réis. At the same time, fields of wheat and barley in Urakami generated a revenue of 200 taels or 132,000 réis for the mission.

Just as important as Urakami and Mogi was another large donation by Arima Harunobu, which included rice paddies and fields in Kazusa—located in the Shimabara Peninsula—and some other areas in his domains. Almeida calculates that these represented a yearly revenue of 1100 koku or 1100 taels or 726,000 réis from the rice paddies, plus 200 taels more from wheat and barley production, totalling 858,000 réis. It is difficult to pinpoint when Kazusa and these other areas Almeida mentions were donated, but the list records the mission had this source of revenue for twenty years or so. Considering the gradually closer relationship developed between the mission and the Arima clan in the 1580s, it is reasonable to assume that these donations happened during this period as well and lasted until the early seventeenth century. That seems to be the case, as Francisco Pires (1563–1632) recorded quite regretfully a land survey in 1602 that greatly diminished revenues for the Shimabara Peninsula.[52]

Almeida also notes there were other smaller areas donated to the mission, which according to the list totalled 150 taels or 99,000 réis in annual revenues. One example is a group of wards donated to the mission in 1584 by Andoku Yasutoshi, Harunobu's maternal uncle, which surrounded the Jesuit seminary.[53]

But not all landholdings obtained by the mission in this period were derived from donations. During the 1580–81 consultation of the mission, the

50   Lucena, "De algumas coisas," 122–24.
51   Shimizu, "Hizen Urakami," 42.
52   MHJ, 418.
53   HJ IV, 72–73.

missionaries discussed whether they should purchase real estate. Although only eight out of twenty-six priests were in favor of openly buying land, these were senior Jesuits: Vice-Provincial Gaspar Coelho, rector of the Nagasaki College António Lopes, veteran Luís de Almeida, among others. They defended these purchases on the grounds they would guarantee sources of revenue to the mission, but also give them the right to summon up residents of acquired villages and fields to work for them. Valignano admitted the possibility of buying land under exceptional circumstances, but only in the domains of converted Japanese warlords, in order to safeguard their investment.[54] In 1583, Valignano wrote to Claudio Acquaviva (1543–1615), general superior of the Society of Jesus, arguing that, because of the uncertainties of the trading ships between India, Macau and Nagasaki, the Jesuits in Japan needed large sums to purchase land and guarantee their subsistence. According to Takase Kōichirō, the General of the Society of Jesus promptly agreed.[55]

Before the battle of Okita-Nawate in 1584, Harunobu had agreed to sell the fields of Hachirao to the mission.[56] It is hard to say exactly what this sale meant, since Jesuit sources do not openly offer details about these businesses. However, looking into Japanese legislation, it is possible to discern among three basic types of sale: definitive sales or *eichi*; temporary sales or *nenkiuri*, according to which one could have a property for an agreed number of years; and finally, conditioned sales or *honsengaeshi*, where the original seller or owner retained the right to take the property back at any moment.[57]

In 1592, the priests decided they should invest in real estate in order to maintain their facilities. In their view, a residence could be maintained with the purchase of six to ten *chō*—one chō being a little more than 9900 m² of land.[58] But the missionaries acquired much larger fields than they had initially agreed on. In a 1593 letter, former superior of the Japanese mission, Francisco Cabral, wrote to Rome saying he had received information concerning the purchase of a large field in the lands of the Arima clan. It seems Japan Jesuits had bought from Arima Harunobu an area of ninety chō, which could represent a revenue of 900 koku, the equivalent of 594,000 réis.[59] Sure enough, Cabral criticized

54   Takase, *Kirishitan Jidai*, 411–17.
55   Josef Wicki and John Gomes, *Documenta Indica*, volume XII (Rome: Institutum Historicum Societatis Iesu, 1948–1988; hereafter DI followed by volume number), 856, mentioned in Takase, *Kirishitan Jidai*, 426–27.
56   MHJ, 431.
57   Maki Hidemasa and Fujiwara Akihisa, *Nihon Hōseishi* (Tokyo: Seirin Shoin, 1993), 152–53.
58   Takase, *Kirishitan Jidai*, 429; Valignano, *Adiciones*, 712–13; DI XVI, 521.
59   According to Alvarez-Taladriz, one chō produced ten koku. See Valignano, *Adiciones*, 712.

the decision: if a "lord in Japan owned 90 chō he had a very large house and more than fifty soldiers, who were obliged to follow him in battle and serve him in other services."[60] Considering the limits imposed in 1592 on these purchases, Takase believes that Japan Jesuits acquired this large area in the domains of the Arima clan before the meeting. Moreover, Takase argues that this specific purchase led to the restriction on the size of land acquisitions.[61]

Almeida's list also records the name of Konishi Yukinaga (1558–1600) as one of the main benefactors of the mission. Baptized Agostinho, the daimyō did not donate any land to the missionaries, but rather foodstuffs and tithes. Furthermore, the amount of rice donated by Yukinaga varied, from 700 to 1000 bales, which amounted to 350 to 500 koku or 231,000 to 330,000 réis.[62] Francisco Pires' *Pontos do que me alembrar* confirms the practice, although there is a large difference in the amount donated: the priest wrote in 1592 that Yukinaga donated two to three thousand koku of rice each year or 1,320,000 to 1,980,000 réis.[63] And when the Bishop of Japan Pedro Martins (1542–1598) arrived in Nagasaki in 1596, the daimyō celebrated the arrival by sending two hundred bales of rice and others of wheat, an act quickly followed by other lords.[64]

Even though Almeida did not list any real estate donation by Yukinaga to the mission, it seems the daimyō did give the missionaries some small sources of income. For example, in 1590, he authorized the Italian Jesuit Organtino Gnecchi-Soldo (1532–1609) to use some of the rice from a piece of land donated by Yukinaga to help the poor. The daimyō also promised to give the priests revenues from Shiki, a village in the archipelago of Amakusa, and donated to the missionaries "a large plot with more than two hundred braças in length and some in width" for them to build a church and their quarters.[65]

Another benefactor listed by Almeida is Amakusa Hisatane (?-1601). The relation of the Amakusa clan with the mission started in 1569, when brother Luís de Almeida entered the region for the first time. Almeida negotiated a five-article treaty with Amakusa Shigehisa (?-1582), according to which the mission was to receive land in the bay of Kawachinoura to build their church. Eventually, the Jesuit ordered the construction of a small church and the installation of two cannons overlooking the inlet. Two years later, mission superior Francisco

---

60   DI XVI, 521.
61   Takase, *Kirishitan Jidai*, 436.
62   *JapSin* 23, fol. 2, 6; BA/JA, 49–IV–66, fol. 99–99v; MHJ, 348.
63   MHJ, 406–407.
64   Torre do Tombo National Archives (Lisbon), Casa de Cadaval, n. 26, "Papeles Varios Curiosos," fol. 357v–358.
65   HJ V, 240.

Cabral baptized Shigehisa as D. Miguel and his son Hisatane as D. João. Ten years later, Jesuit letters described the domains of the Amakusa clan as one of the most important centers of Japanese Christianity, with more than thirty churches and fifteen thousand Christians.[66]

In a letter written in 1583, Cabral mentions that the Japan Jesuits had received a donation of 10 chō in Amakusa to maintain two priests and two brothers.[67] It is uncertain, though, whether this was Kawachinoura, and Sebastião de Almeida does not offer any detail. However, the list refers to donations made by Shigehisa's son, Hisatane. According to Almeida, D. João donated two properties to the priests and brothers. Furthermore, he donated plenty of "floodplains, fields, land plots, forests, wood, and laborers." Calculated in silver, all summed up to about 250 taels, or 165,000 réis. Almeida also wrote that the Jesuits enjoyed this revenue for almost thirty years.[68] Considering their expulsion in 1614, the mission probably received these in the 1580s.

4   Duties and Rights

Since the donation of Yokoseura, Japan Jesuits strengthened their position as political players. It was in the small port offered by Sumitada in 1562 that missionaries obtained access to revenues from taxes and agricultural production, as well as labor and supplies obtained from locals. These were a different kind of donation, which represented not only a source of income but actual and publicly recognized political power. In the fiefs of the Ōmura and Arima clans, Japanese sources clearly specify this authority, known in Japanese as *chigyō*, over some of these spaces.

After the edict expelling the missionaries, in 1588 Toyotomi Hideyoshi appointed Nabeshima Naoshige (1538–1618), a lord from Saga, to govern Nagasaki. The document nominating Nabeshima daikan publicly recognizes that Nagasaki had been a chigyō of the priests until then.[69] According to José Luís Alvarez-Taladriz, the first mention of the term chigyō in missionary sources is a letter written by Luís Fróis in 1569.[70] As recognized by Japanese authorities such as Hideyoshi, Nagasaki, Urakami and Mogi were chigyō of the Jesuits, but

66   Tsuruta Kurazō and Hirata Toyohiro, "Amakusa Goninshū," in *Kirishitan Daimyō—Fukyō, Seisaku, Shinkō no Jissō*, ed. Gonoi Takashi (Tokyo: Miyaobi Shuppansha, 2017), 394–95.

67   Takase, *Kirishitan Jidai*, 434.

68   *JapSin* 23, fol. 2v, 6; BA/JA, 49–IV–66, fol. 99v.

69   Yasutaka Hiroaki, *Kinsei Nagasaki Shihō Seido no Kenkyū* (Tokyo: Shibunkaku, 2010), 120.

70   Valignano, *Sumario*, 319.

the *Nagasaki Nenraiki* mentions three more villages under Jesuit authority or chigyō: Tokitsu, which appears in Almeida's list, Nagayo and Himi.[71] The Jesuit administration depended on negotiation with village authorities, however, which could be called either *tōnin*, *otona*, or even the so-called *shū*: political groups formed by *jizamurai* (samurai gentry or yeomanry) or *hyakushō*, known locally by names such as *hyakushōchū*, *yoriaichū*, *sonchūichimi*, *tonobarashū*, and so on.[72]

It seems the term chigyō referred both to political power and the land itself. In the Latin-Portuguese-Japanese dictionary of 1595, this Japanese word was used to explain not only *possessio*, but also Latin terms such as *fundus* (a defined portion of land), *pascuum* (pasture), *positio* (crop), and *praedium* (immovable things).[73] When explaining to Europeans the notion of chigyō, the 1603–1604 Japanese-Portuguese dictionary translated it as *"terras de renda,"* indicating the term meant arable fields as sources of income or revenue to their owners. That is also the conclusion by Anno Masaki, who reviewing previous research on the meaning of chigyō in Kamakura Japan explained that in early modern Kyūshū the term referred not only to the power or authority over a given land, but also to the real estate itself.[74] This double meaning was well-understood by the Jesuits. Not only that, it seems they saw themselves on an equal footing with other Japanese rulers for a while. In his journal, Afonso de Lucena mentions that when Toyotomi Hideyoshi arrived in Hakata in 1586, all Japanese warlords and their vassals went to the city to recognize his central authority. Among them "was also Fr. Gaspar Coelho, our Vice-Provincial," who had gone to congratulate Hideyoshi on his victory and to ask for the protection of the missionaries and all Japanese converts.[75]

Donating a chigyō meant entrusting the administration of entire villages to a donatary. When explaining in his report to the superior general how properties were distributed in Japan, Valignano wrote that all lands were owned first by the emperor, and whenever a lord gave a piece of property to others, this local ruler would employ the term *depositar*, which can be understood as entrust, commit or deposit.[76] Effectively, depositar is translated as *azukaru* in the

---

71   Anno, *Kyōkairyō Nagasaki*, 143–144.
72   Kitajima Manji, "Tenshōki ni okeru Ryōshuteki Kesshū no Dōkō to Daimyō Kenryoku," in *Kyūshū Daimyō no Kenkyū*, ed. Kimura Tadao (Tokyo: Yoshikawa Kōbunkan, 1983), 271.
73   James J. Robinson, *Selections from the Public and Private Law of the Romans* (New York: American Book Company, 1905).
74   Anno Masaki, "Kyōkairyō Kishin Monjo no Kenkyū," *Shigaku Zasshi* 85, no. 1 (1976): 45.
75   Lucena, "De algumas coisas," 166.
76   Valignano, *Sumário*, 318.

1595 Latin-Portuguese-Japanese dictionary printed in Japan, as seen in entries such as *consigno, depono, depositarius* or *sculna*.[77]

The case of Nagasaki can help us understand the negotiated administration of a chigyō. In an edict enacted by Hideyoshi in 1588 exempting Nagasaki's citizens from taxes, the Japanese ruler refers to the city as a *sōmachi*.[78] The term is derived from the *sōson*, a kind of village administered by an independent body, which paid taxes to its local lord. Nagasaki's administration was then in the hands of the so-called *tōnin*, who would later become the city's *machitoshiyori* or *otona*, each one basically responsible for the administration of a street ward or chō.[79]

In his explanation of how Japanese lords ruled their fiefs, Valignano wrote that those who were entrusted with lands in Japan had *mero et mixto imperio* over said areas; that is to say, the absolute power to execute capital and other punishments against public and other crimes. At the same time, this classification by the Visitor shows that there was still a power superior to these lords. The explanation emulated what happened in Portugal where, according to António Hespanha, the king remained as the maximum authority above others.[80] This legal understanding concerning the authority of Japanese lords over their vassals is reproduced in other Jesuit sources as well, such as a 1571 missive by Francisco Cabral, and in Luís Fróis's *Historia de Japam*.[81] The Visitor also explained how tax collection worked in this system. According to Valignano, those who received the donation benefited from all its revenues, unless determined otherwise by the donating lord. Finally, all those who owned lands had to contribute armed men and other materials to the armies of their lords.[82]

Since receiving real estate gave the missionaries the right to *mero et mixto imperio* over Nagasaki and other areas in Ōmura and Arima, Valignano organized a complex system to divide legal authority over the city and its citizens. Yasutaka Hiroaki argues this was the first case in Japanese history where executive and judicial powers were divided.[83] Reinier Hesselink demonstrates that the Visitor separated criminal law from civil law, as well as distinguishing between civil law and canonical law. Portuguese who committed crimes in

---

77   See "Latin Glossaries with vernacular sources," Toyoshima Masayuki, accessed February 23, 2019, https://joao-roiz.jp/LGR/.

78   *Toyotomi Hideyoshi Monjoshū*, vol. 3 (Tokyo: Yoshikawa Kobunkan, 2017), 239.

79   Shimizu, *Shokuhō Seiken to Kirishitan*, 342.

80   Valignano, *Sumário*, 318; António Manuel Hespanha, *História das Instituições: Época Medieval e Moderna* (Coimbra: Almedina, 1982), 284–85.

81   *JapSin* 7 I, fol. 20v; HJ V, 444.

82   Valignano, *Sumário*, 318–19.

83   Yasutaka, *Kinsei Nagasaki*, 118.

Nagasaki were subject to the power of the Captain Major, the royal representative who led the yearly ship between Macau and Japan. Meanwhile, Japanese were subject to Japanese judges appointed by the Jesuits, but who derived their legitimacy from Ōmura Sumitada, "for he remained 'overlord' of the area."[84] As pointed out by José Luís Alvarez-Taladriz, such a solution replicated the situation of Jesuit missions in India, where secular judges nominated by Jesuits held the necessary legal authority over villages owned by missionaries.[85]

Jesuits also retained hostages from villages they controlled. In early modern Japan, it was usual for warlords to keep relatives or members of other clans as hostages or *hitojichi* in order to secure their political dealings. In his journal, Afonso de Lucena wrote that when Sumitada made a second donation of the five villages of Urakami to the mission in 1586, the warlord handed the political hostages he had from each village to the priest, who in turn sent them to Nagasaki.[86] Accordingly, it is very likely that the Jesuits kept hostages from other villages they controlled as well, or at least from their chigyō.

One important aspect of owning property in Japan was the right to summon laborers. In Jesuit documents, this unpaid labor is referred to as *kuyaku*, or "public service," although Japanese historians refer to this right as *eki* or *yaku*, a kind of corvée.[87] In 1562, when Luís de Almeida explained the donation of Yokoseura, he wrote that Sumitada "wanted to give a source of revenue to the priests, which would be the port of Yokoseura, with all farmers two miles in a circle from the harbour."[88] Almeida seemed to understand these farmers as part of the donation, virtually equating them to serfs handed over to the mission by the warlord. This was radically different from other donations up to this point. Understanding that this was a reference to *kuyaku*, what he meant was that the missionaries would be able to use labor from inhabitants living around the donated port to build their facilities and work in their churches and residences.

As early as 1557, Japan Jesuits had an idea of how the kuyaku worked. In a letter written that year, Gaspar Vilela explained Japanese farmers lived like serfs, since they enjoyed only a very small portion of the revenue generated by their work, while most of it was paid to their lords in the form of taxes and

---

84   Hesselink, *Dream*, 68.
85   Valignano, *Sumario*, 76*.
86   Lucena, "De algumas coisas," 124.
87   Kishimoto Mio, "Eki," in *Rekishigaku Jiten Dai 8 Kan—Hito to Shigoto*, ed. Satō Tsugitaka (Tokyo: Kobundō, 2001), 52–53; Takagi Shōsaku, "Yaku," in *Rekishigaku Jiten Dai 1 Kōkan to Shōhi*, ed. Kawakita Minoru (Tokyo: Kobundō, 1994), 628–29.
88   Cartas 1598 I, fol. 109.

labor.[89] For Japan Jesuits, this meant they had a constant workforce for their fields, churches and residences free of charge. In 1586, Valignano wrote the Japanese mission had no properties or revenue sources, "except for some land donated in some parts by some Christian lords, which matter more for the service paid by people living there than the fruits one could count as revenue."[90] The practice of kuyaku was enough reason to justify its ownership.

Sebastião de Almeida's list notes that the villages donated by the Ōmura clan were plenty with servants—*"gente de serviço"*—stressing the importance of this corvée. Almeida described in similar terms donations by the Arima, Konishi and Amakusa clans. Effectively, he wrote that lands given to the Jesuits by the Arima clan were filled with people ready to work for them, some with four to five thousand souls, "all subjected to the Society of Jesus as if they were their servants, forced by contract to offer the Company a number of men to serve it some days of the week."[91]

In 1593, Francisco Cabral explained how the system worked. According to the former superior of the Japan mission, every day missionaries had three to four men from villages to serve them. Likewise, for each chō, one to three farmers were forced to work in the Jesuits' fields every day.[92] The importance of the kuyaku to the mission must not be overlooked—Almeida wrote that this was how missionaries had access to the necessary labor to build, and also to obtain wood, firewood, and foodstuffs. According to him, the value of these bulk goods amounted to almost the same as the tax revenue obtained from these lands.[93] The corvée was an indispensable source of supplies, thus not only supporting the missionaries' everyday survival, but also allowing them to easily erect new churches and other facilities in times of expansion.

The kuyaku was one of the factors weighed up when the priests debated how they should take back control of Nagasaki when the opportunity arrived. In 1590, when Japan Jesuits still had high hopes of recovering the port-city, they were divided on whether they should accept back the right to govern Nagasaki. The missionaries wanted to make the city a semi-independent republic, self-governed yet cognizant of the power of the Church. The very first reason given by the priests in favour of such solution was that the utility of Nagasaki was in the labor, ships, and other necessary stuffs locals were obliged to offer the

89   Juan Ruiz-de-Medina, *Documentos del Japón 1558–1562* (Rome: Institutum Historicum Societatis Jesu, 1995), 705.

90   MHJ, 187.

91   *JapSin* 23, fol. 2, 6; BA/JA, 49–IV–66, fol. 99.

92   DI XVI, 521–1.

93   *JapSin* 23, fol. 2, 5v–6; BA/JA, 49–IV–66, fol. 98v–99.

Jesuits. If its jurisdiction were to be returned to the Ōmura clan, the mission would not be able to claim such rights.[94] In the end, resorting to the Japanese practice of kuyaku was how Jesuits secured part of the material basis of the mission.

5   Conclusion

Starting in the mid-1580s, the Japan mission was separating itself politically and economically from India. As noted by Takase, this process slowed down land acquisition in South Asia destined to maintain the Japanese mission, thus becoming an incentive for Jesuits to amass real estate locally. Quoting a 1583 letter written by Cabral, the Japanese historian argues that, as revenues obtained from land ownership in Japan were negligible, Almeida's list has no credibility.[95] Surely Almeida's list must not be taken at face value.[96] As shown in this text, even though this is a faulty financial record, it is a testimony of the power and influence Jesuits gathered in Japan, where claims to political authority were backed by land holding. It is also a tool to better evaluate the deep relationship missionaries established with powerful Japanese Christians.

As noted by Vu Thanh, the first donations were not free of ulterior motives. The Ōuchi and Ōtomo clans, for instance, expected the missionaries to intervene with Portuguese merchants in their favor.[97] Until Yokoseura, missionaries obtained very small portions of land, destined almost exclusively for building churches, residences, hospitals and so on. There was no chigyō, they had no income from tax collection—with a few small exceptions from the Ōtomo clan—nor access to labor from obligations residents owed their lords. After that, they slowly began acquiring more landholdings, especially from the Ōmura and Arima clans.

The rhythm of estate acquisition took a sharp turn in the 1580s, when Valignano accepted Nagasaki, thus establishing a strong precedent for accepting donations, and determining the legal conditions for land purchase. During these

---

94   Valignano, *Adiciones*, 602–603.

95   Takase, *Kirishitan Jidai*, 429, and 435. Rodrigues lists pieces of land from the island of Caranjá, as well as the villages of Ponvém, Condotim and Mulgão, all in Bassein, India, acquired between 1571 and 1585 to maintain Jesuits in Japan. Rodrigues, "Local Sources," 117–18. See also Charles J. Borges, *The Economics of the Goa Jesuits, 1542–1759: An Explanation of their Rise and Fall* (New Delhi: Concept Publishing Company, 1994), 118.

96   As did Alvarez-Taladriz. Alessandro Valignano, *Apologia de la Compañia de Jesus de Japón y China (1598)*, ed. José Luís Alvarez-Taladriz (Osaka: private edition, 1998), 207–208.

97   Vu Thanh, " *L'Église des laïcs*," 9.

years, and especially between the donation of Urakami in 1584 and the edict of expulsion in 1587, Jesuits actively acquired more land through purchase and donations. These donations could involve two different attributions: the first, which apparently was the most common, meant Jesuits received annual stipends paid by local lords, or *jishi*. That was the situation of villages such as Yukinoura, "Maxama," Hōshōji, and Kazusa. The second, which followed the model established by Yokoseura, was represented by the actual administrative power over villages, the so-called chigyō. This seems to be the case with Nagasaki, Urakami, Mogi, Nagayo, Tokitsu and Himi. It seems that having the power to administrate a village granted the receiving party some revenue, although the donation of revenues did not necessarily mean the donation of any degree of political power.

Japanese warlords could donate entire villages and reserve for themselves the right to administer them while submitting all revenue to the missionaries, or they could delegate governing powers to the Jesuits while keeping for themselves part of the income obtained from a certain village. All these factors depended on negotiations between priests and the warlord. Nevertheless, access to some rights, such as kuyaku, necessarily depended on missionaries having administrative powers, as shown by concerns expressed by Valignano during their debate over the possibility of a new donation of Nagasaki.

In 1587, right before Hideyoshi stripped the mission of numerous areas under its political control, Japan Jesuits had control over Nagasaki, Urakami and Mogi, as well as income from Yukinoura, Hōshōji, Tokitsu, and "Maxama" in the lands of the Ōmura clan, and Kazusa and Hachirao in the Arima domains, plus a few others in Amakusa. If we consider the values listed by Almeida, not as representative of actual income, but of the political power gained by the missionaries as landowners, Jesuits could be considered lords worth more than two thousand koku (if considering only the yield value of Urakami, Mogi and Tokitsu), but possibly with annual revenues of almost five thousand koku if summing up all rights to income they had accumulated at that point. Albeit very small compared to Ōmura Yoshiaki's 21,427 koku or Arima Harunobu's 40,000 koku in 1587, this was certainly a lot considering the pace of land acquisition after the donation of Nagasaki.[98]

Jesuits were not themelves becoming warlords, however. Anno Masaki believes that after Valignano left Japan in 1582 and Gaspar Coelho took over the mission, they became more militarized. According to the historian, this evidences the military character of the members of the Society of Jesus

---

98   For the *kokudaka* in Kyūshū in 1587, see Ōmura-shi, *Chūseihen*, 415.

themselves: sometimes missionaries, sometime *"secret agents or spies."*[99] On
the other hand, by design or by chance, Jesuits were showing rather common
characteristics of local Buddhist organizations. Japan has a long history of
what historian Fukaya Kōji has called regional temples or *chiiki jiinn*: Buddhist
institutions working as semi-independent local political forces influencing
warlords and controlling small fields or villages located nearby.[100] Jesuits were
neither warlords nor spies, but rather fit a model often found among smaller
religious organizations in Japan.

After 1587, their income increased slowly, as they obtained new donations
from the Ōmura clan. Apparently, they enjoyed all rights from the lands in
Ōmura—tax collection and kuyaku—up to their expulsion from the domain
in 1606, until they had to go into hiding in 1614. Despite large areas such as
Urakami and Kazusa being subjected to Jesuit authorities, Valignano claimed
they had no stable sources of income in 1586.[101] This claim was repeated over
the years. One possible reason could be the Vice-Province of Japan's attempt to
avoid the so-called *finta*, a tribute paid by the mission to the Province of India.
Until 1593, India Jesuits were purchasing real estate in South Asia to support
the mission in Japan, but from that point on the increasing autonomy of the
Japan mission deepened their differences. That year, Cabral accused Valignano
of hiding all revenues obtained from land in Japan to avoid the finta, listing
some villages the mission did not lose in 1587. In 1595, Acquaviva sent separate
Visitors for each province, and the separation became even clearer when the
Japanese mission sent a procurator to Rome that same year.[102] Nevertheless, it
is also possible that Japan Jesuits purposefully underestimated their revenues
in Japan in order to obtain more donations from powerful overseas benefactors.

Owning land in Japan created a series of political problems for the Jesuit
mission, as they were targeted by territorial policies such as Hideyoshi's expansion to Southern Japan. It is interesting to consider that not only the access to
Hideyoshi obtained by the Jesuits, but also the policies directed against them,
can be related to the fact missionaries were actively accumulating land and
political power in the 1580s. Also, it is worth considering that their military

---

99   Anno, *Kyōkairyō Nagasaki*, 128–30.
100   Fukaya Kōji, "Sengokuki Chiiki Jiin he no Shoeki Fuka to sono Futan," in *Shōen to Mura wo Aruku 2*, ed. Fujiki Hisashi and Kuramochi Shigehiro (Tokyo: Azekura Shobō, 2004), 44, and 62–63.
101   MHJ, 187.
102   For more on the *finta* controversy, see BA/JA, 49–V–7, fol. 143–145; *JapSin* 47, fol. 1–2v; *JapSin* 31, fol. 204–205v; DI XVI, 520; DI XVII, 282–286; DI XVIII, 591. Borges defines that the *finta* was a 4 percent charge over the income of Jesuit houses in a given area. See Borges, *The Economics*, 153.

contributions to local warlords could have been related to the obligations attached to donations of political and administrative power. Nevertheless, it was
their project of increasing political and economic autonomy by accumulating
property that gave them some degree of financial and material stability. Overall, this process was evidence of the expertise missionaries had regarding Japanese society, as well as their deep entrenchment in a country outside of the
Portuguese sphere of influence. Still, lack of more detailed sources makes the
task of defining the relationship between land ownership, trade and mission
finances daunting.

Bibliography

Primary Sources

Almeida, Sebastião de. *Catalogo dos fundadores do Collegios e residencias da Prouincia
    de Jappão, e dos benfeitores da mesma Prouincia.* Macau: 1677 [ARSI, *JapSin* 23, and
    BA/JA, 49–IV–66].
Cabral, Francisco. Letter. Nagasaki: September 5, 1571 [ARSI, *JapSin* 7 1].
*Cartas que los Padres y Hermanos de la Compañia de Iesus, que andan em los Reynos
    de Iapon escriuieron a los de la misma Compañia, desde el año de mil y quinientos y
    quarenta y nueue, hasta el de mil y quinientos y setenta y uno.* Alcalá: en casa de Iuan
    Iniguez de Lequerica, 1575.
*Cartas que os Padres e Irmãos da Companhia de Iesus escreuerão dos Reynos de Iapão &
    China aos da mesma Companhia da India, & Europa, desdo anno de 1549 atè o de 1580.*
    2 vols. Évora: Manoel de Lyra, 1598.
Fróis, Luís. *Historia de Japam.* 5 vols. Edited by Josef Wicki. Lisbon: Biblioteca Nacional
    de Lisboa, 1976–1984.
Lucena, Afonso de. "De algumas cousas que ainda se alembra o Pe. Afonso de Lucena
    que pertencem à Christandade de Omura." In *Erinnerungen aus der Christenheit von
    Omura: 1578–1614,* edited and translated by Josef Franz Schütte. Rome: Institutum
    Historicum Societatis Iesu, 1972.
Ōmura Keki. 6 vols [Omura City Archives, n. 101–21 to 101–26].
Papeles Varios Curiosos [Torre do Tombo National Archives, Casa de Cadaval, n. 26].
Rodrigues, Nunes et al. *Assento que se tomou sobre a finta de Jappão.* April 19, 1598
    [ARSI, *JapSin* 31 and 47].
Ruiz-de-Medina, Juan, ed. *Documentos del Japón, 1558–1562.* Rome: Institutum Histori-
    cum Societatis Jesu, 1995.
Schütte, Josef Franz, ed. *Monumenta Historica Japoniae I.* Rome: Institutum Histori-
    cum Societatis Iesu, 1975.
Toyotomi Hideyoshi Monjoshū. 9 vols. Tokyo: Yoshikawa Kobunkan, 2015–2023.

Valignano, Alessandro. *Adiciones del Sumario de Japon.* Edited by José Luiz Alvarez-Taladriz. Osaka: private edition, undated.

Valignano, Alessandro. *Apologia de la Compañia de Jesus de Japon y China (1598).* Edited by José Luiz Alvarez-Taladriz. Osaka: private edition, 1998.

Valignano, Alessandro. *Historia del Principio y Progresso de la Compañia de Jesús en las Indias Orientales (1542–64).* Edited by Josef Wicki. Rome: Institutum Historicum Societatis Iesu, 1944.

Valignano, Alessandro. Letter. Macau: July 1, 1598 [ARSI, *JapSin* 13 I].

Valignano, Alessandro. *Sumario de las Cosas de Japón (1583), Adiciones del Sumario de Japón (1592), Tomo I.* Edited by José Luiz Alvarez-Taladriz. Tokyo: Sophia University, 1954.

Vieira, Francisco. *Rezoens pelas quaes se mostra q[ue] a Vice-Prou[inci]a de Jappão foi aggrauada da Prou[inci]a da India em lhe fazer pagar desdo anno de 96 quatro centos p[arda]os cada anno de finta [...].* Macau: 1618 [BA/JA, 49–V–7].

Wicki, Josef, and John Gomes. *Documenta Indica.* 18 vols. Rome: Institutum Historicum Societatis Iesu, 1948–1988.

Secondary Sources

Alves, Jorge M. dos Santos. "Os jesuítas e a 'contenda da Ilha Verde.' A primeira discussão sobre a legitimidade da presença portuguesa em Macau (1621)." In *A Companhia de Jesus e a Missionação no Oriente*, edited by Nuno da Silva Gonçalves, 423–49. Lisbon: Brotéria, 2000.

Anno, Masaki. "Kyōkairyō Kishin Monjo no Kenkyū." *Shigaku Zasshi* 85, no. 1 (1976): 38–56.

Anno, Masaki. *Kyōkairyō Nagasaki—Iezusukai to Nihon.* Tokyo: Kōdansha, 2014.

Borges, Charles J. *The Economics of the Goa Jesuits, 1542–1759: An Explanation of Their Rise and Fall.* New Delhi: Concept Publishing Company, 1994.

Boxer, Charles R. *The Affair of the Madre de Deus: A Chapter in the History of the Portuguese in Japan.* London; New York: Routledge, 2011.

Brockey, Liam Matthew. *Journey to the East: The Jesuit Mission to China 1579–1724.* Cambridge, MA: The Belknap Press of Harvard University Press, 2007.

Brockey, Liam Matthew. *The Visitor: André Palmeiro and the Jesuits in Asia.* Cambridge, MA: Harvard University Press, 2014.

De Luca, Renzo. "Daidōji Saikyojō to Iezusukai Shiryō no Hikaku Kenkyū." *Kyūshū Shigaku* 135 (2003): 27–56.

Fujiki, Hisashi. *Mura to Ryōshu no Sengoku Sekai.* Tokyo: Tōkyō Daigaku Shuppankai, 1997.

Fukaya, Kōji. "Sengokuki Chiiki Jiin he no Shoeki Fuka to sono Futan." In *Shōen to Mura wo Aruku 2*, edited by Fujiki Hisashi, and Kuramochi Shigehiro, 44–66. Tokyo: Azekura Shobō, 2004.

Hespanha, António Manuel. *História das Instituições: Época Medieval e Moderna.* Coimbra: Almedina, 1982.

Hesselink, Reinier H. *Dream of a Christian Nagasaki: World Trade and the Clash of Cultures 1560–1640.* Jefferson, NC: McFarland, 2016.

Kishimoto, Mio. "Eki." In *Rekishigaku Jiten Dai 8 Kan—Hito to Shigoto*, edited by Satō Tsugitaka, 52–53. Tokyo: Kobundō, 2001.

Kitajima, Manji. "Tenshōki ni okeru Ryōshuteki Kesshū no Dōkō to Daimyō Kenryoku." In *Kyūshū Daimyō no Kenkyū*, edited by Kimura Tadao, 266–309. Tokyo: Yoshikawa Kōbunkan, 1983.

Kudamatsu, Kazunori. "Ōmura Sumitada." In *Kirishitan Daimyō—Fukyō, Seisaku, Shinkō no Jissō*, edited by Gonoi Takashi, 160–78. Tokyo: Miyaobi Shuppansha, 2017.

Maki, Hidemasa and Fujiwara Akihisa, eds. *Nihon Hōseishi.* Tokyo: Seirin Shoin, 1993.

Miyazaki, Katsunori, and Fukuoka Archive Kenkyūkai. *Kenperu ya Shiiboruto tachi ga mita Kyūshū, soshite Nippon.* Fukuoka: Kaichōsha, 2009.

Ōmura-shi, Hensan Iinkai. *Shin'hen Ōmura-shi Shi, Daigokan Furoku.* Ōmura: Ōmura City, 2014.

Ōmura-shi, Hensan Iinkai. *Shin'hen Ōmura-shi Shi, Dainikan Chūseihen.* Ōmura: Ōmura City, 2014.

Robinson, James J. *Selections from the Public and Private Law of the Romans.* New York: American Book Company, 1905.

Rodrigues, Helena. "Local Source of Funding for the Japanese Mission." *Bulletin of Portuguese/Japanese Studies* 7 (2003): 115–37.

Schütte, Josef Franz, ed. *Introductio ad Historiam Societatis Jesu in Japonia, 1549–1650.* Rome: Institutum Historicum Societatis Jesu, 1968.

Shimizu, Hirokazu. "Arima Harunobu." In *Kirishitan Daimyō—Fukyō, Seisaku, Shinkō no Jissō*, edited by Gonoi Takashi, 193–211. Tokyo: Miyaobi Shuppansha, 2017.

Shimizu, Hirokazu. "Hizen Urakami no Bungō Katei." *Kirisutokyō Shigaku* 47 (1993): 34–56.

Shimizu, Hirokazu. *Shokuhō Seiken to Kirishitan—Nichiō Kōshō no Kigen to Tenkai.* Tokyo: Iwata Shoin, 2001.

Takagi, Shōsaku. "Yaku." In *Rekishigaku Jiten Dai 1 Kōkan to Shōhi*, edited by Kawakita Minoru, 628–29. Tokyo: Kobundō, 1994.

Takase, Kōichirō. *Kirishitan Jidai no Kenkyū.* Tokyo: Iwanami Shoten, 1977.

Toyoshima, Masayuki. "Latin Glossaries with vernacular sources." Accessed February 23, 2019, https://joao-roiz.jp/LGR/.

Tsuruta, Kurazō and Hirata Toyohiro. "Amakusa Goninshū." In *Kirishitan Daimyō—Fukyō, Seisaku, Shinkō no Jissō*, edited by Gonoi Takashi, 387–409. Tokyo: Miyaobi Shuppansha, 2017.

Vermote, Frederik. "Financing Jesuit Missions." In *Oxford Handbook of the Jesuits*, edited by Ines G. Županov. New York: Oxford University Press, 2019.

Vu Thanh, Hélène. "Investir dans une Nouvelle Religion. Le Cas de la Mission du Japon (XVIe-XVIIe siècles)." In *L'Église des laïcs. Le sacré en partage (XVIe–XXe siècles)*, edited by Ariane Boltanski, and Marie-Lucie Copete. Madrid: Casa de Velázquez, forthcoming.

Vu Thanh, Hélène. "Un équilibre impossible: financer la mission jésuite du Japon, entre Europe et Asie (1579–1614)." *Revue d'Histoire Moderne et Contemporaine* 63, no. 3 (2016): 7–30.

Yasutaka, Hiroaki. *Kinsei Nagasaki Shihō Seido no Kenkyū*. Tokyo: Shibunkaku, 2010.

Yoshinaga, Masaharu. *Kyūshū Sengokushi*. Tokyo: Ashishobō, 1981.

Zeron, Carlos Alberto de Moura Ribeiro. *Linha de Fé: A Companhia de Jesus e a Escravidão no Processo de Formação da Sociedade Colonial (Brasil, Séculos XVI e XVII)*. São Paulo: Edusp, 2011.

CHAPTER 6

Going Local, Becoming Global

The Connected Histories of Early Modern Missionary Economies in Persia and the Persian Gulf

Christian Windler

Since the 1990s, historians of early modern Catholic missions to Asia have abandoned earlier expansionist narratives to focus on the specific characteristics of the local religious practices that emerged from interactions between the local populations and European missionaries.[1] Adopting a similar decentered perspective, this chapter adds to this growing body of scholarship. However, whereas much of the previous work has examined the interaction between indigenous Christian communities and European clergymen, this contribution focuses on the missionaries themselves.[2] As an analysis of the

---

1 On China, see Eric Zürcher, "The Jesuit Mission in Fujian in Late Ming Times: Levels of Response," in *Development and Decline of Fukien Province in the 17th and 18th Centuries*, ed. Eduard B. Vermeer (Leiden: Brill, 1990), 417–57; Eric Zürcher, "The Lord of Heaven and the Demons: Strange Stories from a Late Ming Christian Manuscript," in *Religion und Philosophie in Ostasien. Festschrift für Hans Steininger zum 65. Geburtstag*, ed. Gert Naundorf, Karl-Heinz Pohl, and Hans Hermann Schmidt (Würzburg: Königshausen/Neumann, 1985), 359–75; Nicolas Standaert, *The Interweaving of Rituals. Funerals in the Cultural Exchange between China and Europe* (Seattle; London: University of Washington Press, 2008); Nicolas Standaert, *Chinese Voices in the Rites Controversy: Travelling Books, Community Networks, Intercultural Arguments* (Rome: Institutum Historicum Societatis Iesu, 2012); Henrietta Harrison, *The Missionary's Curse and Other Tales from a Chinese Catholic Village* (Berkeley, CA; Los Angeles; London: University of California Press, 2013); Eugenio Menegon, *Ancestors, Virgins, and Friars: Christianity as a Local Religion in Late Imperial China* (Cambridge, MA: Harvard University Press, 2009); Nadine Amsler, *Jesuits and Matriarchs: Domestic Worship in Early Modern China* (Seattle; London: University of Washington Press, 2018). On "tropical Catholicism" in South India, see Ines G. Županov, *Missionary Tropics: The Catholic Frontier in India (16th-17th Centuries)* (Ann Arbor, MI: University of Michigan Press, 2005), 24–28, 269–70. On local Christianities in the Syrian provinces of the Ottoman Empire, see Bernard Heyberger, *Les Chrétiens du Proche-Orient au temps de la Réforme catholique* (Rome: École française de Rome, 1994), and *Hindiyya (1720–1798), mystique et criminelle* (Paris: Aubier, 2001). The author gratefully acknowledges Samuel Weber (Bern) for translating an earlier German version of this paper into English.

2 For similar perspectives, see also the contributions to the following volume: Nadine Amsler, Andreea Badea, Bernard Heyberger, and Christian Windler, eds. *Catholic Missionaries in Early Modern Asia. Patterns of Localization* (London; New York: Routledge, 2020). This present

© CHRISTIAN WINDLER, 2021 | DOI:10.1163/9789004444195_007

missionary economy—an aspect that has up until now received scant attention from scholars—the chapter sheds new light on the question of whether,
and to what extent, missionaries became integrated into local societies. One
question in particular merits attention: Did the principals provide missionaries with the material resources they needed to perform their tasks, or were the
missionaries forced to use funds from Europe as "seed capital," which they had
to invest in order to generate enough revenue to cover their expenses in the
long run? By answering this question, we gain a better understanding of the
functioning of early modern ecclesiastical institutions on the one hand, and
the social practices of missionaries on the other.

In the following, the main focus will be less on the Jesuits, whose global activity, partly including its financial aspects, has been studied in recent years,[3]
than on a religious order whose missions have yet to receive attention from
scholars outside the order itself: the Italian congregation of the Discalced Carmelites. Studying the missions to Persia allows us to revise received ideas that
resulted from a one-sided focus on the Society of Jesus of earlier research into
early modern missions: To what extent did the specific norms of each religious
order shape the situation of its members and the relationship to their superiors? Did the practices of the Discalced Carmelites on the ground differ fundamentally from the accommodation that scholarship has traditionally ascribed
to the Jesuits? What conclusions about the extent of missionaries' integration
into local social relations can be inferred from both the differences and similarities of each order's specific everyday practices?

The focus on Persia and the Persian Gulf also means a geographic shift to
a less well-known missionary field. Beginning around 1600, the Safavid Empire became the focal point for a broad variety of expectations, ranging from
political, military, and commercial interests to the hopes of finally finding a

chapter is based on the author's monograph on the Persian missions in the seventeenth
and eighteenth centuries: Christian Windler, *Missionare in Persien. Kulturelle Diversität und
Normenkonkurrenz im globalen Katholizismus (17.–18. Jahrhundert)* (Cologne; Weimar; Vienna: Böhlau Verlag, 2018).

3 On the history of the Society of Jesus, see most recently Markus Friedrich, *Die Jesuiten. Aufstieg, Niedergang, Neubeginn* (Munich; Berlin; Zurich: Piper, 2016), and Ines G. Županov,
ed., *The Oxford Handbook of the Jesuits* (New York: Oxford University Press, 2019). A useful
overview of the state of research is Michela Catto, Guido Mongini, and Silvia Mostaccio,
eds., *Evangelizzazione e globalizzazione. Le missioni gesuitiche nell'età moderna tra storia e
storiografia* (Città di Castello: Società Editrice Dante Alighieri, 2010). Work on the financial
history of the Jesuit missions has until recently focused almost exclusively on missions under
Spanish and Portuguese patronage. For an overview, see Frederik Vermote, "Finances of the
Missions," in *A Companion to Early Modern Catholic Global Missions,* ed. Ronnie Po-Chia Hsia
(Leiden; Boston: Brill, 2018), 367–400.

Muslim population susceptible to the Christian gospel. Towards the end of the sixteenth century, news of the exploits of ʿAbbās I's (1588–1629) armies against the Ottomans had reached European courts and had revived interest in forging an anti-Ottoman alliance with the shah. At the court of Philip III, king of Castile and Portugal, and in the Roman Curia, it was hoped that an alliance with Persia would help realize two dreams at once—military triumph over the Turks and the conversion of numerous Muslims to Christianity. These hopes led to the dispatch of Portuguese Augustinians from Goa and of Discalced Carmelites from Rome, both armed with a religious and diplomatic double mandate. Although the results did not meet initial expectations at all, the Augustinians and the Discalced Carmelites were, in the course of the seventeenth century, joined by Capuchins, Jesuits, Dominicans and some priests of the *Missions étrangères de Paris*.[4]

Unlike other missionaries in Asia and the Americas, the Discalced Carmelites, who were first dispatched to Isfahan in 1604 by Pope Clement VIII (Ippolito Aldobrandini, r. 1592–1605), did not operate under Spanish or Portuguese patronage. Founded by Clement VIII in 1600, the Italian congregation of the Discalced Carmelites was placed under the protection of the post-Tridentine papacy.[5] Significantly, this protection extended to any of the houses the order would establish outside of the territories ruled by the Spanish monarchy. When the Discalced Carmelites reached Isfahan in 1607, they were met by Portuguese Augustinians who had arrived in 1602 and who viewed the local missionary area as an integral part of the *padroado* of Portuguese India.[6] Such claims clashed with Clement VIII's ambitious program of reining in the great Catholic powers of the day, as a number of historians have recently argued.[7] Enlisting the help of his nephews, Pietro Aldobrandini and Cinzio Passeri

---

4   On the Persian missions, see most recently Windler, *Missionare in Persien*, which includes comprehensive bibliographic references.

5   On the Persian mission of the Discalced Carmelites, see Herbert Chick, *A Chronicle of the Carmelites in Persia and the Papal Mission of the XVIIth and XVIIIth Centuries*, 2 vols. (London: Eyre & Spottiswoode, 1939) [Reprint: London; New York: I. B. Tauris, 2012]. On the Persian mission in the context of "Tridentine Orientalism," see Rosemary Virgina Lee, "A Printing Press for Shah ʿAbbas. Science, Learning, and Evangelization in the Near East, 1600–1650" (PhD diss., University of Virginia, 2013). More detailed information on research literature and sources can be found in Windler, *Missionare in Persien*, 19–23.

6   On the missions of the Augustinians, see John M. Flannery, *The Mission of the Portuguese Augustinians to Persia and Beyond (1602–1747)* (Studies in Christian Missions 43) (Leiden; Boston: Brill, 2013).

7   On the Roman Curia's ties to the peripheries of early modern Catholicism in Ireland, England, the Dutch Provinces, East-Central Europe, and the Balkans, see Tadgh Ó hAnnracháin, *Catholic Europe, 1592–1648: Centre and Peripheries* (Oxford: Oxford University Press, 2015), 1–28.

Aldobrandini, as well as other confidantes and the congregations of the Curia, Clement VIII sought to strengthen his hand in the government of the Church to the detriment of the college of cardinals and to increase the powers of the Church at the expense of the Iberian crowns.[8] The dispatch of missionaries under Roman protection was an integral part of this policy, which continued into the 1620s when another reform-minded pope, Gregory XV (Alessandro Ludovisi, r. 1621–1623), set up, against the opposition of the Iberian powers, the Congregation for the Propagation of the Faith (Propaganda Fide), with the aim of promoting and overseeing Catholic missions all over the world as an enterprise of the papacy.[9] As the main beneficiaries of this offensive, the Discalced Carmelites maintained close ties to the papacy; this close connection led to the Discalced Carmelite Domingo de Jesús María becoming the only member of a religious order to be appointed to the Congregation for the Propagation of the Faith founded in 1622.[10]

Their relative proximity to the papacy makes the Discalced Carmelites particularly suitable for gauging the extent to which missionaries became part of local societies. Did their close ties to the Roman Curia mean that Rome financed their missions? In the first part of this contribution I examine the material and symbolic importance of the funds which the Congregation for the Propagation of the Faith and the order itself sent to Persia before I turn to the normative restrictions that these two institutions attempted to impose on the

---

8   On the reorganization of papal government under Clement VIII, see Maria Teresa Fattori, *Clemente VIII e il Sacro Collegio, 1592–1605. Meccanismi istituzionali e accentramento di governo* (Päpste und Papsttum 33) (Stuttgart: Anton Hiersemann, 2004).

9   Besides the reforms of the papal conclave, the establishment of the Congregation for the Propagation of the Faith was the most important reform of the short pontificate of Gregory XV. Both reforms had been attempted under Clement VIII but failed due to Spanish opposition. On the reform of the conclave, see Günther Wassilowsky, *Die Konklavereform Gregors XV. (1621/22). Wertekonflikte, symbolische Inszenierung und Verfahrenswandel im posttridentinischen Papsttum* (Päpste und Papsttum 38) (Stuttgart: Anton Hiersemann, 2010) and Miles Pattenden, *Electing the Pope in Early Modern Italy, 1450–1700* (Oxford: Oxford University Press, 2017), 90–97. On the Congregation for the Propagation of the Faith, see the work of Giovanni Pizzorusso, most recently *Governare le missioni, conoscere il mondo nel XVII secolo. La Congregazione Pontificia de Propaganda Fide* (Studi di storia delle istituzioni ecclesiastiche 6) (Viterbo: Edizioni Sette Città, 2018).

10 Josef Metzler, "Wegbereiter und Vorläufer der Kongregation. Vorschläge und erste Gründungsversuche einer römischen Missionszentrale," in *Sacrae Congregationis de Propaganda Fide Memoria Rerum, 1622–1972*, Vol. I/1: *1622–1700*, ed. Josef Metzler (Rome; Freiburg im Breisgau; Vienna: Herder, 1971), 38–78. Also see Fattori, *Clemente VIII e il Sacro Collegio*, 337–339; Silvano Giordano, *Domenico di Gesù Maria, Ruzola (1559–1630). Un carmelitano scalzo tra politica e riforma nella chiesa posttridentina* (Rome: Institutum Historicum Teresianum, 1991), 220, 226–40.

economic operations members of the order had set up in the missionary area. In the second part, the focus shifts to the local economies in Persia and the Persian Gulf area in which the missionaries operated.

1   Limited Financial Resources but Strict Normative Standards

A superficial reading of the minutes of the Congregation for the Propagation of the Faith may give the impression that the subsidies from Europe constituted the most sizable part of the missions' revenues. It may therefore be surprising to learn that in the day-to-day life of the missions, these subsidies were only of minimal importance. In Basra, where two surviving account books grant quantitative insights into the economy of the local convent, the remittances from Italy made up a mere 2.4 percent of the revenues of the Discalced Carmelites between 1719 and 1753.[11] While there are no exact figures for other convents in the heartland of the Safavid Empire, there is nothing to suggest that they differed starkly from those in Basra, a port city on the Gulf of Persia which had once been under Safavid rule but then became part of the Ottoman Empire in the seventeenth century.

In fact, a close look at the financial situation of the Congregation for the Propagation of the Faith reveals that, in light of its wide-ranging competences, the congregation's financial resources were severely limited. Although little research has been done on the subject,[12] three characteristics that Propaganda Fide shared with other Roman congregations, stand out: first, the congregation's assets were modest, especially when compared to those of the households of wealthy cardinals; second, it depended almost exclusively on the Papal States and, to a lesser extent, on other Italian territories to finance its operations; third, a high percentage of the available resources was spent in Rome. In light of other research on the finances of the papacy,[13] these findings

---

11   Liber accepti et expensi Residentiae nostrae Bassorae mense Ianuario anni 1674 usque ad mensem inclusive decembrem anni 1727 (AGOCD, 483/f); [Liber computum], 1728–1772 (AGOCD, 484/e).

12   The only study thus far is Giovanni Pizzorusso, "Lo Stato temporale della Congregazione de Propaganda Fide nel Seicento," in *Ad ultimos usque terrarum terminos in fide propaganda. Roma fra promozione e difesa della fede in età moderna* (Studi di storia delle istituzioni ecclesiastiche 5), ed. Massimiliano Ghilardi et al. (Viterbo: Edizioni Sette Città, 2014), 51–66. The findings presented here are based on additional research in the material of the series SC. *Stato temporale* of the archives of the Congregation for the Propagation of the Faith. For more detailed references see Windler, *Missionare in Persien*, 39–49.

13   Unfortunately Wolfgang Reinhard's study of 1974 (*Papstfinanz und Nepotismus unter Paul V. (1605–1621). Studien und Quellen zur Struktur und zu quantitativen Aspekten des*

are hardly surprising, though they help put into perspective the role of the Congregation for the Propagation of the Faith and the Roman Curia in the financing of overseas missions.

The revenues of Propaganda Fide lagged far behind those of prominent members of papal families, such as Scipione Borghese, cardinal-nephew of Paul v (Camillo Borghese, r. 1605–1621). In the period between 1651 and 1709, the revenues of Propaganda Fide, according to its *bilanci* (balance sheets), ranged from 21,158 to 25,745 scudi per annum, and the expenditures ranged from 19,027 to 29,335, without there being any clear indication of an upward trend over time.[14] In contrast, the income of Scipione Borghese between 1605 and 1633 had amounted to an average of 225,003 scudi and the expenditures to 224,556 scudi per annum.[15] Thus my research on the finances of Propaganda Fide confirms one of the central findings of Volker Reinhardt's seminal study of the finances of the cardinal-nephew: "All efforts to honour the overarching spiritual and political obligations of the papacy" regularly yielded to the pursuit of "private interests and efforts to secure the advancement and aggrandizement of the status of the papal family."[16]

Other findings help put the total assets of Propaganda Fide into perspective: in 1651, the Congregation for the Propagation of the Faith had assets amounting to a mere 610,196 scudi.[17] In comparison, even Alexander VII (Fabio

---

päpstlichen Herrschaftswesens, 2 vols. [Päpste und Papsttum 6/1 and 11] [Stuttgart: Anton Hiersemann, 1974]) and Volker Reinhardt's monograph of 1984 (*Kardinal Scipione Borghese* [*1605–1633*]. *Vermögen, Finanzen und sozialer Aufstieg eines Papstnepoten* [Bibliothek des Deutschen Historischen Instituts in Rom, 58] [Tübingen: Max Niemeyer Verlag, 1984]) did not usher in a new wave of research on papal finances. As a result the period beyond the early decades of the seventeenth century, which is of interest here, remains woefully understudied.

14   No bilanci survive for the period prior to 1651, and the documentation covering the following years is patchy. It was only in the course of the eighteenth century that both revenues and expenditures seem to have increased. At the same time the growing deficit toward the end of the eighteenth century suggests that the increased activities exceeded the financial capacity of the Congregation. For detailed references see Windler, *Missionare in Persien*, 41–43.

15   Reinhardt, *Kardinal Scipione Borghese*, 96–97.

16   Reinhardt, 549. During his pontificate, Paul v (1605–1621) showered his family with 1,095,130 scudi in monetary donations alone; to this we need to add gifts in kind, as well as the dispensation of lucrative benefices to the cardinal-nephew (Reinhard, *Papstfinanz und Nepotismus*, 53–101). The financial resources of other important curial congregations, in particular the Holy Office, were even more limited than those of Propaganda Fide. See Germano Maifreda, *I denari dell'inquisitore. Affari e giustizia di fede nell'Italia moderna* (Turin: Giulio Einaudi, 2014).

17   Stato temporale 1651 (APF, SC. Stato temporale, vol. 2, fol. 567v).

Chigi, r. 1655–1667), who had initially excluded his relatives from the government of the Church, endowed his nephew Agostino Chigi with approximately 620,000 scudi when the latter married Maria Virginia Borghese in 1659.[18] These numbers lay bare severe shortcomings in the process of institution-building; these shortcomings were shared by the early modern Roman Church and the Papal States and by the secular monarchies of the period. As in the courts of secular princes, so in the Roman Curia, the elaborate ceremonial that exalted the position of the pope did not change the fact that, financially speaking, wealthy noble dynasties, not the developing institutions, continued to pull the strings.[19]

While most resources were raised in the Papal States and in the city of Rome, this was also where most of the Congregation's revenues were spent. Though percentages varied over time, 40 to 50 percent of the expenditures went into stage-managing the missions as a papal enterprise in Rome, where Propaganda Fide, along with the Collegio urbano and the Tipografia poliglotta, was housed in a palace on Piazza di Spagna which had been built by two particularly prestigious architects, Gian Lorenzo Bernini and Francesco Borromini. The sumptuous façade of the Roman palace barely concealed the fact that the institution was at best able to fund only a small part of the missions out of the resources of its stato temporale.[20] This certainly holds true for the Persian mission: although Clement VIII had dispatched the Discalced Carmelites as papal missionaries, the subsidies that were transferred to Persia did not come from the papal household, but from the legacy of a Neapolitan nobleman, Francesco Cimino, baron of Cacurri, who had bequeathed part of his fortune to the order to finance the establishment of a seminary for missionaries. Of the original bequest of the baron, who had ordered his heirs to pay out 2,250 Roman scudi per annum to the order, the Discalced Carmelites eventually managed to secure assets to the tune of 15,827 Roman scudi after reaching a legal settlement in 1622. Yet, even then, the Cimino legacy offered only an irregular income, a situation that was exacerbated by the fact that no additional bequests were made to the missions of the order in the following decades.[21] In 1655, Alexander VII

---

18   Antonio Menniti Ippolito, *Il tramonto della Curia nepotista. Papi, nipoti e burocrazia curiale tra XVI e XVII secolo* (La corte dei papi 5) (Rome: Viella, 1999), 90–93.

19   See Daniel Dessert's conclusion on the court of Versailles: "derrière le rituel servile de Versailles les groupes aristocratiques, qui semblaient avoir été mis au pas par la caporalisation louis-quatorzième, demeurent les véritables maîtres du jeu": Daniel Dessert, *Argent, pouvoir et société au Grand Siècle* (Paris: Arthème Fayard, 1984), 416.

20   Detailed references in Windler, *Missionare in Persien*, 44–49.

21   Chick, *Chronicle*, vol. 2, 757–58, 920; Definitorium generale March 23, 1643 (Fortes, *Acta definitorii generalis O.C.D.*, vol. 1, 363).

devolved the right to manage these resources to the Congregation for the Prop-agation of the Faith.[22] This, combined with the order's inability to secure ad-ditional funding, contributed to the alienation of members of the Discalced Carmelites from the Curia. This alienation manifested itself in the internal correspondence of the order, in which the unquenchable thirst for wealth and power in the court of Rome, as well as the "unbearable Roman slowness" which Propaganda Fide displayed in its dealings with the missionaries, became the target of severe criticism.[23]

If we turn to the eighteenth century, the Dominican missionaries of the re-formed congregation of Santa Sabina and the bishops of Isfahan, who were recruited from the ranks of that order and from the Discalced Carmelites, were the only clergymen in Persia to receive subsidies from the stato temporale of the Congregation for the Propagation of the Faith. What is true elsewhere is also valid in Persia: even in those missions where Propaganda Fide regularly contributed toward missionaries' travel expenses and provided them with addi-tional subsidies, these sums paled in comparison to the mission's total costs.[24] The scarce funds of the Congregation were invested wherever the patronage of secular princes (in particular the Spanish *patronato real* and the Portuguese *padroado*) had left gaps for missionary activities that the Roman Curia could fill, including in parts of the Ottoman Empire and, lagging far behind, in the Polish Armenian communities, in Ireland and Scotland, and in a number of other settings.[25] Given the limited financial capabilities of the Congregation for the Propagation of the Faith, most funds therefore came from those actors whose influence the post-Tridentine papacy was trying to curtail: secular pa-trons and protectors, as well as religious orders. Despite this, it is important to point out that the missions with much looser ties to the Roman Curia also often found themselves in dire financial straits. As a result, missionaries of all orders saw themselves compelled to raise funding from local sources, as I will demonstrate in the second part of this chapter.

By engaging in economic activities, missionaries clearly violated the nor-mative framework which the orders and the Roman Curia were trying to impose on them. The idea that missionaries should not become involved in worldly affairs and engage in trade and finance was a recurrent theme in the texts with which the superiors of the orders and Propaganda Fide sought to regulate the day-to-day lives of missionaries on the ground. In the case of the

22   Chick, *Chronicle*, vol. 2, 763–64.
23   Windler, *Missionare in Persien*, 126–51.
24   Windler, *Missionare in Persien*, 543–48.
25   See the table in Windler, *Missionare in Persien*, 49.

Discalced Carmelites, attempts to keep missionaries apart from worldly affairs emanated from the reform of the order initiated by Teresa of Ávila in the sixteenth century.[26] But the Roman Curia, too, imposed far-reaching restrictions on missionaries' worldly dealings. In 1633, Urban VIII (Maffeo Barberini, r. 1623–1644), acting at the behest of Propaganda Fide, withdrew all missionary areas in Asia that were not under direct Portuguese rule from the exclusive Portuguese padroado. Contrasting with earlier dispensations, such as the one Gregory XIII (Ugo Boncompagni, r. 1572–1585) gave to the Jesuits in Japan for their silk trade, the same bull, Ex debito officii, prohibited members of the regular clergy in these areas from engaging either directly or indirectly in commercial activities or lucrative financial transactions on pain of excommunication or other punishment.[27] In 1669 Clement IX (Giulio Rospigliosi, r. 1667–1669), in the constitution Sollicitudo pastoralis officii, reiterated that the financial distress of the missions was not a valid excuse for disregarding the provisions of his predecessor. Extending Urban VIII's bull to the Americas, he also ordered that excommunications be imposed not only on offending missionaries, but also on those superiors of religious orders who failed to prosecute known violations.[28]

These provisions explain why the missionaries' insistent complaints about insufficient subsidies from Rome never died down. Such complaints remained a fixture in missionaries' letters to the superiors of religious orders and Propaganda Fide, not because they hoped they would change things for the better, but because of the symbolic value that missionaries attached to Roman subsidies as a sign of the superiors' and the Curia's interest in the well-being of the missions. In fact, the frequent complaints about the lack of subsidies helped legitimize fund-raising practices that stood in more or less stark contrast to

---

26   Windler, *Missionare in Persien*, 540–43.

27   Bull *Ex debito pastoralis officii* issued by Urban VIII, February 22, 1633, ed. in: *Collectanea S. Congregationis de Propaganda Fide*, vol. 1, 18–19, here 19, synopsis in: Josef Metzler, "Orientation, programme et premières décisions (1622–1649)," in *Sacrae Congregationis de Propaganda Fide Memoria Rerum, 1622–1972*, Vol. I/1: *1622–1700*, ed. Josef Metzler (Rome; Freiburg im Breisgau; Vienna: Herder, 1971), 170–71; Josef Metzler, "Die Kongregation in der zweiten Hälfte des 17. Jahrhunderts," in *Sacrae Congregationis de Propaganda Fide Memoria Rerum, 1622–1972*, Vol. I/1: *1622–1700*, ed. Josef Metzler (Rome/Freiburg im Breisgau/Vienna: Herder, 1971) 280; Theodor Grentrup, "Das kirchliche Handelsverbot für die Missionare," *Zeitschrift für Missionswissenschaft* 15 (1925): 259. On the silk trade by the Jesuits in Japan, see Hélène Vu Thanh's chapter in this volume.

28   Constitution *Sollicitudo pastoralis officii* issued by Clement IX, June 17, 1669, ed. in: *Collectanea S. Congregationis de Propaganda Fide*, vol. 1, 57–59, synopsis in: Metzler, *Die Kongregation in der zweiten Hälfte des 17. Jahrhunderts*, 280; Grentrup, "Das kirchliche Handelsverbot," 260.

the religious observance which both the orders and the Curia were trying to enforce at the time.[29]

2   Local Convent Economies and Trans-local Economic Integration

The local convent economies set up by missionaries in Persia clearly contravened the provisions of the religious orders and the Roman Curia. However, the neat lines of demarcation that the orders and the Curia were trying to draw between the world of the clergy and the laity flew in the face of material constraints on the ground, most notably insufficient funding from Rome. We can gain some insight into missionaries' fundraising practices from two account books of the house of the Discalced Carmelites in Basra, the first of which covers the period from 1674 to 1727 and the second the subsequent years up to 1772.[30] When assessing these account books it is important to bear in mind that they are not necessarily a reflection of the real economy of the convent. In fact, in 1718 the account-managing vicar added a telling comment to the book: If the expenses recorded over the last two months appeared disproportionately high, he explained, this was because he had only just begun to document all expenses, whereas before he had regularly omitted up to one-third of the effective costs.[31] The year 1718 marks the transition from an earlier period, during which the account-managing vicar tried to show how the Discalced Carmelites in Basra were faithful to the constitutions of their order,[32] and thus only registered those items that would not arouse the suspicion of the visitors sent by the order, to a period of account-keeping practices that more accurately reflected the real convent economy. It should be added that, contrary to his claims in the account book, the accountant was less concerned with concealing generic expenses (which, tellingly, he did not usually specify) than with hiding suspicious sources of revenues, something that was achieved by tampering with the expenses column. Up until 1718 the Discalced Carmelites in Basra documented only income from their activity as priests (alms for masses

---

29   Additional material in Windler, *Missionare in Persien*, 543–48.
30   Liber accepti et expensi Residentiae nostrae Bassorae mense Ianuario anni 1674 usque ad mensem inclusive decembrem anni 1727 (AGOCD, 483/f); [Liber computum], 1728–1772 (AGOCD, 484/e).
31   Liber accepti et expensi Residentiae nostrae Bassorae mense Ianuario anni 1674 usque ad mensem inclusive decembrem anni 1727, entry at the end of 1718 (AGOCD, 483/f).
32   On this point, compare Clément Lenoble, *L'exercice de la pauvreté. Économie et religion chez les franciscains d'Avignon (XIIIe-XVe siècles)* (Rennes: Presses universitaires de Rennes, 2013).

in particular), subsidies from Rome, rent from tenants who lived in their houses, and gifts they had received from grateful guests. Starting in December 1718 they began recording additional sources of income, which, if the vicar is to be believed, had also played an important role even before that date: revenues "ex industria," and from 1724, equally substantial proceeds from the sale of rosewater, which was produced in the city's environs.[33] Given the city's importance as a trading hub and the fathers' close ties to the local Christian merchant community (its members formed their most important spiritual clientele), it is safe to assume that "ex industria" referred to the sale of goods. Since the papacy had threatened to excommunicate members of religious orders who engaged in trade, it stood to reason that they would not record revenues from commercial activities as such.

The account-book entries for the period between 1719 and 1753 reveal the extent to which the convent had become economically independent of the order and the Roman Curia. During this period the subsidies that reached Basra from Europe at irregular intervals covered only a tiny part of the order's expenditures. The house continued to flourish, but this was only due to the fathers' efforts to establish a modest but viable convent economy, which generated 97.6 percent of the house's revenues. So successful were they that they regularly recorded a modest surplus. To finance the mission, the Discalced Carmelites offered services that were sought after by European travellers and local Eastern Christians of various denominations. In doing so, they benefited from the fact that between the 1720s and the early 1770s Basra was witnessing considerable growth as a port of transit, thanks to its integration into trading networks that linked the Indian Ocean and the Gulf of Persia to Aleppo and the Mediterranean Sea. English, Dutch, and French traders were becoming more important in the long-distance trade of the city. Around the same time, Armenian merchants fleeing the growing anarchy and repression in New Julfa also settled in Basra.[34]

It was to this growing community of Christian merchants that the Discalced Carmelites offered accommodation and services as religious specialists. The Venetian Ambrogio Bembo, who stopped over in Basra on his way to India in 1673, describes how the Discalced Carmelites came to pick him up from his

---

33   See Thabit A. G. Abdullah, *Merchants, Mamluks, and Murder: The Political Economy of Trade in Eighteenth-Century Basra* (Albany, NY: State University of New York Press, 2001), 40.

34   René J. Barendse, *Arabian Seas 1700–1763*, vol. 1: *The Western Indian Ocean in the Eighteenth Century* (Leiden; Boston: Brill, 2009), 221–40. On traders based in Basra in the eighteenth century, see Abdullah, *Merchants, Mamluks, and Murder*, 45–82.

ship and escorted him to the convent (the fathers had been informed about the Venetian's imminent arrival in a letter sent to them by the English consul in Aleppo). At the convent the Discalced Carmelites offered their guest much more than a suitable accommodation in keeping with his social status: Bembo was introduced to other European expatriates—a Frenchman and an agent of the Dutch East India Company—in whose company and partly in that of the fathers he visited the canals that surrounded the city. When clearing formalities threatened to delay Bembo's departure to India, the superior of the Discalced Carmelites, who regularly tended to the interests of Frenchmen and Englishmen, helpfully contacted the customs officer on the Venetian's behalf.[35]

Around 1670 the Discalced Carmelites were renting out a house and the rooms of a caravanserai adjoining the convent.[36] Over the years the surplus thus generated was reinvested in the acquisition of additional real estate. Between 1719 and 1753, 41 percent of the revenues of the convent came from letting multiple houses and the rooms of the caravanserai, occasionally even rooms in the convent itself, to travelling merchants. Another 33.6 percent of the revenues consisted of alms and bequests made to the Discalced Carmelites by people who had resided with them and wanted to express their gratitude for the hospitality they had received. Funerals in the courtyard and the church of the convent yielded 6.2 percent. In addition to this, the fathers used their ties to the merchant milieu to sell goods, which between 1719 and 1753 accounted for 16.5 percent of the convent's income. For some time they even seem to have specialized in the rosewater trade: While the sale of rosewater took in a mere 8.1 percent over the whole period, in the years from 1734 to 1738 that percentage soared to almost 23.[37] The categories of revenues, ranging from the proceeds of the sale of goods to alms and bequests, show that the fathers moved between different economies. Whereas the proceeds of the sale of goods in a port town pertained to a market economy, the alms and bequests of grateful guests, which amounted to one third of the revenues, were part of a gift economy based on a Christian system of values. Certain activities of the fathers—in particular the care they offered based on their medical expertise—do not figure as such in the account books because they were part of this gift economy.

---

35   Ambrogio Bembo, *Il viaggio in Asia (1671–1675) nei manoscritti di Minneapolis e di Bergamo*, ed. Antonio Invernizzi (Alessandria: Edizioni dell'Orso, 2012) 109–10, 113–15.

36   Memoria delle cose che devo rappresentare alli nostri signori definitori per le missioni, n.p., n.d. [ca. 1670] (AGOCD, 243/b/3).

37   Liber accepti et expensi Residentiae nostrae Bassorae mense Ianuario anni 1674 usque ad mensem inclusive decembrem anni 1727 (AGOCD, 483/f); [Liber computum], 1728–1772 (AGOCD, 484/e). More details in Windler, *Missionare in Persien*, 548–54.

They were rewarded by counter-gifts in the form of alms and bequests rather than with formal payments, which Propaganda Fide excluded, even in those cases where dispensations for the medical activities of priests were exceptionally granted.[38]

If the account books are a reliable indicator of the convent's revenues from commercial activities, the period under consideration witnessed a significant shift from active participation in the sale of goods to offering services for Europeans and Eastern Christians active in trade. When the vicar decided to adopt sounder bookkeeping practices in 1718, the percentage of recorded revenues from sales soared from 0 to 41.6 percent in 1719. After 1740, however, income from the sale of goods almost disappeared from the account books once again. The fact that the Discalced Carmelites had been acquiring additional real estate that was rented out to travelling merchants might suggest that they were making efforts to specialize as service-providers for merchants and seamen. Nevertheless, it must be mentioned that the lack of records of inadmissible sources of income may have simply been a sign that the fathers had reverted to earlier practices of concealing them from superiors. This is indeed suggested by the writings of a Discalced Carmelite, Cornelio di San Giuseppe, which shed light on the order's close ties to the European trading companies and its resulting involvement in trade during this period. Foreign merchants with no pre-existing ties to the area saw father Cornelio as a trustworthy interlocutor. For a period of time, although of Milanese origin, he looked after the interests of the French East India Company and the French consulate. Furthermore, his remuneration deepened the Discalced Carmelites' involvement in trade: In 1752, to thank father Cornelio for services rendered to the French East India Company and the French nation (merchant colony) in Basra, the trading company sold the convent a barrel of Madeira at a preferential price. The proceeds from the sale of less than half the total of 500 bottles turned out to be sufficient to cover the cost price; the remainder was consumed by the missionaries themselves.[39]

The documentation of the convents of the Discalced Carmelites in Isfahan, New Julfa, and Shiraz, is unfortunately not as detailed as the account books in Basra. From the surviving records it can nevertheless be inferred that the fathers in the heartland of the Safavid Empire had also developed a number of strategies to cope with the desperate financial situation, strategies that all, to some degree, contravened the norms of the religious order to which they

---

38   The medical activities of the Discalced Carmelites in Persia are well-documented. See
      Windler, *Missionare in Persien*, 252–58.
39   *Memorie cronologiche che puonno servire a meglio sovvenirmi de varii altri incidenti di
      mia vita*, written by P. Cornelio di San Giuseppe O.C.D., n.p., n.d., 25, 27 (BA, & 211 sup.).

belonged: Rather than rely on alms and mass offerings alone, as behoved a mendicant order, the fathers appear to have been involved in secular trade.

No sooner had they reached Isfahan in 1607 than the Discalced Carmelites became aware that they were unable to collect sufficient alms and mass offerings in Persia. Despite the latent jurisdictional conflict between the Portuguese padroado and the papacy, the fathers were able to secure the authorization of the archbishop of Goa and the viceroy of Portuguese India to establish convents in Goa and on Hormuz Island. When the Discalced Carmelites finally did found an additional convent in Goa in 1620, it was the prospect of tapping the riches of this wealthy Indian city that led their superiors to retroactively sanction the unauthorized move of the fathers.[40]

As anticipated, the alms shipped in from India went a long way toward solving the financial woes of the missionaries in Persia. In 1649 the procurator of the Persian mission reported to the general chapter of the Discalced Carmelites that, in addition to the subsidies from Rome, a sizeable share of the funds for the Persian mission came from alms and mass offerings from India. In every financial emergency the order dispatched a father or a lay brother to India. The alms which brother Francesco Maria di San Siro brought to Persia in 1701 were reportedly sufficient to service the debts that the mission had run up.[41] Just eight years later, in 1709, however, the simmering conflict between the Portuguese padroado and the Congregation for the Propagation of the Faith culminated in the expulsion of the Discalced Carmelites from Goa, and this critical source of revenue dried up.

In this difficult moment the Discalced Carmelites of Isfahan benefited from the fact that, in addition to securing funding from India, they had been making efforts to tap local resources. These attempts were predicated on two concessions that shah 'Abbās I had made to the Discalced Carmelites. As had the Augustinians before them, the Discalced Carmelites were granted free use of a house surrounded by a large yard that boasted an irrigation plant, good-quality drinking water, and enough space to set up workshops and a horse stable. The fathers would use this property until the end of the mission in the 1750s.[42]

40   Chick, Chronicle, vol. 2, 759–61, 1222–23.

41   P. Felice di Sant'Antonio o.c.d., procurator of the missions in Persia, to the general chapter, Rome, October 15, 1649 (AGOCD, 261/m/1); Chick, Chronicle, vol. 2, 893, 1229.

42   Relatione del P. Benigno di S. Michele sul suo viaggio in Persia, written by P. Redempto de la Cruz and P. Benigno di San Michele o.c.d., Isfahan, August 10, 1609 (AGOCD, 234/e/bis, fol. 30r/v); Voyage de M. [Bénigne] Vachet à travers la Perse, n.p. [account of the author's journey that took place in 1689–1690] (AMEP, vol. 347, 216). For an account from a later period see Memorie concernenti alla Chiesa e diocesi di Persia, written by P. Cornelio di San Giuseppe o.c.d., n.p., n.d., fol. 171r–179v (BA, H 136 suss.).

A few years later, thanks to the ties of father Juan Thadeo de San Eliseo to the court, the order obtained another property outside the city, which was also used throughout the mission's existence.[43]

Together these two properties laid the foundations for a modest convent economy. As in Basra, the Discalced Carmelites in Isfahan let rooms to travellers. While there are no sources allowing the economic impact of the services they provided to be quantified, surviving travel accounts show that the fathers had furnished their houses to welcome travellers. The Venetian Ambrogio Bembo, for example, was quartered in several rooms with a separate kitchen while a second building also served as a guesthouse. According to Bembo, this house was regularly rented to Europeans. During his stay, Bembo met the "heretic Frenchman" (*heretico francese*) Jean Chardin and Antoine Raisin from Lyon, who were both active in the jewellery business.[44] In the yard of the convent the fathers raised chickens and grew fruit, vegetables, grains, and beans, which were watered from an underground canal (*qanāt*) and three draw wells;[45] the trees supplied part of the firewood needed to heat the convent in winter. While the crops from the yard were primarily used for subsistence, Juan Thadeo de San Eliseo in his role as prior of the convent pursued plans to use the property outside the city not only as a burial ground for Catholics but also as a vineyard. According to a report of 1616 to a fellow brother who was staying in Rome, Juan Thadeo was planning to produce several thousand litres of wine each year, a quantity that far exceeded the needs of the convent.[46]

The commercialization of wine, which was in high demand at the court of the shah, gave rise to criticism from Juan Thadeo's fellow brothers and the superiors of the order.[47] In 1630 the *definitorium generale* saw fit to issue an order that the property, which had been designated as a burial ground, be used exclusively for this purpose and not to grow crops.[48] Nevertheless, the Discalced

---

43 P. Juan Thadeo de San Eliseo O.C.D. to P. Benigno di San Michele, subprior O.C.D of the convent of Isfahan, in Rome, Isfahan, March 26, 1616 (AGOCD, 237/m/9).

44 Bembo, *Il viaggio in Asia*, 360–61.

45 P. Filippo Maria di Sant'Agostino O.C.D. to P. Cirillo della Visitazione in Shiraz, New Julfa, September 21, 1724 (AGOCD, 238/u/4); P. Filippo Maria di Sant'Agostino O.C.D. to ?, New Julfa, November 17, 1724 (AGOCD, 238/u/5); Memorie concernenti alla Chiesa e diocesi di Persia, written by P. Cornelio di San Giuseppe O.C.D., n.p., n.d., fol. 177v–179v (BA, H 136 suss.).

46 P. Juan Thadeo de San Eliseo O.C.D. to P. Benigno di San Michele, subprior O.C.D. of the convent of Isfahan, in Rome, Isfahan, March 26, 1616 (AGOCD, 237/m/9).

47 See Windler, *Missionare in Persien*, 557–58.

48 Instruttione per gli nostri padri della missione de Persia et Oriente che si manda d'ordine del definitorio generale del 1630 a 6 di Jenaro, signed P. Fernando de Santa María, *praepositus generalis* O.C.D. (AGOCD, 289/e/1).

Carmelites, enlisting the help of servants, continued to produce wine in quantities that far exceeded their own needs. According to a memorandum an unknown father must have written around 1670, servants of the convent were selling wine and spirits, which caused "scandal" and led to the missionaries being seen as innkeepers. The anonymous author explained that the fathers had been using necessity as a pretext to produce twice as much wine than they needed for subsistence, and urged that they be instructed to refrain from producing more wine than necessary.[49] There are indications that the Discalced Carmelites were also producing wine outside Isfahan. In 1721 the provincial vicar reported that, owing to the lack of funds from Rome, the fathers in Shiraz had borrowed money and produced wine which they then sold to the French consul and the Portuguese agent. Thanks to the proceeds from the sale of the coveted Shiraz wine, which was marketed through the ports on the Gulf of Persia to India, the fathers secured a livelihood and renovated the dilapidated convent.[50]

The sale of wine and spirits was not the only way in which the Discalced Carmelites engaged in trade. The ties to India originally fostered to raise alms and mass offerings soon assumed a commercial dimension, as the revenue from alms could be multiplied if used to acquire Indian goods that could be resold at a profit in Persia. In 1624, for example, the *praepositus generalis* asked the visitor general to invest the alms that he was to collect in Goa in acquiring goods that could be easily transported to and resold in Persia.[51] When he returned from Goa in the 1630s, Dimas della Croce brought back more than 4,000 piaster (approximately 4,000 scudi) in cash and goods, including diamonds.[52] For these goods to be of any use to the local mission, they needed to be resold at a profit.

---

49 Memoria delle cose che devo rappresentare alli nostri signori definitori per le missioni, n.p., n.d. [ca. 1670] (AGOCD, 243/b/3).

50 P. Faustino di San Carolo, provincial vicar O.C.D., to the Definitorium generale O.C.D., Isfahan, May 26, 1721 (AGOCD, 238/g/9, cited in Chick, *Chronicle*, vol. 1, 515–16). By producing Shiraz wine the Discalced Carmelites followed the example of the Portuguese, the Dutch, the English, and the French (Bembo, *Il viaggio in Asia*, 337–38; Francis Richard, *Raphaël du Mans, missionnaire en Perse au XVIIᵉ siècle*, vol. 1: *Biographie. Correspondance* [Paris: L'Harmattan, 1995], 139).

51 Instruction by P. Paolo Simone di Gesù Maria, praepositus generalis O.C.D., to P. Eugenio di San Benedetto, visitor general, [Rome, 1624] (AGOCD, 261/d/1 and 2).

52 P. Giovanni Stefano di Santa Teresa, visitor general O.C.D., to the Definitorium generale O.C.D., Goa, September 15, 1639 (AGOCD, 261/g/1 and 2). Conversion from piaster (probably identical to reales de a ocho) to scudi on the basis of the rates of 1609, 1640, and 1669 in Chick, *Chronicle*, vol. 2, 775–76.

Their involvement in commercial activities was part of the "friendship" and "good correspondence" that the missionaries maintained with merchants of various confessions.[53] The father who criticized the trade in wine and spirits around 1670 lamented the fact that alms from Goa often reached Persia in the form of goods. He also claimed that merchants often bought merchandise in the name of the Discalced Carmelites, which was then brought to Persia and resold in the houses of the order. Thus, he concluded, the fathers were seen as merchants, which was detrimental to their reputation.[54]

Yet another aspect of the close ties to the merchant milieu was the interest that missionaries earned from lending cash to local traders. Although exact figures are difficult to establish, it is clear that the Discalced Carmelites had, at least temporarily, sufficient cash reserves which they could and did lend at high interest rates. The cash thus invested far exceeded the subsidies from Italy (which often failed to reach Persia at all).[55] These controversial investment strategies shed light on the missionaries' economic ties to the laity of other Christian denominations and non-Christians. Besides hinting at involvement with Catholic, Armenian, and Protestant Christians, and Muslims, the correspondence of the Discalced Carmelites sheds light on the relations they cultivated with Indian "pagans," who in Persia were not seen as potential converts and are otherwise rarely mentioned in the sources. Along with Armenian merchants and the various European East India Companies, Indians—"pagans" as well as Muslims—performed a crucial function in linking the Safavid Empire to the monetized economy of South Asia. In the port towns along the Gulf of Persia, as well as in Isfahan, they operated as lenders and money changers.[56] When the missionaries approached the Indians, they were following the example of European and Armenian merchants.[57] It remains unclear at this point to

---

53   Windler, *Missionare in Persien*, 427–62.
54   Memoria delle cose che devo rappresentare alli nostri signori definitori per le missioni, n.p., n.d. [ca. 1670] (AGOCD, 243/b/3).
55   For more details see Windler, *Missionare in Persien*, 560–63, 566–67.
56   Research on the Indian diaspora of merchants and financiers has been hampered by a lack of surviving source material, which has meant that economic histories of the Safavid Empire have largely relied on the records of the European East India companies. Stephen Frederic Dale's important study is largely based on Russian sources from Astrachan, and affords a rare glimpse into the activities and significance of the Indian diaspora in Persia. See Stephen Frederic Dale, *The Muslim Empires of the Ottomans, Safavids, and Mughals* (Cambridge: Cambridge University Press, 2010) and *Indian Merchants and Eurasian Trade, 1600–1750* (Cambridge: Cambridge University Press, 1994), 124–26.
57   On the Armenians as clients of the Bania in South Asia and Persia, see Edmund M. Herzig, "The Armenian Merchants of New Julfa, Isfahan: A Study in Pre-Modern Asian Trade" (PhD diss., University of Oxford, 1991), 208.

what extent this was propelled by the fact that non-Muslim Indians were not subject to the restrictions on interest lending that applied to both Christians and Muslims.[58] At any rate the correspondence of the Discalced Carmelites, which occasionally addressed the issue of interest lending, does not suggest that some practices were specific to one religious group or another; neither in the case of the Discalced Carmelites nor in that of their business partners, do religious reservations about lending money at interest seem to have been seen as a significant obstacle. Even in the correspondence to the superiors of the order, interest rates of up to 24 percent per annum are explicitly mentioned.[59] Significantly, these mentions alone did not provoke controversy within the order, almost as if there had been a sort of implicit consensus not to discuss such delicate questions.

In this and in other cases, then, the lack of subsidies from Italy helped justify practices that contravened the type of observance the post-Tridentine Church was trying to impose on religious orders. The fathers made no attempt to hide from their superiors the economic ties that linked them to the local merchant milieu. Lest this be held against them, they described these fundraising efforts as an unavoidable consequence of the lack of financial support from Europe. Given the chronic underfunding of the missions, it seemed reasonable for missionaries to avail themselves of the services of local merchants, not only to transfer the (admissible) subsidies and alms from Europe and India, but also to take out loans or lend cash at high interest rates, practices that violated the canonical ban on usury. Owing to the material constraints, these violations did not have serious consequences, even when they came to the attention of the Holy Office: In 1709 the Congregation for the Propagation of the Faith sent a report to the Holy Office, according to which some missionaries in Persia who had lent money to merchants claimed that this was a permissible way of generating revenues. The Holy Office ordered that the bishop of Isfahan reprove the missionaries in question and open a formal investigation into the matter, thereby reaffirming the universal validity of canonical norms, but the Congregation failed to follow the enforcement of this decree.[60] Both the normative universalism and its relativization in lived practice were characteristic of a latent conflict that missionaries experienced all over the world. Although the process of confessionalization meant that the superiors of religious orders and the congregations of the Roman Curia tended to deny the legitimacy of local

---

58   See, for example, Rudi Matthee, "Merchants in Safavid Iran: Participants and Perceptions," *Journal of Early Modern History* 4 (2000): 246–48.

59   For more details on this, see Windler, *Missionare in Persien*, 560–63.

60   Relatio; Feria v, November 28, 1709 (ACDF, SO, St.St., M 3 a, fol. 69v–70v, 147v).

normative contexts, in practice they often had no choice but to tolerate them. While the adaptation was in other cases achieved through formal dispensations, the local economy of the Discalced Carmelites was governed by a silence which the actors avoided breaking. This does not mean that the practices were unknown to the superiors of their order and the Roman Curia: In 1709, the Holy Office probably did not intervene because the missionaries had lent money to merchants (something the fathers had often reported on in letters to their superiors), but because some of them had claimed that this practice was permissible.

3   Conclusion: An Isolated Case or a Typical Example?

The discrepancy between the missionaries' actions and the norms of the religious orders to which they belonged was one of the ways in which the missions posed an unintended challenge to the post-Tridentine Church. The gap between the constraints of everyday life on the ground and the standards of religious observance meant that non-observance was not only widespread, but also often thought to be unavoidable. Thus the missions unintentionally relativized values and norms that had formed the backbone of religious orders and their way of life. Although such everyday occurrences were not as striking as the better-known missionary controversies over dogma and rituals, they also more generally undermined the post-Tridentine Church's aspiration to impose its normative standards.

While a systematic comparative analysis of different orders established in the same geographic setting had initially been an aim of my research on missionaries in Safavid Persia, I had to abandon this aim due to the unequal preservation of the documentation. Thus, the question of how the Capuchins, the Augustinians, and the Dominicans completed locally the subsidies they received from outside is probably bound to remain forever unresolved. At least, we know a little more about the Jesuits. The latter had at their disposal an endowment of 15,000 livres tournois (or approximately 5000 scudi) which the queen of Poland had given to them when the mission in Isfahan was founded. Since the mission was part of the province of Lyon, the capital was invested in France in 1654, while the procurator in charge was tasked with transferring the annual returns to Persia.[61] However, the Jesuits on the ground campaigned for

---

61   P. Alexandre de Rhodes S.J. to P. Goswinus Nickel, praepositus generalis S.J., Isfahan, February 21, 1660 (ARSI, Gallia, 103 I, fol. 66r/v). Conversion of livres tournois to scudi according to idem to idem, Isfahan, September 11, 1656 (Ibid., 103 II, fol. 221v).

a transfer of the endowment to Persia. The arguments for this, which the first superior of the Isfahan mission reiterated tirelessly in his correspondence between 1656 and his passing in 1660, included the difficulties of sending letters to Persia, the late and partial payments, and the prospect of returns of more than 10 % (as opposed to the current 4 %) per annum.[62] In 1658, the general of the order came around and ordered an initial transfer of 6000 livres tournois (2000 scudi) to Persia.[63] However, since this decision was sabotaged in France, the Jesuits in Isfahan continued to lack the seed capital they needed to lay the foundations of a local missionary economy. The fathers remained dependent on irregular and partial transfers of the returns from their endowment,[64] and uncertain donations from locals.[65]

Though extremely fragmented, the surviving sources hint at the existence of other sources of income which were, at least in part, less compatible with the order's constitutions and bore similarities with those of the Discalced Carmelites: the sale of produce from the mission's yard, trade deals, and investment of cash at high interest rates. To alleviate the poverty of the Jesuits in Isfahan, father Alexandre de Rhodes wrote in 1659, they had sent commodities to resell them in Goa.[66] Before their move from Isfahan to New Julfa in 1661, the fathers responded to Muslim neighbors' demand for wine, well aware of the risks this presented to their relations to Muslim religious authorities. The convent they acquired in New Julfa in 1661 included a chicken run and a yard supplied with water by an irrigation channel and boasting vines, fruit trees, and land for cultivation, whose produce was in part sold locally. Like the Discalced Carmelites, the superior of the Jesuits made cash investments with local merchants. He learned the hard way that investments at high interest rates were a risky business when the debtor left Isfahan in 1661 without clearing his debts.[67] As with the Discalced Carmelites', the Jesuits' cooperation with merchants and

---

62   Numerous letters from P. Alexandre de Rhodes S.J. to P. Goswinus Nickel, praepositus
      generalis S.J., Isfahan 1656–1660 (ARSI, Gallia, 103 I and II).

63   P. Alexandre de Rhodes S.J. to P. Goswinus Nickel, praepositus generalis S.J., Isfahan, May
      30, 1659 (ARSI, Galllia, 103 I, fol. 53r/v).

64   For example, as of 1663, the fathers in Isfahan had not received money from France in
      more than three years (P. Aimé Chézaud S.J. to P. Claude Boucher, assistant de France S.J.,
      Isfahan, March 25, 1663 [ARSI, Gallia, 97 II, doc. 115, fol. 328r]).

65   Unlike in Syria and Greece, there were no local donors in Isfahan, P. Chézaux complained
      in 1661 (P. Aimé Chézaud S.J. to the assistant de France S.J., Isfahan, November 14 and
      December 16, 1661 [ARSI, Gallia, 97 II, doc. 110 f., fol. 318r, 320v]).

66   P. Alexandre de Rhodes S.J. to P. Goswinus Nickel, praepositus generalis S.J., Isfahan, May
      30, 1659 (ARSI, Gallia, 103 II, fol. 271r).

67   P. Aimé Chézaud S.J. to the assistant de France S.J., Isfahan, November 14 and December
      16, 1661, January 22, 1662 (ARSI, Gallia, 97 II, doc. 110 to 112, fol. 318r, 320r/v, 322r).

financiers was not constricted by religious boundaries: In 1666, father Mercier, in his function as superior, recommended bypassing the Portuguese and entrusting the transfer of cash to China to "our Banyans" who would attend to it "without risks" and at a favourable conversion rate.[68]

The findings on the Discalced Carmelites and the Jesuits in Persia presented here fit a broader picture of predominantly local missionary economies that has been painted of Jesuit missions in other parts of Asia.[69] The poverty of the Jesuits in Persia, who were for the most part left to fend for themselves, stood in stark contrast to the affluence or even prosperity of Jesuit missions in other parts of the world. These findings call into question the picture of the Society of Jesus as a globally integrated enterprise.[70] At the same time, our findings underline the significance the integration of single missions into translocal networks had for their survival.

Studying the Persian missions may act as a corrective to received ideas which can in turn be traced back to the one-sided focus on the Society of Jesus that has informed research on missions. In Persia, the Discalced Carmelites adopted forms of accommodation that did not differ fundamentally from the practices that historians have commonly ascribed to the Jesuits. To be sure, the situation of the members of each order and their relations to the superiors continued to be shaped by the specific norms of each order. Discalced Carmelites who catered to local expectations became embroiled in difficult conflicts which resulted from their order's commitment to strict observance. In the correspondence to their superiors and in interactions with the visitors who were periodically dispatched to Persia, members of that order were careful to portray their comportment and that of their internal adversaries in light of these strict norms. Economic activities had to comply with norms that were characteristic of a mendicant order. While some demanded the strict observance of the order's rule regardless of the cultural environment in which its members operated, others justified the need to accommodate local expectations in clothing and lifestyle by constructing the missionary environment as an antithesis to Catholic Europe.[71]

---

68   P. Claude-Ignace Mercier S.J. to P. Claude Boucher, assistant de France S.J., Isfahan, September 9, 1666 (ARSI, Gallia, 97 II, doc. 121, fol. 336r).

69   See the contributions in this volume.

70   Dauril Alden, *The Making of an Enterprise. The Society of Jesus in Portugal, its Empire, and Beyond, 1540–1750* (Stanford: Stanford University Press, 1996). See also Vermote, "Finances of the Missions," 375–78.

71   See my analysis of observance within the order of the Discalced Carmelites in Windler, *Missionare in Persien*, 499–581.

In comparison to the Discalced Carmelites, the Jesuits found themselves in a more comfortable position: The foundational texts of their order were geared toward missionary activities and, as a result, left the members of that order much greater room for maneuver. Given these differences, the parallels between the orders at the level of everyday practice are all the more important as indicators of the extent to which missionaries of all shades were integrated into local networks. At a practical level, accommodation was a practice shared by members of all orders, constituting as it did a pragmatic response to the expectations that local societies placed in them. Beyond the missionary controversies which periodically caused a stir in Europe and whose faultlines did indeed at times coincide with the boundaries between religious orders, regular clerics, as local actors, differed less from each other than has been suggested by research that has focused on these controversies and the role of the Society of Jesus in them. Indeed, the calls for a decentering perspective on the early modern Catholic Church seem all the more legitimate in light of widespread commonalities that depended more on local conditions than on allegiance to a particular religious order.[72]

Given the diverse constitutions of the orders, the question of the observance of the rule raised by the embeddedness of missionaries in local socio-cultural systems posed itself in ways that differed from order to order. Still, all superiors were equally astounded by the fact that the missions transformed clerics into actors whose lives were being reshaped by local systems of reference—be it their economic behavior, the ways in which they sought to win prestige in a local context, or their handling of the rituals of the Church. The view on missions was, therefore, ambivalent: They were, at one and the same time, a visible sign of the triumph of the Roman Church over its Protestant competitors and a menace to observance and, by corollary, the salvation of the members of the order.

A close look at the economy of the Persian mission reveals how missionaries integrated into local society and how this called into question the universal aspirations of the papacy and the norms of the orders to which the missionaries belonged. Missionaries faced with chronic underfunding of the missions responded to local demands for worldly and spiritual services to secure the long-term survival of the endeavor. While this was an important first step, the example of the Discalced Carmelites in Basra, Isfahan, and New Julfa also shows that convents in Persia not only needed to be embedded in local society; they also needed to be integrated into trans-local trade networks

---

72   See Simon Ditchfield, "Decentering the Catholic Reformation. Papacy and Peoples in the Early Modern World," *Archiv für Reformationsgeschichte* 101 (2010): 186–208.

to South Asia. The missionaries' resulting close ties to Armenian merchants, Indian financial specialists, and the European East India Companies thus shed new light on yet another set of actors who grew increasingly dependent on processes of globalization—processes that had been deepening relations between different parts of the world from the sixteenth century onward.

Indeed, the local and regional embeddedness of missionaries as economic actors needs to be placed in the broader context of a globally connected history. If Rome's central role as a norm-setting authority was challenged in the day-to-day life of the missionaries, this cannot be ascribed solely to the lack of financial resources in the Roman Curia and the many barriers to effective communication between missionaries, superiors of religious orders, and the Curia. Equally important were the circumstances under which European missionaries entered into contact with the great Asian empires: The ties they fostered had little in common with the asymmetrical relations that would emerge under the new circumstances of nineteenth-century colonialism and imperialism. In the eyes of the Safavid shahs, political and economic ties to South Asia were much more important than relations with southern and western Europe. It is no coincidence that the English, Dutch, and French East India Companies, as well as the Portuguese, all used these networks between the Indian subcontinent and Persia to get a foot in the door. Moreover, laymen and clergymen trying to make contact with Asian courts had to accept local court ceremonials which enacted the centrality of local princes. Thus, missionaries became part of non-European centres where they rendered services to Asian princes, who saw Rome, not as the center of the world, but at best the center of a far-away European periphery. This was as true of the Jesuits in the court of Beijing as it was of the various Discalced Carmelites and members of other orders (Capuchins in particular) who became active members of the court of Isfahan. While a global Church depended on the capacity of its clergy to integrate into local social settings in order to secure sufficient funding for its activities, the local missionary economies led them to become part of the globalizing networks of early modern Asia.

Translated by Samuel Weber

Bibliography

Primary Sources

Archivum Congregationis pro Doctrina Fidei, Rome [ACDF]: SO, St.St., M 3 a.
Archivum Generale Ordinis Carmelitarum Discalceatorum, Rome [AGOCD]: 234/e/[bis], 237/m/9, 238/g/9, 238/u/4 and 5, 243/b/3, 261/d/1 and 2, 261/g/1 and 2, 261/m/1, 289/e/1, 483/f, 484/e.

Archivum Romanum Societatis Iesu [ARSI]: Gallia, 97 II, 103 I and II.

Archivio Storico de Propaganda Fide, Rome [APF]: SC. Stato temporale, vol. 1 to 16.

Biblioteca Ambrosiana, Milan [BA]: H 136 suss., & 211 sup.

Archives des missions étrangères de Paris [AMEP]: vol. 347.

Bembo, Ambrogio. *Il viaggio in Asia (1671–1675) nei manoscritti di Minneapolis e di Bergamo*. Edited by Antonio Invernizzi. Alessandria: Edizioni dell'Orso, 2012.

Collectanea S. Congregationis de Propaganda Fide seu decreta instructiones rescripta pro apostolicis missionibus, Vol. 1: *Ann. 1622–1866*. Rome: Ex typographia polyglotta S.C. de Propaganda Fide, 1907.

Fortes, Antonio. O.C.D., *Acta definitorii generalis O.C.D. Congregationis S. Eliae,* Vol. 1: *1605–1658*, Vol. 2: *1658–1710*, Vol. 3: *1710–1766* (Monumenta Historica Carmeli Teresiani. Subsidia, 3–5). Rome: Teresianum, 1985, 1986, 1988.

Secondary Sources

Abdullah, Thabit A. J. *Merchants, Mamluks, and Murder: The Political Economy of Trade in Eighteenth-Century Basra*. Albany, NY: State University of New York Press, 2001.

Alden, Dauril. *The Making of an Enterprise. The Society of Jesus in Portugal, its Empire, and Beyond, 1540–1750*. Stanford: Stanford University Press, 1996.

Amsler, Nadine. *Jesuits and Matriarchs: Domestic Worship in Early Modern China*. Seattle; London: University of Washington Press, 2018.

Amsler, Nadine, Andreea Badea, Bernard Heyberger, and Christian Windler, eds. *Catholic Missionaries in Early Modern Asia. Patterns of Localization*. London; New York: Routledge, 2020.

Barendse, René J. *Arabian Seas 1700–1763*, Vol. 1: *The Western Indian Ocean in the Eighteenth Century*, Vol. 2: *Kings, Gangsters and Companies*, Vol. 3: *Men and Merchandise*, Vol. 4: *Europe in Asia* (European Expansion and Indigenous Response, 3/1–4). Leiden; Boston: Brill, 2009.

Catto, Michela, Guido Mongini, and Silvia Mostaccio, eds. *Evangelizzazione e globalizzazione. Le missioni gesuitiche nell'età moderna tra storia e storiografia* (Biblioteca della Nuova Rivista Storica, 42). Città di Castello: Società Editrice Dante Alighieri, 2010.

Chick, Herbert. *A Chronicle of the Carmelites in Persia and the Papal Mission of the XVIIth and XVIIIth Centuries*, 2 vols. London: Eyre & Spottiswoode, 1939 [Reprint: London/ New York: I. B. Tauris, 2012].

Dale, Stephen Frederik. *Indian Merchants and Eurasian Trade, 1600–1750*. Cambridge: Cambridge University Press, 1994.

Dale, Stephen Frederik. *The Muslim Empires of the Ottomans, Safavids, and Mughals*. Cambridge: Cambridge University Press, 2010.

Dessert, Daniel. *Argent, pouvoir et société au Grand Siècle*. Paris: Arthème Fayard, 1984.

Ditchfield, Simon. "Decentering the Catholic Reformation. Papacy and Peoples in the Early Modern World." *Archiv für Reformationsgeschichte* 101 (2010): 186–208.

Fattori, Maria Teresa. *Clemente VIII e il Sacro Collegio, 1592–1605. Meccanismi istitu-zionali e accentramento di governo* (Päpste und Papsttum 33). Stuttgart: Anton Hiersemann, 2004.

Flannery, John M. *The Mission of the Portuguese Augustinians to Persia and Beyond* (*1602–1747*) (Studies in Christian Missions 43). Leiden; Boston: Brill, 2013.

Friedrich, Markus. *Der lange Arm Roms? Globale Verwaltung und Kommunikation im Jesuitenorden 1540–1773.* Frankfurt am Main; New York: Campus Verlag, 2011.

Friedrich, Markus. *Die Jesuiten. Aufstieg, Niedergang, Neubeginn.* Munich; Berlin; Zurich: Piper, 2016.

Giordano, Silvano. *Domenico di Gesù Maria, Ruzola (1559–1630). Un carmelitano scalzo tra politica e riforma nella chiesa posttridentina* (Institutum Historicum Teresianum, Studia 6). Rome: Institutum Historicum Teresianum, 1991.

Grentrup, Theodor. "Das kirchliche Handelsverbot für die Missionare." *Zeitschrift für Missionswissenschaft* 15 (1925): 257–68.

Harrison, Henrietta. *The Missionary's Curse and Other Tales from a Chinese Catholic Vil-lage.* Berkeley, CA; Los Angeles; London: University of California Press, 2013.

Herzig, Edmund M. "The Armenian Merchants of New Julfa, Isfahan: A Study in Pre-Modern Asian Trade." PhD diss., University of Oxford, 1991.

Heyberger, Bernard. *Les Chrétiens du Proche-Orient au temps de la Réforme catholique* (Bibliothèque des Écoles françaises d'Athènes et de Rome, 284). Rome: École française de Rome, 1994.

Heyberger, Bernard. *Hindiyya (1720–1798), mystique et criminelle.* Paris: Aubier, 2001.

Lee, Rosemary Virginia. "A Printing Press for Shah 'Abbas: Science, Learning, and Evan-gelization in the Near East, 1600–1650." PhD diss., University of Virginia, 2013.

Lenoble, Clément. *L'exercice de la pauvreté. Économie et religion chez les franciscains d'Avignon (XIIIe-XVe siècles).* Rennes: Presses universitaires de Rennes, 2013.

Maifreda, Germano. *I denari dell'inquisitore. Affari e giustizia di fede nell'Italia moder-na.* Turin: Giulio Einaudi, 2014.

Matthee, Rudi. "Merchants in Safavid Iran: Participants and Perceptions." *Journal of Early Modern History* 4 (2000): 233–68.

Menegon, Eugenio. *Ancestors, Virgins, and Friars: Christianity as a Local Religion in Late Imperial China.* Cambridge, MA: Harvard University Press, 2009.

Menniti Ippolito, Antonio. *Il tramonto della Curia nepotista. Papi, nipoti e burocrazia curiale tra XVI e XVII secolo* (La corte dei papi 5). Rome: Viella, 1999.

Metzler, Josef. "Wegbereiter und Vorläufer der Kongregation. Vorschläge und erste Gründungsversuche einer römischen Missionszentrale." In *Sacrae Congregationis de Propaganda Fide Memoria Rerum, 1622–1972,* Vol. I/1: *1622–1700,* edited by Josef Metzler, 38–78. Rome/Freiburg im Breisgau/Vienna: Herder, 1971.

Metzler, Josef. "Orientation, programme et premières décisions (1622–1649)." In *Sacrae Congregationis de Propaganda Fide Memoria Rerum, 1622–1972,* Vol. I/1: *1622–1700,* edited by Josef Metzler, 146–96. Rome; Freiburg im Breisgau; Vienna: Herder, 1971.

Metzler, Josef. "Die Kongregation in der zweiten Hälfte des 17. Jahrhunderts." In *Sacrae Congregationis de Propaganda Fide Memoria Rerum, 1622–1972*, Vol. 1/1: *1622–1700*, edited by Josef Metzler, 244–305. Rome; Freiburg im Breisgau; Vienna: Herder, 1971.

Ó hAnnracháin, Tadgh. *Catholic Europe, 1592–1648: Centre and Peripheries*. Oxford: Oxford University Press, 2015.

Pattenden, Miles. *Electing the Pope in Early Modern Italy, 1450–1700*. Oxford: Oxford University Press, 2017.

Pizzorusso, Giovanni. "Lo Stato temporale della Congregazione de Propaganda Fide nel Seicento." In *Ad ultimos usque terrarum terminos in fide propaganda. Roma fra promozione e difesa della fede in età moderna* (Studi di storia delle istituzioni ecclesiastiche 5), edited by Massimiliano Ghilardi, Gaetano Sabatini, Matteo Sanfilippo, and Donatella Strangio, 51–66. Viterbo: Edizioni Sette Città, 2014.

Pizzorusso, Giovanni. *Governare le missioni, conoscere il mondo nel XVII secolo. La Congregazione Pontificia de Propaganda Fide* (Studi di storia delle istituzioni ecclesiastiche 6). Viterbo: Edizioni Sette Città, 2018.

Reinhard, Wolfgang. *Papstfinanz und Nepotismus unter Paul V. (1605–1621). Studien und Quellen zur Struktur und zu quantitativen Aspekten des päpstlichen Herrschaftswesens*, 2 vol. (Päpste und Papsttum 6/I and II). Stuttgart: Anton Hiersemann, 1974.

Reinhardt, Volker. *Kardinal Scipione Borghese (1605–1633). Vermögen, Finanzen und sozialer Aufstieg eines Papstnepoten* (Bibliothek des Deutschen Historischen Instituts in Rom 58). Tübingen: Max Niemeyer Verlag, 1984.

Richard, Francis. *Raphaël du Mans, missionnaire en Perse au XVIIe siècle*, vol. 1: *Biographie. Correspondance*, vol. 2: *Estats et Mémoire* (Moyen Orient & Océan Indien XVIe–XIXe s., 9/1 and 2). Paris: L'Harmattan, 1995.

Standaert, Nicolas. *The Interweaving of Rituals: Funerals in the Cultural Exchange between China and Europe*. Seattle; London: University of Washington Press, 2008.

Standaert, Nicolas. *Chinese Voices in the Rites Controversy: Travelling Books, Community Networks, Intercultural Arguments* (Bibliotheca Instituti Historici Societatis Iesu 75). Rome: Institutum Historicum Societatis Iesu, 2012.

Vermote, Frederik. "The Role of Urban Real Estate in Jesuit Finances and Networks between Europe and China, 1612–1778." PhD diss., University of British Columbia, Vancouver, 2012.

Vermote, Frederik. "Finances of the Missions." In *A Companion to Early Modern Catholic Global Missions* (Brill's Companions to the Christian Tradition 80), edited by Ronnie Po-Chia Hsia, 367–400. Leiden; Boston: Brill, 2018.

Wassilowsky, Günther. *Die Konklavereform Gregors XV. (1621/22). Wertekonflikte, symbolische Inszenierung und Verfahrenswandel im posttridentinischen Papsttum* (Päpste und Papsttum 38). Stuttgart: Anton Hiersemann, 2010.

Windler, Christian. *Missionare in Persien. Kulturelle Diversität und Normenkonkurrenz im globalen Katholizismus (17.–18. Jahrhundert)* (Externa. Geschichte der

Außenbeziehungen in neuen Perspektiven 12). Cologne; Weimar; Vienna: Böhlau Verlag, 2018.

Županov, Ines G. *Missionary Tropics. The Catholic Frontier in India (16th-17th Centuries)*. Ann Arbor, MI: The University of Michigan Press, 2005.

Županov, Ines G., ed. *The Oxford Handbook of the Jesuits.* New York: Oxford University Press, 2019.

Zürcher, Erik. "The Lord of Heaven and the Demons: Strange Stories from a Late Ming Christian Manuscript." In *Religion und Philosophie in Ostasien. Festschrift für Hans Steininger zum 65. Geburtstag,* edited by Gert Naundorf, Karl-Heinz Pohl, and Hans Hermann Schmidt, 359–75. Würzburg: Königshausen+Neumann, 1985.

Zürcher, Erik. "The Jesuit Mission in Fujian in late Ming times. Levels of Response." In *Development and Decline of Fukien Province in the 17th and 18th Centuries,* edited by Eduard B. Vermeer, 417–57. Leiden: Brill, 1990.

CHAPTER 7

Monsoonal Missions

Asian Trade Diasporas in Spanish Missionary Strategies, 1570–1700

Ryan D. Crewe

In the second half of the sixteenth century, dozens of Spanish missionaries left Spain and Mexico for Asia, along the transpacific galleon route that connected Acapulco with Manila after 1565. For all of their apparent successes in the New World, Spanish missionaries still desired to reach the more fabled destinations of their spiritual cosmography: China and Japan. An ancient set of legends and hopes—which drew from the writings of Marco Polo, medieval mendicant travellers, and cosmographers—led many missionaries to prioritize reaching Asia over their work in America.[1] In 1548, for example, the three most prominent missionaries in Mexico plotted to escape their mission duties to "seek the peoples of Great China," whom they believed to be more advanced.[2] The conversion of Asia was inseparable from their eschatological and universalist vision of a global Christian empire. As fanciful as this may seem, Spanish experience in the Americas seemed to prepare the missionaries for even greater spiritual and temporal conquests across the Pacific.[3] So confident were Spanish mendicant friars in their abilities to convert entire kingdoms, an Augustinian

---

1   Donald F. Lach, *Asia in the Making of Europe*, 3 vols. (Chicago: University of Chicago Press, 1965), vol. I, bk. 1, 36–43; Marco Polo, *El libro de Marco Polo anotado por Cristóbal Colón; El libro de Marco Polo, versión de Rodrigo de Santaella,* ed. Juan Gil (Madrid: Alianza Editorial, 1987); Serge Gruzinski, *The Eagle and the Dragon: Globalization and European Dreams of Conquest in China and America in the Sixteenth Century,* trans. Jean Birrell (Cambridge: Polity, 2014), 37–39, 41–45.

2   The missionaries were Archbishop Fray Juan de Zumárraga, Fray Domingo de Betanzos, Fray Martín de Valencia. Betanzos (1550), Archivo General de la Nación, Mexico City [AGN] Mercedes, tomo 3, fol. 8–9; Fray Gerónimo de Mendieta, *Historia eclesiástica Indiana,* ed. Joaquín García Icazbalceta (Mexico City, 1870), 586–588.

3   Even Fray Bernardino de Sahagún, the foremost missionary scholar of Mesoamerican peoples, concluded after decades of work in Mexico that "God is clearing the path for the faith to enter China, where the people are extremely able, orderly, and of great wisdom." In Mexico, the Faith has "done nothing more than stop on the way … to China." Fray Bernardino de Sahagún, *Historia general de las cosas de Nueva España,* ed. Alfredo López Austin and Josefina García Quintana (Madrid: Alianza Editorial, 1988), vol. II, 813.

chronicler writes, that they "thought themselves the saviours of all Asia."[4] No sooner did the friars land in the Philippines than they scurried to the docks to find a way to China.[5] Before them was their primordial destination, where they hoped to provoke a mass conversion to Christianity on such a scale that it would transform humanity itself. Although they were aware that the Portuguese had already been negotiating obstacles to their mission in China and Japan for decades, they were convinced that their New World experience lent them the ability to surpass their Iberian competitors.[6] "Through God's aid," a missionary predicted in the first feverish years after the conquest of Manila, "easily and with not many people, they will be subjected."[7]

Nevertheless, missionaries quickly had to abandon these certitudes and eschatological designs, at least in practice if not in belief. The headline of this story is well known: their efforts to reach China met with a powerful state that handily repulsed them, and in Japan their mission met with some successes that only ended in state-sanctioned martyrdom on a vast scale. For generations, historians of Spanish missions focused mostly on missionary agency—especially the tragic gap between will and capability—and they concerned themselves with building hagiographies out of so many failures. Recent work on missions around the globe, however, provides fresh avenues for revisiting the story of Spanish Asian missions outside the Philippines. Recent decades have seen a growing emphasis on indigenous agency and the local political, economic, and cultural structures that shaped missionary-indigenous relations. We read of how Kongolese kings strengthened their state by supporting missions; local rulers in Mexico rebuilt states though mission institutions amid devastating population losses; and nomadic peoples in Texas used friars as intermediaries with Spanish colonists.[8] In similar ways, Asian agency and structures forced course-corrections, experimentation, and adaptations.

---

4   Juan de Grijalva, *Crónica de la orden de N.P.S. Agustín en las provincias de la Nueva España* (Mexico City: Porrúa, 1985), 272.

5   Carlos Sanz, *Primitivas relaciones de España con Asia y Oceanía* (Madrid: Librería Suárez, 1958), 361; Juan González de Mendoza, *Historia del gran reino de la China* (Madrid: Miraguano Ediciones, 2008), 251.

6   See, for example Fray Juan de Cobo on Jesuits working under the Portuguese *padroado*, in Antonio de Remesal, *Historia de la prouincia de S. Vicente de Chyapa y Guatemala* (Madrid, 1629), 683.

7   Martín de Rada (1569), Archivo General de Indias [AGI] Filipinas 79, n. 1, fol. 2r.

8   Cécile Fromont, *The Art of Conversion: Christian Visual Culture in the Kingdom of the Kongo* (Chapel Hill: University of North Carolina Press, 2014); Ryan Dominic Crewe, *The Mexican Mission: Indigenous Reconstruction and Mendicant Enterprise in New Spain, 1521–1600* (Cambridge: Cambridge University Press, 2019); Juliana Barr, *Peace Came in the Form of a Woman: Indians and Spaniards in the Texas Borderlands* (Chapel Hill, NC: University of North Carolina Press, 2007). For these approaches in Asian missionary history, see Eugenio

The Spanish mission enterprise became embedded in the circuits and modalities of maritime Asia.[9] Missionaries followed the networks of Asian commerce, which was driven by biannual monsoons that moved people and goods. The seasonal lags between monsoons, in turn, spurred the emergence of *entrepôts* where diverse groups of traders could sojourn while they waited for the winds to shift.[10] Thus the maritime cities of Asia were only as prosperous as they were tolerant.[11] Religious and cultural pluralism and conviviality ensured fluid exchanges, and in all of these ports diverse populations created new hybrid cultures "unshackled from tradition," whose future was "linked not solely to the land of their birth but to a wider community made possible through seaborne connections."[12] Maritime Asia thus provided an infrastructure for missionaries, consisting of sea-routes that stretched from Japan to Malacca, and vibrant multicultural ports whose religious tolerance could allow them to make initial footholds. Ironically, then, the very missionaries who sought to "reduce" all Asia to Roman Catholicism initially took advantage of the open marketplace of goods, peoples, and faiths in Asian port cities.

While maritime Asia inexorably shaped and changed Spanish missionaries, the opposite is also true: Spanish missionaries also became actors in Asian history. Mendicants of the Augustinian, Dominican, and Franciscan Orders, and subsequently Jesuits, landed in Asia in the same transpacific galleons that bore the American silver that accelerated and transformed commerce across the region, and they carried with them a politico-religious ideology that sought to leverage that silver to achieve the salvation of China and all of Asia. Spanish mendicants and Jesuits were thus protagonists in the "Age of Commerce"—the

---

Menegon, *Ancestors, Virgins, and Friars: Christianity as a Local Religion in Late Imperial China* (Cambridge: Cambridge University Press, 2009); Oona Paredes, *A Mountain of Difference: The Lumad in Early Colonial Mindanao* (Ithaca, NY: Cornell University Press, 2013); and Crewe, "Pacific Purgatory: Spanish Dominicans, Chinese Sangleys, and the Entanglement of Mission and Commerce in Manila, 1580–1604," *Journal of Early Modern History* 19 (2015): 337–44.

9   John E. Wills, "Maritime Asia, 1500–1800: The Interactive Emergence of European Domination," *American Historical Review* 98, no. 1 (1993): 83–105; Tonio Andrade and Xing Hang, "Introduction: The East Asian Maritime Realm in Global History, 1500–1700," in *Sea Rovers, Silver, and Samurai: Maritime East Asia in Global History, 1550–1700,* ed. Tonio Andrade and Xing Hang (Honolulu: University of Hawaii Press, 2016), 1–27.

10   Ubaldo Iaccarino, "Manila as an International Entrepôt," *Bulletin of Portuguese/Japanese Studies* 16 (2008): 71–81.

11   Anthony Reid, *Southeast Asia in the Age of Commerce, 1450–1680* (New Haven, CT: Yale University Press, 1988), 11, 64–68.

12   Barbara Watson Andaya and Leonard Andaya, *Port Cities: Multicultural Emporiums of Asia, 1500–1900* (Singapore: Asian Civilizations Museum, 2016), 23.

expansion and diversification of long-distance trade, and its attendant social transformations, which took place when maritime Asia became connected with the American and Atlantic economies.[13] In the interstices between Spanish Manila and the East Asian maritime world, missionaries played a vital role in emerging cross-cultural interactions. Among the diverse array of cross-cultural brokers who translated, financed, and mediated between groups, Spanish missionaries were also "specialized intermediaries."[14] Missionaries carried considerable institutional authority within the Spanish legal and administrative order by virtue of the *patronato real*, the compact between Church and State in the Spanish Empire that granted churchmen and their institutions considerable political power.[15] This authority and influence in the Spanish context was vital for East Asian merchants, who generally lacked sovereign protection overseas and had little recourse to state-sanctioned enforcement. Accordingly, the missionaries' proselytizing strategy in Asia sought to capitalize on the merchants' vulnerabilities. This essay focuses on the mission as a secular and spiritual institution located in the "contact zones" of maritime Asia, sites that held great opportunity but also perils stemming from miscommunications and miscalibrations.[16]

The story of the first seventy years of Spanish mendicant mission enterprises in maritime Asia presents us with an exception to theories that associate expanding commerce with a concomitant expansion of worldviews and "universalizing religions."[17] The missionaries themselves, of course, made every effort

13   Anthony Reid uses this concept to describe early modern Southeast Asia. For maritime East Asia, economic history and transpacific studies provide sufficient evidence to employ the same term. See Reid, *Southeast Asia*; Dennis O. Flynn and Arturo Giráldez, "Born with a Silver Spoon: The Origin of World Trade in 1571," *Journal of World History* 6 (1995): 201–21; William S. Atwell, "International Bullion Flows and the Chinese Economy, 1530–1650," *Past and Present* 95 (1982): 68–90. It also bears noting that this early modern age of commerce had roots in an earlier process of regional commercial exchange and interconnection between the tenth and fourteenth centuries. See Geoff Wade, "An Early Age of Commerce in Southeast Asia, 900–1300 BCE," *Journal of Southeast Asian Studies* 40, no. 2 (2009): 221–65.

14   Francesca Trivellato, "Introduction: The Historical and Comparative Study of Cross-Cultural Trade," in *Religion and Trade: Cross-Cultural Exchanges in World History, 1000–1900*, ed. Francesca Trivellato, Leor Halevi, and Cátia Antunes (Oxford: Oxford University Press, 2014), 1–3, 13–15, 19–20. On missionaries as cross-cultural brokers, see Vu Thanh's chapter in this volume.

15   W. Eugene Shiels, *King and Church: The Rise and Fall of the Patronato Real* (Chicago: Loyola University Press, 1961).

16   On "contact zones," see Mary Louise Pratt, *Travel Writing and Transculturation* (New York: Routledge, 1992), 7–8.

17   Responses to globalizing monotheistic religions in local communities and diasporas appear to differ between Southeast Asia and maritime East Asian encounters. See Reid,

to achieve the outcome outlined in these theories about the power of "macro-cosmic" religions: expanding and globalizing commerce, they believed, would broaden perspectives and make Christianity seem intuitively necessary. Yet they also knew from experience that pragmatic engagement and innumerable local compromises had to take priority over their grand visions. From Grana-da to Tenochtitlán, their missions had settled into local structures—linguistic, political, economic—in order to function. Spanish American missions, for example, followed local paths of least resistance, making themselves seem relevant—if not indispensable—to the continuity of local structures during catastrophic changes.[18] In this vein, Spanish missionaries developed two strat-egies of engagement with maritime Asia: they pursued an outbound strategy that exploited merchant networks and diplomatic contacts to reach mainland kingdoms, and an inbound strategy that focused on the social infrastructure of the port city. While the Spanish mendicant Orders and Jesuits had their fair share of theological and pedagogical differences, not to mention unseemly turf wars over the allocation of mission fields, this dual strategy was their com-mon practice, reflecting both their shared Spanish-American past and their present position in a fledgling Spanish colony at the edge of Asia. Drawing on American precedents, missionaries raised parishes and sought to impose Christian temporal rule over trade diasporas with the intention that new con-verts would serve as vehicles for Christian expansion in their homelands. In both approaches, missionaries were able to establish themselves as important intermediaries in regional networks of commerce and power, but they were unable to parlay these roles into large-scale spiritual transformation. Spanish missions thus successfully became embedded in Asian maritime networks, but in so doing they also became confined by them.

1   The Outbound Strategy: Missionaries and Asian Commercial
       Networks

Cebu, 1569. In this first Spanish foothold in the Philippines, a Chinese merchant named Sanco approached a humble palm-frond structure that was serving as

---

Southeast Asia, vol. II, ch. 1; Barbara Watson Andaya, "Seas, Oceans, and Cosmologies in Southeast Asia," *Journal of Southeast Asian Studies* 48, no. 3 (2017): 349–71. On the appeal of "macrocosmic" religions in globalizing contacts, see Robin Horton, "African Conversion," *Africa: Journal of the International African Institute* 41, no. 2 (1971): 85–108.

18   Crewe, *Mexican Mission*; Crewe, "Bautizando el colonialismo: Las políticas de la con-versión después de la conquista," *Historia Mexicana* 68, no. 3 (2019): 943–1000.

this new city's Augustinian monastery.[19] Sanco had arrived with the monsoon from Fujian Province to trade with the Spanish newcomers. After conducting his business, he then had to wait for the monsoon to turn in order to return to China. In the meantime Sanco had time to reconnoitre his new clients. He made contact with Fray Martín de Rada (1533–1578), a scholar-missionary famed in the Augustinian Order for his "rare ingenuity" in theology, cosmography, mathematics, and linguistics. Fray Martín invited Sanco to stay at his monastery, where he sojourned for "almost half a year."[20] During that time Sanco taught Rada the country's diverse climates and provinces, as well as its government, language, communications, and sophisticated weaponry.[21]

For all their bombast, Spanish missionaries like Rada knew from experience that their mission would only survive through everyday negotiations and compromises with individuals like Sanco, interlocutors who had the power to walk away at any time. When the monsoon carried Sanco back to Fujian, the missionaries gained a future interlocutor and Sanco gained a foothold in an emerging colonial society. These informal relationships laid a foundation for the early communications between Spanish colonists in Luzon and Chinese merchants and authorities. Over the concerns of Spanish authorities who feared that missionary ambitions might thwart commerce and diplomacy, the missionaries leveraged new commercial relationships to reach the mainland—even if this meant taking on non-religious roles as intermediaries and interpreters.[22] By so doing, they sought to make themselves relevant, even necessary, in the emerging trade relationship.

Unlike the Spaniards, Chinese merchants were by no means new to the Philippine archipelago. Hemmed in and isolated from the rest of China by rugged mountains, the coastal people of Fujian, or Hokkiens, "used the seas as their fields"—as one Ming official put it—and had long engaged in trade from Japan to Sumatra.[23] These trading ventures moved with the monsoons,

19   Gaspar de San Agustín, *Conquistas de las islas Filipinas* (Madrid: 1698), 117–205.
20   Rada studied at Paris and Salamanca and as a missionary in Mexico learned the notoriously difficult Otomí language. His theological and linguistic expertise, and his study of cosmography and mathematics, led to his appointment to the Philippine mission. San Agustín, *Conquistas*, 363–72. Rada (1571), AGI Patronato 24, R. 22.
21   Rada (1571), AGI Patronato 24, R. 22.
22   José Antonio Cervera, *Tras el sueño de China: Agustinos y dominicos en Asia Oriental a finales del siglo XVI* (Madrid: Plaza y Valdés, 2013), 156–57; San Agustín, *Conquistas*, 366; Mendoza, *Historia*, 162, 249.
23   Geoff Wade, trans., *Southeast Asia in the Ming Shi-lu: An Open Access Resource* (Singapore: Asia Research Institute, 2005), accessed September 11, 2013, http://epress.nus.edu.sg/msl/entry/586.

southward in the fall and winter and northward in spring and summer. Merchants sojourned in trading ports between the monsoons, a practice known as "passing the winter." Hokkiens were trading with lowland peoples in the islands as early as the ninth century.[24] Indigenous Filipinos called them Sangleys, after the Hokkien *sing-li*, meaning "trade" or "doing business."[25] Hokkiens managed the risks of long-distance commerce by allying clans through intermarriage and by sealing bonds of fictive kinship known as "sworn brotherhoods," which functioned as mutual-aid agreements. It was not uncommon for some members of these brotherhoods to ingratiate themselves with local merchants and authorities by adopting their religions or intermarrying with their elites, a decision some would make in Spanish Manila.[26] Hokkien commerce flourished with official support for private ventures and peaked in the fourteenth century, but it diminished in the fifteenth century after Ming rulers severely restricted overseas trade.[27] By the time the Spaniards arrived at the Muslim port of Maynilad in 1570, they found just forty Sangleys residing there.

The Spanish conquest of the Philippines could not have occurred at a more propitious time for Hokkien merchants. In 1567, a severe monetary crisis in China forced the government to seek specie abroad by lifting its ban on foreign trade.[28] A rising Chinese demand for silver coincided with the rising supply of American silver across the Pacific. Supply and demand then converged with the Spanish conquest of Manila in 1571. Spaniards sensed the gravity of the opportunity—and with supply lines stretching across the Pacific, their very survival depended on Chinese commerce. Accordingly the Spanish commander, Miguel de Legaspi (1502–1572), condemned his subordinates for plundering Chinese vessels and set out to establish a good name among Hokkien merchants and Chinese officials. In Mindoro, he ransomed thirty Chinese merchants held captive by local rulers, and during his

---

24   James K. Chin, "Junk Trade, Business Networks, and Sojourning Communities: Hokkien Merchants in Early Maritime Asia," *Journal of Chinese Overseas* 6 (2010): 162; Berthold Laufer, "The Relations of the Chinese to the Philippine Islands," *Smithsonian Miscellaneous Collection*, 50 (1908): 251–54.

25   Martín de Goyti reported in 1570 that indigenous people called Hokkiens *sangleys*: AGI Patronato 24, R. 17. See also Chin, "Junk Trade," 188; Charles Boxer, *South China in the Sixteenth Century* (Bangkok: Orchid Press, 2004), 260.

26   Chin, "Junk Trade," 161.

27   Chin, 162.

28   Richard von Glahn, *Fountain of Fortune: Money and Monetary Policy in China, 1000–1700* (Berkeley, CA: University of California Press, 1996), 117–18; Flynn and Giráldez, "Silver Spoon."

conquest of Manila he protected Chinese junks from crossfire.[29] For their part, Hokkien merchants promised to return if Spanish promises of New World silver materialized. Legaspi's diplomatic acumen—and the arrival of galleons from Mexico—paid quick dividends. Just a year after Manila came under Spanish rule, ten Hokkien junks appeared in Manila Bay with an array of luxuries and necessities.[30] For missionaries, all this augured well for their hopes of converting China.

Spanish missionaries in the sixteenth century were forever on the watch for subtle signs of divine aid as they navigated foreign geographies and cultures. Having ventured far beyond the pale, they looked for signs in the decisions and habits of people they little understood but yearned to convert. On the docks of Manila, where the unprecedented exchange of American silver for Asian goods attracted ever-greater numbers of Hokkien traders, Spanish mendicants saw nothing less than a divinely-ordained opportunity. The polyglot Fray Martín de Rada wasted no time in learning Chinese so that Hokkien networks would carry the "seed of the Gospel" to the mainland.[31] Rada and his companions understood that in this new context the friars needed to be understated about their religious mission; Instead, they should seek to make themselves useful to Sangley merchants by taking on worldly roles as interpreters and mediators. This was not an unusual strategic decision for Spanish mendicant missionaries. In indigenous local polities in the New World and the Philippine Islands, their Orders had assumed worldly roles in negotiating peace, rebuilding indigenous political structures, and reorganizing local economies. The underlying idea was that the worldly order, including native secular structures, should be directed towards the service of evangelization.[32] On several occasions they even took this secular strategy to the extreme by commodifying themselves: on

---

29   Emma Helen Blair and J. A. Robertson, eds. *The Philippine Islands, 1493–1803* (Cleveland: A. H. Clark, 1903), III, 58; Legaspi (1573), AGI Patronato 24, N. 23; Boxer, *South China*, xli–xliii; San Agustín, *Conquistas*, 224.

30   Guido de Lavezaris (1573), AGI Filipinas 6, R. 2, N. 15, fol. 16v. According to San Agustín, by 1572 Chinese merchants were already setting prices for mercury in line with reported prices in Mexico: see *Conquistas*, 246.

31   Rada (1586), AGI Filipinas 79, N. 15, fol. 1; Mendoza, *Historia*, 162.

32   Crewe, "Pacific Purgatory," 341–43, 349–51; Crewe, *Mexican Mission*, chapter 3; Synod of Manila (1582), in Valentín Marín y Morales, *Ensayo de una síntesis de los trabajos realizados por las corporaciones religiosas* (Manila, 1901), 199. For a description and critique of mission efforts in the Philippines and the mission's accommodation with secular powers, see Bishop Fray Domingo de Salazar's letter to the Third Mexican Council (1585), in Alberto Carrillo Cázares, ed. *Manuscritos del concilio tercero* (Zamora: El Colegio de Michoacán, 2006), vol. I, 363–65.

the docks mendicants offered themselves to Hokkiens as slaves.[33] This is the essence of the missionaries' strategy of outbound engagement: the haste, even desperation, to begin a new sacred story in their fabled Cathay. Their sole objective was to arrive, work in any capacity, and proselytize on Chinese soil. In this respect, the missionaries' strategy paralleled that of Spanish merchants and civil authorities, who also wanted to trade and negotiate directly with China without having to work through Sangley middlemen in the Philippines.[34]

Amid the frenetic trading that began to unfold on the shorelines of Manila and Mindoro, friars searched high and low for a Hokkien captain who might unwittingly pilot Christianity into China. Yet this was a nearly impossible favor to ask of them. No Spanish protestations of good intentions could convince junk captains to risk the severe punishments that mainland officials would inflict upon them for illegally bringing foreigners to China.[35] Even Sanco, Rada's acquaintance who wintered with him in Cebu, proved difficult to persuade. When Sanco arrived in Manila in 1573 to trade silks and porcelain for American silver, Fray Martín approached him. "After pestering and begging him," Sanco agreed to take two friars with him upon his return to Fujian. But when the time came to leave Sanco balked. "He either said yes in bad faith, or he did not dare take them," Rada stated. Surely the likelihood of punishment at the hands of magistrates back home weighed heavily. Sanco "raised anchor and set sail," leaving the disappointed Augustinians ashore.[36]

Such scenes repeated over the next two decades. Friars would negotiate with Hokkien merchants; occasionally a captain would show some curiosity about their religion. The friars would then ask for passage in their silver-laden junks. According to the friars, some junk captains would initially agree, only to backtrack, disappear, or mislead them afterwards.[37] Of course, such tales of betrayal are one-sided accounts—and here it bears remembering that mendicant authors were never immune to overstating their suffering. Scholars have yet to find Chinese accounts of these interactions, but Spanish civil sources

---

33 By all accounts no Hokkiens accepted the offers. Rada (1571), AGI Patronato 24, R. 22, fol. 1v; San Agustín, *Conquistas*, 251; Mendoza, *Historia*, 250.

34 Paulo Jorge de Sousa Pinto, "Enemy at the Gates: Macao, Manila, and the 'Pinhal Episode,'" *Bulletin of Portuguese/Japanese Studies* 16 (2008): 17–18; Francisco Colín, Pablo Pastells, eds., *Labor evangélica de los obreros de la Compañía de Jesús en las Islas Filipinas* (Barcelona, 1904), I, 197–98.

35 Rada, (1586), AGI Filipinas 79, N. 15, fol. 1v; Rada (1571), AGI Patronato 24, R. 22; Boxer, *South China*, xlii; San Agustín, *Conquistas*, 251–53.

36 Rada (1586), AGI Filipinas 79, N. 15, fol. 1v.

37 San Agustín, *Conquistas*, 251–53, 325–29; Rada (1586), AGI Filipinas 79, N. 15, fol. 2; Boxer, *South China*, lxxiv; Mendoza, *Historia*, 251–53.

note the pestering that Hokkien captains received from anxious friars.[38] If the mendicant accounts are indeed accurate, this begs the question: why would the junk captains initially agree to smuggle friars into China in the first place? Here the story of Sanco provides us with some context. Ever since he arrived in Cebu in 1569, he must have perceived the central importance that religious authorities held among the Castilian newcomers. As on other early modern frontiers, it must have been obvious that the friars held the keys to legitimacy in the Spanish political and legal system.[39] And like Sanco, other Hokkien junk traders must have understood that the best way to de-escalate misunderstandings and protect themselves was by maintaining good relations with the friars, especially during the trading season. In the captains' sudden changes of mind, we are perhaps witnessing a tortured effort to balance priorities between new clients abroad and the rigorous demands of home.

The friars also found an obstacle in their own civil authorities, who came to fear the severity of Chinese mandarins as much as Hokkien traders. Legaspi and his successor, Guido de Lavezaris (1499–1581), were aware of Manila's vulnerable strategic position and sought cordial relations with the Middle Kingdom. The hubris of Spaniards who dreamed of conquering China "in the Mexican style" is notorious, but at the same time security concerns motivated civil authorities to expressly forbid friars from going to China without permission from local officials.[40] Mendicants despaired in the face of these obstacles. "They lost hope that they would ever reach China," Rada wrote, "unless the Lord guided them by some other means."[41] The mission's commercial path to China, so promising for its simplicity, had closed. Yet precisely when it seemed the missionaries had run out of options, a "conjuncture and opportunity" for the Faith came in the least expected of ways.[42]

In November 1574, Manila suffered a sudden and devastating attack at the hands of Lin Feng, a corsair who commanded an armada of about seventy ships and several thousand warriors.[43] Known in Spanish and Filipino history as Limahong, Lin Feng had long menaced coastal populations and shipping in the waters off Southeastern China. Chinese authorities deployed sea and

---

38   Boxer, *South China*, xlii–xliv.

39   Paredes, *Mountain*; Crewe, "Pacific Purgatory."

40   Manel Ollé, *La empresa de China: De la armada invencible al galeón de Manila* (Barcelona: El Acantilado, 2003), 42; Rada (1571), AGI Patronato 24, R. 22; Rada (1586), AGI Filipinas 79, N. 15, fol. 1r–1v; Mendoza, *Conquistas*, 251.

41   Rada (1586), AGI Filipinas 79, N. 15, fol. 2.

42   Rada (1586), AGI Filipinas 79, N. 15, fol. 2; Mendoza, *Historia*, 163.

43   Rada (1586), AGI Filipinas 79, N. 15, fol. 2v.

land forces to defeat him, but Lin Feng always managed to escape.[44] The corsair "pointed his prows towards Manila" after he seized a Hokkien junk brimming with silver, gold, cottons, and wax blocks acquired in the Spanish port. The captured junk captain is said to have informed him that Manila lay defenceless.[45] By dint of luck—some advance warning and a contrary wind that slowed the assault—*manileños* managed to repulse the attack, but their new city was reduced to ashes.[46] Down but not out, Lin Feng retreated northward to Pangasinan. Spanish forces under Captain Juan de Salcedo followed in pursuit, and after setting much of Lin Feng's fleet aflame, they laid siege to the corsair's camp.[47]

By no intention of his own, Lin Feng's path of destruction across the South China Sea produced a diplomatic opening for the Spanish. At Salcedo's siege camp, a Chinese captain named Wan Kao unexpectedly arrived in March 1575. Known as Omoncon in Spanish sources, Wan Kao had been sent by the viceroy of Fujian to locate Lin Feng. With their common enemy surrounded, Salcedo invited Wan to meet Governor Lavezaris in Manila. Accompanying Wan was Sinsay, a trusted Hokkien merchant who provisioned Spanish military forces on credit.[48] Lavezaris regaled his guest and promised cooperation. Wan Kao was no doubt relieved to find his fugitive surrounded, and he decided to return to Fujian with the good news. As an added courtesy he offered to bring Spanish envoys to Fujian. For Lavezaris, this was an opportunity to finally extend Spanish commerce and missions to the mainland. He appointed two Augustinians as his emissaries: Fray Martín de Rada and Fray Jerónimo Marín. Accompanying them was Sinsay, who provided his skills as a mediator, and two soldiers.[49] Diplomacy mattered above all else. On Lavezaris' orders, the emissaries were to keep their disrespect for Chinese religion to themselves, avoiding the open iconoclasm of Cortés and Magellan a generation earlier.[50] This call for discretion and moderation in religious matters conformed with

---

44   Wade, *Ming Shi-lu*, accessed July 10, 2019, http://www.epress.nus.edu.sg/msl/reign/wan-li/year-1-month-5-day-14; http://www.epress.nus.edu.sg/msl/reign/wan-li/year-2-month-2-day-12.

45   Rada (1586), AGI Filipinas 79, N. 15, fol. 2v.

46   Rada lost his prized library to the flames. Boxer, *South China,* lxxv; Cabildo of Manila (1576), AGI Filipinas 84, N. 6, fol. 5.

47   San Agustín, *Conquistas,* 292–97.

48   San Agustín, *Conquistas,* 294, 313. Boxer, *South China,* xliv; Rada (1576), AGI Filipinas 84, N. 5, fol. 1.

49   Mendoza, *Historia,* 179; Elviro Pérez, *Catálogo bio-biográfico de los religiosos agustinos de la Provincia del Santísimo Nombre de Jesús de las Islas Filipinas* (Manila, 1901), 11.

50   San Agustín, *Conquistas,* 305–306.

the royal "Ordinance regarding New Discoveries" of 1573, which sought to eliminate iconoclasm and religious violence from Spanish encounters with non-Christians on frontiers.[51]

Rada's mission to Fujian shifted the missionaries' outbound strategy from commerce to the realm of high diplomacy. Wan Kao brought the Spanish party to meet the principal mandarin in Zhangzhou, and along the way the visitors were fêted and given tours of prosperous towns. Ever the scholar, Rada purchased hundreds of volumes in the city's bookstores.[52] The Spanish party sought to obtain rights to directly access the Chinese mainland for commerce and preaching.[53] Knowing that the success of their embassy hinged on the fate of Lin Feng, Rada assured his Chinese interlocutors that the corsair's capture was imminent.[54] It turned out, however, that the negotiations did not carry the importance that the Spanish emissaries had assumed: they met with exceeding politeness and bureaucratic run-arounds, exquisite banquets and delayed negotiations.[55] The mandarins declared they had to remit all Spanish requests to the emperor, and after some weeks they showed the delegation the door, dispatching them in a fleet of warships under Wan Kao's command. As an incentive, the authorities promised to entertain the Spaniards' requests if they delivered Lin Feng.[56]

Ultimately, the entire visit appears to have been a courtesy paid by Chinese authorities. The Spanish in Luzon had been useful in pursuing one of their most notorious outlaws, and Rada's visit helped ensure they would finish the task. Yet the outcome of the visit also fits into a longer-term pattern, honed through interactions with the Portuguese. Chinese authorities kept Iberians at arm's length, trading with them while keeping a wary eye on their brusque expansionism. It is telling that the *Ming Shih*, the annals of the Ming state, only mentions the Spanish once during Lin Feng's war and Rada's embassy. Luzon, the annals read, was "a non-tributary country" that was "incline[d] towards righteousness"—undoubtedly a reference to Spanish battles against Lin Feng.[57] Rada's embassy, that divine conjuncture in missionary accounts, receives no mention.

---

51   Paulino Castañeda Delgado, *Memoriales del Padre Silva sobre la predicación pacífica y los repartimientos* (Madrid: CSIC, 1983), 77–78.

52   Boxer, *South China,* lxxxiii.

53   Boxer, lvi; Rada (1576), AGI Filipinas 84, N. 5, fol. 1.

54   Rada (1576), AGI Filipinas 84, N. 5, fol. 1.

55   Boxer, *South China,* 247–57; Mendoza, *Historia,* 220–23.

56   Mendoza, *Historia,* 222.

57   Wade, *Ming Shi-lu,* accessed July 9, 2019: http://www.epress.nus.edu.sg/msl/reign/wan-li/year-4-month-1-day-25.

Having left Manila with the prospect of establishing a foothold in China, the Spanish emissaries returned with nothing—and to make matters worse, they and their Chinese companions met with even worse news in Manila. Some weeks earlier, Lin Feng had built a fleet under the very noses of the Spaniards and managed to escape their siege; his whereabouts were anyone's guess.[58] That the Spaniards were unable to fulfil the Chinese conditions in such a spectacular way, Rada wrote, "was a great outrage [considering] all the work that [we] had started."[59] To make matters worse, the new Spanish governor, Francisco de Sande (1540–1602), was far less adept at diplomacy. Due to the timing of the monsoon, Wan Kao and his five hundred soldiers had to winter in Manila, which further exacerbated relations.[60] When Wan Kao and his forces left Manila, Sande convinced Wan Kao to take Rada and another friar back to Fujian. A few days later, after attempting to dissuade the missionaries from following through with their plan, Wan Kao simply abandoned the friars on a beach in Zambales before tacking homeward.[61]

The Augustinians' debacle was followed by similar attempts to reach China and other parts of mainland Asia. The mendicants who followed them to the Philippines—Discalced Franciscans and Dominicans—were not to be deterred. In 1579, the Franciscan Fray Pedro de Alfaro and three of his brethren arranged a passage to Canton despite Spanish prohibitions. Within weeks the friars wound up expelled.[62] A year later, yet another Franciscan interloper found himself in prison.[63] By 1590, when it was the Dominicans' turn to chase the Chinese mirage, the Discalced Franciscans warned their colleagues that they "would end up with nothing more than to suffer prisons, death threats, without any hope in saving any souls." Undaunted, the Dominicans made the crossing with the assistance of Sanco, now baptized as Don Francisco, and another Christian Sangley named Don Tomás Siguan.[64] Like their dejected predecessors, they accomplished "nothing more than what the Discalced

---

58   Rada declared that "God was not served" by Lin Feng's escape. Rada (1576), AGI Filipinas 84, N. 5, fol. 1v; Mendoza, *Historia*, 222.

59   Rada (1576), AGI Filipinas 84, N. 5, fol. 1v.

60   Cabildo of Manila (1576), AGI Filipinas 84, N. 6, fol. 5v.

61   San Agustín, *Conquistas*, 251–53, 325–29; Rada (1586), AGI Filipinas 79, N. 15, fol. 2; Boxer, *South China*, lxxiv.

62   Mendoza, *Historia*, 250–59.

63   Carmen Y. Hsu, "Writing on Behalf of a Christian Empire: Gifts, Dissimulation, and Politics in the Letters of Philip II of Spain to Wanli of China," *Hispanic Review* 78, no.3 (2010): 328–29.

64   The honorific *don* indicates that Sanco and Siguan enjoyed elite status among Sangleys. Blair, *Philippine*, VII, 233–37.

Franciscans had foreseen." Upon his return to Manila, Fray Miguel de Bena-
vides summed up the lesson of these mendicant attempts: "[T]he preaching
and entry into the kingdoms of China cannot be accomplished with mere
human plans, because the devil, with the laws of state at his disposal, has
slammed that door shut in such a way that only the powerful arm of God
would be enough to open it."[65]

The missionaries' strategy of outbound engagement was based on an underlying assumption that Spaniards possessed a right to trade and preach the Gospel on Chinese soil. This right was reciprocal with that of Sangleys to trade (but
not spread paganism) in the Philippines. The seventeenth-century chronicler of
the early Augustinian missions in Asia, Fray Gaspar de San Agustín (1654–1721),
argued that their mission enterprise sought to instil in Sino-Hispanic relations
the principle of *ius gentium*, or the universal right of peoples "to establish commerce and gain an opportunity to introduce [Christian] preachers."[66] This clearly
echoes Francisco de Vitoria (1483–1546), who in the 1530s made the case for *ius
predicandi*, the right to evangelize anywhere.[67] It followed that the violation of
these universal rights constituted a *casus belli*. In 1576, after Wan Kao abruptly
ended Rada's second visit to China, Governor Sande channeled Vitoria for some
sabre-rattling: the Chinese could be justifiably conquered because "they prohibit
foreigners from entering their country."[68]

As the door to China slammed shut, however, it seemed another was opening in Japan.[69] In the 1580s and 90s, Spanish mendicants pursued the same
outbound strategy in Japan as they had in China. Due to its temperate climate the archipelago appealed to Spaniards as "another Spain," but initially
missionaries like Augustinian Fray Francisco Manrique viewed Japan as just
another means to their eternal end. By converting Japan, they posited, they
could amass an army to conquer China.[70] The opportunity opened in the 1580s
due to a conjuncture of three processes: feudal lords in the south were bris-
tling at attempts to centralize power; Japanese merchants were seeking ways
to circumvent Portuguese monopolization of Japanese access to the Chinese

---

65   Sanz, *Primitivas*, 292–93.

66   San Agustín, *Conquistas*, 366.

67   Fernando de los Ríos, *Religión y estado en la España del siglo XVI* (Seville: Editorial
      Renacimiento, 2007), 181–83.

68   Blair, *Philippine*, IV, 21.

69   Maria Fernanda de los Arcos, "The Philippine Colonial Elite and the Evangelization of
      Japan," *Bulletin of Portuguese/Japanese Studies* 4 (2002): 63–89.

70   Juan Gil, *Hidalgos y samurais: España y Japón en los siglos XVI y XVII* (Madrid: Alianza,
      1991), 30.

market; and likewise, some Japanese Christians were considering spiritual alternatives to the Portuguese Jesuits.[71]

As Rada had attempted in China, the Spanish mendicants in Japan sought to leverage commercial networks and diplomatic relations to establish a foothold for their missions. Spanish missionaries depended on Spanish and Sangley commercial routes to Japan, while merchants depended on missionaries as go-betweens.[72] For Japanese rulers, meanwhile, maintaining relations with Spanish friars enabled them to expand their commerce with Manila, which appealed as an alternative to Portuguese Macau for obtaining Chinese goods.[73] Spanish mendicants gained access to Japanese rulers by serving as diplomats and mediators. In 1584, Fray Francisco Manrique led efforts to bring the feudal lord (*daimyo*) of Hirado, Matsuura Takanobu, into the Spanish orbit; in 1592, the Dominican Fray Juan de Cobo (1546–1592) and a Christian Sangley named Juan Sami represented Spanish Manila before Hideyoshi (1537–1598); and in the most intriguing twist of fate, in 1610 the Franciscans Fray Luís Sotelo (1574–1624) and Fray Alonso Muñoz were named by the Shogun Tokugawa as emissaries before the viceroy of Mexico and the king of Spain.[74] Mendicants steadily established a network of missions, developed a following among the poor, and cultivated their relationships with local rulers.

Yet these diplomatic openings were volatile and fleeting, and the Christian mission, though it achieved thousands of converts, was ultimately doomed by Japanese security concerns.[75] Persecutions of Christians were on-going, most notably in the crucifixion of Franciscans and Japanese Christians at Nagasaki in 1597, and the persecutions from 1613 onward that drove Christianity underground. Ultimately, though missionary efforts to gain footholds in China and Japan unfolded in entirely different contexts, the difference is only one of degree. If engagement with Chinese authorities brought quick disappointments, engagement with Japanese rulers was a far more drawn out affair that passed through highs and lows, only to arrive at the same closed door. The underlying commonality between these two enterprises has to do with native power: these missions were only successful to the extent that local powers perceived the

---

71   Charles Boxer, *The Christian Century in Japan, 1549–1650* (Manchester: Carcanet, 1993), 160–62; Gil, *Hidalgos*, 32–36.

72   Hélène Vu Thanh, "Les liens complexes entre missionaires et marchands ibériques: Deux modèles de présence au Japon (1549–1639)," *Le Verger* (2014): 6.

73   Boxer, *The Christian Century*, 160–62.

74   Vu Thanh, "Les liens," 5; Gil, *Hidalgos*, 34, 43–48, 258–61; Rodrigo de Vivero, *Relación del Japón* (Barcelona: Linkgua, 2019), 35.

75   Birgit Tremml-Werner, "Friend or Foe? Intercultural Diplomacy between Momoyama Japan and the Spanish Philippines in the 1590s," in Andrade and Xing, *Sea Rovers*, 65–85.

missionaries as useful in pursuit of their own ends. As Hélène Vu Thanh states, "local powers were able to set the terms."[76]

The results of the missionaries' outbound strategy illustrates the considerable leverage that Asian merchants and officials wielded in their relations with the Spaniards of Luzon. Spanish missionary strategy evolved from networking with Hokkien merchants on the shores of the Philippines to high-stakes negotiations with viceroys, mandarins, and shoguns, but to little avail. Local rulers and merchants wielded enough leverage in their relations with Spaniards that they were able to render the missionaries' religious message largely irrelevant in the great contests for commercial and political power, even as missionaries facilitated those diplomatic and commercial relations. The missionaries would find this a hard lesson to learn, and for decades mendicants continued to entertain outbound policies of various kinds, from landing ashore unprotected to endorsing flat-out military and spiritual conquests throughout Southeast Asia and China. Fray Diego de Aduarte (1570–1636), for example, urged Spaniards to intervene militarily in Cambodia and use the kingdom as a mainland base for Christianity. The plan initially had the enthusiastic support of Governor Luís Pérez Dasmariñas (1567–1603), but two disastrous expeditions in the late-1590s divided the civil authorities.[77] By the early seventeenth century, such proposals were gaining less traction as Spanish civil and ecclesiastical authorities came to grips with their own strategic limitations. For missionaries, their stalling outbound strategy obliged them to reconsider their options—and in the diverse port city that was emerging just outside Spanish Manila's city walls, some believed they found a new pathway for Christianity.

2   The Inbound Strategy: Trade Diasporas in Manila

By the 1580s, missionaries in Manila began to revise their strategies for extending Christianity into Asia. Augustinians, as well as the Discalced Franciscans, Dominicans, and Jesuits who followed them, had to set aside the urgency of reaching the mainland in favour of a longer-term approach. Manila, along with other port cities in the region like Cebu, Macau, Keelung, and Nagasaki, housed diasporas that missionaries believed could transmit the Christian message to other corners of Asia. In Manila, a diverse array of trading communities

---

76   Vu Thanh, "Les liens," 2.
77   Aduarte (1600), AGI Filipinas 84, N. 81; Antonio de Morga, *Sucesos de las Islas Filipinas*, ed. W. E. Retana (Madrid, 1909), 241–42; Charles Boxer, "Portuguese and Spanish Projects for the Conquest of Southeast Asia," *Journal of Asian History* 3, no. 2 (1969): 129–33.

emerged around the Spaniards' fortified city of Intramuros: Sangleys, Japanese, Bruneians, Malays, and Indians arrived with the monsoons and sojourned during trading seasons. Many, especially Sangleys and Japanese, settled permanently. Missionaries drew upon American experience in building mission parishes under Christian spiritual and temporal rule, known as *doctrinas*, in the hopes that new Chinese and Japanese Christian communities based in Manila would irradiate Christianity into their homelands. "Not only will the Chinese be ministered to here," a Dominican argued, "but in their own lands ... [for] in brief time they themselves will become priests and friars."[78]

Given the volume of their traffic and their connections to the friars' most desired destination, the Sangley community in Manila became enmeshed in the missionaries' plans, preaching, and internal competition. The attraction was mutual. The arrival of Spaniards, awash with their silver wealth of Zacatecas and Potosí, turned Luzon into a New World for Hokkiens.[79] By 1603, roughly six hundred wealthy Hokkien merchants resided in Manila with their adopted sons and slaves, who served as their agents, and their fortunes made them indispensible brokers and financiers in the transpacific trade.[80] Meanwhile, thousands of poorer Chinese tradesmen also migrated to meet Manila's labor demands.[81] Virtually every trade in Manila came to be dominated by Sangley immigrants.[82] By the mid-seventeenth century, the Sangley population reached thirty thousand people, far surpassing the Spanish population of two thousand.[83] Transformed by trade and immigration, Manila had become what one Dominican called *las Indias para los chinos*—"the Indies for the Chinese, just as the Western Indies in America are for our Spaniards."[84]

Augustinians were the first missionaries to engage the Sangley immigrants in Manila. In 1572 and 1573, while Rada continued to beg junk captains for passage, his older colleague Fray Alonso de Alvarado founded a monastery in

---

78 Sanz, *Primitivas*, 290.

79 Blair, *Philippine*, III, 74, 167.

80 Chin, "Junk Trade," 188–92, 195–96; Lin Renchuan, "Fukien's Private Sea Trade in the 16th and 17th Centuries," in *Development and Decline of Fukien Province in the 17th and 18th Centuries*, ed. E. B. Vermeer (Leiden: Brill, 1990), 183–93; Antonio de Morga, *Sucesos de las Islas Filipinas*, ed. Francisca Perujo (Mexico City: Fondo de Cultura Económica, 2007), 189.

81 Remesal, *Historia*, 684; Lin, "Sea Trade," 183.

82 Blair, *Philippine*, VII, 33; Lucille Chia, "The Butcher, the Baker, and the Carpenter: Chinese Sojourners in the Spanish Philippines and their Impact on Southern Fujian," *Journal of the Economic and Social History of the Orient* 49 (2006): 519–34.

83 A. García Abásolo, "Los chinos y el modelo colonial español en Filipinas," *Cuadernos de Historia Moderna* 10 (2011): 223–42.

84 Archivo Provincial del Santo Rosario/Archive of University of Santo Tomás [APSR-AUST], Sangleyes vol. 1, fol. 695r; AGI Filipinas 6, R. 10, N. 180, fol. 25v.

Tondo and Baybay, a settlement north of Spanish Manila where Hokkiens resided among Tagalogs. Alvarado began to learn Chinese and won some converts.[85] The Augustinians then drew upon New World precedents to set up Tondo as a doctrina, an entity defined in Spanish law as a native parish under the spiritual care of missionaries and the temporal discipline of converted indigenous rulers or elites. Royal legislation stipulated that doctrinas were the exclusive domain of the mendicant order assigned to it, and doctrina boundaries were to correspond with those of local native governments.[86] The doctrina was thus both a spiritual monopoly and a semi-autonomous polity under colonial rule. In Mexico, this fusion of secular and spiritual territoriality triggered unbecoming turf wars among competing mendicant orders.[87] Missionaries carried these institutional rivalries to the Philippines. As soon as the missionaries realized the benefits of working with Sangleys, the mendicant orders jostled to claim a monopoly over them.

As the first to establish a Sangley doctrina, the Augustinians held an initial advantage over the other orders that followed them.[88] However, the deaths of the veterans Alvarado and Rada and the resulting staff turnaround meant that friars on staff did not know enough Chinese to preach to their converts, much less win new ones. Then the political winds shifted: the favor of the Mexican viceroyalty that the Augustinians had enjoyed was overshadowed by the arrival of Bishop Fray Domingo de Salazar (1512–1594), a Dominican who worked hard to expand his order. The Sangleys were among the bishop's top priorities.[89] Since the Augustinians could not preach in Chinese, Salazar wrote, God himself handed the Sangleys to the Dominicans.[90] Divine intervention aside, it also took plenty of political manoeuvring. In 1589, steady Dominican lobbying led Governor Santiago de Vera to grant the Dominicans exclusive jurisdiction over the Parián, a district that Spanish authorities had assigned to Sangleys so that *infieles* would not mingle with—nor, in their view, contaminate—Filipino neophytes. The governor also lent some of his court interpreters to ease the Dominicans into their new ministry.[91]

---

85   San Agustín, *Conquistas*, 253.
86   Jesús Gayo, *Doctrina Cristiana* (Manila: University of Santo Tomás, 1951), 95; Blair, *Philippine*, IV, 142.
87   Crewe, *Mexican Mission*, ch. 6.
88   On the first decades of the Augustinian mission in the Philippines, see Romain Bertrand, *Le long remords de la conquête* (Paris: Seuil, 2015), 137–216.
89   Sanz, *Primitivas,* 310; Morga, Retana ed. *Sucesos*, 398–400.
90   Sanz, *Primitivas,* 317.
91   Spanish missionaries referred to non-Christian Sangleys as *infieles*. Blair, *Philippine*, VI, 89.

Yet the Chinese community was still divided between the two orders. Across the Pasig River, the Chinese community in Tondo still lay within the Augustinian doctrina. To establish a unified Chinese doctrina under their monopoly, the Dominicans crossed the Pasig River on St. John's Day in 1589 to conquer Sangleys with the Word. Armed with legal authorizations to preach in Chinese to the residents, Tondo passed to the Dominicans. The Dominicans had managed to create a single mission doctrina that included several thousand Chinese *infieles* and a handful of converts. For their part, the Augustinians took the Dominicans to court, and in a dispute that lasted decades, they excoriated their rivals at every turn.[92] During one tense period in 1596, two exasperated Dominicans pleaded for help from Spain, writing: "the Augustinians are making war on us."[93]

To consolidate their mission to the Sangleys, the Dominicans followed a familiar script from the colonization of America. In a city where Spanish officials subjected Sangleys to abuses, the friars presented themselves as their natural protectors. Dominicans sought to establish a legal regime that regulated Spanish relations with Sangleys. This approach had deep roots, recalling the actions and ideals of Dominicans Fray Antonio de Montesinos (1475–1540) in Santo Domingo, Fray Bartolomé de las Casas (1474–1566) in transatlantic colonial policymaking, and Fray Francisco de Vitoria's philosophical works, as well as the activism of the Franciscan Archbishop Fray Juan de Zumárraga (1468–1548) in Mexico.[94] In Manila, Dominicans opposed the Spanish practice of forcing Sangleys to perform *repartimiento* labor—the same type of levy that compelled Andean peoples to mine the very silver that attracted the Sangleys to Manila.[95] They also condemned Spanish officials for demanding bribes from Sangleys. "As soon as the ships arrived," a chronicler in Fujian wrote, "they sent out men to hurry with all dispatch to bring [the Spanish governor] presents of silk."[96] Bishop Salazar underlined his order's campaign by declaring himself the "Protector of the Sangleys," a title that recalled that of "Protector of the Indians" adopted by his confrères in the New World such as Las Casas

---

92   Blair, *Philippine*, VI, 130, VII, 109; Sanz, *Primitivas*, 315.

93   Manila Dominicans (1596), AGI Filipinas 84, N. 66.

94   Before crossing the Atlantic to serve as a missionary in Florida and Mexico, Salazar
      studied under Vitoria in Salamanca. See Horacio de la Costa, "Church and State in the
      Philippines during the Administration of Bishop Salazar, 1581–1594," *Hispanic American
      Historical Review* 30, no. 3 (1950): 318–19.

95   Most notorious was the levy in which Sangleys rowed Spanish galleys throughout the
      Philippines.

96   Laufer, "Relations," 279; Morga, Perujo ed. *Sucesos,* 311; Salazar (1582), AGI Filipinas 6, R. 10,
      N. 180, fol. 25v; Benavides (1596), AGI Filipinas 76, N. 41, fol. 1r.

and Zumárraga. Spanish authorities and settlers opposed the bishop's public activism with a flurry of personal attacks and efforts to reduce Sangley commerce.[97] This did not diminish the Dominican campaign. In court, Salazar's diocesan lawyers defended Sangleys who were subjected to abuses and bribes from Spanish officials, and in the arena of policy they were instrumental in defeating the settlers' attempts to curb Sangley commerce and immigration in Manila.[98]

Sangleys recognized that the Dominicans occupied a vital position as intermediaries with Spanish authorities. A remarkable document illustrates their emerging alliance. In 1596, twenty-seven Sangleys—eight junk captains and eighteen merchants—petitioned Philip II to end Spanish abuses. Instead of protecting them as the king commanded, the Sangleys declared his agents were demanding bribes and arbitrarily seizing their goods, "something akin to plunder and robbery." Sangleys were defenceless before Spanish law: judges "did not deal with our cases impartially, nor did they order any compensation to be paid to us." As a result "we merchants have lost everything." Merchants new to the Manila trade "lost all of their original capital," while long-established Sangley brokers went bankrupt. The only Spaniards who helped them were the *Ba-Li*—the Dominican padres. "Thanks be to God," they wrote, that they could count upon Dominicans, "the Great Wall of the Eastern Barbarian," who stood as their "emancipators" and "protectors."[99]

Having won the support of many Sangleys, Dominicans followed a New World script: they built governing institutions in the Parián that could support their efforts at mass conversion.[100] Spanish missionaries in the sixteenth century placed great value on visible signs of conversion: on structures raised and processions held to bear witness to a new faith.[101] A handful of wealthy merchants converted and formed a local government consisting of a *gobernador* (governor) and deputies who kept order, collected a wide array of taxes, and managed a

---

97   General *junta* of Manila (1586), Blair, *Philippine*, VI, 166–69; Luís Pérez Dasmariñas (1592), Blair, *Philippine*, VII, 273–80.

98   Benito de Mendiola (1585), AGI Filipinas 84, N. 35, fol. 1r–v; Crewe, "Pacific Purgatory," 353–54.

99   I am extremely grateful to James K. Chin for translating this petition. *Tang-min* [Chinese people] to Felipe II (1596), AGI Filipinas 76, N. 41, fol. 3r. For a longer excerpt see Crewe, "Pacific Purgatory." On "Ba-Li" and other Hokkien renderings of Spanish, see Menegon, *Ancestors*, 39–40.

100   Crewe, "Pacific Purgatory," 337–65.

101   Diego de Aduarte, *Historia de la provincia del Santo Rosario* (Zaragoza, 1693), 95–97; See, for example, on Philippine missions: Perujo ed. *Sucesos,* 272–73.

treasury.[102] Missionaries hoped that Christian governance would produce mass conversions in the Parián like those they had overseen in America. The chronicler Fray Diego de Aduarte noted the devotion of Sangleys such as Bartolomé Tamban, who travelled from Fujian to work at the Dominicans' hospital, converted, and went on to serve the friars for eighteen years as a catechist; or Juan de Vera, a merchant who paid for a printing press, which enabled the friars to disseminate doctrinal works in Chinese and Tagalog.[103] A small but consistent number of wealthy Sangley merchants converted and moved into administrative positions. These converts gained considerable power in Manila by situating themselves as mediators between their countrymen and Spanish authorities. Among these were Siguan and Sanco, both of whom served as gobernadores.[104]

Yet for every exemplary neophyte, Spaniards could also name an apostate. Li Dan, baptized Andrea Dittis in Manila, ended up working for the Spaniards' English enemies in Japan; their former convert and gobernador Eng Can was suspected of plotting the devastating uprising against Spanish rule in 1603; and Zheng Zhilong, a baptized immigrant from Fujian who worked as a tailor in Manila, apostatized and went on to build a great corsair armada that endangered Manila's very existence.[105] The Sangleys wielded enough economic leverage through both trade and labor power that even the poorest could disregard the friars' exhortations. Consequently most Sangleys never converted even as they acknowledged the missionaries' temporal power.[106] This led the missionaries to pin the Sangleys to a narrative of betrayal that settled deep into seventeenth-century Spanish stereotypes of Sangleys. No sooner did Sangley Christians board their vessels, Spaniards alleged, than they jettisoned their false Christian cover into the sea.[107] Such tales only reinforced doubts surrounding the ultimate loyalties of Chinese Christians. In the midst of interethnic tensions, these suspicions became utterly lethal, as can be seen in four rebellions and massacres that took place in the seventeenth century.[108]

102   Juan Gil, *Los chinos en Manila* (Lisbon: Centro Científico e Cultural de Macau, 2011), 162, 171; AGI Filipinas 7, R. 1, N. 12, fol. 2r.

103   Aduarte, *Historia*, 99, 102.

104   Gil, *Chinos*, 28; San Agustin, *Conquistas*, 463–64; Aduarte, *Historia*, I, 189; Blair, *Philippine*, VII, 237.

105   Chin, "Junk Trade," 172–73; Morga, Perujo ed. *Sucesos*, 174–78, 187–200; Cathedral Chapter (1603), AGI Filipinas 84, N. 118; Audiencia (1603) AGI Filipinas 19, R. 4, N. 73; AGI Filipinas 28, N. 131, fol. 983r.

106   Menegon, *Ancestors*, 49–57.

107   Pedro Murillo Velarde, *Geographía histórica de las Islas Philipinas* (Madrid, 1752), 57; AGI Filipinas 28, f. 983r; Crewe, "Pacific Purgatory," 357–62.

108   Crewe, "Pacific Purgatory"; Gil, *Chinos*, 323, 325; Aduarte, *Historia*, I, 57.

Despite the limited success of the Parián doctrina, mendicants used it as a model for their ministry to Japanese residents and sojourners, the second largest Asian immigrant population in Manila. Japanese Christians had been present in Manila since the Spanish conquest, when they found a merchant named Pablo who had been baptized by Jesuits in Japan.[109] Missionaries initiated evangelization efforts among Japanese merchants in 1586, when eight were baptized by Bishop Salazar. Not long thereafter, the Discalced Franciscans raised a humble mission church in Dilao, a district south of the Chinese Parián that the government assigned to Japanese merchants and migrants. Like the Chinese quarter, Dilao demarcated a doctrina jurisdiction and established a marketplace.[110]

Spanish mendicants intended the Japanese community in Manila to reinforce Christianity in a kingdom where their mission was making difficult progress. The missionaries' engagement with the Japanese community in Manila had a far greater effect on Christianity in Japan than their mission among the Sangleys had on China. One of the early objectives of ethnic doctrinas was to produce native clergies that could bring Christianity from Manila to their homelands. Whereas no Sangleys were ordained until later in the colonial period, by the early seventeenth century Japanese Christians affiliated with mendicants were voyaging to Manila to study for their ordination. The Japanese friar Jacobo de Santa María, for example, took orders in Manila and returned to Japan with a recently-ordained Japanese Jesuit. Both were executed by Japanese authorities.[111]

Intensifying persecutions in the 1610s, however, irreversibly changed the missionaries' strategy for Dilao and the Japanese Christian community in Manila. Instead of serving as a base from which to extend Christianity into Japan, Manila became a refuge for Japanese Christians fleeing persecution. Among them was Don Juan Nayto Toquan, a nobleman forced to flee for sponsoring the Church, who settled in Manila in 1614, and wound up making a living as an expert in Chinese medicine. That same year, Iulia Nayto, a nun who had pursued a hermitic life in Japan, arrived in Manila with thirteen nuns and

109 Goytí (1570), AGI Filipinas, 24, R. 17, fol. 1; Madalena Ribeiro, "The Japanese Diaspora in the 17th Century According to Jesuit Sources," *Bulletin of Portuguese/Japanese Studies* 3 (2001): 53–83.

110 Colín and Pastells, *Labor*, I, 357–359; Robert Reed, *Colonial Manila: The Context of Hispanic Urbanism and Process of Morphogenesis* (Berkeley, CA: University of California Press, 1978), 53–55.

111 Aduarte, *Historia*, 652, 683–86.

established a convent with Spanish backing.[112] But some Spaniards and Japanese resisted the one-way relationship that led from persecution to refuge, and sought to restore Manila's role as an exporter of Christianity. In 1624, Japanese Christians and Spanish missionaries proposed to establish a seminary for Japanese students, not unlike the Jesuit college for Japanese Christians founded three decades earlier in Macau.[113] Once ordained, the alumni would return to Japan to preach "until the Lord opens the door that is now slammed shut to Europeans." Japanese petitioners in Nagasaki urged Spaniards to follow the example of seminaries for English Catholics in Rome and Spain. However, Manila's ecclesiastical and civil leadership blocked the plan. A seminary dedicated to training Japanese clergymen, they argued, might provoke an already-hostile regime to deepen their ties with the Dutch, and it would scuttle any hopes for reviving trade between the Philippines and Japan.[114] These worldly concerns closed the debate, and the plan was shelved.

The quiet cancellation of a project that would have ordained and exported Japanese priests illustrates how Manila's strategic vulnerabilities foreclosed missionary plans to leverage conversions in this port city into a broader spiritual transformation. Manila had become a refuge, not a springboard, for the faith. This only proved the long reach of Japanese persecution campaigns: deep within the headquarters of Spanish missionary activity in Asia, officials suppressed their most ambitious plans to export Christianity from Manila.

3   Local Demand and the Limits of Missionary Agency

Fuan, 1631. On a late winter's day in an isolated corner of northern Fujian Province, a local mandarin named Guo Bangyong received news of a rare opportunity for his small Christian community. A diplomatic mission that Spanish commanders had sent from northern Taiwan to the viceroy of Fujian had foundered after a mutiny and shipwreck. With their credentials lost in the fracas, most of the Spanish party was sent back to Taiwan. However one of the

---

112   Colín, *Labor*, 710, 725–86. Aduarte provides biographies of refugee nuns and lay brothers: *Historia*, 101, 582, 683–86, 698–700, 758; Haruko Nawata Ward, *Women Religious Leaders in Japan's Christian Century* (Farnham: Ashgate, 2009), 61–82. A Christian refugee petitioned the Spanish government to employ him as an interpreter: Juan Antonio, *japón* (1624), AGI Filipinas 39, N. 21.

113   Diego Yuuki, "O Colégio de São Paulo de Macau e a igreja do Japão," *Revista de Cultura* 30 (1997), 127–30.

114   Colín and Pastells, *Labor*, II, 258–60.

emissaries, Fray Angelo Cocchi, escaped and arrived in Fuzhou. Cocchi had received strict orders not to discuss religion, since the commanders in Taiwan were only seeking trade and an alliance against the Dutch.[115] After so many failed missions to China over the previous six decades, Spanish authorities were resigned to focus strictly on their strategic needs. But in this case, the Faith appeared when it was least expected.

For Guo Bangyong, who had been baptized as Joaquín Guo by an itinerant Jesuit a decade earlier, Cocchi's shipwreck was a godsend for the Christians of Fuan: finally, after years without a priest, they might receive the sacraments and live their lives in an established Church. Guo led ten Christians to Fuzhou, found Cocchi, and brought him to their community. Over the next several years, Guo served as a catechist and translator at this accidental mission, and when persecutions drove the Dominicans out of Fuan in 1637, Guo followed them to Manila and became a lay brother. Guo then guided the Dominicans back to Fuan a few years later, and over the next decades a small but thriving local Christianity developed around the Dominican parish.[116]

Dominicans surely welcomed their serendipitous mission in Fuan, but the story of how it emerged nonetheless confirmed the futility of their best-laid plans. For sixty years Spanish mendicants had struggled to use merchant networks, diplomatic relations, and diasporas in Manila to instigate the spiritual transformation of Asia. Instead, after countless frustrations, it took a handful of dedicated local converts—*not* friars—to open the door, for reasons entirely their own.[117] The result was a modest, local, Chinese church that bore no resemblance to grand expectations shaped by the friars' readings of Polo or Pordenone.[118] Over the next two centuries, small numbers of local Christians would affiliate with Spanish mendicants in other parts of China, and in Cochinchina.[119] In no place outside the Philippines would Spanish missionaries meet their objectives of transforming political structures and reducing them to serve mass evangelization.

---

115   Aduarte, *Historia*, 620–21; Fray Juan Peguero, *Compendio* (1690), APSR-AUST, fol. 27–31. Aduarte does not acknowledge Guo's efforts. Peguero referred to Guo as Ioachin Ko.

116   Peguero, *Compendio*, fol. 31; Menegon, *Ancestors*, 18, 23–36 on Guo and Cocchi; see subsequent chapters on later decades.

117   Menegon, *Ancestors*, 12, 18. Menegon states that Aduarte was "uneasy" about Chinese agency since it decentered the friars' role: see Aduarte, *Historia*, 620–21.

118   Rada (1570) AGI Filipinas 79. N. 15, fol. 1; Lach, *Asia*, 36–43.

119   Peguero, *Compendio*, fol. 19r–v.

That indigenous peoples, together with their structures and cultural mores, would determine the success of Spanish missions was not new, of course. While missionaries catalogued their successes and failures, local structures prevailed in the long run. Even in Mexico, which missionaries remembered as an unmitigated triumph, missionaries succeeded because they were needed to rebuild indigenous structures.[120] In the seas of Asia, it was in the interests of Sanco, the lord of Hirado, or the Sangleys to work with missionaries because they lent access to Spanish legal institutions and commercial ties, but the need for engagement did not morph into a hegemonic force of mass conversion. The Spanish mission enterprise formed an important part of cross-cultural relations, such that it contributed to an emerging system of exchange that connected Asia and America via Manila. Yet its spiritual agenda was enmeshed in these secular processes. As a result, missionaries waited for what must have felt like eons for someone in their desired destination to respond and engage with them out of spiritual longing. And when the moment came, as it did in Fuan and a handful of other locales, they had to conform to the context of their converts and leave imperial illusions behind.

Bibliography

Primary Sources

Archivo General de las Indias, Seville [AGI], Filipinas 6, R. 2, N. 15; 6, R. 10, N. 180; 7, R. 1, N. 12; 19, R. 4, N. 73; 24, R. 17; 28, N. 131; 39, N. 21; 76, N. 41; 79. N. 15; 84, N. 5; 84, N. 6; 84, N. 35; 84, N. 66; 84, N. 81.

Patronato 24, R. 17; 22; 23; 24.

Archivo Provincial del Santo Rosario/Archive of University of Santo Tomás, Manila [APSR-AUST], Sangleyes vol. 1.

Archivo General de la Nación, Mexico City [AGN] Mercedes, tomo 3.

Aduarte, Diego de. *Historia de la provincia del Santo Rosario*. Zaragoza, 1693.

Blair, Emma Helen, and J. A. Robertson, eds. *The Philippine Islands, 1493–1803*. 55 vols. Cleveland, OH: A. H. Clark, 1903.

Carrillo Cázares, Alberto, ed. *Manuscritos del concilio tercero*. Zamora: El Colegio de Michoacán, 2006.

Colín, Francisco. *Labor evangélica de los obreros de la Compañía de Jesús en las Islas Filipinas*. 3 vols. Edited by Pablo Pastells. Barcelona, 1904.

---

120   Crewe, *Mexican Mission*.

González de Mendoza, Juan. *Historia del gran reino de la China*. Madrid: Miraguano Ediciones, 2008.

Grijalva, Juan de. *Crónica de la orden de N.P.S. Agustín en las provincias de la Nueva España*. Mexico City: Porrúa, 1985.

Mendieta, Fray Gerónimo de. *Historia eclesiástica Indiana*. Edited by Joaquín García Icazbalceta. Mexico City, 1870.

Morga, Antonio de. *Sucesos de las Islas Filipinas*. Edited by W. E. Retana. Madrid, 1909.

Morga, Antonio de. *Sucesos de las Islas Filipinas*. Edited by Francisca Perujo. Mexico City: Fondo de Cultura Económica, 2007.

Murillo Velarde, Pedro. *Geographía histórica de las Islas Philipinas, del África y de sus islas adyacentes*. Madrid, 1752.

Polo, Marco. *El libro de Marco Polo anotado por Cristóbal Colón; El libro de Marco Polo, versión de Rodrigo de Santaella*. Edited by Juan Gil. Madrid: Alianza Editorial, 1987.

Remesal, Fray Antonio de. *Historia de la prouincia de S. Vicente de Chyapa y Guatemala*. Madrid, 1629.

Sahagún, Fray Bernardino de. *Historia general de las cosas de Nueva España*. 2 vols. Edited by Alfredo López Austin and Josefina García Quintana. Madrid: Alianza Editorial, 1988.

San Agustín, Gaspar de. *Conquistas de las islas Filipinas*. Madrid, 1698.

Vivero, Rodrigo de. *Relación del Japón*. Barcelona: Linkgua, 2019.

Wade, Geoff, trans. *Southeast Asia in the Ming Shi-lu: an open access resource*. Singapore: Asia Research Institute, 2005. Accessed November 9, 2013. http://www.epress.nus.edu.sg/msl.

Secondary Sources

Andaya, Barbara Watson. "Seas, Oceans, and Cosmologies in Southeast Asia." *Journal of Southeast Asian Studies* 48, no. 3 (2017): 349–71.

Andaya, Barbara Watson, and Leonard Andaya. *Port Cities: Multicultural Emporiums of Asia, 1500–1900*. Singapore: Asian Civilizations Museum, 2016.

Andrade, Tonio, and Xing Hang. "Introduction: The East Asian Maritime Realm in Global History, 1500–1700." In *Sea Rovers, Silver, and Samurai: Maritime East Asia in Global History, 1550–1700*, edited by Tonio Andrade and Xing Hang, 1–27. Honolulu: University of Hawaii Press, 2016.

Arcos, María Fernanda de los. "The Philippine Colonial Elite and the Evangelization of Japan." *Bulletin of Portuguese/Japanese Studies* 4 (2002): 63–89.

Atwell, William S. "International Bullion Flows and the Chinese Economy, 1530–1650." *Past and Present* 95 (1982): 68–90.

Barr, Juliana. *Peace Came in the Form of a Woman: Indians and Spaniards in the Texas Borderlands*. Chapel Hill, NC: University of North Carolina Press, 2007.

Bertrand, Romain. *Le long remords de la conquête*. Paris: Seuil, 2015.

Boxer, Ralph. *South China in the Sixteenth Century*. Bangkok: Orchid Press, 2004.

Boxer, Ralph. *The Christian Century in Japan, 1549–1650*. Manchester: Carcanet, 1993.

Boxer, Ralph. "Portuguese and Spanish Projects for the Conquest of Southeast Asia." *Journal of Asian History* 3, no. 2 (1969): 118–36.

Castañeda Delgado, Paulino. *Memoriales del Padre Silva sobre la predicación pacífica y los repartimientos*. Madrid: CSIC, 1983.

Chia, Lucille. "The Butcher, the Baker, and the Carpenter: Chinese Sojourners in the Spanish Philippines and their Impact on Southern Fujian." *Journal of the Economic and Social History of the Orient* 49 (2006): 519–34.

Chin, James K. "Junk Trade, Business Networks, and Sojourning Communities: Hokkien Merchants in Early Maritime Asia." *Journal of Chinese Overseas* 6 (2010): 157–215.

Costa, Horacio de la. "Church and State in the Philippines during the Administration of Bishop Salazar, 1581–1594." *Hispanic American Historical Review* 30, no. 3 (1950): 315–35.

Crewe, Ryan Dominic. *The Mexican Mission: Indigenous Reconstruction and Mendicant Enterprise in New Spain, 1521–1600*. Cambridge: Cambridge University Press, 2019.

Crewe, Ryan Dominic. "Pacific Purgatory: Spanish Dominicans, Chinese Sangleys, and the Entanglement of Mission and Commerce in Manila, 1580–1604." *Journal of Early Modern History* 19 (2015): 337–44.

Crewe, Ryan Dominic. "Bautizando el colonialismo: Las políticas de la conversión después de la conquista." *Historia Mexicana* 68, no. 3 (2019): 943–1000.

Flynn, Dennis O. and Arturo Giráldez. "Born with a Silver Spoon: The Origin of World Trade in 1571." *Journal of World History* 6 (1995): 201–21.

Fromont, Cécile. *The Art of Conversion: Christian Visual Culture in the Kingdom of the Kongo*. Chapel Hill, NC: University of North Carolina Press, 2014.

García Abásolo, A. "Los chinos y el modelo colonial español en Filipinas." *Cuadernos de Historia Moderna* 10 (2011): 223–42.

Gayo, Jesús. *Doctrina Cristiana*. Manila: University of Santo Tomás, 1951.

Gil, Juan. *Hidalgos y samurais: España y Japón en los siglos XVI y XVII*. Madrid: Alianza, 1991.

Gil, Juan. *Los chinos en Manila*. Lisbon: Centro Científico e Cultural de Macau, 2011.

Gruzinski, Serge. *The Eagle and the Dragon: Globalization and European Dreams of Conquest in China and America in the Sixteenth Century*. Translated by Jean Birrell. Cambridge: Polity, 2014.

Horton, Robin. "African Conversion." *Africa: Journal of the International African Institute* 41, no. 2 (1971): 85–108.

Hsu, Carmen Y. "Writing on Behalf of a Christian Empire: Gifts, Dissimulation, and Politics in the Letters of Philip II of Spain to Wanli of China." *Hispanic Review* 78, no. 3 (2010): 323–44.

Iaccarino, Ubaldo. "Manila as an International Entrepôt." *Bulletin of Portuguese/Japanese Studies* 16 (2008): 71–81.

Laufer, Berthold. "The Relations of the Chinese to the Philippine Islands." *Smithsonian Miscellaneous Collection* 50 (1908): 248–83.

Lin, Renchuan. "Fukien's Private Sea Trade in the 16th and 17th Centuries." In *Development and Decline of Fukien Province in the 17th and 18th Centuries*, edited by E. B. Vermeer, 183–93. Leiden: Brill, 1990.

Los Ríos, Fernando de. *Religión y estado en la España del siglo XVI.* Seville: Editorial Renacimiento, 2007.

Marín y Morales, Valentín. *Ensayo de una síntesis de los trabajos realizados por las corporaciones religiosas.* Manila, 1901.

Menegon, Eugenio. *Ancestors, Virgins, and Friars: Christianity as a Local Religion in Late Imperial China.* Cambridge: Cambridge University Press, 2009.

Nawata Ward, Haruko. *Women Religious Leaders in Japan's Christian Century.* Farnham, UK: Ashgate, 2009.

Ollé, Manel. *La empresa de China: De la armada invencible al galeón de Manila.* Barcelona: El Acantilado, 2003.

Paredes, Oona. *A Mountain of Difference: The Lumad in Early Colonial Mindanao.* Ithaca, NY: Cornell University Press, 2013.

Pérez, Elviro. *Catálogo bio-biográfico de los religiosos agustinos de la Provincia del Santísimo Nombre de Jesús de las Islas Filipinas.* Manila, 1901.

Pratt, Mary Louise. *Travel Writing and Transculturation.* New York: Routledge, 1992.

Reed, Robert. *Colonial Manila: The Context of Hispanic Urbanism and Process of Morphogenesis.* Berkeley: University of California Press, 1978.

Reid, Anthony. *Southeast Asia in the Age of Commerce, 1450–1680.* 2 vols. New Haven, CT: Yale University Press, 1988.

Ribeiro, Madalena. "The Japanese Diaspora in the 17th Century According to Jesuit Sources." *Bulletin of Portuguese/Japanese Studies* 3 (2001): 53–83.

Sanz, Carlos. *Primitivas relaciones de España con Asia y Oceanía.* Madrid: Librería Suárez, 1958.

Shiels, W. Eugene. *King and Church: The Rise and Fall of the Patronato Real.* Chicago: Loyola University Press, 1961.

Sousa Pinto, Paulo Jorge de. "Enemy at the Gates: Macao, Manila, and the Pinhal Episode." *Bulletin of Portuguese/Japanese Studies* 16 (2008): 11–43.

Tremml-Werner, Birgit. "Friend or Foe? Intercultural Diplomacy between Momoyama Japan and the Spanish Philippines in the 1590s." In *Sea Rovers, Silver, and Samurai: Maritime East Asia in Global History, 1550–1700*, edited by Tonio Andrade and Xing Hang, 65–85. Honolulu: University of Hawai'i Press, 2016.

Trivellato, Francesca. "Introduction: The Historical and Comparative Study of Cross-Cultural Trade." In *Religion and Trade: Cross-Cultural Exchanges in World History,*

1000–1900, edited by Francesca Trivellato, Leor Halevi, and Cátia Antunes, 1–20. Oxford: Oxford University Press, 2014.

Von Glahn, Richard. *Fountain of Fortune: Money and Monetary Policy in China, 1000–1700*. Berkeley, CA: University of California Press, 1996.

Vu Thanh, Hélène. "Les liens complexes entre missionaires et marchands ibériques: Deux modèles de présence au Japon (1549–1639)." *Le Verger – bouquet V* (2014): 1–19.

Wade, Geoff. "An Early Age of Commerce in Southeast Asia, 900-1300BCE." *Journal of Southeast Asian Studies* 40, no. 2 (2009): 221–65.

Yuuki, Diego. "O Colégio de São Paulo de Macau e a igreja do Japão." *Revista de Cultura* 30 (1997): 127–30.

PART 3

Funding the Missions: Finances and Evangelization

∵

CHAPTER 8

Funding the Propagation of the Faith

Noble Strategies and the Financial Support of Jesuit Colleges in France and Italy (c.1590–c.1650)

Ariane Boltanski

This chapter is based on a close analysis of a dozen cases within the broader scope of a long-term study of the pious foundations of the nobility and their support of missions in Europe, in particular in France and Italy. The focus is the financial support given by the local secular nobility to Jesuit colleges and the domestic missions of the Society of Jesus at the end of the sixteenth and during the first half of the seventeenth century. The nature and extent of these lay capitalizations and their effects on the financial situation of Jesuit establishments are at the heart of the analysis.

At the end of the sixteenth and during the first half of the seventeenth century, the founders of Jesuit establishments were mostly nobles holding fiefdoms and born from the ranks of the high and medium nobility of the sword (*noblesse d'épée*). Thanks to their considerable material and socio-political resources, they helped support, in various ways, missions of evangelization within the territories under their domination.[1] In the cases presented here, these nobles were at the forefront of campaigns to propagate the faith, a task that relied largely on the network of Jesuit colleges and which was part of the universal missionary project of the Society.[2] These colleges were both the starting

---

1 Ariane Boltanski and Aliocha Maldavsky, "Laity and Procurement of Funds," in *The Aquaviva Project: Claudio Aquaviva's Generalate (1581–1615) and the Emergence of Modern Catholicism*, ed. Pierre-Antoine Fabre and Flavio Rurale (Chestnut Hill, PA: Institute of Jesuit Sources, Boston College, 2017), 191–216; Sabina Pavone, *I gesuiti dalle origini alla soppressione, 1540/ 1773* (Rome: Laterza, 2004); John W. Padberg, Martin O'Keefe, John L. McCarthy, eds., *For Matters of Greater Moment: The First Thirty Jesuit General Congregations; A Brief History and a Translation of the Decrees* (St. Louis, MO: Institute of Jesuit Sources, 1994), xv, 8; Ronnie Po-chia Hsia, *The World of Catholic Renewal, 1540–1770* (Cambridge: Cambridge University Press, 1998); François de Dainville, "Le collège et la cité," in *L'éducation des jésuites: XVIᵉ-XVIIIᵉ siècles*, ed. Marie-Madeleine Compère (Paris: Éd. de Minuit, 1978), 153–54.

2 For more on the missionary project, see Pierre-Antoine Fabre and Bernard Vincent, eds., *Missions Religieuses Modernes: Notre lieu est le monde* (Rome: Presses de l'École française de Rome, 2007); Frédéric Meyer and Christian Sorrel, eds., *Les missions intérieures en France et en Italie du XVIᵉ au XXᵉ siècle* (Chambéry: Institut d'études savoisiennes, 2001); Louis

points and epicentres of various religious, devotional, and especially pastoral activities, which the Society saw as essential for the spread of the Catholic faith and for anchoring Christian doctrine in the hearts of the faithful.[3]

The comparative approach used here highlights the intertwining of religious and worldly interests in the investments made by such lay nobles. I consider the ultimate subordination of multiple socio-political, seigniorial and territorial issues—including those associated with the pursuit of honor and the perpetuation of a family name—to a fundamentally spiritual goal and a soteriological quest. By studying the difficult and sometimes contentious financial arrangements, which required later recapitalizations and which bound a whole network of actors to a noble founder, the aim is to assess the impact of lay *agency* in the funding of Jesuit institutions and missionary actions. What is ultimately at stake is an understanding of the active lay support behind the Catholic post-Tridentine wave of evangelization.[4]

Of course, such an approach also takes into account the fundamental differences between the foundations under scrutiny. The first type of foundation was those missions of evangelization targeting the conversion of Protestants to Catholicism. This was the case with the residences and colleges of the Gévaudan-Vivarais-Cévennes group, and, to a certain extent, with the colleges of Charleville and Chambéry. In the second type of foundation, the aim was to bring "heterodox" Catholics and populations considered to be bordering on heresy to a Counter-Reformed Catholicism, because of their ignorance of the faith and non-conformist practices. This was the case with the colleges of Corsica and in the Kingdom of Naples, especially in Apulia.[5] Finally, the foundations

Châtellier, *La religion des pauvres. Les missions rurales en Europe et la formation du catholicisme moderne, XVIe-XIXe siècles* (Paris: Aubier, 1993); Adriano Prosperi, *Tribunali della coscienza: inquisitori, confessori, missionari* (Turin: Einaudi, 1996); Bernadette Majorana, "Une pastorale spectaculaire. Missions et missionnaires jésuites en Italie (XVIe-XVIIe siècle)," *Annales. Histoire, Sciences Sociales* 57, no. 2 (2002): 297–320; Carla Faralli, "Le missioni dei Gesuiti in Italia (sec. XVI-XVII): problemi di una ricerca in corso," *Bollettino della Società di studi valdesi* 82, no. 138 (1975): 97–116.

3   John O'Malley, *The First Jesuits* (Cambridge, MA; London: Harvard University Press, 1994), 200–42.

4   For missions outside Europe, from a comparative perspective, see especially, Aliocha Maldavsky, ed., *Les laïcs dans la mission. Europe et Amériques, XVIe-XVIIIe siècles* (Tours: Presses Universitaires François-Rabelais, 2017); Hélène Vu Thanh, "Investir dans une nouvelle religion. Le cas de la mission du Japon (XVIe-XVIIe siècles)," in *L'Église des laïcs. Le sacré en partage (XVIe–XXe siècles)*, ed. Ariane Boltanski and Marie-Lucie Copete (Madrid: Casa de Velázquez, Collection de la Casa de Velázquez, forthcoming).

5   On the perceptions of the missionaries during the evangelization of the "rudes," also qualified as "the local Indians," read among other texts, Adriano Prosperi, " 'Otras Indias': missionari della Controriforma tra contadini e selvaggi," in *Scienze, credenze occulte, livelli di*

served, in the third type of establishment, to strengthen the faithful in post-Tridentine Catholicism. This was the case in several colleges in France (Nevers, Chaumont-en-Bassigny) or in Mirandola in Italy. These were not, strictly speaking, missions, even though the various religious activities of the colleges were essentially directed towards the local urban and rural populations.

In all the cases examined, however, missionary action and, generally speaking, the religious activities deployed in the direction of the local populations, had as their point of departure a Jesuit college or a residence. Moreover, the founders and/or main benefactors of such establishments were all members of secular noble families. When raising funds, these nobles were associated with other actors of the local community. Founding Jesuit establishments and maintaining them over time represented *joint ventures,* possible only through the collaboration of consortiums of benefactors. Such consortiums were necessary because the founding process, like the material and financial arrangements on which the foundations rested, had to last over time. A foundation could not be considered established and finished at the moment of its initial opening. In what follows I closely examine the process through which the funding arrangements were negotiated in the Jesuit missions.

1   Powerful, Noble, Secular Investors

By assuming a ministry in education, the Jesuits accepted, under Ignatius' Generalate (1491–1556; gen. 1540–1556), the principle that their order would own and manage property.[6] This meant a *de facto* renunciation of their collective poverty, and was also a means of guaranteeing the lasting existence of free-of-charge establishments.[7] The first two decades of the Society were thus largely dedicated to the development of "seduction" strategies. These were aimed at finding investors capable of raising funds to support the proper establishment of colleges. Gradually, the Jesuits perfected their techniques, targeting

cultura (Florence: Olschki, 1982), 205–34; Bernard Dompnier, "La France du premier XVIIᵉ siècle et les frontières de la mission," *Mélanges de l'École française de Rome. Italie et Méditerranée* 109, no. 2 (1997): 621–52; Bernard Dompnier, "Les missions des capucins et leur empreinte sur la Réforme catholique en France," *Revue de l'histoire de l'Église de France* 70, no. 184 (1984): 131–32.

6   This acceptance can be seen with the first college foundations of the 1540s (Valencia in Spain, Messina and Palermo in 1548–1549 in the Italian peninsula): see O'Malley, *The First Jesuits,* 200 *sq.*; Miguel Batllori, *Cultura e finanze: studi sulla storia dei gesuiti da S. Ignazio al Vaticano II* (Rome: Storia e letteratura, 1983), 121 *sq.*

7   On the principle of free admission in particular, see O'Malley, *The First Jesuits,* 219.

potential donors and forming networks of friends and supporters.[8] Following the 1560s and throughout the second half of the sixteenth century, came
a concern for moderation and caution when accepting requests for foundations, however, as many colleges were then finding it difficult to sustain their
existence.[9] In France, notably, the economic context and impact of inflation
meant some inadequately endowed establishments remained closed. Illustrating the economic hardships of the 1560s and 1570s was, for example, the case
of Chambéry, where, despite insufficient funding, a college was established to
please the Duke of Savoy.[10] Another project that did not come to fruition was
a novitiate in Rethel, which the Duke and Duchess of Nevers (Louis de Gonzague, 1539–1595 and Henriette de Clèves, 1542–1601) wanted to see established
in 1579. Cerignola, in Apulia, first established in 1578 thanks to the endowment
granted by the Marquise of Arienzo, Anna de Mendoza, was later shut down in
1592.[11] However, despite these setbacks, the secular elite, and especially the nobility, became increasingly important for the Jesuits in the second half of the

---

8   Olwen Hufton, "The Widow's Mite and Other Strategies: Funding the Catholic Refor-
      mation. The Prothero Lecture," *Transactions of the Royal Historical Society* 6e Series, 8
      (1999): 117–37; Olwen Hufton, "Altruism and Reciprocity: The Early Jesuits and their Fe-
      male Patrons," *Renaissance Studies* 15 (2001): 328–53; Olwen Hufton, "Every Tub on Its
      Own Bottom: Funding a Jesuit college in Early Modern Europe," in *The Jesuits II. Cultures,
      Sciences, and the Arts, 1540–1773*, ed. John O'Malley et al. (Toronto: University of Toronto
      Press, 2006), 5–23; O'Malley, *The First Jesuits*, 200–42.
9   Boltanski and Maldavsky, "Laity and Procurement of Funds," 201.
10   Archivum Romanum Societatis Iesu [hereafter ARSI], *Gal.* 56, fol. 127, October 3, 1564.
      400 *écus* were assigned by the Duke of Savoy to found a Jesuit college in Chambéry. The
      sum was to be levied, but the inhabitants did not pay the tax willingly. More financial dif-
      ficulties came later too; *Gal.* 56, fol. 126, 132–33; Henri Fouqueray, *Histoire de la Compagnie
      de Jésus en France, des origines à la suppression, 1528–1762* (Paris: A. Picard, Firmin-Didot,
      1910), 5 vols., t. 1, 452 *sq.*; A. Lynn Martin, *The Jesuit Mind: The Mentality of an Elite in Early
      Modern France* (Ithaca, NY: Cornell University Press, 1988), 52–53 and 57–58; A. Lynn
      Martin, "The Jesuit Mission to France," in *The Mercurian Project: Forming Jesuit Culture,
      1573–1580*, ed. Thomas McCoog (Rome: IHSI, 2004), 253.
11   ARSI, *FRANC.* 1-II. *Epp. Gen.*, fol. 275v–276, May 18, 1586, letter by the General to the Duke
      of Nevers; Ariane Boltanski, "Des fondations pieuses de nobles français dans la deuxième
      moitié du XVIe siècle. Défense de l'orthodoxie et territoire," in *Le Salut par les armes.
      Noblesse et défense de l'orthodoxie, XIIIe-XVIIe siècles*, ed. Ariane Boltanski and Franck
      Mercier (Rennes: PUR, 2011), 256; Pierre Delattre, *Les établissements des jésuites en France
      depuis quatre siècles: Répertoire topo-bibliographique publié à l'occasion du quatrième cen-
      tenaire de la fondation de la Compagnie de Jésus, 1540–1940* (Enghien: Institut supérieur de
      théologie, 1949), 5 vols., t. 4, col. 381–82; Alberto Tanturri, "La provincia napoletana della
      Compagnia di Gesù: Serie storica delle fondazioni, geografia degli insediamenti e identità
      dei fondatori (1558–1767)," in *I patrimoni dei gesuiti nell'Italia moderna: una prospettiva
      comparativa*, ed. Niccolò Guasti (Bari: Edipuglia, 2013), 85–106.

sixteenth century, and even more so at the turn of the seventeenth. As private investors, they were instrumental in actively supporting the Society alongside other, more traditional partners, such as princes, bishops and town halls. When considering the Jesuit institutions in the province of Naples in 1628 and the quality of their founders and benefactors, it is apparent that the patrons were mostly lay and that many were nobles. Indeed, in nineteen institutions out of twenty-two, the founders or main benefactors were lay and ten were nobles.[12]

The association of lay nobles with Jesuit projects was therefore very much a reality at the beginning of the seventeenth century, whenever the possibility of a foundation was deemed sufficiently strong and reliable by the Jesuits. In the first years of the seventeenth century, it was usually on the very initiative of secular noble benefactors that the residences or colleges examined in this chapter were established. For example, the Count of Montlaur (Louis de Modène, 1551–1604) went to Rome in 1600 to ask the Society of Jesus to establish themselves in the main town of his barony, Aubenas. For this, he met the pope and the General of the Society.[13] Likewise, in August 1610, the Duke of Modena and the Cardinal of Este supported the Prince of Mirandola's request to the General to found a college in his capital city. For this purpose they invited the Provincial to assess the situation.[14] The requests therefore came from the nobles, who endeavored to persuade the authorities of the Society that their city was an interesting site for the opening of a Jesuit establishment and that they would provide all the necessary— financial—guarantees. Solicited from many sides, the Society did not wish to become dispersed; indeed, the crucial question was the stability and financial and material security of the founded institutions.

It appears that for the Jesuits, colleges had to be financially autonomous institutions, fully sustained by endowments of stable assets and/or annuities.[15]

---

12   ARSI, Fondo Gesuitico [hereafter *FG*], Titulus XVIII, collegia, vol. 1473, fol. 117–29, probably dating 1628, State of the Province of Naples; Tanturri, "La provincia napoletana della Compagnia di Gesù," 103; and see Niccolò Guasti, "Tra élites cittadine e baroni: le strategie politico-economiche dei gesuiti nel Regno di Napoli (secoli XVI-XVII)," in *Élites e reti di potere. Strategie d'integrazione nell'Europa di età moderna*, ed. Marcella Aglietti et al. (Pisa: Pisa University Press, 2016), 31–45.

13   ARSI, *FG* 1368, fol. 14–15, 1625; *FG* 1368, fol. 22–25v, 1638–1640, fundatio collegii Albenacensis Societatis Jesu, here fol. 22; Édouard de Gigord, *Les jésuites d'Aubenas (1601–1762)* (Paris: Picard, 1910), 18.

14   ARSI, *EPP. EXT.* 30, fol. 130, August 15, 1610, letter from the Duke of Modena to the General; *EPP. EXT.* 30, fol. 131, August 18, 1610, letter from the Cardinal d'Este to the General. The Prince of Mirandola was married to Laura, the daughter of Cesare d'Este, the Duke of Modena.

15   Hufton, "The Widow's Mite," 120; Martin, "The Jesuit Mission to France," 252; Batllori, "Le città italiane e i collegi gesuitici," in *Città italiane del '500 tra Riforma e Controriforma: atti*

Any new foundation therefore required two levels of financing, both considered essential by the Generalate. One level paid first for the construction (or, as was sometimes the case, the refurbishment) of buildings sheltering classrooms and living spaces, and second, of a church. The other level of financing ensured the regular maintenance of the fathers and the school staff.[16] For this, the Society set thresholds below which any foundation was theoretically impossible. In 1553, Loyola established that the financial minimum for a college was the ability to support at least fourteen Jesuits.[17] The Fifth General Congregation of 1593 specified later that, for the teaching of the humanities, the most modest of colleges had to be able to support thirty Jesuits on an annual basis, and that a university required the upkeep of no less than a hundred.[18] In practice these thresholds were rarely reached or respected. The income statements of twenty-one Jesuit colleges and of a residence in the province of Naples dating back to approximately 1628 clearly show that none of the twenty-one colleges employed more than twenty-eight Jesuit fathers. Furthermore, only five colleges out of the twenty-one actually supported more than twenty Jesuits. According to the statements, maintaining a Jesuit father cost between 78 to 100 écus per year, and roughly 90 écus on average.[19]

What distinguished the residences from the colleges was their financial basis, which largely determined the size of the establishment, as well as the size of its workforce. Residences with few resources were subsequently smaller. In principle, they did not have the right to hold assets and did not have the same degree of financial autonomy as the colleges. For the Society of Jesus to allow the foundation of a residence, or for an existing residence to be granted college status, the endowment had to reach adequate levels. For example, one nobleman of Genoa, Tomaso Raggio, inscribed in his will of July 24, 1593, his desire to fund various pious foundations. One of these was for a Jesuit college in Corsica.

---

del Convegno internazionale di studi, Lucca, 13–15 ottobre 1983, ed. Martin Koerner (Lucca: M. Pacini Fazzi, 1988), 294 and 296; Miguel Batllori, *Cultura e finanze*, 122; Flavio Rurale, "La provincia milanese della Compagnia di Gesù tra Cinque e Seicento: Struttura organizzativa e problemi politico-finanziari," in *La Compagnia di Gesù e la Società piemontese*, ed. Bruno Signorelli and Pietro Uscello (Vercelli: Archivio di Stato di Vercelli, 1995), 47–59.

16   Hufton, "Every Tub," 16. See various examples in Jean Vallery-Radot, *Recueil de plans d'édifices de la Compagnie de Jésus conservé à la Bibliothèque nationale de Paris* (Bibliotheca Instituti Historici Societatis Iesu, xv, Rome-Paris: Institutum historicum-Bibliothèque nationale, 1960); Tanturri, "La provincia napoletana," 89.

17   Martin, *The Jesuit Mind*, 48.

18   Padberg, O'Keefe, and McCarthy, *For Matters of Greater Moment*, 211.

19   ARSI, FG 1473, fol. 117–29, probably from 1628. In France, in 1628, the upkeep of a Jesuit was estimated by Gigord at 150 livres per annum, or 12 livres and 10 sols per month: Gigord, *Les jésuites d'Aubenas*, 139.

Raggio was aware that the annuity of 1,500 *lira* (roughly 400 écus) he wished to donate would be insufficient to adequately establish a college. He hoped that other legacies might come to increase his initial bequest. It was only in April 1603, however, that a further annuity of 800 écus, twice that of Raggio's initial endowment, was offered by Marc'Antonio Garbarino and the foundation of a residence in Bastia was finally authorized.[20] In Charleville, Chaumont and Aubenas, and in other locations, a residence was first created before the General conceded that all the financial barriers had been cleared and that the residence could become a college. In all these cases, the laity applied for the transformation of the residence into a college, but the General hesitated or, at least, proved to be in no hurry. As early as 1602, Louis de Modène asked for the residence in Aubenas to be transformed into a college, a request that his heirs had to reiterate regularly. The General finally allowed the transformation in 1621, after a priory providing an extra annuity of roughly 100 écus per year (and stable assets) was annexed, supplemented by further donations by the Vivarais States.[21]

In all the cases studied, the gathering of capital began with an initial and substantial donation by a noble founder. Most of the time this endowment took the form of an annuity. In Ajaccio, an annuity of nearly 2,000 ducats (or écus) was donated. In Bastia, in 1603, the total annuity was of 1,200 écus. In Charleville, Charles de Gonzague (1580–1637) donated 2,400 livres per year, beginning in 1620. In Tournon, the Count, Just-Louis de Tournon (died 1617), grandnephew of the cardinal (who was the initial founder), granted 4,000 livres, allowing, in 1606, for the stabilization of the university and the upkeep of over sixty Jesuits.[22]

---

20   The contract is signed with Marco Antonio Garbarino on April 13, 1603. The General gives his approval on August 30, 1603: ARSI, *Med.* 82–1, fol. 181; *Med.* 82–1, fol. 185–87; Alessandro Monti, *La Compagnia di Gesù nel territorio della provincia torinese* (Chieri: M. Ghirardi, 1914–1920) 5 vols., vol. 2, 166–69 and 171; Ilario Rinieri, *I vescovi della Corsica* (Livorno: Raffaello Giusti, 1934), 88.

21   ARSI, *Tolos.* 19, fol. 2, May 22, 1602; fol. 3, July 20, 1602, letters by the Marquis de Montlor to the General; *Tolos.* 19, fol. 10, October 6, 1604, letter by Jacqueline, Marquise de Montlor to the General; *Tolos.* 19, fol. 15, May 22, 1613, letter by Colonel d'Ornano to the General; ARSI, *Tolos.* 1–II, fol. 342v, April 18, 1622, letter by the General to Father Robert de La Haye, Rector of the college of Aubenas; ARSI, FG 1368, doc. 10, fol. 16–17, 1627, letter by Forcaud, Rector of the college of Aubenas; Gigord, *Les jésuites d'Aubenas,* 77; Delattre, *Les établissements des jésuites en France,* t. 1, col. 366.

22   ARSI, *Tolos.* 22, fol. 154–59, February 5, 1606, contract for the foundation of the university of Tournon. In Italy, at the beginning of the seventeenth century, there was a 1 to 4 ratio between the écu or ducat and the lira. In France, the ratio was 1 to 3 between the écu and the livre.

Moreover, in all the cases in France, the annuities were based on local sources of income, income from the very land where the foundations were established. In Italy, the situation was different. For the Corsican colleges, the founders—who all belonged to the good nobility of Genoa (at the same rank as the high nobility of the Robe in France), and who came from the senatorial *milieu*—mobilized annuities raised elsewhere. This was the case with the Doria family, founders in Ajaccio through an annual income levied in the Kingdom of Naples.[23] In Mirandola, the prince financed the college through "extraterritorial" funds: stable assets from the region of Modena and Mantua. The founding document of July 1, 1611 established the payment of 1,500 écus per year for the maintenance of thirty Jesuits, of which 500 écus actually came from these latter assets. The document also stipulated that the Jesuits were not allowed to own property in the principality of Mirandola or any local land being under the jurisdiction of the prince. If the Jesuits became landowners in the principality through legacies in their favour, they would have to sell the land within a year and use the funds to buy property outside of the prince's jurisdiction. If they did not find a buyer from the principality, they would have to sell the property—at a low price—to the ducal Chamber.[24]

Founding new establishments therefore involved several agreements with different local stakeholders.[25] The town hall, for instance, always contributed to the founding capital through financial donations, purchases or bequests of buildings for the college. For example, in Eu (Normandy), at the request of the Duke of Guise (1550–1588), the governor of the city assembled the inhabitants and read aloud the Duke's letters concerning his plans to open a Jesuit college. Following this, the assembled inhabitants agreed, unanimously it seems, to the cession of the premises to the Jesuits for the purposes of a college.[26]

The bishop and other local notables could also participate in the founding negotiations. In Ajaccio, the process of foundation involved the city council,

---

23   ARSI, *FG* 81, fol. 287, on the act of January 5, 1617; ARSI, *FG* 81, fol. 290–92, January 16, 1617, contract signed by the Doria; *FG* 1389, doc. 18, non-folioted, 1621; Rinieri, *I vescovi*, 104–105; Monti, *La Compagnia di Gesù*, 199 *sq*.

24   ARSI, *FG* 1468, doc. 1, not foliated, July 1, 1611; ARSI, *Ven.* 115, fol. 277, July 1, 1611; *Ven.* 115, fol. 290; *Ven.* 115, fol. 292–94: state of the income and property of the college of Mirandola.

25   See also, on this aspect, Miriam Turrini, *Il 'giovin signore' in collegio. I gesuiti e l'educazione della nobiltà nelle consuetudini del collegio ducale di Parma* (Bologna: CLUEB, 2006); Miriam Turrini, "Tra Farnese, gesuiti e nobiltà: il Collegio ducale di Parma nei secoli XVII-XVIII," in *Il Collegio dei Nobili di Parma. La formazione della classe dirigente (secoli XVII-XIX), Atti del Convegno nazionale, Fornovo, Sala Baganza, Fontevivo, 22–24 maggio 2008*, ed. Alba Mora (Parma: MUP, 2013), 153–72.

26   Delattre, *Les établissements des jésuites en France*, t. 2, col. 412–13.

the Magnificent Elders ("les Magnifiques Anciens," the main representatives of the urban oligarchy), the Senate of Genoa and the city's bishop. In the ancillary endowments, which were necessary for purchasing the buildings that would house the college, the Senate, in 1616, replaced the town hall in providing the main funding. This was perhaps a way of keeping the Ajaccian municipal patriarchate at bay while simultaneously strengthening the Senate's authority in relation to the foundation. It also seems linked to the more general desire of the Senate to consolidate its political hold on a portion of the island shaken by popular unrest during the 1610s, and especially after the violent uprising during the night of Saint Lawrence of 1615.[27] The Senate, therefore, strongly supported the founding of the college of Ajaccio.[28] The founding document was signed by both the Doria and the Society and clearly states the donors' wish to please the Senate of the Republic by favouring the establishment of this college.[29] The bishop of Ajaccio also supported the Jesuit cause on their arrival on October 8, 1617, by hosting the fathers in the cathedral with much pomp and pageantry during their urban mission, especially for the Forty Hours' Devotion.[30]

New foundations also depended on the appeals made by founders to other lay donors. By meeting the larger part of the material needs and providing the authority, the influence and the necessary network for a foundation, the initiative of a noble family was crucial, but would later be buttressed by others. Foundations were thus collective enterprises, *joint ventures* of sorts. Groups of donors came together to raise an initial capital or to finance an annuity. These multiple stakeholders: town halls, often the bishop, sometimes representatives of the state (the governor or, for example, the Vivarais States[31] for Aubenas and Tournon), all participated in the local negotiations and were brought to collaborate. A foundation was the start of an intricate social network that brought together actors from various categories of society and collectively involved them in the creation and maintenance of a religious institution. However, stakeholders sometimes failed to reach a satisfactory agreement, and the foundation of

27   Antoine-Marie Graziani, José Stromboni, *Les feux de la Saint-Laurent: une révolte populaire en Corse au début du XVIIᵉ siècle* (Ajaccio: A. Piazzola, 2000).

28   Monti, *La Compagnia di Gesù*, 189–190, 193–99; Rinieri, *I vescovi*, 103–104.

29   ARSI, FG 81, fol. 290.

30   ARSI, *Med.* 76-II, fol. 410.

31   In a large part of Languedoc, the diocese (i.e., the ecclesiastical but also administrative subdivision, from which taxes were raised by the King) was represented by an Assembly (*Assemblée d'Assiette*), which had an important fiscal and administrative role in the seventeenth century. In that region, this assembly had merged with the Vivarais Estates (an institution dating back to medieval times) in which representatives of the nobility, of the clergy and of the main towns met.

colleges could be met with opposition. The Jesuits first attempted to found a college in Bergamo in 1569 and repeatedly failed to secure an agreement, despite the support of various notables and powerful city figures. The Jesuits had to wait until 1771 to settle in Bergamo, only to encounter difficulties.[32] Though in Aubenas the funding of the Jesuits provoked local conflicts and tensions, most of the time the process generated a community bond around the development of the Jesuit project.

2   Long-Term Investments

Foundations did not spring from a single initial investment which suddenly guaranteed the financial autonomy of a Jesuit institution. They were instead long-term projects of capitalization. The transactions that associated the Society of Jesus with its donors were only sustainable because of the way they were financed (as detailed below) and because of the expectations of the investors, and their perceptions of the role they played in the whole process. Indeed, foundations were considered worldly investments likely to foster salvation of the benefactors and were designed to last, maintaining themselves from one generation to another. They were a means for individuals and their descendants to find eternal salvation. Because they were seen by the laity to be similar to the properties (*estates*) of the church based on perpetuity, foundations were, by definition, eternal. They were also considered part of the *habitus* of patronage: the secular, noble and elite tradition of protecting churches.

The Society, for its part, rejected any transformation of the founder or principal donor into a "patron," a person in charge or a manager with a *jus patronatus*. It denied its benefactors both patronage, and jurisdiction or seigneurial-type ownership, which would have conferred rights over the earthly existence of the colleges and over their temporal goods.[33] The Jesuits did, however, encourage the founders and their successors to ensure that the foundations were properly maintained and financially lasting. They wished to establish a durable link between generations. Beyond funeral ceremonies and burials in college churches, this connection between generations was apparent in the regular offering of masses, in the honorary privileges granted to the donor families, and in the commemorative inscriptions of founders and their descendants on the walls of the buildings and of the churches. In short, the link was in the lasting

---

32   Christopher Carlsmith, *A Renaissance Education: Schooling in Bergamo and the Venetian Republic, 1500–1650* (Toronto: University of Toronto Press, 2010), 171–2 and 176–93.

33   Boltanski and Maldavsky, "Laity and Procurement of Funds," 204.

nature of the religious order itself, which, unlike lineage, was immune to biological extinction (although not to political extinction, as the Jesuits would find out in the eighteenth century).

The Society thus maintained a form of ambiguity that, in practice, accommodated the perpetuation of families, their reputation and the defence of their honor. Fundamentally, the soteriological aims pursued through the noble foundations were closely tied to the exaltation of lineage and the need to be remembered. Given the noble houses often faced risk of extinction and oblivion, their association with the foundations contributed to their lasting reputation, by highlighting their piety and their deeds in the defence of the faith.[34]

In most cases, later legacies had to come to shore up the initial donation. Successive recapitalizations were commonplace and explain the irregularity of the deployment of established foundations. These rose and declined, irregularly and in a non-linear fashion, over time and space. In Eu, for example, in 1607 and throughout the 1610s, the Duchess of Guise (1548–1633) made several donations. For the construction of the college church alone, the Duchess' endowments amounted to 35,000 livres and these added to donations made by the Duke during the last decades of the sixteenth century. The town hall and other donors also supplemented the investments of the Duke and Duchess. One instance was Anne de Roncherolles' (c.1540-after 1576?) legacy of an annuity of 150 livres, conceded at the request of the Guises, in September 1581. The donations in favour of the Jesuits in Eu were spread out over decades. Nevertheless, the college was left poor, became indebted, and the number of fathers maintained in this establishment declined during the second half of the seventeenth century.[35] Thus, the capital of an establishment did not rest solely on an initial bestowment, a lump sum of money or a single perpetual annuity.

---

34   See Ángela Atienza López, *Tiempos de conventos, una historia social de las fundaciones en la España moderna* (Madrid: Marcial Pons, 2008); Anne-Valérie Solignat, "Les fondations pieuses de la noblesse auvergnate à la Renaissance," *Histoire et mesure* 27 (2012): 133–60. See also Paul Shore, *Jesuits and the Politics of Religious pluralism in Eighteenth Century Transylvania: Culture, Politics and Religion, 1693–1773* (Aldershot: Ashgate, 2007), chapter V, about the case of Cluj in Transylvania and, especially, about the relationships between Stephanus, Count of Apor, and the Jesuits at the end of the seventeenth century. The Count was an important benefactor of the Jesuits in this city; he was buried in their church and celebrated by the Society as a defender of the faith.

35   Archives Nationales (France), Minutier Central, Et. VIII, 389, fol. 23–25, January 9, 1582, Foundation contract of the college of Eu; Archives Départementales Seine Maritime, D. 15 and D. 16, two inventories of the property titles of the college and D. 552, declaration of its assets and income in 1730; Delattre, *Les établissements des jésuites en France*, t. 2, col. 411 *sq.*

It is important to emphasize, in addition, the gap between the financial commitments of the founders and the actual resources the colleges collected. It was quite usual for founders to make financial promises that were only partially realized. Indeed, part of the capital donated could be property or a source of income, secular or ecclesiastical, which was finally worth less than the value estimated at the time of negotiation for the foundation. In other cases, after an agreement was signed, the Jesuits still had to take possession of the property to actually benefit from any derived revenues. This could take decades and drag the Society into multiple lawsuits. For example, following several contracts signed in 1618, two families allied by marriage, the Rose and the de Hault families, donated the foundation capital for the college of Chaumont-en-Bassigny (Champagne province). The Rose family donated 16,420 livres through three people: Nicolas Rose's widow, Catherine des Fours, and his two sons, Claude and Guillaume (the latter—probably died 1657—entering the Society and bequeathing his share through his brother Claude).[36] As for the de Hault (or Haut) family, the capital they donated amounted, in theory, to 23,000 livres. This was given by the widow of Nicolas de Hault, Marguerite Rose,[37] and her son, Galaad (c.1598-c.1681), who, like his uncle Guillaume, also entered the Jesuit order. Of the 20,000 livres given by Marguerite, 12,000 depended on *taille* levied in the election of Troyes. These were supposed to provide a regular annual income of 1,000 livres. The Jesuits discovered, however, that the Grand Council had decided to decrease the expected annuity to only 500 livres per year. The Jesuits blamed this on Marguerite Rose's "bad faith" as they considered she was certainly aware of the change in situation when the agreement with them was made. The very capital of 20,000 livres was also composite. It was a mixture of annuities and property, and included two houses and a nearly ruined "*gaignage*" (real estate) which had been grossly overestimated and offered very little real return.[38] The reduction in annuity and the overestimations reduced the true value of the capital granted. To make matters worse, the profits reaped from the assets and/or annuities on which the foundations were based could drop suddenly, not simply because of a reduction in the actual annuity, but because of an adverse economic context. For example, in Mirandola, a balance sheet drawn up by the Society in 1663 or 1664, indicates that the annual income of the college remained roughly stable, at around 1,500 écus

---

36   Catherine des Fours donated 1,200 livres of capital and Claude Rose promised 2,000 more. Guillaume Rose donated 13,220 livres. And see *infra*.

37   Marguerite donated a lump sum of 3,000 livres and her son gave 20,000 livres, which he first gave to his mother to donate to the Society.

38   ARSI, *Camp.* 1, fol. 147–50, not dated; FG 1385, doc. 7 and 24, not dated.

per year, between 1619 (the year the founder actually delivered the goods and annuities promised) and 1629. This amount dropped throughout the 1630s because of the Mantua war, the plague, and a major flooding of the Po River. It rose again to 545 écus a year in the 1640s, then to 593 in the 1650s. From 1660 to 1663, it reached 930 écus.[39]

More generally, various recurring factors tended to combine in reducing the financial stability of the Jesuit establishments. There were economic difficulties, such as inflation, over the last decades of the sixteenth century and financial assets were always more or less precarious. There were legal conflicts too, often within families (see the case of Barletta below) and promises only partially kept by the donors. There were also new needs leading the Jesuits to ask for more donations. This tangle of causes and consequences, rather than disjoining the relations between the Society and the founders or their families, perpetuated them and increased the dependence of the Jesuits on their sponsors. Within the process of foundation, the initial agreement, from an initiative instigated by powerful lay families and endorsed by the Society, reinforced the lineage, giving the title and the privileges of founder to these noble main investors, without leaving the Jesuit institution fully independent financially. The Society and, more particularly, its local representatives, had to participate in a whole series of further negotiations and transactions, which maintained the influence of the nobles within the Jesuit institutions.

The perpetuation of the financial bases of the Jesuit establishments raises the issue of the solidarity between the generations, with the latter now committed as a result of the initial donation. In Chaumont, for example, the foundation of the Jesuit college was linked to the admission of Guillaume Rose (pronouncing the three simple vows around 1614–1615)[40] and of his nephew, Galaad de Hault (*idem* after November 1617), to the Society.[41] Before pronouncing their vows, their respective relatives promised to financially support the creation of the college of Chaumont they were to join. It was through his brother Claude, his executor, that Guillaume donated all his property to the college. Galaad gave the college 20,000 livres through his mother (as noted above). The

---

39   ARSI, *Ven.* 115, fol. 294v.

40   Guillaume Rose, then a novice, made his will on October 9, 1614 and renounced all his possessions before he was allowed to take his vows (in all likelihood the three simple vows of poverty, obedience and chastity) in 1615: ARSI, *Camp.* 1, fol. 154–155v.

41   In 1617, Galaad, then a novice enrolled at the Society's university in Pont à Mousson, made several donations to his sisters in April, then made his will to the benefit of his mother on November 7, before taking his vows (again, the three simple vows). ARSI, *Camp.* 1, fol°153, November 7, 1617.

initial success of this operation, based on a necessary understanding between kin, demonstrated the strength of family ties. Simultaneously, it consolidated the privileges of the family and its hold on the foundation, especially since, throughout their careers, the two Jesuits, Guillaume and Galaad, served as rectors of the college of Chaumont.[42]

These intergenerational ties were undoubtedly essential when it came to legacies towards the Society, but also in a much more general way.[43] Indeed, the descendants of the noble founders regularly emphasized their desire and even their duty to carry on the charitable work of their ancestors. In so doing, they added to the prestige of their lineage, by appearing to be good Christians and defenders of the faith, which was indispensable to the identity of the nobility. This apparent loyalty to the family name did not necessarily translate into concrete financial transactions, however. In practice, descendants did not always respect the financial commitments of their predecessors. They sometimes even challenged them, including in court, or tried to reduce their impact. In Aubenas, for example, between the initial commitment of Louis de Modène (in 1600–1601) and the endorsement by the Society of a formal act of foundation (in 1643), more than forty years elapsed. Meanwhile, the Jesuits were materially supported, but only somewhat precariously. The main heiress of the barony, Marie de Raymond-Modène, Countess of Montlaur (1584–1672) and her husband, Jean-Baptiste d'Ornano (1581–1626), Marshal of France, regularly renegotiated with the Society. The couple first reduced the initial annuity donated, from 500 écus to 200 écus in 1607, and then brought it down to only 100 in 1617. The union of an ecclesiastical benefice was, in theory, to compensate for this cutback, but in reality it was slow to come.[44] It was therefore only the considerable donation, granted in 1638 by Marguerite de Raymond-Modène (Marie's sister) and her husband that finalized the foundation.[45] Another

---

42   Émile Jolibois, *Histoire de Chaumont* (Paris: J.-B. Dumoulin, 1856), 208–209; Émile Jolibois, *La Haute-Marne ancienne et moderne, dictionnaire géographique, statistique, historique et biographique* (Chaumont: Vve Miot-Dadant 1858), 467–68.

43   Solignat, "Les fondations pieuses"; Christian Kuhn, "Les fondations pieuses dans la représentation historique. L'exemple du *Grand livre* des Tucher de Nuremberg, 1590," *Société française d'histoire urbaine* 1, 27 (2010): 59–74; Florian Mazel, "Les aléas de la protection seigneuriale," in *Structures et dynamiques religieuses dans les sociétés de l'Occident latin, 1179–1449*, ed. Marie-Madeleine de Cevins and Jean-Michel Matz (Rennes: PUR, 2010), 423–32.

44   I.e., the incorporation into the Jesuit residence's estate of the properties and rights associated with an ecclesiastical benefice and of the income derived therefrom; see also *infra*. The annexation of a benefice is granted by the pope.

45   An act of foundation was signed on September 17, 1638, but was considered out of conformity with the *Constitutions* on several points. It was rewritten and only signed by the

example, in 1592, is the foundation of the college of Barletta in Puglia, as a result of the joint intervention of the town hall and private legatees, one of whom was Ippolita di Prato, the Baronessa of Sava (died 1630). The foundation was plagued after Ippolita's death by disputes between her heirs and the Society.[46] On July 22, 1624, Ippolita irrevocably bequeathed 30,000 ducats to the college, to be transferred, upon her death and that of her son Andrea. The 30,000 ducats had to be taken on the value of the fiefdom of Sava, located near Taranto. This became effective on November 16, 1630. Ippolita's will also stipulated, however, that in exchange the Society should pay 6,000 ducats out of the 30,000 it was hoped would be raised from the sale of the fiefdom for the upkeep of her niece, Petronilla Francone. In 1632, Petronilla entrusted her legacy to Nicolo Zucchetti so that he and Antonio Messi (Zucchetti's partner in this deal), might pay the creditors of her late husband. The Society therefore found itself embroiled in complex negotiations and disputes over this legacy. Moreover, the fiefdom of Sava was valued at only 20,000 ducats in 1634 instead of the 30,000 expected. When, in 1642, the Jesuits finally took possession of the property, they discovered that the tenants had not paid their rents for several years, and that the farms, for lack of maintenance, had fallen into disrepair. The resulting reclamation costs nearly reduced to zero any profits reaped from the farms during the following few seasons.[47]

In Italy, there were also special cases, which did not exist in French territory, because of the use of "mounts of piety" to finance the foundation and pay the running costs of certain establishments. In the seventeenth century, the main families of the Neapolitan aristocracy founded *monti di pietà* for charitable

---

General in 1643. Despite the importance of the financial donation made by Marguerite and her spouse, it is Marie who bears the official title of a founder: namely ARSI, *FG* 1368, fol. 14–15, 1625; *FG* 1368, fol. 16–17, June 16, 1627, letter from the Rector of the college of Aubenas; *FG* 1368, doc. 14, fol. 22–25v, 1638–1640; *FG* 1368, doc. 13, fol. 20–21, September 23, 1643; *Tolos.* 19, fol. 10 and 12, October 6,1604, two letters from the Marquise to the General; *Tolos.* 19, fol. 15, May 22,1613, letter from the Colonel of Ornano to the General; *Tolos.* 19, fol. 17–19, a memoire concerning the residence, here fol. 17; Gigord, *Les jésuites d'Aubenas*, 147.

46   Guasti, "Tra élite cittadine e baroni," 40–42; Tanturri, "La provincia napoletana," 103; Mario Spedicato, "Il patrimonio dei Gesuiti nel Mezzogiorno moderno. Alcune linee di lettura," in *I patrimoni dei gesuiti nell'Italia moderna*, ed. Guasti, 41–53, here 48.

47   ARSI, *FG* 1369, fol. 38, 1632, and fol. 39, 1633; *FG* 1369, fol. 40, capitolo del testamento della sig. di Prato; *FG* 1369, fol. 41 *sq.* After 1642, memoirs on the donation of I. di Prato. Archivio di Stato di Napoli, Azienda Gesuitica, vol. 5, Cabreo dei beni posseduti dal collegio di Barletta in Sava, fol. 1 *sq.*, instruzioni della terra di Sava, here fol. 1: The effective assignation of the land of Sava to the college of Barletta, which, until then "had no foundation," was finalized in October 1645.

purposes.[48] These were established by the local clans known as the *seggio*. From the last decades of the sixteenth century onwards, the Neapolitan aristocracy also invested largely in the funding of Jesuit institutions in the Kingdom of Naples.[49] The College of the Nobles in Naples, supported by the *Monte Manso* (created in 1608) is at the intersection of these two phenomena.[50] Initially, the Marquis of Villa, Giovani Battista Manso (1561–1645), created a classic type of a monte, which was destined to finance the education of impoverished young nobles and pay for the dowries of young noble ladies wishing to enter a convent. Between 1626 and 1629, however, Giovani Battista Manso transformed this initial project and decided to aggregate his monte to the foundation of a college for nobles. He entrusted this task to the Jesuits, who took the direction of the college on June 29, 1629. The foundation therefore relied on the capital of the monte, which amounted to 50,000 ducats in the 1620s. When the establishment was formally inaugurated in 1634, the monte was administered collegially by governors, who were nobles but not necessarily members of the *seggi*. They managed the capital of the college. They paid for the annuity of 420 ducats required to maintain the Jesuit fathers. The 400 ducats in rental fees for the housing of the fathers (a sum which exceeded what was originally planned) was paid by Giovani Battista Manso until 1643, after which date he suspended payment, forcing the Jesuits into debt and generating much

---

48   About the *monti*, in general, see, among other, Paola Avallone, ed., *Prestare ai poveri. Il credito su pegno e i Monti di pietà in area mediterranea (secoli XV-XIX)*, Naples, Consiglio Nazionale delle Ricerche, Istituto di Studi sulle Società del Mediterraneo, 2007. Emerging in Italy as early as the fifteenth century, the monti are first linked to the exercise of charity and assistance to the poor, then, usually, to forms of credit, mainly for the poor, sometimes without interest or with low interest. For the monti in the kingdom of Naples during the seventeenth century, see in particular, Tommaso Astarita, *The Continuity of Feudal Power: The Caracciolo di Brienza in Spanish Naples* (Cambridge: Cambridge University Press, 2004), 183 *sq.*

49   Astarita, *The Continuity of Feudal Power*, 183. The author indicates in particular that: "By the seventeenth century, one or more Monti existed for almost every clan." Unusually, the Monte di Manso included among its governors both noblemen of the clans (*Seggi*) and noblemen of other families; Spedicato, "Il patrimonio dei Gesuiti nel Mezzogiorno moderno," 45–47; Tanturri, "La provincia napoletana," 99 and 102–104; Guasti, "Tra élites cittadine e baroni"; Carolina Belli, "La fondazione del collegio dei nobili di Napoli," in *Chiesa, assistenza e società nel Mezzogiorno moderno*, ed. Carla Russo (Galatina, Lecce: Congedo, 1994), 183–280.

50   See also, about this monte, Michele Manfredi, *Gio. Battista Manso, nella vita e nelle opere* (Naples: N. Jovene, 1919), 133 *sq.*; and Astarita, *The Continuity of Feudal Power*, 183, 189; Belli, "La fondazione del collegio dei nobili di Napoli." See also the case of Jesuit college for young nobles in Parma, in Turrini, *Il 'giovin signore' in collegio*; Turrini, "Tra Farnese, gesuiti e nobiltà," 153–72.

tension. In 1646, after the death of the Marquis of Villa, the Society and the governors of the monte drew up a new convention.[51] The creation of a monte and of a subsequent collegial administration, even if it somewhat anticipated an elitist Evergetism (linked to more contemporary charitable forms),[52] did not, therefore, contribute to any greater financial autonomy of the Jesuit college from its noble founder.

Such complex capitalizations and donations—more or less honored pledges of financing, and constantly renewed negotiations between the Society and the relatives and right holders of the main founder—effectively maintained the Jesuit establishments in a state of dependence and entangled them in a web of financial constraints with secular donors.

3   The Fragmentation of the Assets of Jesuit Establishments, and Their Inscription within Economic Circuits

The fragmentation of the capital and sources of income of the Jesuits, as the case of Barletta demonstrates, meant the noble foundations locked the establishments of the Society of Jesus within complex economic circuits. In the French cases studied—except in Chaumont, and unlike the case studied in Italy—foundations depended on a further combination of one or more ecclesiastical benefices. Only through the amalgamation of several benefices was it possible to form a sufficiently solid financial basis for a residence or a college. For example, during the 1560s, Cardinal Tournon contributed to the annexation of the priory of Andance (established in the diocese of Vienne) with all its derived income and dependencies for the Jesuit college. In 1577, this priory generated 1,000 livres. Later, in 1606, the Count of Tournon helped to annex the priory of Saint-Sauveur (which was a dependence of the Benedictine Abbey of la Chaise-Dieu in the diocese of Clermont). It was decided in the founding contract that as soon as the annexation became effective, the Count would

---

51   ARSI, *Neap.* 190, fol. 290 *sq.*, here especially, f. 293 and 295; *Neap.* 190, fol. 324–25, May 1644, a memoire from the Provincial of Naples; *Neap.* 190, fol. 383, October 24, 1630, letter from the Marquis of Villa and fol. 384, letter concerning the college; *Neap.* 190, fol. 394–95, Jesuit complaints about college housing; *Neap.* 190, fol. 398–399, June 7, 1630, letter from the Marquis of Villa; *Neap.* 74, fol. 17–22v, memoire to the Marquis; *Neap.* 74, fol. 23–24, September 19, 1640, letter from the Marquis; FG 91 (Instrumententorum), fol. 338 *sq.*, November 14, 1664, here fol. 338, contract between the *seminarium nobilium* and the *Monte Manso*; Belli, 198, 203–204, 217–18, 231 and 236.

52   To the extent that charity and good works were run by a secular framework, involving a collective effort on behalf of this local aristocracy.

cease paying the annuity of 4,000 livres. The annexation was slowed down by the hesitation of the monks of La Chaise-Dieu, however, who finally consented, but only on the condition that the Jesuits of Tournon pay them an annuity of 300 livres and maintain five of their monks.[53] In the act of foundation, it was usually the noble founder who committed to secure the adjunction of at least one benefice, either in substitution for an annuity, or over and above it. This required, not financial power, but the ability to intercede and influence the ecclesiastical institutions or convents into granting one of their benefices, often a priory, and for the pontifical authorities to ratify the annexation. Again, such annexations were often time-consuming and, because of this, the founder had to attend to all these transactions over a long period of time. In 1620, Duke Charles de Gonzague (1580–1637) negotiated the union of the priory of Saint-Julien, a dependency of the Benedictine abbey of Notre-Dame-de-Mouzon, with the Jesuit college of Charleville, with the proviso that the abbot should keep the advowson of several cures. For this the Duke no doubt largely forced the hand of the abbot and monks of Mouzon. He also tried to persuade the pope that he should incorporate this benefice into the capital of the college free of charge. The union was not effective, however, in 1626 and Charles de Gonzague appealed to the General of the Society to speak to the pope and have him intercede in his favour.[54]

It is also important to emphasize the many types of property and derived revenues gathered by the founders. Particularly fragmented contributions enrolled the Jesuit settlements in a variety of economic circuits. The college of Charleville is an example of economic amalgamation and of the diversity of the subsequent exchanges and economic relations. In Charleville, the accumulation of substantial capital and of sufficient derived income took time: varied donations took place from 1612 to 1647, and there were even some later contributions. The process involved the founder, the Duke of Nevers (1580–1637), then, in 1647, his successor, Charles II de Gonzague (1629–1665), as well as three ancillary donors: a relative (the Princess of Conti), a seigneurial officer (Claude Morel, a noble of the robe, in 1642), and the abbot of Saint-Michel-en-Thiérache.

---

53   ARSI, FG 1642, doc. 1 and 3, about Andance; Tolos. 24, fol. 6, June 18, 1605, letter from the Provincial of Lyon; various documents from Tolos. 22, in particular fol. 111, April 19, 1607; Tolos. 22, fol. 154–59, Contract of foundation, here fol. 157; Tolos. 22, fol. 228, 1608, act from Henry IV; and other documents.

54   ARSI, FG 1385, fol. 2, November 27, 1620; and other documents in this volume; ARSI, EPP. EXT. 32, fol. 1, 1626, letter from Charles of Gonzague to the General; Delattre, Les établissements des jésuites en France, t. 1, col. 1290–1291; C. Dubroux, "Le collège des jésuites de Charleville (1612–1762)," Revue historique ardennaise 13 (1906): 144–45.

To supplement this, there were donations from the town hall. The basis of the college's capital was thus extremely varied and diverse in its components. It can be broken down as follows: first, perpetual annuities amounting, in 1647, to 3,150 livres a year; second, real estate in Charleville, i.e., the buildings and the church of the college, plus new housing estates built in the new city, a manor, and shops that were all rented out; third, cuts of wood from two acres of Mont-cornet Forest; and fourth, land, pastures and fields that were geographically dispersed all over the sovereignty of Arches and the Duchy of Rethelois. These latter properties and lands were rented out under different types of leaseholds. The rents were collected either in cash or in kind: a percentage of the harvest in cereals, hay, poultry and vegetables was paid to feed the college. With the land also came seigniorial rights and many tithes. Yet, despite these revenues, the college experienced persistent difficulties and accumulated debts. The fourth part of its patrimony—the land, and especially all the tithes—came from its union with the priory and its outbuildings. Tithes were raised in nine different cities and localities of the Rethélois (among them major centres such as Mézières, Lumes and Warnécourt). These were most often shared, to a third or a quarter, between the Jesuits and other shareholders. When information is available concerning the second half of the seventeenth and the eighteenth century, it appears that the collection of these tithes was leased out and not undertaken directly by the Jesuits, or more concretely, by their agents.[55] Apparently, this subcontracting was in response to the difficulties experienced by the Society when collecting tithes during the second half of the sixteenth century—mainly the resistance of the local population. This was the case with the residents in the dependencies in Megève linked to the college of Chambéry and, for Tournon, in the priory of Andance.[56] The possession of these ecclesiastical benefices brought obligations for the colleges that can appear incompatible with the *Constitutions* of the Society: the advowson of cures, the celebrations of masses for donators in chapels founded by them or their families, or, in the case of the college of Charleville, the payment of one third of the *portion congrue*[57] to the resident *curé* of Mézières and the maintenance and repair of the parish churches.[58]

---

55   This income statement is drawn from the summary of the documents consulted at ARSI, most of them already mentioned; and Delattre, *Les établissements des jésuites en France*, t. 1, col. 1313–1316; Dubroux, "Le collège des jésuites de Charleville," 143–55.

56   A. Lynn Martin, "Jesuit Encounters with Rural France in the Sixteenth Century," *Australian Journal of French Studies* 18 (1981): 202–11, here 209–11.

57   That is, the share of the tithe that was given by its recipient to the parish priest or vicar.

58   Dubroux, "Le collège des jésuites de Charleville," 153–55 and 157.

4   Conclusion

The noble founders studied here, either French or Italian, did not merely donate an initial sum to the Society and then withdraw from the affairs of the
Jesuit residence or college they helped to found. On the contrary, the financial
relations between the Society of Jesus and its benefactors ran over time and
lastingly associated the Jesuits with privileged investors. Pious foundations
were long-term processes, more complex than expected. They created for the
Jesuits a dependency on secular investors, because new donations and inter-
cessions were later needed, and because of ongoing conflicts and constant negotiations. Most of the time the families of the founders enticed other actors
from various strata of the local society to join the foundation and invest their
resources in its perpetuation or growth. It is therefore necessary to insist on the
agency, that is to say, on the strong capacity for autonomy deployed by the laity in these operations. Donors did not passively follow convention, nor, more
importantly, did they submit to the injunctions of the Church. They adapted
to their own agendas the Catholic imperatives of good works and pious donations, which they had effectively internalized, by modulating their investments
according to their financial capacities, their needs and their expectations. The
donations placed the Society in a relationship of obligation, which maintained
the superiority of the donor in the general scheme of gift and counter-gift.[59]
In part, the obligations of the Society towards its benefactors stemmed from a
"theology of gratitude" inscribed in the *Constitutions* and in the spirit of the order, by Ignatius Loyola himself.[60] These obligations were translated in material
terms, into titles and privileges granted to the founders and their descendants,
offering various advantages, which could also benefit, to a lesser degree, secondary donors who helped with the financing of Jesuit establishments. For the
families, these were honorific counterparts, which further strengthened their
presence and power within the institutions they contributed to finance. The
daily masses and the prayers of the fathers gave them hope of an ultimate compensation in the afterlife. Salvation, as seen by these lay donors, was a return
on investment.

The Jesuit establishments were therefore entangled in a web of financial
constraints. Accordingly, by simultaneously fulfilling the worldly needs of the

---

59   Marcel Mauss, "Essai sur le don: forme et raison de l'échange dans les sociétés archaïques,"
        in *Sociologie et anthropologie* (Paris: PUF, 1950), 143–279; see also Maurice Godelier,
        L'énigme du don (Paris: Fayard, 1996) and Natalie Zemon Davis, *The Gift in Sixteenth-
        Century France* (Oxford; New York: Oxford University Press, 2000), 167–208.
60   Hufton, "The Widow's Mite," 127.

order and the desires of powerful noble investors, the Society of Jesus became integrated in the circuits of local economies and became a major stakeholder of a broader financial network. Because of their superior social status—these founders were members of the nobility or of a "category" that was seen as the "best part" (*sanior pars*) of the society—the support they gave to the Order contributed to a crowding effect as more actors in the seventeenth century gathered around the Jesuit project and backed it. Foundations were thus economic powerhouses, which explains to some degree the expansion of the colleges, and of the Catholic evangelization of the Society of Jesus.

Bibliography

Primary Sources

Archivum Romanum Societatis Iesu [ARSI]: *Camp.*1; *Epp. Ext.* 30; *Franc.* 1-11; *Fondo Gesuitico* 81, 91, 1368, 1369, 1385, 1389, 1468, 1473; *Gal.* 56; *Med.* 76–11, 82-1; *Neap.* 74, 190; *Tolos.* 1–11, 19, 22, 24; *Ven.* 115.

Archives Nationales (France): *Minutier central*, Et. VIII, 389.

Archives Départementales de la Seine-Maritime (France): D15, 16, 552.

Jolibois, Émile. *Histoire de Chaumont*. Paris: J.-B. Dumoulin, 1856.

Jolibois, Émile. *La Haute-Marne ancienne et moderne, dictionnaire géographique, statistique, historique et biographique*. Chaumont: Vve Miot-Dadant, 1858.

Padberg, John W., Martin O'Keefe and John L. McCarthy, eds. *For Matters of Greater Moment: The First Thirty Jesuit General Congregations; A Brief History and a Translation of the Decrees*. St. Louis, MO: Institute of Jesuit Sources, 1994.

Vallery-Radot, Jean. *Recueil de plans d'édifices de la Compagnie de Jésus conservé à la Bibliothèque nationale de Paris*. Bibliotheca Instituti Historici Societatis Iesu, XV, Rome; Paris: Institutum historicum-Bibliothèque nationale, 1960.

Secondary Sources

Astarita, Tommaso. *The Continuity of Feudal Power: The Caracciolo di Brienza in Spanish Naples*. Cambridge: Cambridge University Press, 2004.

Atienza López, Ángela. *Tiempos de conventos, una historia social de las fundaciones en la España moderna*. Madrid: Marcial Pons, 2008.

Avallone, Paola, ed. *Prestare ai poveri. Il credito su pegno e i Monti di pietà in area mediterranea (secoli XV-XIX)*. Naples: Consiglio Nazionale delle Ricerche, Istituto di Studi sulle Società del Mediterraneo, 2007.

Batllori, Miguel. "Le città italiane e i collegi gesuitici." In *Città italiane del '500 tra Riforma e Controriforma: atti del Convegno internazionale di studi, Lucca, 13–15 ottobre 1983*, edited by Martin Koerner, 293–97. Lucca: M. Pacini Fazzi, 1988.

Batllori, Miguel. *Cultura e finanze: studi sulla storia dei gesuiti da S. Ignazio al Vaticano II.* Rome: Ed. di Storia e letteratura, 1983.

Belli, Carolina. "La fondazione del collegio dei nobili di Napoli." In *Chiesa, assistenza e società nel Mezzogiorno moderno,* edited by Carla Russo, 183–280. Galatina; Lecce: Congedo, 1994.

Boltanski, Ariane. "Des fondations pieuses de nobles français dans la deuxième moitié du XVIe siècle. Défense de l'orthodoxie et territoire." In *Le Salut par les armes. Noblesse et défense de l'orthodoxie, XIIIe-XVIIe siècles,* edited by Ariane Boltanski and Franck Mercier, 251–64. Rennes: PUR, 2011.

Boltanski, Ariane, and Aliocha Maldavsky. "Laity and Procurement of Funds." In *The Aquaviva Project: Claudio Aquaviva's generalate (1581–1615) and the Emergence of Modern Catholicism,* edited by Pierre-Antoine Fabre and Flavio Rurale, 191–216. Chestnut Hill, PA: Institute of Jesuit Sources, Boston College, 2017.

Carlsmith, Christopher. *A Renaissance Education: Schooling in Bergamo and the Venetian Republic, 1500–1650.* Toronto: University of Toronto Press, 2010.

Châtellier, Louis. *La religion des pauvres. Les missions rurales en Europe et la formation du catholicisme moderne, XVIe-XIXe siècles.* Paris: Aubier, 1993.

Dainville, François de. "Le collège et la cité." In *L'éducation des jésuites: XVIe-XVIIIe siècles,* edited by Marie-Madeleine Compère, 150–64. Paris: Éd. de Minuit, 1978.

Davis, Natalie Zemon. *The Gift in Sixteenth-Century France.* Oxford; New York: Oxford University Press, 2000.

Delattre, Pierre. *Les établissements des jésuites en France depuis quatre siècles: Répertoire topo-bibliographique publié à l'occasion du quatrième centenaire de la fondation de la Compagnie de Jésus, 1540–1940.* 5 vols. Enghien: Institut supérieur de théologie, 1949.

Dompnier, Bernard. "La France du premier XVIIe et les frontières de la mission." *Mélanges de l'École française de Rome. Italie et Méditerranée* 109 (1997): 621–52.

Dompnier, Bernard. "Les missions des capucins et leur empreinte sur la Réforme catholique en France." *Revue d'histoire de l'Église de France* 70 (1984): 127–47.

Dubroux, C. "Le collège des jésuites de Charleville (1612–1762)." *Revue historique ardennaise* 13 (1906): 137–208.

Fabre, Pierre-Antoine, and Bernard Vincent, eds. *Missions Religieuses Modernes: Notre lieu est le monde.* Rome: Presses de l'École française de Rome, 2007.

Faralli, Carla. "Le missioni dei Gesuiti in Italia (sec. XVI-XVII): problemi di una ricerca in corso." *Bollettino della Società di studi valdesi* 82, 138 (1975): 97–116.

Fouqueray, Henri. *Histoire de la Compagnie de Jésus en France, des origines à la suppression, 1528–1762.* Paris: A. Picard, Firmin-Didot, 1910.

Gigord, Édouard de. *Les jésuites d'Aubenas (1601–1762).* Paris: Picard, 1910.

Graziani, Antoine-Marie and José Stromboni. *Les feux de la Saint-Laurent: une révolte populaire en Corse au début du XVIIe siècle.* Ajaccio: A. Piazzola, 2000.

Godelier, Maurice. *L'énigme du don.* Paris: Fayard, 1996.

Guasti, Niccolò. "Tra élites cittadine e baroni: le strategie politico-economiche dei gesuiti nel Regno di Napoli (secoli XVI–XVII)." In *Élites e reti di potere: Strategie d'integrazione nell'Europa di età moderna*, edited by Marcella Aglietti, Alejandra Franganillo and José Antonio Lopez Anguita, 31–45. Pisa: Pisa University Press, 2016.

Hsia, Ronnie Po-chia. *Noble Patronage and Jesuit Missions: Maria Theresia von Fugger-Wellenburg, 1690–1762, and Jesuit Missionaries in China and Vietnam*. Rome: Institutum Historicum Societatis Iesu, 2006.

Hufton, Owlen. "Every Tub on Its Own Bottom: Funding a Jesuit College in Early Modern Europe." In *The Jesuits II: Cultures, Sciences, and the Arts, 1540–1773*, edited by John O'Malley, Gauvin Alexander Bailey, Steven J. Harris, and T. Frank Kennedy, 5–23. Toronto: University of Toronto Press, 2006.

Hufton, Owlen. "Altruism and Reciprocity: The Early Jesuits and Their Female Patrons." *Renaissance Studies* 15 (2001): 328–53.

Hufton, Owlen. "The Widow's Mite and Other Strategies: Funding the Catholic Reformation; The Prothero Lecture." *Transactions of the Royal Historical Society* Sixth Series 8 (1999): 117–37.

Kuhn, Christian. "Les fondations pieuses dans la représentation historique. L'exemple du *Grand livre* des Tucher de Nuremberg, 1590." *Société française d'histoire urbaine* 1, no. 27 (2010): 59–74.

Majorana, Bernadette. "Une pastorale spectaculaire. Missions et missionnaires jésuites en Italie (XVIe-XVIIe siècle)."*Annales, Histoire, Sciences Sociales* 57, no. 2 (2002): 297–320.

Manfredi, Michele. *Gio. Battista Manso, nella vita e nelle opere*, Naples: N. Jovene, 1919.

Martin, A. Lynn. "Jesuit Encounters with Rural France in the Sixteenth Century." *Australian Journal of French Studies* 18 (1981): 202–11.

Martin, A. Lynn. *The Jesuit Mind. The Mentality of an Elite in Early Modern France*. Ithaca, NY: Cornell University Press, 1988.

Martin, A. Lynn. "The Jesuit Mission to France." In *The Mercurian Project: Forming Jesuit Culture, 1573–1580*, edited by Thomas McCoog, 249–93. Rome: Institutum Historicum Societatis Iesu; St. Louis, mo: Institute of Jesuit Sources, 2004.

Mazel, Florian. "Les aléas de la protection seigneuriale." In *Structures et dynamiques religieuses dans les sociétés de l'Occident latin, 1179–1449*, edited by Marie-Madeleine de Cevins and Jean-Michel Matz, 423–32. Rennes: PUR, 2010.

Mauss, Marcel. "Essai sur le don: forme et raison de l'échange dans les sociétés archaïques." In *Sociologie et anthropologie*, 143–279. Paris: PUF, 1950.

Meyer, Frédéric, and Christian Sorrel. *Les missions intérieures en France et en Italie du XVIe au XXe siècle*. Chambéry: Institut d'études savoisiennes, 2001.

Monti, Alessandro. *La Compagnia di Gesù nel territorio della provincia torinese*, 5 vols., vol. 2. Chieri: M. Ghirardi, 1914–1920.

O'Malley, John. *The First Jesuits*. Cambridge, MA; London: Harvard University Press, 1994.

Pavone, Sabina. *I gesuiti dalle origini alla soppressione, 1540–1773*. Rome: Laterza, 2004.

Prosperi, Adriano. *Tribunali della coscienza: inquisitori, confessori, missionari*. Turin: G. Einaudi, 1996.

Prosperi, Adriano. " 'Otras Indias': missionari della Controriforma tra contadini e selvaggi." In *Scienze, credenze occulte, livelli di cultura*, 205–34. Florence: Olschki, 1982.

Rinieri, Ilario. *I vescovi della Corsica*. Livorno: Raffaello Giusti, 1934.

Rurale, Flavio. "La provincia milanese della Compagnia di Gesù tra Cinque e Seicento: Struttura organizzativa e problemi politico-finanziari." In *La Compagnia di Gesù e la Società piemontese*, edited by Bruno Signorelli and Pietro Uscello, 47–59. Vercelli: Archivio di Stato di Vercelli, 1995.

Shore, Paul. *Jesuits and the Politics of Religious pluralism in Eighteenth Century Transylvania: Culture, Politics and Religion, 1693–1773*. Aldershot: Ashgate, 2007.

Solignat, Anne-Valérie. "Les fondations pieuses de la noblesse auvergnate à la Renaissance." *Histoire et mesure* 27 (2012): 133–60.

Spedicato, Mario. "Il patrimonio dei Gesuiti nel Mezzogiorno moderno. Alcune linee di lettura." In *I patrimoni dei gesuiti nell'Italia moderna: Una prospettiva comparativa*, edited by Niccolò Guasti, 41–53. Bari: Edipuglia, 2013.

Tanturri, Alberto. "La provincia napoletana della Compagnia di Gesù: Serie storica delle fondazioni, geografia degli insediamenti e identità dei fondatori (1558–1767)." In *I patrimoni dei gesuiti nell'Italia moderna: Una prospettiva comparativa*, edited by Niccolò Guasti, 85–106. Bari: Edipuglia, 2013.

Turrini, Miriam. *Il 'giovin signore' in collegio. I gesuiti e l'educazione della nobiltà nelle consuetudini del collegio ducale di Parma*. Bologna: CLUEB, 2006.

Turrini, Miriam. "Tra Farnese, gesuiti e nobiltà: il Collegio ducale di Parma nei secoli XVII-XVIII." In *Il Collegio dei Nobili di Parma. La formazione della classe dirigente (secoli XVII-XIX), Atti del Convegno nazionale, Fornovo, Sala Baganza, Fontevivo, 22–24 maggio 2008*, edited by Alba Mora, 153–72. Parma: MUP, 2013.

CHAPTER 9

The College of San Hermenegildo in Seville

The Centerpiece of a Global Financial Network

Sébastien Malaprade

In his monumental overview of the Society of Jesus' expansion in the Portuguese empire, Dauril Alden notes the frequent financial scandals tarnishing the image of the Jesuits during the Ancien Régime.[1] The most sensational of these was the 1761 bankruptcy of the trading house of the superior of the Windward Islands, Antoine Lavalette (1708–1767). This event furnished a weighty argument to the Jansenist parliamentarians, who were calling for the Jesuits to be expelled from the kingdom of France in the wake of comparable measures by Sebastião José de Carvalho (better known as Marquês de Pombal) in Portugal four years earlier. In Martinique, Lavalette had got into the habit of negotiating and exporting bulk sugar from his plantations back to ports in France. But amidst the turmoil of the Seven Years' War, he was unable to honor his debts to traders in Marseille, who took the case to court.[2] In the minds of the Jesuits' detractors, these practices confirmed the cupidity of Ignatius de Loyola's disciples, who were seen as wont to break their vow of poverty and behave "as trafficking merchants … rather than as apostles."[3] Such judgements are a tribute to a long-established rhetorical trope exaggerating the order's profits by land and sea, within and outside the Society. This perception may be traced in particular to memories of a misfortune that struck in Seville in 1645, when the College of San Hermenegildo went bankrupt.

Alden sketches some analogies between these two affairs in a few lines. In addition to the Atlantic connection, and the desire in each case to heap guilt on individuals so as to clear the Society's good name, both display a global dimension. The scandal in Seville echoed far beyond the frontiers of

---

1 Dauril Alden, *The Making of an Enterprise: The Society of Jesus in Portugal, its Empire, and Beyond, 1540–1750* (Stanford, CA: Stanford University Press, 1996), 555–56.

2 D. G. Thompson, "The Fate of the French Jesuits' Creditors under the Ancien Régime," *The English Historical Review* 91, no. 359 (1976): 255–57; Andrew Dial, "The 'Lavalette Affair,' Jesuits and Money in the French Atlantic" (PhD Diss., McGill University, 2018).

3 Anonymous, *Les jésuites, marchands, usuriers, usurpateurs et leurs cruautés dans l'ancien et le nouveau continent* (La Haye: chez les frères Vaillant, 1759), 2.

Andalusia. In his letter of indictment sent to Pope Innocent x (1644–1655) on January 8, 1649,[4] the Bishop of Puebla in Mexico, Juan Palafox (1600–1659), expressed his indignation at the intrigue of the Sevillian fathers. Protestant and Jansenist propagandists composing the anti-Jesuit legend could draw inspiration from this severe condemnation and did not refrain from evoking the "bankruptcy" of the college and the sufferings endured by its creditors. In the eighth pamphlet published under the title *Écrits des curés de Paris* in 1659, Blaise Pascal—or more probably Pierre Nicole and Antoine Arnaud—referred to the "shameful affair" of the "bankrupt priests."[5] No sooner had the San Hermenegildo trial started than it was commented upon in Portugal, France, and Mexico, to the great regret of the prelates of the Holy See. Palafox feared the reaction of foreign traders in Seville. Enemies of the Catholic faith would assuredly alert their European partners to the miscreants' dishonesty, thus hampering trade: "[W]hat will Dutch heretics say ... what will English and German Protestants say who boast of maintaining inviolable faith in their contracts." During the Ancien Régime, the economic sphere was beset with uncertainty, and hence regulated through trust-based relations.[6] The Jesuits thus agreed that the trial had devastating effects. In Palafox's opinion, it harmed colleges in Andalusia, the Society, and the Roman Church more generally.

There is a striking contrast between the mass of documentation this event generated and the subsequent historiographical silence. Nevertheless, in the early twentieth century, the Jesuit Antonio Astrain, known for his compendium on the history of the Spanish assistancy, nevertheless described the Sevillian bankruptcy as "resounding" and as "famous" as that of Lavalette.[7] Astrain lamented that such a "disaster" should darken his hagiography of Spanish Jesuits. For his research, he had drawn on printed material held by the *Archivo di Stato* in Rome, particularly reports by judges in charge of the investigation and a virulent indictment of the Society signed by Juan Onofre y Salazar, attorney to the Jesuits. In fact, since 1645 a wave of factums, memoranda and pamphlets had circulated in Spain and its imperial territories, where the fate of the college was just as much on trial in the court of public opinion as it was in the tribunals. The legal battle pitting claimants against the Seville college lasted from

---

4 *Carta del venerable siervo de Dios Juan de Palafox y Mendoza al sumo Pontífice Inocencio X, Puebla de los Angeles*, January 8, 1649 (Madrid: Imprenta de D. Gabriel Ramirez, 1768), 152–56.

5 Blaise Pascal, *Œuvres*, vol. III (La Haye: chez Detune, 1779), 313–14.

6 Pierre-Yves Grenier, *L'économie de l'Ancien Régime, un monde de l'échange et de l'incertitude* (Paris: Albin Michel, 1996).

7 Antonio Astrain, *Historia de la Compañía de Jesús en la asistencia de España*, vol. 5 (Madrid: Administración de razón y fe, 1912), 40–47.

1645 to 1657, providing extensive material in the form of twenty-odd printed documents.[8] Yet despite being abundantly documented,[9] the affair has not sparked the curiosity of historians. Three articles published in low-key publications merely rehearse the judicial stages, with no analytic ambitions.[10] One paper, by Jesús Aguado de los Reyes, sets out the chronological underpinnings of San Hermenegildo's fortune prior to its bankruptcy. This was conceived as the foundation stone for a project about the college's trading and banking functions, which did not reach fruition.[11]

Several hypotheses may explain this superficial treatment. Although the sources are numerous, the corpus is scattered between distant archives depositories—in Madrid, Seville, Granada, Cadiz, Paris, London, Rome, and Mexico; any in-depth enquiry into the college's fortune and speculative practices entails searching through these and triangulating sources of differing nature—letters, chronicles, legal documents and so on. As things currently stand, it is not possible to locate the proceedings of this protracted trial in the un-catalogued boxes of the archives of the Court of Castile in Madrid. But this gap should not impede research, for the variety of available factums provides a way of partially circumventing this handicap. More generally, the profusion of studies about the Society of Jesus in the fields of culture (the Jesuit interventions in scientific, intellectual, and educational fields), religion (their missionary and evangelical zeal accompanying colonization) and politics (their relationship to power) have tended to eclipse questions about material underpinnings and interactions with capitalist and trading milieus.[12]

---

8   The Spanish National Library holds most of them in its collection of factums (*porcones*). The extensive holdings of the university libraries of Seville and Granada complete the corpus.

9   The collection of documents compiled by the *Memorial Histórico Español* contains several about the trial.

10   Ricardo Torres Muñoz, "La quiebra del colegio San Hermenegildo de Sevilla. Aproximación a un concurso en la España del siglo XVII," in *Estudios sobre la ley concursal, libro homenaje a Manuel Olivencia* (Madrid; Barcelona: Marcial Pons, 2005), 523–38; Elena Martín Mayoral, "La quiebra del colegio de San Hemenegildo de Sevilla, 1643," in *Nuevos estudios sobre historia de la contabilidad*, ed. Esteban Hernández Esteve and Begoña Prieto Moreno (Burgos: Diputación provincial de Burgos, 2008), 373–90; Antonio Cortes Peña, "La quiebra del colegio de San Hermenegildo," in *Actas de las II Jornadas de Metodología y Didáctica de la Historia* (Cáceres: Universidad de Extremadura, 1983), 191–202.

11   Jesús Aguado de los Reyes, "Negocios de sotanas: los jesuitas y el mercado financiero sevillano en la primera mitad del siglo XVII," in *La Compañía de Jesús en España: otra mirada*, ed. Joaquín Morales Ferrer and Agustín Galán García (Madrid: Anaya, 2007), 55–76. In a book in honor of Jesús Aguado de los Reyes, José Antonio Ollero states that this task was interrupted by the deteriorating health of the former.

12   Monographs about the Jesuits in Spain neglect this aspect. See for example Teófanes Egido López, *Los jesuitas en España y en el mundo hispánico* (Madrid: Marcial Pons,

Frederik Vermote has recently commented on persisting historiographical shortcomings concerning the way the Society's financial machinery
functioned.[13] In fact, we have significantly better understanding of the
instruments supporting its missionary and educational enterprise in the
Americas than on the Iberian peninsula.[14] Since François Chevalier's pio-
neering work on the expansion of the great estates in Mexico,[15] some historians have argued that the Jesuits were expert administrators.[16] Some even
grant the Jesuits a form of intrinsic modernity, said to have transpired in the
economic thought of their theologians and in their accounting and commercial practices. These scholars emphasize the rationality of Jesuit investments, their spirit of innovation facilitating the birth of agrarian capitalism, their capacity to break into market economy circuits and to establish
information and distribution procedures. In the field of doctrine, this dy-
namism is said to have been shaped by a moral laxity which authorized a
more flexible relation to money.[17] Such a conception is far from unified or
consensual, covers a variety of different shades, and stretches as far as the
debatable thesis of Charles Boxer, who argues the Society was the first ever
multinational.[18] In Italy, mediaevalists work alongside early modernists on
the spiritual implications of the enrichment of the clergy, placing emphasis

---

2004); Wenceslao Soto Artuñedo, *Los Jesuitas en Andalucía, estudios conmemorativos
del 450 aniversario de la fundación de la provincia* (Granada: Facultad de Teología de
Granada, 2007).

13   Frederik Vermote, "Finances of the Missions," in *A Companion to Early Modern Catholic
Global Missions*, ed. Ronnie Po-Chia Hsia (Leiden; Boston: Brill, 2018), 367–400.

14   Nicholas Cushner, *Farm and Factory: The Jesuit and the Developement of Agrarian
Capitalism in Colonial Quito, 1600–1767* (Albany, NY: State University of New York Press,
1982); Aliocha Maldavsky, Roberto Di Stefano, eds., *Invertir en lo sagrado: salvación y dom-
inación territorial en América y Europa* (*siglos XVI-XX*) (Santa Rosa: EdUNLPam, 2018);
Frederik Vermote, "Financing Jesuit Mission," in *The Oxford Handbook of Jesuits*, ed. Ines
G. Županov (New York: Oxford University Press, 2019), 128–49.

15   François Chevalier, *La formation des grands domaines au Mexique: terre et société aux
XVIe-XVIIe siècles* (Paris: Institut d'ethnologie, 1952).

16   Markus Friedrich, "'Government in India and Japen is Different from Government in
Europe': Asian Jesuits on Infrastructure. Homogeneity of Administrative Space, and the
Possibilities for a Global Management of Power," *Journal of Jesuit Studies* 4, no. 1 (2017):
1–27.

17   Paola Vismara, "Les jésuites et la morale économique," *Dix-septième siècle* 4 (2007): 739–54.

18   Charles R. Boxer, *Portuguese India in the Mid-Seventeenth Century* (New Delhi: Oxford
University Press, 1980), 50. Alden criticized Boxer's opinion in *The Making of an Enterprise*,
Appendix B, 668–69. See Luke Clossey, *Salvation and Globalization in the Early Jesuit
Missions* (Cambridge: Cambridge University Press, 2008).

on the Jesuits' strategic choices in developing productive land, in contrast to a regular economy said to be more conservative.[19] In Spain, an analogous diagnosis has been advanced by Antonio Luis López Martínez, one of the few historians to have enquired into these aspects. In his monograph about the economy of religious orders in the province of Seville, he argues that the Jesuits invented a management model that provided a source of inspiration for clergy and for laypeople.[20]

Irrespective of their differences, these works form an intellectual cluster that views the Catholic Church as a matrix for the Ancien Régime economy. They cast aside preconceptions about its supposed entrepreneurial faint-heartedness in implicit comparison with the Protestant states of Northern Europe. Leaving to one side the debate about the wealth or poverty of the Society of Jesus—which can only be resolved by considering the extraordinary diversity of contexts in which they were operating around the globe—this article endeavors to show that the college of San Hermenegildo was an influential operator in the Seville credit market in the first half of the seventeenth century. The college's credit, determined by its reputation among the population, empowered it to compensate for the lack of banking institutions and make profitable inroads into merchant networks. The trial enables us to ascertain the limit beyond which indebtedness became intolerable, and the reasons why the college was suddenly stripped of its power. This article makes no claim to any monographic treatment; its purpose is to examine the college's role in a financial system spanning the Atlantic, and combining Andalusian, Roman and American strands. These interlocking scales of action resulted less from any geographical presupposition—the place of Seville in the Spanish Atlantic system—than from a deliberate policy based on the mobilization and circulation of clerical and lay go-betweens steeped in merchant culture.[21]

---

19   Giacomo Todeschini, *Richesses franciscaines. De la pauvreté volontaire à la société de marché* (Paris: Verdier, 2008); Fiorenzo Landi, *Accumulation and Dissolution of Large Estates of the Regular Clergy in the Early Modern Europe* (Rimini: Guaraldi, 1999); Niccolò Guasti, ed., *I patrimoni dei gesuiti nell'Italia moderna: una prospettiva comparativa* (Bari: Edipuglia, 2013).

20   Antonio Luis López Martínez, *La Economía de las órdenes religiosas en el Antiguo Régimen. Sus propiedades y rentas en el reino de Sevilla* (Seville: Excma. Diputación Provincial de Sevilla, 1992).

21   Go-betweens were used in the context of colonization, see Alida C. Metcalf, *Go-betweens and the Colonization of Brazil, 1500–1600* (Austin, TX: University of Texas Press, 2005).

1   The Fortunes and Misfortunes of San Hermenegildo

While the judicial ins and outs of the San Hermenegildo bankruptcy are of
secondary importance here, we need to briefly separate the various strands
so as to understand how one of the wealthiest colleges in Spain came to be on
the verge of ruin. The college's insolvency, the first symptoms of which came
to light in 1642, coincided with the climax to the Spanish economic crisis. No
doubt the risks taken on by the Jesuits lent credence to those blaming them for
their misadventure. Nevertheless, it was primarily the combined effects of the
downturn in Atlantic trade—no shipment of silver reached Seville in 1640[22]—
and decisions aggravating the monetary and fiscal disorder that precipitated
their downfall. Since the revolt of the Catalan peasants in May 1640, followed
shortly after by the Portuguese, Philip IV (1621–1665) and his ministers had
been deploring the string of "misfortunes" battering Spain. Since 1635 and the
French intervention in the Thirty Years' War, new military fronts had opened,
compelling Spain to turn to ever greater financial expedients: increasing the
fiscal burden, a half-annate tax on salaries and interest from public bonds (*juros*) in 1635, the sequestration of precious metals unloaded in Seville (*reme-
sas*),[23] and a raft of taxes on Seville merchants.[24] In 1642 a further devaluation
of copper money was decreed (*vellón*), and the silver premium—paid in compensation on monetary conversions—reached new heights. These measures
heightened the distrust of merchants, acting as a brake on consumption and
draining liquidity channels.

    In this context of uncertainty, it is easy to understand why civilians, having
entrusted their savings to the college, hastened to call in these debts, totaling
450,000 ducats. Fearing danger, the college Superiors devised remedies in 1642
to renegotiate the sums owed and when payments were due.[25] While certain
privileged creditors were fully reimbursed, others were obliged to accept partial repayments in various instalments via the transfer of interest on public
bonds. The less fortunate were asked to make do with half of their due.[26] With
discontent growing, the dispute reached the courts. The aggrieved Sevillians

22   Antonio Domínguez Ortiz, "Los caudales de Indias y la política exterior de Felipe IV," in
      Estudios Americanistas (Madrid: Real Academia de la Historia, 1998), 29–116.
23   Ramón Lanza García, ed., *Las instituciones económicas, las finanzas públicas y el declive de
      España en la Edad moderna* (Madrid: UAM ediciones, 2018).
24   José Manuel Díaz Blanco, *Así trocaste tu gloria: guerra y comercio colonial en la España del
      siglo XVII* (Valladolid: Instituto Universitario de Historia Simancas, Marcial Pons 2012).
25   Aguado de los Reyes, "Negocios de sotanas," 55–76.
26   Biblioteca Nacional de España [hereafter BNE], VE, 1408–34–1, Memorial que se dio a S.M
      (que Dios guarde) en su real mano por los acreedores … .

launched a joint action under the aegis of a lawyer, Juan Onofre y Salazar, who was party to the case. The concourse of creditors—as proceedings to recover debts against a common debtor are called—was recorded on March 14, 1645, numbering 300 people from various social strata. Its purpose was to seize the college's assets.[27] Arbitration was drawn out, and went through many twists and turns. Between 1645 and 1648 there were countless appeals and requests against ecclesiastical decisions (*recursos de fuerza*), to determine whether or not ecclesiastical jurisdiction was competent. Actions to get a case reallocated to a more favorable judge were commonplace in monarchies ruled by more than one normative and jurisdictional order.[28] On April 3, 1657, when a ruling had just been issued after twelve years, Juan Onofre de Salazar summed up the torturous proceedings in the following terms: "I have never been in the army, but I have read and always heard it said that the sinews of war are money. And you need it to plead in Seville, Rome, [and Madrid] in front of the Council of Castile and the court of the nuncio."[29] A week earlier, the apostolic judge Miguel Muñoz de Ahumada had ordered that the college pay its debts by auctioning off its temporal goods, while retaining possession of its spiritual goods.[30]

Indeed, the college's lawyers had stated during the trial that most of its capital came from benefices, chaplaincies, and its pious foundation, and that, as such, these goods were inalienable and subject to the regime of mortmain.[31] The objective was to minimize the value of temporal property, which alone could be used to clear debts. Additionally, the Jesuits sought to pin the blame for the bankruptcy on the person in charge of the college's economic management between 1632 and 1645, the procurator, Andrés de Villar. They said they knew nothing of the brother coadjutor's accounting and banking practices, described as "fraudulent," nor of the transactions he had carried out on behalf of the college. According to them, his calamitous administration, "the dissimulation in his books and in his accounts," and the contract of loans totaling 800,000 ducats had plunged the college into insolvency and poverty.[32] In the 1650s, the financial repercussions of this led to classes being closed and to

---

27   Gisela von Wobeser, *El crédito eclesiástico en la Nueva España, siglo XVIII* (Mexico: Fondo de cultura económica, 2010), 148–53.
28   For a summary of the stages in proceedings, see Archivo Histórico Nacional [Hereafter AHN], Clero, Jesuitas, 218.
29   AHN, Clero, Jesuitas, 218.
30   Cortes Peña, "La quiebra del colegio," 191–202.
31   The state or condition of goods (land, buildings), inalienably held.
32   AHN, Clero, Jesuitas, 218; BNE, R, 38922 (18), *Traslado de una petición de querella contra Villar*.

deteriorating material conditions for residents.[33] Andrés de Villar, on the other hand, with the backing of his creditors, accused his hierarchy—the rector, Pedro de Marmol, and the provincial of Andalusia, Pedro de Áviles—of having encouraged bankruptcy proceedings in order to try to shirk their contractual obligations.[34] Especially, he praised his own financial and asset management, for which he had obtained his superiors' prior approval throughout his thirteen years in tenure. On this point, the college's defense is undermined by an internal document of the Society. It was drawn up by Pedro Fonseca, a Jesuit in charge of assisting San Hermenegildo during the trial. He admitted having proof in his possession that de Villar's operations had been approved subsequent to the accounts being checked: "and this is a source of great dismay to me, for if [Áviles] approved his accounts after viewing them and approved his traffics, that confirms all the attacks against the Society's credit published by our adversaries ... and in that case we lose not just our fortune but our honor too."[35] These admissions are fundamental, confirming that the system introduced by Andrés de Villar was in response to a deliberate college enrichment policy.

Although disagreements over the value of San Hermenegildo's income and assets were part of a war of figures seeking to discredit or uphold de Villar's actions, the trial casts light on the resources of one of the most prosperous colleges in Spain.[36] It is true that its income needed to rise in step with the number of pupils, for, in accordance with the Constitutions of the Society of Jesus, its teachers dispensed instruction free of charge.[37] Founded in 1580, San Hermenegildo took five-hundred pupils on opening, rising to over a thousand by the beginning of the seventeenth century.[38] The buildings, described as "sumptuous" after their embellishment, housed a large of staff of over a hundred people, including many servants.[39] Of course, depicting the college as an

33   AHN, Clero, Jesuitas, 218; Antonio Domínguez Ortiz, *Orto y ocaso de Sevilla* (Seville: Universidad de Sevilla, 1991) 122–23. The number of residents plummeted, for in 1668 there were only thirty left in the college. In addition to this drop in revenue, the 1649 plague killed a certain number of Sevillian Jesuits.

34   Biblioteca Universitaria de Granada [Hereafter BUG], Fondo antiguo, siglo XVII, Don Andrés de Villar Goitia, vezino, y natural de la villa de Oñate ... (1653).

35   AHN, Clero, Jesuitas, 218.

36   Astrain, *Historia de la Compañía de Jesús*, 40–47.

37   Ignace De Loyola, *Écrits*, ed. Maurice Giulani (Paris; Montréal: Desclée de Brouwer and Bellarmin, 1991).

38   Astrain, *Historia de la Compañía de Jesús*, 40–47; Biblioteca Universitaria de Sevilla [Hereafter BUS], Fondo antiguo, A 109/088(27), *Traslado del informe que hizo a su Magestad el señor don Juan de Santelices y Guevara* (1646).

39   BUG, Fondo antiguo, *Don Andrés de Villar* ... (1653).

opulent palace suited the purposes of its creditors, and the figures put forward by plaintiffs are best treated with caution. Several estimates during the trial reckoned San Hermenegildo to control over 500,000 ducats.[40] Such sums, beyond the reach of many monastic institutions, placed the college on an equal footing with wealthy aristocratic houses. But like these, it was in danger of being undermined by the volume of its debts. In 1645 it was burdened with debts of 400,000 ducats.[41] Villar apparently inherited 205,000 ducats in debt, and contracted a further 200,000 ducats in loans invested in expanding and modernizing San Hermenegildo's landholdings.[42] Concurring figures place the college's revenue, free of encumbrances and liens, at 8,248 ducats per year in 1632. Still, the judge at the Seville hearing estimated the college's revenue to stand at 15,000 ducats in 1644, while the Jesuits asserted that with bankruptcy it had collapsed to 5,070 ducats.[43] By way of comparison, calculations by López Martínez attribute an average income of 13,527 reales (1,229 ducats) to the houses of regular clergy in the province of Seville in 1717.[44]

Although attempts to arrive at an exact figure for the college's income are necessarily vain in the absence of complete accounts, and although endeavors to estimate assets are clouded by a series of unknowns—the capacity to collect money from landholdings, property leases and public bonds, dissimulation of the true volume of debts, the inclusion or otherwise in its assets of nonproductive goods such as the church and buildings, the impossibility of determining the price of nontransferable and indissoluble possessions—this string of figures nevertheless gives an idea of the college's ability to borrow on the Seville credit market, and of the capital passing through the hands of its procurator. In the Spanish Empire few religious institutions could pride themselves on channeling such large flows of money, especially in decades marked by liquidity shortages. While during the first half of the seventeenth century religious and aristocratic orders[45] saw their income from landholdings eroded,[46] San

---

40   AHN, Clero, Jesuitas, 218.

41   Since 1632, 800,000 ducats had been borrowed, meaning 350,000 ducats had been reimbursed.

42   BUG, Fondo antiguo, *Don Andrés de Villar* ... (1653).

43   According to Villar, revenue from 1635 to 1645 was 7,700 ducats; and according to the Jesuits, 5270 ducats in 1644; Memorial Histórico español, t. XVIII (Madrid: imprenta nacional, 1864), *Informe audiencia de Sevilla*, 107–14.

44   López Martínez, *La economía de las ordenes*, 106–11.

45   Bartolomé Yun Casalilla, *La gestión del poder, Corona y Economías aristocráticas en Castilla (siglo XVII-XVIII)* (Madrid: Akal, 2003).

46   Julián J. Lozano Navarro, "El dinero de los jesuitas: una aproximación a la realidad económica del colegio de Marchena (Sevilla). Siglos XVI–XVIII," *Krypton* 4 (2014): 12–23.

Hermenegildo's assets grew, and inspired the confidence of investors who were forsaking depreciated state bonds.[47] Some of the capital was tied up in renovating college buildings—the church, a new refectory at the exorbitant cost of 20,000 ducats, the library, the school and so on. Some was employed in enhancing the college's landholdings by making purchases intended to guarantee a stable income. With the remaining sums, the Jesuits intended to maximize their profit by speculating on merchandise for the *Carrera de Indias*. As we shall see, these investments were correlated, and the extent to which regional and Atlantic markets were interlinked determined how good the college's credit was.

2   Land Accumulation and Atlantic Commercial Opportunities

In Spain, the wealth of regular orders was based on three sources: public bonds issued on consolidated debt (*juros*), mortgage-backed loans supported by collateral (*censos*), and real estate, generating income from farmland and from urban buildings.[48] In contrast, the Christian ethic and doctrine forbade ecclesiastics from indulging in mercantile and secular activities, restricting the produce from land to domestic uses.[49] Nevertheless, historiography has shown how religious orders, far from cutting themselves off from the world, had ever since the eleventh century fostered economic development by inculcating in merchants the norms for legitimate enrichment, indexed on the common good and the rejection of hoarding.[50] Until the waves of Spanish confiscations in the first half of the nineteenth century, religious orders fueled the economy, stimulating production and consumption.[51] This dynamic led in some cases to active participation in trade, such

47   Alberto Marcos Martín, "Deuda pública, mercado crediticio y actividades económicas en la Castilla del siglo XVII," *Hispania* 243 (2013): 133–60.
48   Ceferino Caro López, "El patrimonio de los regulares madrileños en los siglos XVII y XVIII," *Hispania Sacra* 102 (1998): 509–50.
49   Robert-Henri, Bautier, "'Clercs mécaniques' et 'clercs marchands' dans la France du XIIIᵉ siècle," *Comptes rendus des séances de l'Académie des Inscriptions et Belles-Lettres* 125, no. 2 (1981): 209–42.
50   Giacomo Todeschini, *Les Marchands et le Temple, La société chrétienne et le cercle vertueux de la richesse du Moyen Âge à l'époque moderne* (Paris: Albin Michel, 2017).
51   Kathryn Burns, *Convents and the Spiritual Economy of Cuzco, Peru* (Durham, NC; London: Duke University Press, 1999); Arnold Bauer, "The Church in the Economy of Spanish America: Censos y Depósitos in the Eighteenth and Nineteenth Centuries," *The Hispanic American Historical Review* 63, no. 4 (1983): 707–33.

as at San Hermenegildo, which drew on its close ties with capitalist circles in Seville.

In the late sixteenth century, the college expanded its landholdings in the immediate surroundings of Seville, acquiring property on the banks of the Guadaíra, an affluent of the Guadalquivir flowing south of the town. According to Andrés de Villar, in the mid-seventeenth century these lands were deemed "the best, the most precious, and the most estimable in all Andalusia."[52] On exploring this area in the late eighteenth century, the traveler and physiocrat Antonio Ponz (1725–1792) was equally full of praise, admiring the quality of the olives—"the biggest in Europe"—and the wheat-producing bread of proverbial whiteness.[53] The Guadaíra was indeed the breadbasket of Seville, with dozens of mills extracting the flour needed to feed the second-largest town in the kingdom. The Jesuits, in addition to being involved in local supply circuits, also produced olives for capitalist purposes (illustration 9.1). This specialization in crops (vines and olive oil) for the American market modified the landscape of the Seville hinterlands.[54]

San Hermenegildo built up its landholdings via a classical process combining the aggregation of ecclesiastical benefices, religious bequests, gifts from laypeople—chaplaincies, charitable and pious foundations—and a targeted acquisition policy. As in Italy or in France, the college's economic base depended on the charity of the nobility.[55] In 1566, a chaplaincy was granted to the Jesuits, who opened the first classes in a house prefiguring the college. The landholdings attached to this chaplaincy lay in Huelva, and in 1573, San Hermenegildo was granted the capacity to replace them so as to acquire estates in Tizón and Pitaña, half a league south of Seville. The college then launched a process of concentrating its holdings along the Guadaíra, which, in addition to its hydraulic power, provided water for irrigation, essential in the Mediterranean climate. Between 1578 and 1612, it aggregated lands adjacent to these two estates over the course of thirteen transactions.[56] In 1612 it received a bequest from a powerful Seville lawyer, Marco Antonio de Alfaro. The value of this pious foundation was estimated at over 80,000 ducats. The money was used to purchase three chunks of land, further extending the Society's holdings

---

52   BUG, Fondo antiguo, *Don Andrés de Villar …* (1653).
53   Quoted by Álvaro Recio Mir, "De la compañía de Jesús al XII Duque de Alba: la hacienda de los Ángeles de Álcala de Guadaíra," *Laboratorio de arte* 20 (2007): 309–37.
54   Juan José Iglesias Rodríguez, José Jaime García Bernal and José Manuel Díaz Blanco, eds., *Andalucía en el mundo atlántico moderno* (Madrid: Sílex Universidad, 2016).
55   See Ariane Boltanski's chapter in this book.
56   AHN, Clero, Jesuitas, 157.

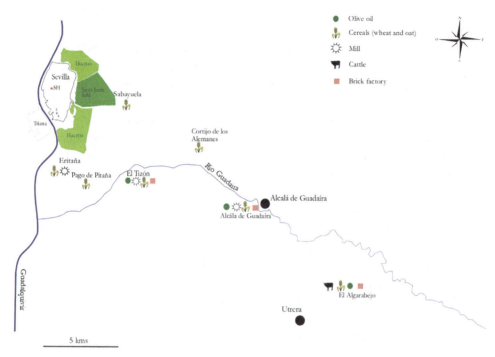

ILLUSTRATION 9.1   Localization of Jesuits' landholdings near Seville

along the Guadaíra: the first lay in the urban perimeter of Álcala de Guadaíra, the second—San Francisco Javier de los Ángeles—five kilometers to the west, while the third—Algarabejo—covered over 1500 hectares fifteen kilometers east of Álcala.[57] The Jesuits' other landholdings—San Augustín de Burguillos, La Pisana, etc.—derived from the legal portion of inheritances bequeathed by ecclesiastics residing in San Hermenegildo, or from pious works instituted by the Sevillian elite.

My purpose here is not to draw up an inventory of these landholdings, but rather to note that, in 1632, 61 percent of the college's income came from agriculture and livestock rearing (19 percent came from interest on censos and juros, the rest from pious works, benefices, and rental income). In 1644, the college was the owner of impressive herds—441 oxen, 800 cows, 700 donkeys, 148 mares, 17 horses, 6 mules, 13,500 ewes, 450 goats, and over 1000 pigs. Accounts for the same year show that wheat and barley were sown on over 1,720

57   See the Mexican case in James D. Riley, "The Wealth of the Jesuits' in Mexico, 1670–1767," *The Americas* 33, no. 2 (1976): 226–66.

hectares (2,700 *fanegas*).[58] San Hermenegildo directly oversaw the farming of these lands with the help of dozens of farm laborers, prioritizing highly profitable commercial crops to meet demand in Andalusia and the Americas. Between 1632 and 1644, the college borrowed 156,000 ducats, used to increase the land under cultivation, particularly olive groves. Oil was popular as a currency on the Seville marketplace, and difficulties in acclimatizing olive trees overseas meant there was strong demand from the Indies. This agricultural rationalization in response to near or distant markets also transpired in the desire to modernize production infrastructures. Mills were renovated at great expense, such as the grain mill at Tizón. First it was equipped with two additional grindstones (taking the total to five), before being fitted in 1642 with a new water-wheel whose manufacture involved over a hundred men at a cost of 5000 ducats.[59] The Tizón site was enclosed by walls, and had a *huerta* with three dammed reservoirs, an oil mill, a brick oven, and a bread oven. This quest for profitability, whether it took the form of diverting more water from the Guadaíra,[60] or enclosing plots of land,[61] altered the equilibrium in the community, triggering increased disputes with the neighborhood. Lastly, however sophisticated this administration was, it did not rid San Hermenegildo of the uncertainty defining ancient economies. In 1635, and again in 1643, poor harvests and episodic outbreaks meant profits failed to offset losses.[62]

On the basis of a document not hitherto used by historians, it is possible to examine how these local activities were intertwined with the college's Atlantic trading. Although during the trial the Jesuits denied any involvement in distant commerce, an accounts' sheet of August 1643 proves the contrary.[63] Its author, Domingo de Arechavala, was sent to Cadix and San Lúcar de Barrameda by Andrés de Villar and Francisco de Aleman, the rector of San Hermenegildo at the time. These towns were outports of Seville, with facilities for unloading ships from the Indies, where the fleet escorted by General Pedro de Ursua dropped anchor during July and August 1643. Once there, Arechavala was tasked with recovering consignments to Andrés de Villar. Silver was delivered in exchange for the shipment of olive oil cargoes to New Spain in 1642. The transaction enabled the college to procure valued silver coins at a time when poor alloy copper coins were saturating the market. Some of this profit was used to finance

58   AHN, Clero, Jesuitas, 157.
59   BUG, Fondo antiguo, *Don Andrés de Villar* ... (1653).
60   AHN, Clero, Jesuitas, 157.
61   Recio Mir, "De la compañía de Jesús al XII Duque de Alba," 313.
62   BUG, Fondo antiguo, *Don Andrés de Villar* ... (1653).
63   AHN, Clero, Jesuitas, 157.

the college's routine business—paying the mule drivers, laborers, and shepherds working on the San Hermenegildo estates. As the harvest had been poor, grain was purchased for the impending planting season at Algarabejo. Other payments indicate that refined products from far away were purchased, such as 90 quintals of Breton cod, and bedspreads manufactured in China. Lastly, the rest of the consignment was made up of dyeing plants grown in New Spain—cochineal and indigo—and chocolate. The former were sold at a good price: in all 59 arrobes of cochineal, weighing 678 kilos, were sold for 82,258 silver reales, either directly or by promissory notes, proving the Jesuits were familiar with the financial instruments favored by merchants. As for the chocolate, it would appear to have been an excellent means of negotiation for the Society, and its dispatch to centers of power in Madrid and Rome engendered abundant epistolary reports.[64] These dealings were all the more lucrative as the fiscal privileges granted to ecclesiastics enlarged their profits. The Jesuits were exempt from the *alcabala* on each sale of oil, a tax normally levied on all transactions.[65] The Jesuits also continually defrauded the royal customs, and were regularly accused of dissimulating merchandise or infringing the obligation to record precious metals with the clerks at the *Casa de Contratación*. Hence, according to some of his enemies, Andrés de Villar had indulged in such abuses.[66]

San Hermenegildo was thus involved in the Seville land market and in global trade. It owed its fortune to a circular Atlantic economy which saw American profits reinjected locally to expand and to specialize in capitalist farming operations. This organization binding the college's fortune to the articulation of different scales—the landholdings along the Río de Guadaíra, Seville, the Guadalquivir and its ports, the Atlantic—even seems to have applied in the field of culture. In 1740, once the college had recovered from collapse, it commissioned a baroque *reredos* (altarpiece) of classical manufacture for its chapel at the Algarabejo *cortijo*. Its base, however, was decorated with Oriental-style patterns, presenting a peaceful Chinese landscape.[67] Was this simply a matter of fashion, showing that chinoiseries had reached as far as the agricultural countryside? Or in tribute to missionary action in China, was it presented as

---

64   Samir Boumediene, *La colonisation du savoir, Une histoire des plantes médicinales du "Nouveau Monde" (1492–1750)* (Vaulx-en-Velin: Éditions des Mondes à faire, 2016), 139–40.

65   The clergy were exempted from taxes on commercial transactions by virtue of their Estate—*alcabalas, almorajifazgo*: BNE, Porcones, 489-6, f. 7v.

66   AHN, Clero, Jesuitas, 218, Letter of the father Tello (May 28, 1654).

67   Alvaro Recio Mir, "Notas sobre el cortijos de Algarbejo de Álcala de Guadaíra y el retablo de su capilla," *Laboratorio de arte* 14 (2001): 87–107.

the archetype of the mission? Or did it instead indicate an awareness of San Hermenegildo's global destiny? While this third interpretation is no more than a hypothesis, it is certain that ever since the late sixteenth century the college had been playing a full part in the transatlantic network built up by the Jesuits.

3   Building Atlantic Networks: The San Hermenegildo Trading House

The material management of Jesuit institutions necessitated the assistance of qualified agents recruited from both inside and outside the Society. At the various levels of its hierarchy, decisions about temporal goods, accountancy, the recovery of rents, communication, and financial relationships with other Society trading houses were carried out by procurators (*procuradores*).[68] These functions meant they were similar to cellarers, the brothers who administered monastic goods. They were sometimes described as "business agents,"[69] and enjoyed extensive leeway thanks to their procuracies, a decisive legal instrument bestowing the power to act and be represented at a distance. Most were selected from among the coadjutor brothers. The reluctance to confide this type of mission to Jesuits with the title of priest shows that ecclesiastics assigned to secular affairs operated in a grey area. At San Hermenegildo, they were recruited largely on the grounds of their skill, their background, and their relational capital. The *Instrucción para el procurador de Indias*, drawn up in 1574, is one of the few normative provisions establishing guidelines for the work of procurators.[70] All those who held this strategic office, which consisted particularly in ensuring the proper functioning of financial links with all the provinces in America (Peru, Mexico, New Granada, Paraguay, Quito, and the Philippines), were based in San Hermenegildo. The propinquity between the college procurator and the procurator for the Indies explains the volume and quality of the trading conducted by the Seville college.

During the trial, it was noted that the affairs of the college were so commixed with those of the procurator for the Indies that certain witnesses were

---

68   Fabian Fechner, "Las tierras incógnitas de la administración jesuita: toma de decisiones, gremios consultivos y evolución de normas," *Historica* 38, no. 2 (2014): 11–42. On procurators, see also Hélène Vu Thanh's chapter in this volume.

69   Carlos Urani Montiel, "Procuradores jesuitas y mercados en conflicto: el caso de Felipe del Castillo de la Misión de Moxos (1737)," *Anuario de estudios bolivianos, archivísticos y bibliográficos* 18 (2012): 203–31.

70   Félix Zubillaga, "El procurador de las Indias occidentales de la compañía de Jesús," *Archivum Historicum Societatis Iesu* 22 (1953): 367–417.

unclear about their respective activities.[71] The two agents worked within the same walls.[72] The San Hermenegildo library held "the books and papers of the office of the procurator for the Indies,"[73] and the college enclosure housed a store where excess stock from the Indies was held together with merchandise for supplying Jesuits in the Americas.[74] As the interface between the "old" and the "new" worlds, the procurator for the Indies carried out many of the various tasks set out in a 1651 treatise by Pedro Salinas.[75] He helped with the reception of Jesuits arriving from America and the attendant administrative procedures. He received cases unloaded in Seville and dispatched them to their benefi-ciaries. He imported from all over Europe that which Jesuits were unable to procure on the other side of the Atlantic. He was sometimes referred to as a "*factor*," and his work resembled that of commissioners sent as delegates by the heads of international firms: his epistolary relations did not cover solely the Indies, but extended to "all parts of Spain, Italy, France, and Flanders, whence were dispatched the books, cloth, and other objects these provinces [in Amer-ica] needed."[76] Given their proximity, he probably shared his bulging address book with his San Hermenegildo counterpart. Besides, they were known to co-operate financially. This was grounded in a set of shared interests facilitating the the the circulation of money between their coffers.[77] According to Andrés de Villar, the college had lent 54,000 reales in 1635 to Fabian López, the procurator for the Indies, at rates lower than those available on the Seville money mar-ket.[78] The two men pooled their credit to expand their field of action, working as one in 1638 to invite new funders to underwrite loans before Miguel de Bur-gos, the college's lawyer and close friend of Villar.[79] These Jesuits frequented the same places of power and channels of commercial knowledge—Villar's procuracy authorized him to "withdraw from the *Casa de Contratación* of the

---

71   J. Gabriel Martínez-Serna, "Procurators and the Making of the Jesuit Atlantic Network," in *Soundings in Atlantic History: Latent Structures and Intellectual Currents, 1500–1830*, ed. Bernard Bailyn and Patricia L. Denault (Cambridge, MA; London: Harvard University Press, 2011), 181–209.

72   The São Roque college in Lisbon hosted the procurator for the Portuguese Assistancy.

73   BUG, Caja 040, Papeles varios jurídicos, fol. 2.

74   Real Academia de la Historia [hereafter RAH], 9-3617, *Satisfación que da el Padre Jacinto Perez ...*, fol. 218.

75   Antonio Domínguez Ortiz, "La Procuraduría de Indias en la Compañía de Jesús en Sevilla," in *Estudios americanistas* (Madrid, Real Academia de la Historia, 1998), 311–30.

76   Ortiz, 311–30.

77   BNE, Porcones, 489-6, *Los acreedores de Sevilla con el colegio San Hermenegildo*.

78   AHN, Clero, Jesuitas, 218, Letter from Andrés Villar dated January 29, 1656.

79   Aguado de los Reyes, "Negocios de sotanas," 55–76.

Indies all the quantities and merchandise he needed."[80] Lastly, they shared a merchant culture and taste for risk, which turned out to be fatal: in 1635, the balance of López's accounts showed the volume of his liabilities, and, like Villar, he was declared bankrupt.

In light of the intense trading and financial flows passing through and energized by San Hermenegildo, it is not surprising that the town's population became convinced that the college was acting as a "trading house." In his pamphlet denouncing the Society, Palafox deplored the way that the Seville house issued "bills of exchange" and had turned into a "bank." Such judgements seeped into statements by witnesses who, during the 1645 trial, declared "that ordinarily many people arrived at the college who had come to trade there."[81] Though Seville's center of gravity had shifted towards the Atlantic in the late fifteenth century, it still conducted large-scale exchanges with the Mediterranean and Oriental worlds. San Hermenegildo took advantage of its position as a crossroads between two seas, optimizing its returns by exporting spices from the Indies bought using gold and silver from America: "many witnesses have seen cases of cinnamon, flacons of saffron, and quantities of canvas destined for the Indies" inside the college. The agricultural-commercial arrangements devised by Andrés de Villar transcended the limits of the Spanish Empire. They were international in nature, connecting the college to the main trade routes.

In response to the college superiors, who insisted they had been hoodwinked by de Villar, many witnesses stated that they could not have been ignorant of the scale of this trafficking, conducted openly and beknown to all. Nevertheless, such activities called for caution, to ward off potential criticism of merchants in cassocks. One such technique, which was commonplace among men of business[82] and financial officers,[83] consisted in enlisting dummy nominees to dissimulate business dealings. Although the historiography on these intermediaries is largely incomplete, they played a decisive role in the functioning of economic institutions, and the existing literature affords a glimpse of the role that servants played. Their status as laypeople allowed them to take part in operations from which ecclesiastics were debarred. Andrés de Villar employed Alonso Barba and Juan de Lara as nominees, both servants at the college. During the trial, Barba was described as the "personal agent and

---

80   BUG, Fondo antiguo, *Don Andrés de Villar ...* (1653).

81   BNE, Porcones, 489-6, *Los acreedores.*

82   Francisco Andújar Castillo, "Negocios privados, cargos públicos. El recurso a testaferros en la etapa del cambio dinástico," *Tiempos Modernos* 30, no. 1 (2015).

83   Sébastien Malaprade, *Des châteaux en Espagne, gouvernement des finances et mobilité sociale au XVIIe siècle* (Limoges: Pulim, 2018).

confidant of de Villar" by the Jesuits, who denounced collusion between the
two to enrich themselves at the expense of the college. Yet given certain declarations in court, it is likely that the Jesuit hierarchy knew and approved of
the missions entrusted to this subaltern. The canon of the cathedral of Seville,
Duarte Pereira, certified that Barba used to receive letters of exchange from
Rome and was seen receiving and paying large quantities of money belonging to the college, "as if he were a bank cashier."[84] According to de Villar's adversaries, he had rented a house in the name of Alonso Barba a stone's throw
from the college. The rent was paid by another nominee, Lorenzo de Villar,
brother of Andrés, a merchant who was well-known in seafaring circles and
had a strong foothold in the *Carrera de Indias*. This stratagem was reputedly
used to discreetly prepare shipments for the Indies without the consent of the
Jesuits, who claimed that "all the merchandise that the aforementioned Villar
sent to the Indies was placed in the name of his brothers, Juan and Lorenzo de
Villar, and of his cousin Gregorio de Villar, as attested by the declarations of
the commanding officers of the ships where the cargoes were."[85] The college
thus sought to exculpate itself by entrusting the running of this trading house
to Andrés de Villar, and by condemning family relations it felt to be an aggravating factor at the time of the trial. Once again, this defense was undermined
by statements and letters from the superiors at San Hermenegildo proving that
this setup had received their blessing.

Indeed, Villar's relational resources had actually been one of the key considerations in his promotion to procurator in 1632. When filling this post, the
college, wishing to expand the volume of its business dealings, gave priority to
individuals with ties to the world of trade. Thus both Andrés de Villar and his
successor Domingo de Arechavala were Basques whose families' fortunes were
built on trade. In the seventeenth century, a significant part of the Basque community, with long-standing Atlantic experience, lived in Seville and Cadiz.[86]
Since the early days of the conquest of the Americas, its sailors and merchants
had succeeded in obtaining privileged positions in the administration of the
merchant consulate, in the *Casa de la Contratación*, and on board ships in the
Carrera de Indias where they accounted for one third of the commanding officers.[87] More generally, while the Basques made up only a small portion of the

---

84 BNE, Porcones, 489-6, *Los acreedores*.

85 AHN, Clero, Jesuitas, 218.

86 Xabier Lamikiz, "Basques in the Atlantic World, 1450–1824," *Oxford Research Encyclopedia
    of Latin American History*, 2017, Doi: 10.1093.

87 Lutgardo García Fuentes, "Los vascos en la carrera de indias en la edad moderna: una
    minoría dominante," *Temas americanistas* 16 (2003): 29–49.

population of the kingdom, they gravitated in the king's orbit and dominated senior government offices for the Indies and for finance. In recruiting Basques for the position of procurator, San Hermenegildo was seeking to capture some of the power and influence of this network, which was prepared to cooperate with religious orders, particularly the disciples of Loyola.[88] The merchandise crossing the Atlantic on college business was escorted by Basques. For instance, in 1643 the cochineal and indigo awaited by Villar were delivered to Domingo de Arechavala by the ship's captain Juan de Lizaralde. All three came from the same nation, with their "ethnic solidarity" supposedly precluding any of the swindling that could occur in Atlantic exchanges.[89]

The power of the Seville college resided partly in the dense family and re- lational network of its procurators, particularly their siblings. The brothers Villar—Lorenzo, Juan, and Andrés—originated from Oñate, a small town in Guipúzcoa.[90] Andrés was only fifteen when he became procurator for the San Luis novitiate in Seville, where he learnt how to handle accounts, before en- tering San Hermenegildo in 1632. A procuracy Andrés granted to Lorenzo in 1640 describes his brothers as "captains."[91] It was usual for sailors crossing the Atlantic to combine their merchant activities with the role of intermediary.[92] On his death, Juan bequeathed assets and sums due in New Spain and in New Granada. Lorenzo, for his part, settled in Veracruz, on the east coast of Mexico, in one of the most strategic ports in the *Carrera de Indias*. Grown rich through trade and the legacy of a wealthy American cousin, he purchased in 1646 the office of *alguazil* from the Holy Office of the Inquisition for Veracruz, and then for Mexico, completing his fine social ascent.[93] The interests of the San Herme- negildo Jesuits were thus closely bound up with those of procurators and their families, blurring the frontiers between the religious and the secular worlds. In this regard, the accusations brought by the college's superiors against Vil- lar, claiming his sole ambition was to "enrich his brothers, his relatives, in the

88   José Ramón Díaz Durana and Alfonso de Otazu, *El espíritu emprendedor de los vascos* (Madrid: Sílex, 2008).

89   Francesca Trivellato, *The Familiarity of Strangers: The Sephardic Diaspora, Livorno, and Cross-Cultural Trade in the Early Modern Period* (New Haven, CT: Yale University Press, 2009).

90   Juan Carlos de Guerra, *Ensayo de un padrón histórico de Guipuzca segun el orden de sus familias pobladoras* (San Sebastian: Joaquín Muñoz-Baroja de la primitiva casa Baroja, 1928), 606.

91   Archivo Histórico Provincial de Cadíz, Juan de Alcaudete, 1404, fol. 467–469.

92   Xabier Lamikiz, *Trade and Trust in the Eighteenth-Century Atlantic World: Spanish Merchants and their Overseas Networks* (Woodbridge, UK; Rochester, NY: The Boydell Press, 2010).

93   AHN, Inquisición, 1305, exp. 13.

purpose of changing his status,"[94] may seem cynical. Indeed, the affairs of the Villar brothers, and then of the Arechavalas family, were propitious for the college's trading operations and vice versa. From Seville, Andrés acted as his brother's representative (*apoderado*), receiving precious merchandise such as leather and Pernambuco wood from New Spain.[95] From Veracruz, where part of Mexico's riches transited, Lorenzo de Villar paid for orders placed by his brother. In a memorandum written after 1654, Andrés explained the reasons that had led him to delegate the sale of the college's cargoes to his brother in 1643: it was in no case a matter of misleading his hierarchy by using nominees, but of "profiting from [Lorenzo's] credit" to find purchasers at a time when the college's liquidity was drying up due to the delay of the fleet.[96] Lorenzo was used as a broker, providing "always good advice" to the Jesuits, according to his brother. This family setup continued once Domingo de Arechavala became procurator, as news of San Hermenegildo's bankruptcy was spreading. In 1646 and 1647, de Arechavala put his signature to letters of exchange, receipts, and payment orders on behalf of his brother, Bartolomé, a rich merchant in Bilbao whose business took him to Seville, Cadiz, and the Americas.[97]

This brief incursion into the Basque-dominated financial network of San Hermenegildo casts light on the Society of Jesus's financial brokers and sources of information. The secrecy surrounding their activities is not without heuristic consequences, and though they played decisive roles in colleges' business operations, they are not always easy to identify in the archives. This group of lawyers, transporters, sailors, traders, money changers, ships' captains, and officers of the king proves that the financial involvement of laypeople in favor of the Society was not restricted to pious donations. These individuals' assistance increased the volume of the college's business affairs, hence the solidity of its credit. From this perspective, the 1645 bankruptcy indicates the extent to which reputational issues were significant in the functioning of a college that had become a banking institution during the 1630s.

4   Credit and Banking Reputation

The expression "moral economy" is used by historians of the Ancien Régime involved in sifting carefully through the values guiding social, economic, and

---

94   AHN, Clero, Jesuitas, 218.
95   Aguado de los Reyes, "Negocios de sotanas," 55–76.
96   BUG, Fondo antiguo, *Don Andrés de Villar* ... (1653).
97   AHN, Clero, Jesuita, 157.

political life.[98] An anthropology of these old societies would no doubt distil from this list a quintessence based on the principles of honor, loyalty, faith, and trust. The polysemous notion of credit lies at the intersection of these concepts expressing social, religious, and economic phenomena. It is equally useful for apprehending the complex assemblage of relations and obligations structuring the societies—based on family, corporative, and clientelist ties— and for understanding how the societies dealt with the instability of economic markets and uncertainties of trade. On this point, lack of liquidity and weak banking institutions led to the very extensive use of credit and a diversification of sources of money supply, such as pawning foodstuffs, granaries, and turning to merchants who bought gold and silver.[99] From peasants borrowing seed to aristocrats *achetant à terme*, everybody used such means to defer payments. Though banks operating under royal license had supported the Seville economy in the sixteenth century, none remained after 1610.[100] It was in this context that San Hermenegildo developed banking services offered to Sevillians, to the extent that its creditors described the college as a "private bank."[101] The visibility of its resources and the trust the population placed in an institution toiling for the common good—through its preaching, education of the young, and evangelization of slaves—explains the increase in its credit until the 1642 downturn. There were three areas to the college's banking activities: loans, borrowing against remuneration, and financial intermediation.

Religious institutions in the Spanish Empire played an essential role in the circulation and provision of capital.[102] Convents, cathedral chapters, parish churches, and brotherhoods had supported the expansion of the main long-term credit instrument, mortgage-backed loans, known as *censos*. San Hermenegildo was no exception, and held over a dozen in 1632.[103] But the financial pull exerted by the college also enabled it to grant short-term loans, with Jesuits being the main beneficiaries. In the seventeenth century, the Society had six houses just in Seville—San Hermenegildo, the professed house, the English College, the novitiate, the Irish seminary, and the Concepción seminary[104]—and

---

98   Laurence Fontaine, *L'économie morale, Pauvreté, crédit et confiance dans l'Europe préindustrielle* (Paris: Gallimard, 1993).

99   Felipe Ruiz Martín, *La banca en España hasta 1782* (Pamplona: Urgoiti Editores, 2016).

100   Carlos Álvarez Nogal, "Los bancos públicos de Agustín y Julio Spinola en la Corte y Sevilla entre 1602 y 1610," in *Las instituciones económicas*, 223–58.

101   AHN, Clero, Jesuita, 218.

102   José Antonio Álvarez Vázquez, *Rentas, precios y crédito en Zamora en el Antiguo Régimen* (Zamora: Colegio Universitario, 1987).

103   AHN, Clero, Jesuitas, 157.

104   Diego Ortiz de Zúñiga, *Anales eclesiásticos y seculares de la muy noble y muy leal ciudad de Sevilla, t. V* (Seville: Imprenta real, 1796), 51–52.

Andalusia was home to forty Jesuit colleges at the time.[105] In 1645, San Hermenegildo lent nearly 5,000 ducats to the Santiago de Cadiz college at an interest
rate of 5 percent.[106] According to Andrés de Villar, all the colleges and novi-
tiates in Andalusia "benefited from the wealth of San Hermenegildo," whither
their representatives came to procure money to conduct their missions. Solidarity between Jesuits did not simply facilitate internal loans. In 1645, de Villar's
accounts show that 25,000 ducats were lent to private individuals. In 1658, the
procurator for the Indies was accused of buying and selling silver and gold in
the college store.[107] The charge was dismissed, but showed that its banking reputation persisted several years after its bankruptcy.

The college's volume of accumulated debt in 1645—450,000 ducats—is
testament to its borrowing capacity. Estimates based on meticulous work in
notarial archives by Jesús Aguado de los Reyes are revealing: for the period
1632–1645, he has identified 235 loans for a total of 51,426,025 silver maravedis
and 99,242,904 billon maravedis. He draws attention to Villar's responsibility
in the vicious circle of debt—in 1644, interest payments cost 88,000 ducats
per year.[108] Villar sought in vain to pay down old debts by concluding new
private loan agreements or renegotiating them against usurious rates of interest. Rather than discussing whether these choices were appropriate, what
matters here is to emphasize the trust the college inspired during these years
of crisis.

Examining lists of creditors gives a clearer picture of who they were and of
the spheres they issued from. The loans were taken out locally from Seville inhabitants. The San Hermenegildo estates on the outskirts of town were known
by all, and seemed to grant lenders security. The college capitalized on its ac-
ademic reputation: it was appreciated for the quality of its teachers, and the
oligarchy sent their children there, prior to attending university. The list of
creditors shows a significant proportion of women among the subscribers, accounting for half of lenders, such as Ana de Llamas, a widow who handed over
1,500 ducats in 1640, and Antonia de Ávila, a nun at the Santa Isabel convent.[109]
But we need to unravel the ties binding these women to members of the college if we are to avoid reductive explanations based on feminine devotion and
piety. As widows or nuns they knew how to use their financial autonomy by
placing their money where it was likely to generate the highest yield, with the

---

105   Soto Artuñedo, *Los Jesuitas en Andalucía*, 104.
106   AHN, Clero, Jesuitas 157.
107   RAH, 9-3617, fol. 215.
108   BNE, R, 38922 (18).
109   AHN, Clero, Jesuitas, 218.

promised rates of interest peaking at 16 percent.[110] At a time when the yield on censos and juros was being eroded, and their holders were running into difficulties in recovering payment, the prestige of San Hermenegildo enabled it to channel some of the money from disappointed savers. This moral and financial authority incited private individuals to entrust their assets portfolios to the ecclesiastics. Andrés de Villar had thus specialized in the recovery of arrears on juros, acting on behalf of powerful patriots such as Gregorio López de Mendizábal, a Castile councilor from Oñate.[111] Trust in the Jesuit institution thus conditioned the credit of San Hermenegildo. In 1651, Pedro de Salinas bitterly noted that the loss of trust had caused bankruptcy, "and it is hard to bear seeing that these quantities of money were lent to the Society due to the esteem and trust that [people] had in it, and that despite this confidence they neglected their assets."[112]

The image of the college had been tarnished by the publicity surrounding the scandal. The Jesuits thus unanimously viewed the purpose of the trial as restoring San Hermenegildo's credit, otherwise "the Society's closest friends and the most devout will take their distance, and deprive it of their gifts and alms."[113] On coming to the assistance of his fellow Jesuits after nine years of judicial proceedings, in 1654 Pedro de Fonseca summed up his mission in the following terms: "we resolved to first re-establish the credit and renown of this college, and of the Society, against the hurtful tongues and pens of Andrés de Villar and some creditors."[114] In this regard, the college's initial calculations had proved wrong. Faced with pamphlets by Villar and creditors, the Jesuits had initially cloaked themselves in silence. But as the provincial of Andalusia in person admitted, "these memoranda and pamphlets had spawned others which were equally scandalous and spread against the Society." Hard pressed, the college responded by waging war through ink and pen. Factums were liked by businesspeople, and were assimilable to instruments of credit, with writing being used as a weapon to strengthen or destroy reputations. By distributing them at their own expense "to ecclesiastics and dignitaries in the Republic of Seville," "by reproducing over 100 copies," and by disseminating them "throughout the kingdom," Villar and the creditors had managed to discredit the Society by giving the affair a political significance.[115] In Oñate, in the

---

110   AHN, Clero, Jesuitas, 218.
111   Aguado de los Reyes, "Negocios de sotanas," 55–76.
112   Domínguez Ortiz, "La Procuraduría de Indias," 311–30.
113   BNE, VE, 1408–34–1, Memorial que se dio a S.M.
114   AHN, Clero, Jesuitas, 218.
115   AHN, Clero, Jesuita, 218.

Basque country, the superior of the Jesuit college admitted in 1654 that he was defeated: "[T]his country is narrow and the people enjoy seeing the fathers of the Society mocked and vanquished."[116] In sharp contrast, attempts by the Jesuits to cleanse their good name by discrediting de Villar and his brothers— accused of having fraudulently enriched themselves—had fallen flat.[117]

Although San Hermenegildo managed to retain its assets at the issue of the trial, the symbolic cost of the trial was considerable, and there was no doubt it had lost the communication battle for public opinion. The pen of Onofre y Salazar had wrought devastation, and his attacks had been extensively relayed. His many stylistic effects sought to elicit the reader's commiseration and iden- tification. The Jesuits had set upon the most vulnerable inhabitants: "defense- less widows," "women separated from their husbands," "orphans," "girls," "nuns expelled [from their order]," "despairing nobles." From a theological point of view, failure to pay a debt, usury, and profiting from illicit trade were among the gravest of sins. These moral failings were the indirect expression of the Jesuits' *avaritia*, as crystallized in details that creditors repeated with relish, such as the *jeu de paume* court purchased from the Duke of Medina Sidonia for 5,000 ducats. The discursive strategy consisted in suggesting that Jesuits used it for recreational purposes, in contradiction with their status, while the latter assert- ed that it had been acquired so as to put an end to the cries of players disturbing the reading of mass. Thus, the Society's enemies' stragegy to inflict reputational bankruptcy' on the College was based on both moral and juridical arguments emphazising accounting fraud, usurious interest and wilful misconduct.

In the middle of the sixteenth century, the Dominican theologian Tomás de Mercado (1525–1575) condemned the abuses of interest-bearing loans, which, to his mind, were damaging the *Carrera de Indias* by inflating the price of mer- chandise and ruining lenders.[118] In the seventeenth century, *arbitrista* literature took up as one of its favorite themes the extraction of gold and silver outside Spain. Gold from the Indies enriched foreign manufactures and impoverished Spaniards, who were unable to abandon their rentier mentality and were proud of living on credit. These *topoi* retain a certain topicality in the historiography, despite studies, which through a combination of various methods—case stud- ies, pragmatic approaches focusing on the role of agency, biographical prisms, etc.—set out an alternative account of the Spanish seventeenth century, viewed less in terms of declinism. By seeking to link up local and global scales and priv- ileging an interactional approach to the Society's financial intermediaries and

---

116   AHN, Clero, Jesuita, 218.
117   AHN, Clero, Jesuita, 218.
118   Tomás de Mercado, *Suma de tratos y contratos* (Salamanca, 1569).

actors, this paper has analyzed how the San Hermenegildo college turned itself into the centerpiece of the Society of Jesus's financial system.

Viewed in the light of the college's sensational bankruptcy, de Mercado's harsh judgements on the noxious influence of credit may seem legitimate. However, this chapter has shown that the Jesuits took on debt in response to a rational economic program: improving the productive capacity and yield of their lands, exporting some of their produce to the Indies, and recapitalizing their landholdings thanks to the produce of a circular economy between Andalusia and the American territories. Sevillians' capital, rather than being immobilized, was dynamizing local and more distant markets. These conclusions tie in with theses highlighting the Society's financial and administrative skills and its role in driving the process of Iberian globalization. It is important to be clear about their scope. By pooling its resources with those of the procurator for the Indies, the college placed itself at the heart of a remarkable communications setup. The information sent to it by the dense network of European and American correspondents was supplemented by that transiting via the financial intermediaries of the Basque procurators and by agents in Rome. By concentrating monetary, commercial, and agricultural flows, the college could display the extent of its wealth. This situation confronted it with a difficult circle to square. While the visibility of its wealth secured the confidence of lenders, at the same time it fed feelings of resentment and jealousy at its economic might. In this respect, the financial bankruptcy of San Hermenegildo was primarily the result of its reputational bankruptcy.

Bibliography

Primary Sources

Biblioteca Nacional de España [BNE], VE, 1408–34–1; R, 38922 (18); Porcones, 489-6.

Biblioteca Universitaria de Granada [BUG], Fondo antiguo, siglo XVII, Caja 040 and *don Andrés de Villar.*

Biblioteca Universitaria de Sevilla [BUS], Fondo antiguo, A 109/088(27).

Real Academia de la Historia [RAH], 9-3617.

Archivo Histórico Nacional [AHN], Clero, Jesuitas 157 and 218; Inquisición 1305.

Archivo Histórico Provincial de Cádiz, 1404.

Anonymous. *Les jésuites, marchands, usuriers, usurpateurs et leurs cruautés dans l'ancien et le nouveau continent.* La Haye: chez les frères Vaillant, 1759.

Carta del venerable siervo de Dios Juan de Palafox y Mendoza al sumo Pontífice Inocencio X, Puebla de los Angeles, January 8, 1649. Madrid: Imprenta de D. Gabriel Ramirez, 1768.

Mercado, Tomás de. *Suma de tratos y contratos*. Salamanca, 1569.

Ortiz de Zúñiga, Diego. *Anales eclesiásticos y seculares de la muy noble y muy leal ciudad de Sevilla, t. V*. Seville: Imprenta real, 1796.

Pascal, Blaise. *Œuvres*, vol. III. La Haye: chez Detune, 1779.

Secondary Sources

Aguado de los Reyes, Jesús. "Negocios de sotanas: los jesuitas y el mercado financie-ro sevillano en la primera mitad del siglo XVII." In *La Companía de Jesús en España: otra mirada*, edited by Joaquín Morales Ferrer and Agustín Galán García, 55–76. Madrid: Anaya, 2007.

Alden, Dauril. *The Making of an Enterprise: The Society of Jesus in Portugal, its Empire, and Beyond, 1540–1750*. Stanford, CA: Stanford University Press, 1996.

Álvarez Vázquez, José Antonio. *Rentas, precios y crédito en Zamora en el Antiguo Régimen*. Zamora: Colegio Universitario, 1987.

Astrain, Antonio. *Historia de la Compañía de Jesús en la asistencia de España*, vol. 5. Madrid: Administración de razón y fe, 1912.

Bauer, Arnold. "The Church in the Economy of Spanish America: Censos y Depósitos in the Eighteenth and Nineteenth Centuries." *The Hispanic American Historical Review* 63, no. 4 (1983): 707–33.

Bautier, Robert-Henri. "'Clercs mécaniques' et 'clercs marchands' dans la France du XIIIe siècle." *Comptes rendus des séances de l'Académie des Inscriptions et Belles-Lettres* 125, no. 2 (1981): 209–42.

Boumediene, Samir. *La colonisation du savoir, Une histoire des plantes médicinales du "Nouveau Monde" (1492–1750)*. Vaulx-en-Velin: Éditions des Mondes à faire, 2016.

Boxer, Charles R. *Portuguese India in the Mid-Seventeenth Century*. New Delhi: Oxford University Press, 1980.

Burns, Kathryn. *Convents and the Spiritual Economy of Cuzco, Peru*. Durham, NC; London: Duke University Press, 1999.

Chevalier, François. *La formation des grands domaines au Mexique: terre et société aux XVIe-XVIIe siècles*. Paris, Institut d'ethnologie, 1952.

Clossey, Luke. *Salvation and Globalization in the Early Jesuit Missions*. Cambridge: Cambridge University Press, 2008.

Cortes Peña, Antonio. "La quiebra del colegio de San Hermenegildo." In *Actas de las II Jornadas de Metodología y Didáctica de la Historia*, 191–202. Cáceres: Universidad de Extremadura, 1983.

Cushner, Nicholas. *Farm and Factory: The Jesuit and the Developement of Agrarian Capitalism in Colonial Quito, 1600–1767*. Albany, NY: State University of New York Press, 1982.

Dial, Andrew. "The 'Lavalette Affair': Jesuits and Money in the French Atlantic." PhD Diss., McGill University, 2018.

Díaz Blanco, José Manuel. *Así trocaste tu gloria: guerra y comercio colonial en la España del siglo XVII.* Valladolid: Instituto Universitario de Historia Simancas, Marcial Pons 2012.

Domínguez Ortiz, Antonio. "Los caudales de Indias y la política exterior de Felipe IV." In *Estudios Americanistas,* 29–116. Madrid: Real Academia de Historia, 1998.

Fechner, Fabián. "Las tierras incógnitas de la administración jesuita: toma de decisiones, gremios consultivos y evolución de normas." *Historica* 38, no. 2 (2014): 11–42.

Fontaine, Laurence. *L'économie morale, Pauvreté, crédit et confiance dans l'Europe préindustrielle.* Paris: Gallimard, 1993.

Friedrich, Markus. " 'Government in India and Japen is Different from Government in Europe': Asian Jesuits on Infrastructure. Homogeneity of Administrative Space, and the Possibilities for a Global Management of Power." *Journal of Jesuit Studies* 4, no. 1 (2017): 1–27.

García Fuentes, Lutgardo. "Los vascos en la carrera de Indias en la edad moderna: una minoría dominante." *Temas americanistas* 16 (2003): 29–49.

Grenier, Pierre-Yves. *L'économie de l'Ancien Régime, un monde de l'échange et de l'incertitude.* Paris: Albin Michel, 1996.

Guasti, Niccolò, ed. *I patrimoni dei gesuiti nell'Italia moderna: una prospettiva comparativa.* Bari: Edipuglia, 2013.

Lamikiz, Xabier. *Trade and Trust in the Eighteenth-Century Atlantic World: Spanish Merchants and their Overseas Networks.* Woodbridge, UK; Rochester, NY: The Boydell Press, 2010.

Lamikiz, Xabier. "Basques in the Atlantic World, 1450–1824." In *Oxford Research Encyclopedia of Latin American History,* 2017, Doi: 10.1093.

Landi, Fiorenzo. *Accumulation and Dissolution of Large Estates of the Regular Clergy in the Early Modern Europe.* Rimini: Guaraldi, 1999.

Lanza García, Ramón, ed. *Las instituciones económicas, las finanzas públicas y el declive de España en la Edad moderna.* Madrid: UAM ediciones, 2018.

López, Martínez and Antonio Luis. *La Economía de las órdenes religiosas en el Antiguo Régimen. Sus propiedades y rentas en el reino de Sevilla.* Seville: Excma. Diputación Provincial de Sevilla, 1992.

Lozano Navarro, Julián J. "El dinero de los jesuitas: una aproximación a la realidad económica del colegio de Marchena (Sevilla). Siglos XVI–XVIII." *Krypton* 4 (2014): 12–23.

Malaprade, Sébastien. *Des châteaux en Espagne, gouvernement des finances et mobilité sociale au XVIIe siècle.* Limoges: Pulim, 2018.

Maldavsky, Aliocha and Roberto Di Stefano, ed. *Invertir en lo sagrado: salvación y dominación territorial en América y Europa (siglos XVI-XX).* Santa Rosa: EdUNLPam, 2018.

Marcos Martín, Alberto. "Deuda pública, mercado crediticio y actividades económicas en la Castilla del siglo XVII." *Hispania* 243 (2013): 133–60.

234

MALAPRADE

Martínez-Serna, J. Gabriel. "Procurators and the Making of the Jesuit Atlantic Network." In *Soundings in Atlantic History: Latent Structures and Intellectual Currents, 1500–1830*, edited by Bernard Bailyn and Patricia L. Denault, 181–209. Cambridge, MA; London: Harvard University Press, 2011.

Ramón Díaz Durana, José and Alfonso De Otazu. *El espíritu emprendedor de los vascos*. Madrid: Sílex, 2008.

Riley, James D. "The Wealth of the Jesuits' in Mexico, 1670–1767." *The Americas* 33, no. 2 (1976): 226–66.

Ruiz Martín, Felipe. *La banca en España hasta 1782*. Pamplona: Urgoiti Editores, 2016.

Soto Artuñedo, Wenceslao. *Los Jesuitas en Andalucía, estudios conmemorativos del 450 aniversario de la fundación de la provincia*. Granada: Facultad de Teología de Granada, 2007.

Todeschini, Giacomo. *Richesses franciscaines. De la pauvreté volontaire à la société de marché*. Paris: Verdier, 2008.

Todeschini, Giacomo. *Les Marchands et le Temple, La société chrétienne et le cercle vertueux de la richesse du Moyen Âge à l'époque moderne*. Paris: Albin Michel, 2017.

Torres Muñoz, Ricardo. "La quiebra del colegio San Hermenegildo de Sevilla. Aproximación a un concurso en la España del siglo XVII." In *Estudios sobre la ley concursal, libro homenaje a Manuel Olivencia*, 523–38. Madrid; Barcelona: Marcial Pons, 2005.

Trivellato, Francesca. *The Familiarity of Strangers: The Sephardic Diaspora, Livorno, and Cross-Cultural Trade in the Early Modern Period*. New Haven, CT: Yale University Press, 2009.

Urani Montiel, Carlos. "Procuradores jesuitas y mercados en conflicto: el caso de Felipe del Castillo de la Misión de Moxos (1737)." *Anuario de estudios bolivianos, archivísticos y bibliográficos* 18 (2012): 203–31.

Vermote, Fred. "Finances of the Missions." In *A Companion to Early Modern Catholic Global Missions*, edited by Ronnie Po-Chia Hsia, 367–400. Leiden; Boston: Brill, 2018.

Vermote, Frederik. "Financing Jesuit Mission." In *The Oxford Handbook of Jesuits*, edited by Inès G. Županov, 128–49. New York: Oxford University Press, 2019.

Vismara, Paola. "Les jésuites et la morale économique." *Dix-septième siècle* 4 (2007): 739–54.

Von Wobeser, Gisela. *El crédito eclesiástico en la Nueva España, siglo XVIII*. Mexico: Fondo de cultura económica, 2010.

Zubillaga, Félix. "El procurador de las Indias occidentales de la compañía de Jesús." *Archivum Historicum Societatis Iesu* 22 (1953): 367–417.

PART 4

Moralizing the Economy: Religious
Controversies and Debates

∴

CHAPTER 10

Missionaries as Merchants and Mercenaries

Religious Controversies over Commerce in Southeast Asia

Tara Alberts

1　Introduction: Funding the Missions

In 1666, missionary Jacques de Bourges (c.1634–1714) arrived back in France. He had been one of a group of French secular priests sent to found new missions in mainland Southeast Asia and in China. These missionaries were members of a new religious organization, the Société des Missions Étrangères de Paris (MEP), established in 1658. By 1660 three members of the society—Pierre Lambert de la Motte (1624–1679), François Pallu (1636–1684) and Ignace Cotolendi (1630–1662)—had been ordained in Rome as bishops and as vicars apostolic with wide-ranging authority over missions in East and Southeast Asia. Missionaries from a variety of religious orders—including Jesuits, Franciscans, Dominicans, Augustinians—already operated in these mission fields under Iberian patronage and authority. These new French missionaries, funded by patrons in Paris and Rome, and vested with authority by the papal Congregation of Propaganda Fide, represented a re-organization of the ecclesiastical landscape in Asia and a reform of the evangelical economy of salvation.[1]

In 1660 de Bourges had departed Marseilles with bishop Lambert de la Motte and fellow priest François Deydier (1634–1693), and had reached Siam (modern-day Thailand) after an arduous eighteen-month journey. After spending a year in the Siamese capital Ayutthaya, in 1663 de Bourges was sent back to Europe to report on the progress of the mission, and to seek advice and support from patrons in Paris and Rome. In particular, he was to present a sheaf of letters from the French bishops to the pope and the cardinals of the Propaganda Fide, reporting on several "difficulties" relating to the behaviour and

---

[1]　On the foundation of the MEP and their early missions, see especially Henri Chappoulie, *Aux origines d'une église: Rome et les missions d'Indochine au XVIIe siècle*, 2 vols (Paris: Bloud et Guy, 1943–1948); Jean Guennou, *Les Missions Étrangères* (Paris: Saint-Paul, 1963); Françoise Fauconnet-Buzelin, *Aux sources des Missions Étrangères: Pierre Lambert de la Motte 1624–1679* (Paris: Perrin, 2006) and Alain Forest, *Les missionnaires français au Tonkin et au Siam. Analyse comparée d'un relatif succès et d'un total échec,* 3 vols (Paris: L'Harmattan, 1998).

practices of the religious orders currently operating in the region. These were serious and urgent issues, he reported, as "abuses introduced into a country with Religion easily take on the force of custom."[2]

In Europe de Bourges also made a broader pitch for support, publishing a detailed account of the French mission to Siam: his *Relation du voyage de Monseigneur l'Evêque de Beryte*. First printed in Paris in 1666, this quickly went through several editions and was translated into Dutch and German.[3] De Bourges' narrative appealed to readers, and has been discussed by later scholars, as a travelogue—being the first French account of Siam—and as an example of a new genre of French missionary writing designed for the edification of a wide audience of pious lay men and women.[4] It was published at a time when the French public was hungry for new details of Catholic missions in the East. In the 1650s, wildly popular accounts by Jesuit Alexandre de Rhodes (1591–1660) of the missions in Tonkin and Cochinchina had fired up the imaginations of a generation of devout men and women, and had added impetus to the creation of a new French mission to Asia.[5] The first members and patrons of the MEP had heard de Rhodes' call; de Bourges' volume covered their response and thereby continued the story. It was also a polemic: part of the opening salvo in the war of words between the MEP and other missionary orders, in particular the Jesuits, over the governance and management of missionary work in Asia. Like most seventeenth-century mission accounts, Bourges' was speaking simultaneously to a number of audiences. It sought to move pious lay men and women to pray for the success of the mission; to inspire priests with the necessary vocation and ability to offer themselves as missionaries; and to win over the well-connected to pledge their time and influence to the service—and defense—of the MEP.

---

2 Jacques de Bourges, *Relation dv voyage de Monseigneur l'Evêque de Beryte, Vicaire Apostolique dv Royavme de la Cochinchine* (Paris: Denys Bechet, 1668; first published 1666), 8, 208.

3 Bourges, *Relation*. On value and significance of this account in history of Franco-Siamese relations, see Dirk Van De Cruysse, *Louis XVI et le Siam* (Paris: Fayard, 1991), 155ss. See also Donald F. Lach and Edwin J. Van Kley, *Asia in the Making of Europe, Vol. III: A Century of Advance. Book Three; Southeast Asia* (Chicago: University of Chicago Press, 1993), 143, 1186. Portions of Bourges' account have been translated into English by Michael Smithies, "Jacques de Bourges (c.1630–1714) and Siam," *Journal of the Siam Society* 81 (1991): 113–128.

4 See Jean Pierre Duteil, "Introduction," in Jacques de Bourges, *Relation du voyage de Mgr l'évêque de Béryte,* ed. Jean Pierre Duteil (Paris: Gérard Montfort, 2000), 1–14; Michael Harrigan, *Veiled Encounters. Representing the Orient in Seventeenth-century French Travel Literature* (Amsterdam: Editions Rodopi, 2008).

5 On the role of de Rhodes, see Adrien Launay, *Histoire générale de la Société des Missions Étrangères*. 3 vols (Paris: Téqui, 1894), 14–15; Fauconnet-Buselin, *Aux sources,* 60.

However, we can also read the text in another way. Against a backdrop of competition for funds and support between religious orders, we can read de Bourges' text—and other missionary accounts like it—as investment prospectuses. They were documents that knit together worldly and spiritual economies; that demonstrated how the pious reader could use the former in the service of the latter. Most importantly, they set out the religious society's distinctive spirituality that would underpin the success of the mission–and thus the spiritual "return" on donors' investments—while highlighting rivals' comparative unsuitability.

As an "investment prospectus," de Bourges' account is animated throughout by an illuminating tension. On the one hand, money is necessarily an important theme. Through detailed accounting, De Bourges makes clear that the project of spreading Christianity around the world is extremely costly, and vulnerable to changes in fortune and to catastrophe. Existing donors—and the precise value of their gifts—feature prominently. De Bourges begins and ends his voyage—and his book—visiting, praying with, and praising existing patrons of the mission: itemizing their donations, lauding their generosity and the "ardent and pure charity which animates them to procure the advancement" of the mission.[6] The security and effective management of donors' investments is also highlighted. De Bourges peppers his account with anecdotes which illustrate the missionaries' financial prudence, often in the form of advice to future missionaries to imitate or learn from the sensible conduct of these practical pioneers. Through their wise choices they were able to marshal their resources to reach their destination and begin efficiently converting donations into souls saved.

Yet behind the refrain of careful financial management we hear a second theme: of renunciation, abjection, and disregard for all things of the world. At times the two themes are almost discordant: de Bourges treads a fine line between expressing on the one hand the need for sufficient liquidity to provide for the mission and the capability of missionaries to manage effectively the logistics of the mission and, on the other, describing the missionaries' determination to eschew worldly concerns and to trust in providence. Money takes on a different color in this second theme. It is one of the many snares set by the devil to catch the unwary missionary and divert him from his path. Because this fundamental truth had been overlooked, grave errors had crept into the missions of Southeast Asia. De Bourges had returned to Europe in part to present testimony to Rome that other missionary groups had become fixated on

---

6 Bourges, *Relation,* 241.

things of the world, adopting unwise and sinful financial practices and turning from matters of the spirit to matters of commerce, accumulation, and profit maximization.

Through a close reading of texts like de Bourges', this chapter explores how missionaries marketed their spiritual lives in their pitches for support and investment from a pious European public. Histories of missionary finances, of the economics of evangelism and of conversion have been explored from a variety of angles by a number of scholars. A number of studies have provided crucial insights into the various sources and structures of missionary funding.[7] Historians of the Iberian empires have illuminated the complexities of funding missions through annual remittances.[8] A number of important works have elucidated the changing role and nature of *latifundia*—grants of large tracts of land—in the economics of global missions, from the *prazos* of Mozambique, to slave plantations of Brazil, to land and villages accumulated in South Asia.[9] Historians of mission in Southeast Asia have similarly considered how colonial and religious authorities experimented with new approaches to grants of land, labor and tribute rights—from the friar estates of the Philippines, to the fortress on Solor from which friars of the Dominican order profited from the sandalwood trade, to the villages in western India purchased by the Jesuits of the Province of Japan to finance their missions in Tonkin.[10] Recently Barbara

---

7   A detailed overview of recent historiography is given by Fred Vermote, "Finances of the Missions," in *A Companion to Early Modern Catholic Global Missions*, ed. Ronnie Po-Chia Hsia (Leiden: Brill, 2018), 367–400.

8   See for example George Bryan Souza, *The Survival of Empire: Portuguese Trade and Society in China and the South China Sea 1630–1754* (Cambridge: Cambridge University Press, 2004), 24; Isabel dos Guimarães Sá, "Ecclesiastical Structures and Religious Action," in *Portuguese Oceanic Expansion, 1400–1800*, ed. Francisco Bethencourt and Diogo Ramada Curto (Cambridge: Cambridge University Press, 2007), 255–82; Jorge M. Pedreira, "Costs and Financial Trends in the Portuguese Empire, 1415–1822," in Bethencourt and Curto, *Portuguese Oceanic Expansion,* 78–79; James C. Boyajian, *Portuguese Trade in Asia Under the Habsburgs, 1580–1640* (Baltimore, MD: Johns Hopkins University Press, 1993), 30; Catarina Madeira Santos, *"Goa é a chave de toda a Índia." Perfil político da capital do Estado da Índia (1505–1570)* (Lisbon: Comissão Nacional para as Comemorações dos Descobrimentos Portugueses, 1999).

9   For example, Nicholas P. Cushner, *Lords of the Land. Sugar, Wine and Jesuit Estates of Coastal Peru, 1600–1767* (New York: SUNY Press, 1980); Alden, *Making of an Enterprise,* 434–50; Anthony Disney, *History of Portugal and the Portuguese Empire,* vol. 2 (Cambridge: Cambridge University Press, 2006), 250–1, 361. Dauril Alden, "Some Considerations Concerning Jesuit Enterprises in Asia," in *A Companhia de Jesus e a missionação no Oriente*, ed. Nuno de Silva Gonçalves (Lisbon: Brotéria, 2000), 56. Souza, *Survival,* 24; Charles J. Borges, *The Economics of the Goa Jesuits, 1542–1759: An Explanation of Their Rise and Fall* (New Delhi: Concept Publishing Company, 1994). For the Japanese case, see Rômulo Ehalt's chapter in this volume.

10   On the friar estates, see Denis Morrow Roth, *The Friar Estates of the Philippines* (Albuquerque, NM: University of New Mexico Press, 1977). On Solor, see John Villiers, "As

Watson Andaya has offered an excellent comparative account of missionary economics in the Philippines and Indonesia.[11] The importance—and pitfalls—to all missionary orders of reliance on widening and shifting networks of lay donors in Europe and on the mission fields have been highlighted.[12] The key role of non-Christian donors has also been explored. Patronage from royal courts keen to establish trading links with European powers provided a foundation for the missions in Cambodia, Siam, Laos, and Tonkin, for example, where a number of missionaries obtained donations or pensions from royal courts on the strength of their knowledge of mathematics, astrology, medicine, engineering, and technologies such as clockwork and hydraulics.[13]

Such studies have highlighted the broader tensions and difficulties that each method of funding could create. Accumulation of land by religious orders, for example, was opposed by colonial authorities and others who condemned the superfluity and splendor of such holdings and cavilled against clerical exemption from tithes and taxes.[14] In Portuguese Melaka measures were taken at the beginning of the seventeenth century to prevent secular holdings being converted into ecclesiastical property without royal assent.[15] In the Philippines, friars' exploitation of the tribute system led to accusations of cruelty that rendered Christianity odious.[16]

---

derradeiras do mundo: The Dominican Missions and the Sandalwood Trade in the Lesser Sunda Islands in the Sixteenth and Seventeenth Centuries," in *Seminário Internacional de História Indo- Portuguesa, II Actas*, ed. Luís de Albuquerque and Inácio Guerreiro (Lisbon: IICT, 1985): 573–86; Leonard Andaya, "The 'Informal Portuguese Empire' and the Topasses in the Solor Archipelago and Timor in the Seventeenth and Eighteenth Centuries," *Journal of Southeast Asian Studies* 41 (2010): 391–440.

11   Barbara Watson Andaya, "Between Empires and Emporia: The Economics of Christianization in Early Modern Southeast Asia," *Journal of the Economic and Social History of the Orient* 53 (2010): 357–92.

12   See for example Luke Clossey, *Salvation and Globalization in the Early Jesuit Missions* (Cambridge: Cambridge University Press, 2008), 136–215; Catherine Marin, "Du refus d'un patronat royal à la française: un soutien du Roi et des Grands contrôlé," in *La Société des Missions Étrangères de Paris—350 ans à la rencontre de l'Asie (1658–2008)*, ed. Catherine Marin (Paris: Karthala, 2010), 81–94; Jean Guennou, *Les Missions Étrangères* (Paris: Saint-Paul, 1963), 57–60.

13   Alain Forest, *Les missions françaises*, vol. 2, 127; Tara Alberts, *Conflict and Conversion, Catholicism in Southeast Asia, 1500–1700* (Oxford: Oxford University Press, 2013), 107–109; and Tara Alberts, "Missions in Vietnam," in *A Companion to the Early Modern Catholic Global Missions*, ed. Ronnie Po-Chia Hsia (Leiden; Boston: Brill, 2018), 269–302.

14   Alden, *Making of an Enterprise*, 434–50; Alden, "Some Considerations," 61.

15   Manuel Teixeira, *Macau e a sua diocese, vol. 3* (Macau: Tipografia Soi Sang, 1956–1976), 101.

16   John Leddy Phelan, "Free versus Compulsory Labor: Mexico and the Philippines, 1540–1648," *Comparative Studies in Society and History* 1 (1959): 189–201; J. S. Cummins and

Distance from centers of ecclesiastical and colonial authority also inspired missionaries to experiment with a wide range of funding methods, many of which were immediately controversial. This was certainly the case in the scattered mission fields of Southeast Asia. Religious orders around Asia loaned out capital to converts (or indeed to non-Christians), ostensibly to save them from exorbitant rates of interest offered by other lenders, which may push them into debt bondage.[17] Between 1661 and 1670, the Jesuits in Siam loaned out capital of 9170 pardãos—obtained from legacies and other donations—at 10 percent.[18] François Pallu also suggested to the Propaganda Fide that French missionaries in Siam be permitted to loan capital at a limited interest rate as an alternative to engaging in commerce.[19] Of course, the question of whether money could ever be lent by Christians without committing the sin of usury had been hotly debated in Europe, not least given the development of pious credit organizations and pawnbrokers such as the *Montes Pietatis* in Italy.[20]

Few methods of raising or liquidizing sufficient funds were more controversial than missionary engagement in commerce.[21] This topic inspired particularly vehement denunciations and vicious polemic. Anxieties over this matter are threaded through de Bourges' narrative. Examining this issue, this chapter

---

Nicholas P. Cushner, "Labor in the Colonial Philippines: The *Discurso Parenetico* of Gomez de Espinosa," *Philippine Studies* 22 (1974): 117–48.

17   Souza, *Survival of Empire*, 24–25; Alden, *Making of an Enterprise*, 552–67.

18   Thomas Valguarnera, "Treslado do Titulo da Missaõ de Siao," Archivum Romanum Societatis Iesu [hereafter ARSI], *JapSin* 76, fol. 29.

19   "Cong.°," fol. 16.

20   As outlined in the 10th Session of the Fifth Lateran Council (1512–17). See Norman J. Tanner, *Decrees of the Ecumenical Councils,* Vol. 1 (London: Sheed & Ward, 1990), 625–27. On the development of the moral discourse concerning usury on the seventeenth-century missions see especially Paolo Vismara, "Les Jésuites et la morale économique," *Dix-septième siècle* 237 (2007): 739–54. See also Diego Quaglioni, Giacomo Todeschini, et Gian Maria Varanini (eds), *Credito e usura fra teologia, diritto e amministrazione : linguaggi a confronto, sec. XII-XVI* (Rome: École française de Rome, 2005) On the *Montes Pietatis* in Italy, see Ariane Boltanski's chapter in this volume.

21   See especially Andaya, "Between Empires and Emporia"; Henri Chappoulie, *Une controverse entre missionnaires à Siam au XVIIᵉ siècle. Le Religiosus negotiator du jésuite français J. Tissanier. Suivi de quelques documents concernant le commerce des clercs* (Paris: s. n., 1943); Dauril Alden, *The Making of an Enterprise: The Society of Jesus in Portugal, its Empire, and Beyond* (Stanford, CA: University of California Press, 1996); John Villiers, "Doing Business with the Infidel: Merchants, Missionaries and Monarchs in Sixteenth Century Southeast Asia," in *Maritime Asia: Profit Maximisation, Ethics and Trade Structures,* ed. Karl Anton Sprengard and Roderich Ptak (Wiesbaden: Harrassowitz Verlag, 1994), 160–70; Nicholas P. Cushner, "Merchants and Missionaries: A Theologian's View of Clerical Involvement in the Galleon Trade," *The Hispanic American Historical Review* 47 (1967): 360–69; Roth, *Friar Estates,* 83–85.

will unpack the intractable paradox at the heart of missionary discussions of financial issues: the unseemliness of concerns about, and engagement with, worldly matters by men tasked with spiritual conquest. Money and resources could take on new meanings depending on how they were acquired, and no method of funding missionary endeavor was practically or spiritually unproblematic. Tensions between different groups often resulted in every aspect of missionary behavior and organization being held up to intense and sometimes uncharitable scrutiny. The line between legitimate and inappropriate management of mission finance was subject to fierce dispute. In accounts such as de Bourges', the threads of material and spiritual economies are necessarily interwoven, creating an intriguing tension. Untangling these issues, this chapter illuminates how, out of debates over the probity and propriety of missionary behavior, a new rhetoric of missionary spirituality was forged. New religious societies of the seventeenth century such as the MEP thereby differentiated themselves from their rivals, and offered pious patrons a unique investment opportunity.

2 Missionary Accounts: Managing Money

Detailed narratives like de Bourges', or companion pieces like Pierre Duval's "Carte du voyage de Mr l'Evesque de Beryte" (illustration 10.1) made imaginable the voyage for which donations had paid or would pay. These representations made graphic the scale of the endeavor—the costs, the risks, the sheer globe-spanning magnitude even of the initial journey, let alone the difficult task of evangelizing. Over more than two hundred pages, de Bourges provides an exhaustive account of the missionaries' journey between Europe and their mission fields in the east, building a picture of the expense of sending a missionary to Southeast Asia, and of strategies used to make funds last. Allowing donors to travel along with the missionaries, de Bourges' narrative offers two assurances about investments entrusted to the MEP: that their management will always be financially and spiritually prudent.

Let us consider first the fiscal prudence of the missionaries as recounted by de Bourges. The profusion of detail in de Bourges' account provides a sense of pseudo-precision: as though almost every *sou* is accounted for, albeit in a confusing welter of prices and currencies.[22] We learn, for example, that the

---

22   De Bourges refers to a large number of currencies, but most often describes prices in terms of (French) écus and livres or (Spanish) pistoles and piastres. The relative value of French écus and livres fluctuated, from time to time fixed by royal edict. In this period an

ILLUSTRATION 10.1 Travel map of Bishop de Beryte to Cochinchina (1660–1662) in Pierre
                   Duval, *Carte du voyage de Mr. l'Evesque de Beryte, vicaire apostolique au
                   Royaume de la Cochinchine* (Paris: Pierre Duval, 1677)
                   REPRODUCED WITH PERMISSION OF THE BIBLIOTHÈQUE NATIONALE
                   DE FRANCE (PARIS)

missionaries spent a quarter *piastre* per animal-load to cross the Euphrates, two
piastres per head payable by all "Franks" (Christians) in Anah, and two *piastres*
per head as a city-fee at the gates of Bagdad.[23] Wherever possible the missionaries rely on the hospitality and charity of fellow Christians and others for accommodation and sustenance. Yet throughout the journey, costs mount: fees
to hire transport (a ship berth, a place on a caravan with animals and fodder);
wages for personnel (guards, guides, animal handlers, carters, muleteers, boat

---

écu was worth between three and six livres, and each livre could be divided into 20 sous.
The golden Spanish pistole (the term was also used in France for the gold Louis d'Or) and
the silver piastre (piece of eight) were widely used in international trade. A royal arrêt
of 1666 valued the pistole at 11 livres. See G.A. Valleyre, *Histoire des divers changemens et
mutations des monnoyes de France, ou leur valeur depuis 1666 jusqu'à present* (Paris: Claude
Cellier, 1705), 4–7. For comparison, in the 1660s in Paris the daily wage of a skilled mason
was around 40 sous per day, while a general laborer on a building site could often earn
around 16–20 sous per day. Micheline Baulant, "Le salaire des ouvriers du bâtiment à Paris
de 1400 à 1726," *Annales. Histoire. Sciences Sociales* 26 (1971): 478.

23   Bourges, *Relation,* 41–45; 60; 62.

crew, a "spokesman" [*un truchement*] or dragoman, interpreters); accommodation and subsistence along the way; and taxes, tolls, and customs charges.

De Bourges explains that he hopes that his account will assist those who follow, and to this end provides snatches of advice throughout. He notes which legs of the journey were reasonably priced, and those which were surprisingly expensive. Thus we hear that travel between Isfahan and Gomeron (Bandar Abbas) in Persia, cost only 10 piastres per head, while in Siam, river transport from the coast required three boats at 12 *écus* each, and travel passes at 10 *écus* each—a figure de Bourges found very high.[24] He highlights a number of incidental costs which required unplanned outlay: as they crossed Ottoman lands, for example, they felt obliged to win over "with various little presents" their Janissary guide, and to buy clothes to allow them to dress as "Turks."[25] He also warns of the costly consequences of accidents and misfortunes: a capsized riverboat in Siam, for example, resulted in the loss of their expensive travel passes, and incurred the costs of an extra journey back to Tenassarim (Tanintharyi, Myanmar) to replace them.[26]

Of course, God's favor and regard for the endeavor is revealed periodically, even in the minutiae of managing quotidian expenses. De Bourges often credits providence with allowing them to escape duty charges and taxes, for example. Thus they paid relatively little in custom charges at Bagdad, thanks to the intervention of the Topigi Bachi (Master of Ordnance) who was a Venetian Catholic and who under-valued their possessions.[27] In Corna (al-Qurnah), despite the assayers being "very strict," they escaped "by a particular assistance from God" as inspectors only inspected one box of books and another of church ornaments, and levied no charge.[28] However in Basra their "curiosities" were examined and valued at 500 piastres, which was, de Bourges consoled himself, "hardly much more than they had cost in Paris": they were obliged to pay 7.5 percent, he relates, which came to 37-and-a-half piastres.[29]

For the most part, however, de Bourges emphasizes the missionaries' canny and capable management of resources. He relates various stratagems to avoid custom duties. In Surat, for example, they escaped some duties after consulting with the commander of the Dutch factory.[30] Similarly, in Masulipatan they

---

24   Bourges, 32–35; 128, 131–6.

25   Bourges, 33, 43.

26   Bourges, 128, 131–36.

27   Bourges, 45. He valued what had cost over 400 écus in Paris at 100 écus.

28   Bourges, 45, 48.

29   Bourges, 49.

30   Bourges, 98.

borrowed a servant from the Dutch factory, which meant "we were taken for Dutchmen, and we avoided the customs fees," which were not payable by English or Dutch merchants.[31] In Mergui (Myeik in what is now Myanmar), the customs inspection cost the missionaries dearly due to their rosary beads, which were mistaken for coral, a material taxed at 8 percent. De Bourges advised future missionaries to sneak things through customs: "[T]hey do not search one's person, nor take any silver currency, and it isn't difficult ... to hide the little curiosities which one might bring from Europe to give as presents, which one is obliged to do on many occasions."[32]

De Bourges also warns missionaries to pay close attention to exchange rates and local currency markets. His account is littered with references to the price of specie. It is possible for the wise traveler to save "more than the expense of their voyage from Europe" through awareness of such things.[33] For example, the advice the missionaries had received in France to take Spanish pistolles had proven mistaken: they lost 10 sols per pistolle in Aleppo and Basra and around 23 sols 6 derniers per pistolle in Persia due to the low price of gold there.[34] Instead, he recommends, in terms of silver currency, Spanish piastres (from Spain, not Peru, which were of a poor alloy) are the most useful coinage to take. These pass for écus in Alexandrette, Aleppo, and Bagdad, but are weighed more exactly in Basra, meaning a profit of 7–8 percent could be made on them in the first three cities, and 10–12 percent in Basra. A *louis d'or* in the latter city would also net a profit of 10 percent. Of gold coins, Venetian and Hungarian sequins were profitable—coins costing 6 livres 3 sols in Lyon sold for a profit at up to 7 livres 10 sols in Aleppo and Basra.[35]

This attention to currency markets should continue in the mission fields. Once in "the Indies," the value of one's gold can fluctuate radically, he reports. In Masulipatan the missionaries made 12 sols on each pistolle and could have made more if they had changed écus d'or, *lys de France* or *sequins* of Venice.[36] Gold was worth around 30 sols per pistolle less in Siam than in the rest of the Indies, while in Tonkin and Cochinchina the value was also dropping due to a recent increase in the import of gold from China and Manila. "And so one should dispose of whatever one has of gold, and change it into the coin of the country," de Bourges recommends.[37] "One can find Siamese silver in Masulipatan, of the

---

31   Bourges, 114.
32   Bourges, 127.
33   Bourges, 62.
34   Bourges, 62, 88, 101.
35   Bourges, 61–62.
36   Bourges, 113.
37   Bourges, 212.

same alloy as that in the Indies, without any further expense to change it. It is very strongly recommended that you take this opportunity, because the norm is to give five percent in Siam."[38]

It is unwise to load oneself down with silver, however. De Bourges advises that the most useful items to bring on the voyage, "especially by laymen [i.e. secular auxiliaries] who can, when the opportunity presents itself, trade and sell them, are the most brilliant yellow amber, and the largest and most vermillion coral, because European coins are not marketable." These materials can be hidden from customs agents in a saddlebag or valise. De Bourges also advises missionaries to bring a few "good watches," which can be sold for a decent price in Persia: "this type of minor trade (*petit commerce*) being necessary to obtain more easily and as required the currency of the country."[39]

This practical money management allows the missionaries to reach their destination despite many obstacles. Yet the real guarantee of the success of the mission is in their piety and disinterest. For all the pragmatism of de Bourges' account, he emphasized the priests' pious detachment from the world and submission to God's will. There were important limits to their resource-maximization practices. In the busy trading port of Masulipatan, for example, de Bourges and his companions had been advised to entrust their silver to certain merchants who would guarantee a return of 35 percent, payable in Tenasserim. They demurred, which proved a wise decision, prompting Bourges to intone that "it is always remiss for an Evangelical Worker to accept anything that does not come to him via permitted routes, and about which there is any suspicion of being less than pure and not in conformity with the sanctity of his condition."[40] Reflecting on the nature of commerce in general, de Bourges notes that foreigners in Masulipatan suffer terribly, "seized by a dysentery or a flux, caused by the bad water one drinks there," and tormented by the terrible heat.[41] "And thus God wished to make merchants pay dearly," he concludes primly, "for the riches they seek in foreign lands, and to combat the extreme ardor which they have for profit by other extreme arduousness, as it is clear to see that in the places in which Europeans are the most keen to practice their commerce, it is there that the heat is the most insupportable."[42]

Missionary writers like de Bourges were participating in an ongoing project of describing and creating a normative framework to fashion the ideal

---

38   Bourges, 212–13.
39   Bourges, 61, 89.
40   Bourges, 119.
41   Bourges, 116.
42   Bourges, 117.

evangelist. Along the way they were also contributing to a growing literature that described the nature and consequences of commerce, and the "spirit" of the merchant, in an age of increasing global trade. In France, new rhetorics of profit maximization, interest, and advantage were developing as new commercial companies were founded and sought investors.[43] Subtle and complex intellectual analyses of the nature of profit-seeking, wealth, and associated sins such as avarice developed, introducing ambivalence to definitions and discussions of such matters.[44]

3   Controversies over Commerce

As we turn to consider these questions of commerce in more detail, we see how, in many of their interventions on this matter, the MEP pledged a new way of proceeding. Indeed, their guarantee of spiritual profit lay in the inversion of the usual interests of worldly investors in commercial enterprises. Thus de Bourges makes a clear distinction between the profit-hunger and mercenary motives of the merchants on the one hand, and the MEP missionaries who were soldiers of Christ on the other. Merchants and their commercial activities belonged to a separate, incommensurate sphere from that of clerics; the "ardor" of merchants for worldly wealth contrasted with the MEP missionaries' scorn for the same. The return on patrons' investment—the souls saved and good works accomplished—were guaranteed by the MEP missionaries attention to these distinctions.

As we can see from de Bourges' account, the realities of the mission field obliged missionaries to articulate exactly what commerce *was* and what fundamental aspects of the endeavor either made it inimical to the priestly state, or else permitted in certain circumstances. Where did the line fall between bartering and currency trading of the sort recommended by de Bourges and his companions, and scandalous speculation?

---

43   See especially Andrea Finkelstein, *The Grammar of Profit: The Price Revolution in Intellectual Context* (Leiden; Boston: Brill, 2006); Elisabeth Heijmans, *The Agency of Empire: Connections and Strategies in French Overseas Expansion (1686–1746)* (Leiden; Boston: Brill, 2020).

44   See especially Nannerl O. Keohane, *Philosophy and the State in France. The Renaissance to the Enlightenment* (Princeton: Princeton University Press, 1980), 161–63; Mathieu de la Gorce, "Blâme et éloge de l'avarice dans le *Livre des marchans*," *Seizième Siècle* 4 (2008): 89–112; Jonathan Patterson, *Representing Avarice in Late Renaissance France* (Oxford: Oxford University Press, 2015); Henry C. Clark, "Commerce, the Virtues, and the Public Sphere in Early-Seventeenth-Century France," *French Historical Studies* 21 (1998): 415–40.

According to many theologians, ecclesiasts were numbered alongside nobles and soldiers as categories of people whose position precluded involvement in trade.[45] In 394, St. Jerome (347–420) set out the duties of a cleric in
a letter to Nepotian, who had recently taken holy orders. He urged him to flee
"like the plague" clergymen who engaged in business. By engaging in commerce, such a man had chosen to turn away from the poverty of the cross. To
fraternize with him would be corrupting: "You despise gold; he loves it. You
spurn wealth; he eagerly pursues it. You love silence, meekness, privacy; he
takes delight in talking and effrontery, in squares, and streets, and apothecar-
ies' shops."[46] Injunctions against clerical engagement in trade proliferated in
the medieval Church. Alexander III (1159–1181), for example, prohibited clerics from engaging in commerce for the sake of profit (*causa lucri*) under pain
of excommunication.[47] Behind such injunctions lay the understanding, later
clearly articulated by Thomas Aquinas (1225–1274), that "certain occupations
are so inconsistent with one another, that they cannot be fittingly exercised
together. Human Laws, for example, forbid soldiers whose business it is to fight
to engage in commerce. ... [C]ommercial enterprises are forbidden to clerics,
since they entangle the soul too much. *No man being a soldier to God entangles
himself with secular business.*"[48]

By the sixteenth century, canon law to some commentators seemed very
clear: it was not legitimate for priests to engage in commerce—an action several jurists had defined as "buying a commodity with the intention of selling
it again unchanged and gaining from the transaction."[49] The Council of Trent
re-affirmed all previous decrees about clerics "fleeing worldly commerce" (*sae-
cularibus negotiis fugiendis*).[50] Further injunctions reiterated these points: in

---

45   Giovanni Vignali, *Comento su le leggi di eccezione per gli affari di commercio messe in
      relazione tra la loro tuttel le leggi di commercio degil stati d'Italia non che delle parti più
      colte di Europa, vol. 1* (Naples: Vico Figurari, 1855), 204.

46   St. Jerome to Nepotian (Letter LII) in Philip Schaff and Henry Wace, ed., *Nicene and Post-
      Nicene Fathers, Second Series, Vol. VI—Jerome: Letters and Select Works* (New York: Cosimo,
      2007), 91. For broader context, see especially William Bright, *The Canons of the First Four
      General Councils of Nicaea, Constantinople, Ephesus and Chalcedon: with Notes,* 2nd ed.
      (Oxford: Clarendon Press, 1892), 149–52.

47   Vignali, *Comento,* 204.

48   Thomas Aquinas, *Summa Theologica, vol. 35 (2a2ae. 34–46) Consequences of Charity,* ed.
      Thomas R. Heath (London: Blackfriars, 1972): 87.

49   They were, however, permitted to sell items that they had made or improved. Alden,
      Making of an Enterprise, 529 fn. 2. On the complex definition of commerce and trade see
      J. Dede, "Business Pursuits of Clerics and Religious: Further Considerations," *The Jurist* 23
      (1963): 50–60.

50   Council of Trent, Session 22, canon 1. Tanner, *Decrees* II, 738.

1563, for example, Pius IV issued a Brief explicitly forbidding all Portuguese ecclesiasts from engaging in trade.[51]

However, this was far from the end of the matter. Commerce and religious conversion were closely intertwined in Southeast Asia. The trade winds tended to bring new gods as well as new commodities and business opportunities. The spread of Islam, Christianity, and movements of Buddhist reform were facilitated by trade.[52] From the beginning, there was an intimate connection between trade and religion in the Iberian empires. Indeed, one Dominican treatise, setting out the Portuguese crown's title to exclusive jurisdiction over Southeast Asian missions, listed commerce as one of the grounds that permitted the Portuguese to establish churches: where the king had no temporal power or bishops, he had patronage rights "by reason of conquest, discovery, and commerce."[53] The interests of merchants and missionaries were often interdependent: "souls and revenue down one path" (*de um caminho ganhar almas e fazenda*), or as Jesuit Antonio Vieira put it, "The preachers take the Gospel and the merchants take the preachers."[54] Missionaries knew that their reports would be mined for information about local markets and commercial opportunities, and often became deeply embroiled in commercial interests. Despite their professed distaste for trade, the missionaries of the Missions Étrangères did not escape this interdependency: later, in return for free passage on the ships of the newly formed Compagnie des Indes Orientales, they would be expected to provide useful intelligence. Indeed, many of their investors and patrons, members of the Compagnie du Saint Sacrement,

---

51   "Bolle Pontificie sul Patronato della corona di Portogallo nelle Indie," Archivio Segreto Vaticano [hereafter ASV] *Archivio della nunziatura apostolica*: Divisoni I. Sezione 1°: fol. 69.

52   See Anthony Reid, *Southeast Asia in the Age of Commerce, 1450–1680. Vol. Two: Expansion and Crisis* (New Haven, CT and London: Yale University Press, 1993), 132–201.

53   Untitled account of the Portuguese Empire, around 1651, Archivum Generalis Ordinis Prædicatorum, *XIII.56900.2:* fol. 42. Numerous individual countries between India and China, including Siam, are listed and Portugal's claim to influence is similarly defined: "In Omnibus istis Regnis habent Lusitani comercium": fol. 7. See also Malyn Newitt, "Formal and Informal Empire in the History of Portuguese Expansion," *Portuguese Studies* 17 (2001): 1–21; Andaya, "Between Empires and Emporia."

54   The first quote is used by John Villiers as the title of his article, "De um caminho ganhar almas e fazenda: Motives of Portuguese Expansion in Eastern Indonesia in the Sixteenth Century," *Terrae Incognitae* 14 (1982): 23–39; Vieira is cited in Glen J. Ames, *Renascent Empire? The House of Braganza and the Quest for Stability in Portuguese Monsoon Asia, c. 1640–1683* (Amsterdam: Amsterdam University Press, 2000), 59.

were also closely involved in the establishment of this French commercial enterprise.[55]

Most religious orders made use of lay adjuncts to trade and handle money on their behalf, leading in some cases to internal disputes about the relationship between the revenues of the order and vows of apostolic poverty. By necessity, whatever their theological bent, most missionary orders developed complex networks of exchange on a global level. Studies by Charles J. Borges, Nicholas P. Cushner, and Dauril Alden have uncovered the systems developed by the Jesuits to facilitate the flow of resources, specie, materials, and manpower.[56] Other orders also relied on complex economic networks, as recent research has begun to illuminate.[57]

Responding to the complexities and difficulties of sustaining missionary work in distant lands, missionaries and canon lawyers tested the boundaries of injunctions against clerical trade. The definition of "commerce" was explored, and the soundness of the rule against it was examined against the realities of the mission field. Francis Xavier, for example, suggested that cloth bought in Bassein could be sold licitly for fivefold profit in the Moluccas to fund a mission there.[58] Similarly, Alessandro Valignano argued that trade for the sake of charity, to save so many souls, "is not trade, nor commerce" (*nao he mercancia, nà negoceacão*).[59] Jesuits in Japan came to depend on trading silk, which had been authorized by Pope Gregory XIII (Ugo Boncompagni, p. 1572–1585), as long as this was only in order to raise enough money to live.[60] Alternative funds—6,000 cruzados from the pope and promised revenues from the King of Spain and from remittances from Bassein and Melaka—proved insufficient

55   On the development of French mercantile companies, see Philippe Haudrère, *Les Compagnies des Indes orientales. Trois siècles de rencontre entre Orientaux et Occidentaux* (Paris: Desjonqueres, 2006).

56   Charles J. Borges, "The Portuguese Jesuits in Asia: Their Economic and Political Networking within Asia and Europe," in Silva Gonçalves, *A Companhia*, 203–24; Alden, "Some Considerations," 53–62; Alden, *Making of an Enterprise*, 528–51; Cushner, "Merchants."

57   See for example, Julia McClure, *The Franciscan Invention of the New World* (London: Palgrave Macmillan, 2017); Julia McClure, "The Globalisation of Franciscan Poverty," *Journal of World History*, 30 (2019): 335–62; Felicita Tramontana, "Trading in Spiritual and Earthly Goods. Franciscans in Semi-Rural Palestine," in *Catholic Missions in Early Modern Asia. Patterns of Localization*, ed. Nadine Amsler, Andreea Badea, Bernard Heyberger and Christian Windler (London: Routledge, 2020): 126–41.

58   Alden, *Making of an Enterprise*, 528.

59   Summary of Valignano's position given in "Informação do trato q' temos da China Japao," February 10, 1620, Macao, ARSI, *JapSin* 45, fol. 234. Valignano's interpretation was, of course, hotly debated amongst Jesuits in Japan.

60   On the silk trade by the Jesuits in Japan, see Hélène Vu Thanh's chapter in this volume.

to discontinue the trade.[61] These debates were felt keenly in the Southeast Asian missions, where trade seemed crucial. As the Jesuits were forced out of Japan and re-settled in Cochinchina, Tonkin, Siam and elsewhere in Southeast Asia, trade continued to provide for their needs. In 1631, the Visitor André Palmeiro recommended that the Jesuits in Tonkin appoint secular assistants, and ask some local Christians to help with selling and buying merchandise.[62]

In de Bourges' account too, we see the blurred edges of the prohibition, as missionaries utilize "minor trade" and currency trading in order to maintain liquidity. De Bourges' recommendations about currency are particularly interesting. Currency could be a particularly astute investment. Contemporary accounts make clear the importance of gold, silver, and copper, monetized or not, as commodities throughout Southeast Asia. Simon de la Loubère, for example, details the value of the Siamese tical (illustration 10.2) relative to the comparative weight of monetized French silver, reporting that although it weighs no more than a demi-écu, it is worth 37-and-a-half sols, and adding that "they have no money of gold, nor copper. Gold is merchandise for them, and is worth twelve times as much as silver."[63] *Negotiatio argentaria* is specifically banned in later glosses of canon law: currency exchange where money is bought or sold for profit "is definitely not lawful for clerics."[64] Clearly de Bourges does not see these activities as falling within the bounds of the provision: perhaps because they are not motivated by a desire for profit, and are not habitual.[65]

The issue became a lightning rod in the conflict between the MEP and other religious orders in Southeast Asia. It was used in their appeals for support in order to draw a clear distinction between their way of proceeding and that of their rivals. The letters which de Bourges carried back to Rome, for example complained that the secular clergy of the missions were all "as ignorant of things of science as they are disinclined to spiritual things, and totally given to games and commerce," gaining a reputation amongst the populace as "avaricious, lacking

---

61   "Exponuntur R.P.N. Gli rationes propter quas Prouᵃ Japoniæ exercebat aliquam speciem mercaturæ," 1669, ARSI, *Fondo Gesuitico* 721/11/7/1, fol. 1r–v.

62   "Instrucção que a Padre Andre Palmeiro Visitador da Provincia de Japam, e China, deu ao Padre Gaspar de Amaral," February 16, 1631, Biblioteca da Ajuda, *Jesuítas na Asia*, 49–V–31, fol. 41v–42.

63   Simon de la Loubère, *Du Royaume de Siam, vol. I* (Paris: la Veuve de Jean Baptiste Coignard, 1691), 280.

64   John P. Beal, James A. Coriden and Thomas J. Green, *New Commentary on the Code of Canon Law* (New York: Paulist Press, 2000), on canon 286 prohibiting business or trade, 378.

65   On the significance of the act of trading being a habitual practice, see Dede, "Business Pursuits," 59.

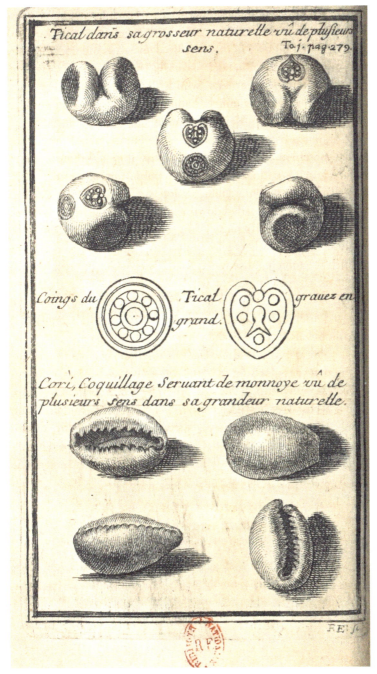

ILLUSTRATION 10.2 Ticals and cowrie shells of Siam in Simon Loubère, *Du Royaume de Siam*
vol. I (Paris: la Veuve de Jean Baptiste Coignard, 1691), 278–79

in zeal, dishonest, and engaged in commerce."[66] The mendicant friars were no better: "[T]he Dominicans, who are three, are also engaged in commerce. One of them, having enriched himself in this way, lived such a scandalous life that his superior was obliged to send him back to Goa."[67] The Jesuits were described as the worst of all. Tomaso Valguernera, "who is the superior in order to accumulate riches" was accused of publicly trading in Manila, Japan and other places, and of adopting the courtesies and manners of the Mandarins of the royal court, "the better to rise to their status," while Emmanuel Miranda "has a great name as a merchant and employs 12 servants. It is said that he has in Siam 60,000 scudi, and it is certain that he trades publically, under the pretext of doing it through a Portuguese merchant."[68] Moreover, the French priests had seen dock in Ayutthaya a ship "loaded down with merchandise, the most part belonging to Father Rocca, a Portuguese Jesuit, who was on the boat and who publically supervised some workers who built a little shop near to the Jesuit residence, to which the merchandise was carried." The Jesuits' interest in commerce drove them as far as collaboration with the heretic Dutch. Jesuit Andrea Gomez, they alleged, "arrived in Siam on a boat belonging to the Dutch East India Company, and immediately had unloaded many bales of merchandise ... and invested his money in other goods, to re-export to Goa."[69]

Through these reports, the MEP drew clear distinctions between their way of proceeding and that of their rivals, marking themselves as a more secure investment prospective. In Ayutthaya Pierre Lambert de la Motte had made public his disgust in a pastoral letter which contained a vehement condemnation of the city's clergy. His intemperate approach to the issue alienated many, but his uncompromising position appealed to two Jesuits in the city: fellow Frenchmen Pierre Albier and Joseph Tissanier. The two collaborated with Lambert de la Motte and Pallu to produce a treatise, *Religiosus Negotiator*.[70] This slight but

---

66   "Cong.° par'lais super rebus sinarum habita die 24 Dec.ris 166," Archivio Storico della Congregazione de Propaganda Fide [hereafter APF], *Acta Congregationis Particularis super rebus Sinarum et Indiarum Orientalium*, vol. 1A: fol. 13–14. The document draws together various written reports, sent to the Propaganda Fide by the vicars apostolic. Cardinal Piccolomani presented this summary of the key points of these reports to the assembled congregation of cardinals for discussion.

67   "Cong.°," fol. 14.

68   "Cong.°," fol. 13–14v.

69   "Cong.°," fol. 14v.

70   References here are taken from the copy found in the archives of the Propaganda Fide: Joseph Tissanier and Pierre Albier, "Religiosus Negotiator. Sivè Dissertatio brevis in qua quærituran Societatis Jesu Relgiosis liceat in Indijs Oriantalibus negotiari," 1665, in APF, *Scritture Riferite, Indie Orientali e Cina,* Miscellanea 37, Relazioni sul Siam,

influential document set out a rigorous position on the legitimacy of clerical trade, and would color a number of later polemics directed against perceived missionary laxity and self-interest.[71]

The opening salvo of the treatise made it clear that the document would pull no punches, as it reports on the "sordid and filthy commerce which profanes the Church of God" found not only amongst secular clergy, but also within the Society of Jesus. Following Jesuit theologian Paul Laymann (1574–1635) "and other doctors," the authors simply and rigidly defined commerce as the act of buying something with the intent to take it elsewhere and sell it at a higher price, in order to gain from the action.[72] The treatise considered whether it was licit for the Jesuits to engage in this practice on four levels: as clerics, as religious, as members of the Society of Jesus and as missionaries. It concluded that each of these conditions excluded them from commerce. As clerics, they should look to the story of Jesus whipping the traders (*negotiatores*) out of the temple as a model of the necessary separation of sacred and profane.[73] As religious, they should, as St. Jerome had urged, renounce things of the world.[74] As Jesuits, they should seek to emulate the spirit of their founder, Ignatius Loyola, and in particular his conception of the spiritual value of poverty.[75] Finally, as missionaries, commerce was incompatible with their holy duty to labor in the vineyard of the Lord: one who was dedicated to being a merchant was not worthy of the title of apostle.[76] Missionaries must put their faith in God, and seek alms in Rome and from pious patrons.

MEP accounts of other missionary groups made clear to potential donors and supporters that any investment in these rival missions would fail to achieve an adequate return. They indicated that investment in these missions would be unwise and could possibly even cause harm in several ways. First, they argued that any group engaged in commerce at any level would be less successful at the primary task of conversion. Clerical engagement in commerce risked damaging the prestige of priests in the eyes of local populations. The instructions of the Propaganda Fide to the vicars apostolic emphasized the importance of personal disinterest: how they must not make themselves

---

Cochincina e Tonkino, f. 2. Another exemplar, translated into Portuguese, is found in ARSI, *Fondo Gesuitico*: 721/11/7/4, fol. 11–21v: "Religiozo Negoziador. Ou disputa breue na qual se inquire, se aos Religiozos da Compa de IESU, he licito contrar em as Indias Orientais."

71   See Chappoulie, *Une controverse*, 3–27.

72   "Religiosus Negotiator," fol. 2.

73   "Religiosus Negotiator," fol. 2v.

74   "Religiosus Negotiator," fol. 4v. Drawing on letter to Nepotian cited above.

75   "Religiosus Negotiator," fol. 5r–v.

76   "Religiosus Negotiator," fol. 6.

"odious due to material questions."[77] Once provided with food and clothing, they must "abstain from lowly profiteering, not demand alms, not amass money, gifts, riches. If certain faithful, despite your refusal, impose their offerings you, before their eyes distribute them to the poor, understanding that nothing astonishes people, nothing attracts their esteem like contempt for temporal things, like that evangelical poverty which, elevating one above all human and terrestrial realities, prepares one for the treasures of heaven."[78] In Siam Lambert de la Motte fulminated that the Jesuits should consider, "the advantage that the priests of the idols gain against the ministers of the Gospel in seeing them entirely occupied in worldly interests, they being, in contrast, very distant from such things."[79]

Second, missionaries engaged in commerce could not be sure of God's favor. In 1665, Pallu related, a ship carrying Jesuit cargo from Macau had arrived in Siam only to spontaneously burst into flames. "This is not the only punishment that God has given to the Jesuits for ignoring the prohibitions and censures of the Holy Church against trade," he asserted. Soon afterwards, another ship was taken by Chinese pirates in a clear example of divine intervention.[80] Surely patrons would prefer to support an endeavor which had the approval and support not only of the great and the good of Paris and Rome, but of God, over the dubious enterprise of worldly clerics?

Finally, there was a risk that in contributing to rivals' coffers, donors may inadvertently feed their chief vices. Profit, money, and worldly commodities took on their own agency in MEP discourse. They become a corrupting force, filling the mind and spirit and inducing avarice. MEP writing depicted existing missions as having been laid waste by this sin, which could strip a priest of his "interior peace" and render him "incapable of giving himself to God and working for the salvation of souls."[81] This evil had spread across the Indies, "to the extent that the three vows of religion [e.g. the vows of poverty, chastity and obedience taken by regular clergy], which should have been the most efficacious remedies, have been unable to preserve certain religious from its deadly

---

77   Propaganda Fide, *Instructions aux vicaires apostoliques des royaumes du Tonkin et de la Cochinchine (1659)* ed. Bernard Jacqueline (Paris: Archives des Missions Étrangères de Paris, 2008), 61.

78   Propaganda Fide, *Instructions*, 61.

79   "Relation du voyage du Tonkin par Mgr de Berithe," AMEP, vol. 677, fol. 198.

80   "Replica del Vescouo d'Eliopoli alla Risposta dei Padri della Compagnia," ASV, *Missioni*, vol. 108, fol. 16.

81   François Pallu, and Pierre Lambert de la Motte, *Monita ad missionarios: Instructions aux missionnaires de la S. congrégation de la propagande rédigées à Ayuthaya, Siam, en 1665.* (Paris: Archives des Missions Étrangères de Paris, 2000), 26.

ravages."[82] For Lambert de la Motte, Jesuit trade was motivated not by a need to support the mission, but by avarice: their intention "is to render themselves powerful in material goods and to make the world dependent on them due to the need which the Portuguese have for trade."[83]

Avarice, or the desire for riches, was seen by some theologians as a special category of sin: St. Thomas Aquinas, following Ecclesiastes, declared covetousness to be the root of all sin as "by riches man acquires the means of committing any sin whatever."[84] Commerce thus became both the symptom and the cause of moral degeneracy. Condemning the failure of the Iberians to ordain local Christians as priests, for example, the priests of the Missions Étrangères frequently lauded the innate morality of Southeast Asian converts, emphasizing their lack of self-interest and concern for trade. The population of the Philippines, for example, was depicted as existing in a state of pre-Lapsarian innocence, degraded only to the extent that they had been exposed to Spanish colonists: away from this influence, "there are no games, no drunkenness, no vanity, no amusements, no commerce, no fraud, no flattery, no, or little knowledge of the luxury and the debauchery of the Spanish, but much natural goodness, lots of spirit, and a great disposition to virtue and to the most abstract sciences: who will doubt that we couldn't make good priests from amongst these people."[85]

In contrast, the first Missions Étrangères priests offered a new approach to and conception of the spiritual characteristics of the ideal missionary. The MEP aimed to inculcate in each missionary a "spirit of mortification and prayer" in which he would find "a means of perfection of the self; the exercise of these same virtues will equally help him to work effectively for the salvation and sanctification of others."[86] Indeed, the missionary should embrace those moments when the mission seems close to collapse due to material want, when a thousand problems were pressing, when nothing seemed to be succeeding in his work of evangelism, and when those who were embracing worldly methods seemed to be reaping a better harvest. This was the "furnace in which his metal is stripped from his ore and increases in purity." In this enviable state "he feels in himself the triumph of grace, the inhumation of the old man and the

---

82   Pallu and Lambert de la Motte, *Monita*, 27.

83   AMEP, vol. 677, fol. 199.

84   Cited by Juliann Vitullo and Diane Wolfthal, "Introduction," in their *Money, Morality and Culture in Late Medieval and Early Modern Europe* (Farnham, UK: Ashgate, 2010), 1.

85   "Plan qui doit être présenté à la Sacré Cong.n," Archives des Missions Étrangères de Paris [hereafter AMEP], vol. 129, 97–98.

86   Pallu and Lambert de la Motte, *Monita*, 32.

rebirth of the new, in a word, total renunciation [*le dépouillement total*]. A sort of transport sets him outside of himself, and makes him live for God alone and for his glory. ... He is certain of possessing the most perfect ressemblance to Christ his master, derided by the populace, and contributing nevertheless to the salvation of souls even though the fruit of his labors remain hidden from his own eyes."[87]

The MEP missionary, donors were assured, even in extremis would not stumble and allow "human means" to expose him to the besetting sins of the mercantile world. "What is there more shameful than an apostolic man," Pallu wrote, "whose conversation, once he has renounced the things of this world, must be of heaven, mixing himself in secular affairs." It is not only commerce itself which must be avoided, but "even the desire and spirit of the merchant which is forbidden to clerics." He compared the missionary to an elite soldier, who, in contrast to the base and unreliable mercenary, is forbidden from engaging in trade as it may distract him from his duty. "How much more reason, then, for the Christian militia to abstain from all trafficking? ... It is better for the missionary to return to his country or to be reduced to the greatest extremes than to engage in commerce."[88]

Criticisms of commerce, then, were not only about canon law: they were also part of the performance of a particular sort of spirituality, which would, at one time, have found a sympathetic audience in France amongst the *dévots*. MEP letters, reports, and journals were inflected with a very distinctive spirituality: austere, and concerned with human nature and the battle against the passions. Radical and self-abnegating, this spirituality reflected multiple, varied currents of French spirituality of the Catholic reform. It owed a debt to what historian Henri Brémond called the *école française* of spirituality of Pierre de Bérulle and his followers, and drew inspiration from a range of writers including Vincent de Paul, François de Sales, Jean Eudes, Louis Abelly, Jean de Saint-Sanson, Jean-Baptiste de la Salle, and Louis Lallement.[89] The

---

87   Pallu and Lambert de la Motte, *Monita*, 49–59.
88   Pallu, cited and analyzed in the anti-Jesuit polemic of Antoine Arnauld, *Œuvres de Messire Antoine Arnauld. Tome Trente-Deuxième* (Paris & se vend à Lausanne, Chez Sigismond D'Arnay & Compagnie, 1780), 450.
89   See especially Henri Bremond, *Histoire littéraire du sentiment religieux. Depuis la fin des guerres de religion jusqu'à nos jours Vol. III: La conquête mystique. L'École Française* (Paris: Librarie Bloud et Gay, 1923); Louis Cognet, *Origines de la spiritualité française au XVIIe siècle* (Paris: Fayard 1987); Yves Krumenaker, *L'École française de la spiritualité. Des mystiques, des fondateurs, des courants et leurs interprètes* (Paris: Le Cerf, 1998); Jean Guennou, "Préface," in *La divinisation par Jésus-Christ*, trans. Louis Laneau and Jean-Paul Lenfant (Paris: Missions Etrangères de Paris, 1987; private press).

emphasis above all was on abandonment to the will of God, abnegation of self, perfection of the spirit, and identification with the divine in the person of Christ. Turning away from worldly means, becoming indifferent to material comforts and submitting to a complete renunciation of the will were necessary first steps in becoming an effective missionary.

De Bourges' account depicts how this mentality sustains the missionaries. Tossed in a stormy sea, for example, and facing death, for example, those aboard "undergo the trial by combat which occurs between the rational and the inferior parts of the soul. If the disturbance was great outside due to the vehemence of the storm, it was no less strong inside due to the pain suffered by the sensual man—who always wishes to live—when he finds himself close to death."[90] The missionaries, however, in their renunciation, are sanguine. "It is also in these moments that the spiritual man conforms to Jesus-Christ his Lord and his model, sacrificing with a glad heart all, as it pleases God, who plays with the life of creatures like flotsam on the sea."[91]

While varied currents of French spiritual thought shaped the main channels of Missions Étrangères spirituality in the Ayutthayan seminary, equally important was the local context of Buddhist monasticism in Siam, and more generally in Southeast Asia. Missions Étrangères priests studied Pali and discussed religious matters with Buddhist monks. In the early days of the mission, they spent many years dressed in saffron robes, practicing the sort of spiritual and temporal austerity admired by local populations.

Eventually the Propaganda Fide denied permission for this way of proceeding and the missionaries reverted to their soutanes, but they retained a keen awareness of local standards of spirituality. The importance of these experiences is clear in a number of documents which sought to describe and even codify MEP spirituality. It is clear, for example, in a set of proposed rules for missionaries of the Society, submitted to Rome, where they were discussed in 1669. These rules would have made defined a new "chrism" for the Society, rooting their activities in a strict and demanding program of contemplation and interior spiritual development, and binding the missionaries with a series of vows.[92] They were inspired by the observation that the missionaries would not achieve the conversion of the population without matching the "rigors" of the local Buddhist monks: they "believed themselves to be obliged

---

90   Bourges, *Relation*, 215–6.

91   Bourges, *Relation*, 216.

92   "Institutione di Vita che si proposti gli Vicari Apostolici della China, Cocincina, e del Tunchino," APF, Acta Congregationis Particularis super rebus Sinarum et Indiarum Orientalium (Acta CP), 1A, fol. 168–87. See Alberts, *Conflict and Conversion*, 98–99.

to embrace the harshness and austerity of their conduct and behavior."[93] These "interior" vows—so called to distinguish them from those taken by regular clergy—were of poverty, chastity and obedience, with additional promises to live as austerely as Buddhist monks (in particular by abstaining from meat), and to refrain from the use of medicine.[94] Each vow required rigorous prayer and mortification. The vow of poverty, for example, not only involved renunciation of all goods, but "absolutely stripping oneself of every intentional love towards oneself, and promising his divine Majesty to love nothing but to the extent that it served his divine glory."[95] One can see the seminary in Ayutthaya as an outpost of continuing French spiritual reform, where these varied but complementary strains of spirituality came together, transplanted into and reinvigorated by the Buddhist context. The product of all of these trends can be seen in a pair of works conceived of and created in Ayutthaya. Louis Laneau (1637–1696) received almost all of his spiritual formation on the missions. He left France for Siam at the age of twenty-three. In the seminary in Ayutthaya, under the tutelage of Lambert de la Motte, he absorbed the approach of writers including de Sales, Bérulle, and Lallemant.[96] He also spent around three years in a Buddhist monastery learning Pali and some of the fundamentals of Buddhist teaching.

In 1688, a succession crisis following the death of King Narai of Siam brought an end to the royal patronage of the French priests. Laneau, along with many others, was imprisoned and used the time until his release in 1690 to begin his spiritual work, *De deificatione justorum per Jesus Christum,* which drew together the threads of his spiritual training and experience. As a part of the mystical body of Christ, he wrote, the missionary must not permit himself "any action which would be unworthy of Christ, anything that does not have the perfume of the sanctity of the members of Christ" such that "in them, like in a mirror, through them, like a transparent body, we see the Christ who dwells within them, who operates within them by the Holy Spirit, who shows himself in them by their good works."[97] Priests must therefore, for the good of the mission, renounce behaviors and habits which may be permitted by the Church, but which would scandalize local populations.[98]

---

93   "Institutione," fol. 168v.
94   "Institutione," fol. 171r-179v.
95   "Institutione," fol. 171r.
96   Krumenacker, *L'École Française*, 551–53.
97   Louis Laneau, and Jean-Paul Lenfant, trans., *La divinisation par Jésus-Christ* (Paris: Missions Etrangères de Paris, 1987), 253.
98   Laneau and Lenfant, *La divinisation*, 264.

In 1691 Laneau composed a catechistical dialogue in Siamese between a Buddhist monk and a Catholic which wove together this spiritual sense with his understandings of Buddhist teachings and values. Renunciation forms a point of contact between the two world views. Christ had been born as a lowly man, the Christian explains, "as riches lead to covetousness," and he taught us "not to allow oneself to get lost in this world of the *Saṃsāra* [in Buddhism, the cycle of existence], not to trust one's happiness to goods and riches."[99] To reach salvation, he urges the monk, "endeavor to lead a pure life until death, desiring to have no attachment to goods, nor the changing world of the *Saṃsāra*, nor any other human interest: thus, limiting your interest for things of the world, you will become capable of fixing your attention permanently on God."[100]

In Laneau's work we see how the French and Southeast Asian priests who trained in the MEP seminary of Ayutthaya tested the spiritual concepts of the *siècle des saints* in the crucible of the mission field, leading to the creation of a new approach to mission rooted in a distinctive type of Christo-centric contemplative spirituality. The spirituality of the Missions Étrangères priests was distinct and novel enough to provoke dark (and unfair) allegations of heterodoxy from rivals.[101] Having fallen out with Lambert de la Motte, for example, in 1669 Jesuit Joseph Tissanier reported that "it seems that our French bishop intends to exterminate us [Jesuits]: the passion that he shows against us, his extravagant principles, and his way of life make many people believe that he is an *alumbrado* or Jansenist."[102] Louis Laneau's magnum opus was not published in Europe "due to the anti-quietist reaction which hit all works which dealt with the mystical life," but also perhaps because of the ongoing controversy between the two missionary societies.[103]

In France, by the end of the seventeenth century, the spirit of heightened interiority, of mystical abnegation and extreme renunciation that characterized so many works of spiritual writing from the first half of the century, was already on the wane. Nervousness concerning the potentially seditious nature of confraternities and sodalities had led to the circumscription and suppression of organizations that had promoted this sort of piety, such as the Compagnie

---

99   Louis Laneau, *Rencontre avec un sage bouddhique. Traduit du siamois d'après un manuscrit conservé aux archives des Missions étrangères de Paris*, ed. Pierre-Yves Fux (Geneva: Ad Solem, 1998), 99–100.

100   Laneau, *Rencontre*, 116.

101   See especially Fauconnet-Buzelin, *Aux sources*, 299–320.

102   Joseph Tissanier, Siam, September 10, 1669, ARSI, *JapSin* 76, fol. 25.

103   Guennou, *Les Missons,* 551.

du Saint Sacrement and other associations of *"Bons Amis."*[104] Yet if the *siècle des saints* was giving way to the *siècle des lumières* in France, amongst the first generation of Missions Étrangères priests in Southeast Asia the fervent spirituality of the *école française* was given new life. This, the MEP argued, promised success where other missionary orders had hitherto fallen to sin, offering an unprecedented return on donors' investments. Already, de Bourges' account relates, converts were being made, plans for the ordination of local clergy were well developed, and for the first time a stable church could be founded, with no stain of sin.

4   Conclusion

What could be worse than a man of God who turned his mind from the heavens to the squalid exigencies of the marketplace? In forgetting his obligations, the worldly priest became no better than a merchant—damned to dysentery as they were—or even, a mercenary: quitting the battalions of Christ to sell himself into the services of Mammon. Such wounding rhetoric was deployed ruthlessly in the conflicts between the different missionary orders, in person, in letters and in print, as each side sought supporters and patrons.

Accounts like de Bourges', in their appeal for patrons, struck an intriguing balance between highlighting the practical and spiritual qualities which would allow a missionary to succeed. Missionaries clearly could not afford to remain ignorant of matters of exchange and profit. They were largely dependent on networks of trade. De Bourges was scathing about those who engaged in commerce, but he was careful to outline how those who followed him could maximize profit by exploiting the fluctuating values of specie, and how they could use dissimulation and deceit to avoid taxes and customs charges. Without astutely observing and engaging with the murky world of accumulation, profit maximization, and commerce, missionaries would quickly run out of resources before they reached their mission fields. It was entirely necessary to know where to change one's money (and into what), where best to buy everything: from bread, to fabric, to intriguing trinkets for gifts or bribes, to precious materials for altar ornaments. De Bourges laid out the practical abilities and resourcefulness of the MEP missionaries which enabled them to overcome a large number of challenges. He thereby reassured his audience of potential

---

104   Fauconnet-Buzelin, *Aux sources,* 73, 75; Raoul Allier, *La Cabale des Dévots 1627–1666* (Paris: Armand Colin, 1902), 153–54.

patrons that the MEP would be able to put their donations to work in the great endeavor of evangelization.

Examining interaction between financial and spiritual worlds in missionary rhetoric opens up a range of intriguing vistas. As Giacomo Todeschini has demonstrated for an earlier period, the importance of spiritual writing to the development of broader intellectual frames and mentalities cannot be understated.[105] Missions could also play an important role in shaping beliefs, attitudes, and moral understandings concerning trade. As Claude Prudhomme has demonstrated, connections and divergences between networks of evangelism and trade in the colonial context are particularly complex at the conceptual or ideological level, with missions playing an important role in the construction of what he calls the "imperial economic spirit," and of the identities and value systems of market participants.[106] Equally, as we have seen, rhetoric concerning economic realities could be important in shaping missionary spirituality as orders sought to carve out their own niches in the spiritual economy, and to demonstrate to their benefactors the value of their spiritual and financial investments.

Bibliography

Primary Sources

Archivio Storico della Congregazione de Propaganda Fide [APF]: *Acta Congregationis Particularis super rebus Sinarum et Indiarum Orientalium*, vol. 1A; *Scritture Riferite nei Congressi. Indie Orientali e Cina,* vol. 1, 4, Miscellanea 37.

Archivum Romanum Societatis Iesu [ARSI]: *JapSin* 45, 76; *Fondo Gesuitico* 721/11/7/1.

Archivum Generalis Ordinis Prædicatorum: *XIII.56900.2*.

Archivio Segreto Vaticano [ASV]: *Archivio della nunziatura apostolica*: Divisoni I. Sezione 1; *Missioni*, vol. 108.

Biblioteca da Ajuda: *Jesuítas na Asia*, 49-V-31.

Archives des missions étrangères de Paris [AMEP]: vols. 129, 677.

---

105   See especially Giacomo Todeschini, *I mercanti e il tempio: la società cristiana e il circolo virtuoso della ricchezza fra Medioevo ed età moderna,* (Bologna: Il Mulino, 2002) and Giacomo Todeschini, *Ricchezza francescana: dalla povertà volontaria alla società di mercato* (Bologna: Il Mulino, 2004).

106   Claude Prudhomme, "Le missionnaire et l'entrepreneur dans les colonies françaises," in *L'esprit économique impérial (1830–1970). Groupes de pression & réseaux du patronat colonial en France & dans l'empire,* ed. Hubert Bonin, Catherine Hodeir, and Jean-François Klein (Paris: Société française d'histoire d'outre-mer, 2008), 149–66.

Aquinas, Thomas. *Summa Theologica, vol. 35 (2a2ae. 34–46) Consequences of Charity.* Edited by Thomas R. Heath. London: Blackfriars, 1972.

Arnauld, Antoine. *Œuvres de Messire Antoine Arnauld. Tome Trente-Deuxième.* Paris & Lausanne: Sigismond D'Arnay & Compagnie, 1780.

Bourges, Jacques de. *Relation dv voyage de Monseigneur l'Evêque de Beryte, Vicaire Apostolique dv Royavme de la Cochinchine, Par la Turquie, la Perse, les Indes, &c., jusqu'au Royaume de Siam, & autres lieux.* Paris: Denys Bechet, 1668 (first published 1666).

Bright, William. *The Canons of the First Four General Councils of Nicaea, Constantinople, Ephesus and Chalcedon: with Notes*, 2nd ed. Oxford: Clarendon Press, 1892.

Brisacier, Jacques-Charles. *Discours funèbre pour Madame la Duchesse d'Aiguillon prononcé a Paris dans la Chapelle du Séminaire des Missions étrangères.* Paris: Charles Angot, 1675.

Laneau, Louis and Pierre-Yves Fux, ed. *Rencontre avec un sage bouddhique. Traduit du siamois d'après un manuscrit conservé aux archives des Missions étrangères de Paris.* Geneva: Ad Solem, 1998.

Laneau, Louis and Jean-Paul Lenfant, trans. *La divinisation par Jésus-Christ.* Paris: Missions Etrangères de Paris, 1987.

Loubère, Simon de la. *Du Royaume de Siam.* Paris: la Veuve de Jean Baptiste Coignard, 1691.

Pallu, François and Pierre Lambert de la Motte. *Monita ad missionarios: Instructions aux missionnaires de la S. congrégation de la propagande rédigées à Ayuthaya, Siam, en 1665.* Paris: Archives des missions étrangère de Paris, 2000.

Propaganda Fide, *Instructions aux vicaires apostoliques des royaumes du Tonkin et de la Cochinchine (1659)* ed. Bernard Jacqueline. Paris: Archives des Missions Étrangères de Paris, 2008.

Schaff, Philip and Henry Wace, ed. *Nicene and Post-Nicene Fathers, Second Series, Vol. VI—Jerome: Letters and Select Works.* New York: Cosimo, 2007.

Tanner, Norman J. *Decrees of the Ecumenical Councils*, 2 vols. London: Sheed & Ward, 1990.

Tissanier, Joseph. *Lettre d'un Pere de la Compagnie de Iesvs écrite du Tunquin le 25 Nouembre 1658 au P. Procureur de la Prouince de France.* Paris: [?] 1659.

Valleyre, G.A., *Histoire des divers changemens et mutations des monnoyes de France, ou leur valeur depuis 1666 jusqu'à present.* Paris: Claude Cellier, 1705.

Secondary Sources

Alberts, Tara. *Conflict and Conversion: Catholicism in Southeast Asia, 1500–1700.* Oxford: Oxford University Press, 2013.

Alberts, Tara. "Missions in Vietnam." In *A Companion to the Early Modern Catholic Global Missions*, edited by Ronnie Po-Chia Hsia, 269–302. Leiden; Boston: Brill, 2018.

Alden, Dauril. *The Making of an Enterprise: The Society of Jesus in Portugal, its Empire, and Beyond*. Stanford, CA: University of California Press, 1996.

Alden, Dauril. "Some Considerations Concerning Jesuit Enterprises in Asia." In *A Companhia de Jesus e a missionação no Oriente*, edited by Nuno de Silva Gonçalves, 53–62. Lisbon: Brotéria, 2000.

Allier, Raoul. *La Cabale des Dévots 1627–1666*. Paris: Librairie Armand Colin, 1902.

Ames, Glen J. *Renascent Empire? The House of Braganza and the Quest for Stability in Portuguese Monsoon Asia, c. 1640–1683*. Amsterdam: Amsterdam University Press, 2000.

Andaya, Barbara Watson. "Between Empires and Emporia: The Economics of Christianization in Early Modern Southeast Asia." *Journal of the Economic and Social History of the Orient* 53 (2010): 357–92.

Andaya, Leonard. "The 'Informal Portuguese Empire' and the Topasses in the Solor Archipelago and Timor in the Seventeenth and Eighteenth Centuries." *Journal of Southeast Asian Studies* 41 (2010): 391–440.

Baulant, Micheline. "Le salaire des ouvriers du bâtiment à Paris de 1400 à 1726." *Annales. Histoire. Sciences Sociales* 26 (1971): 463–83.

Beal, John P., James A. Coriden and Thomas J. Green, ed. *New Commentary on the Code of Canon Law*. New York: Paulist Press, 2000.

Borges, Charles J. *The Economics of the Goa Jesuits, 1542–1759*. New Delhi: Concept Publishing Company, 1994.

Borges, Charles J. "The Portuguese Jesuits in Asia: Their Economic and Political Networking within Asia and Europe." In *A Companhia de Jesus e a missionação no Oriente*, edited by Nuno de Silva Gonçalves, 203–24. Lisbon: Brotéria, 2000.

Boxer, Charles. *The Affair of the "Madre de Deus" (A Chapter in the History of the Portuguese in Japan)*. London: Kegan Paul, Trench, Trubner, 1929.

Boyajian, James C. *Portuguese Trade in Asia Under the Habsburgs, 1580–1640*. Baltimore, MD: Johns Hopkins University Press, 1993.

Bremond, Henri. *Histoire littéraire du sentiment religieux. Depuis la fin des guerres de religion jusqu'à nos jours Vol. III: La conquête mystique. L'École Française*. Paris: Librairie Bloud et Gay, 1923.

Chappoulie, Henri. *Une controverse entre missionnaires à Siam au XVIIe siècle. Le Religiosus negotiator du jésuite français J. Tissanier. Suivi de quelques documents concernant le commerce des clercs*. Paris: s. n., 1943.

Chappoulie, Henri. *Aux origines d'une église : Rome et les missions d'Indochine au XVIIe siècle*. 2 vols. Paris: Bloud et Guy, 1943–1948.

Clark, Henry C. "Commerce, the Virtues, and the Public Sphere in Early-Seventeenth-Century France." *French Historical Studies* 21 (1998): 415–40.

Clossey, Luke. *Salvation and Globalization in the Early Jesuit Missions*. Cambridge: Cambridge University Press, 2008.

Cognet, Louis. *Origines de la spiritualité française au XVIIe siècle*. Paris: Fayard 1987.

Cummins, J. S. and Nicholas P. Cushner. "Labor in the Colonial Philippines: The *Discurso Parenetico* of Gomez de Espinosa." *Philippine Studies* 22 (1974): 117–48.

Cushner, Nicholas P. "Merchants and Missionaries: A Theologian's View of Clerical Involvement in the Galleon Trade." *The Hispanic American Historical Review* 47 (1967): 360–69.

Cushner, Nicholas P. *Lords of the Land. Sugar, Wine and Jesuit Estates of Coastal Peru, 1600–1767*. New York: SUNY Press, 1980.

Dede, J. "Business Pursuits of Clerics and Religious: Further Considerations." *The Jurist* 23 (1963): 50–60.

Disney, Anthony. *History of Portugal and the Portuguese Empire*, 2 vols. Cambridge: Cambridge University Press, 2006.

Duteil, Jean Pierre. "Introduction," in Jacques de Bourges, *Relation du voyage de Mgr l'évêque de Béryte,* edited by Jean Pierre Duteil, 1–14. Paris: Gérard Montfort, 2000.

Fauconnet-Buzelin, Françoise. *Aux sources des Missions étrangères: Pierre Lambert de la Motte 1624–1679*. Paris: Perrin, 2006.

Finkelstein, Andrea. *The Grammar of Profit: The Price Revolution in Intellectual Context*. Leiden; Boston: Brill, 2006.

Forest, Alain. *Les Missions Français, au Tonkin et au Siam XVIIe-XVIIIe siècles. Analyse comparée d'un relatif succès et d'un total échec*. 3 vols. Paris: L'Harmattan, 1998.

Gorce, Mathieu de la. "Blâme et éloge de l'avarice dans le *Livre des marchands*." *Seizième siècle* 4 (2008): 89–112.

Guennou, Jean. *Les missions étrangères*. Paris: Saint-Paul, 1963.

Guennou, Jean. "Préface." In *La divinisation par Jésus-Christ*, translated by Louis Laneau and Jean-Paul Lenfant. Paris: Missions Etrangères de Paris, 1987.

Harrigan, Michael. *Veiled Encounters. Representing the Orient in Seventeenth-century French Travel Literature*. Amsterdam: Rodopi, 2008.

Haudrère, Philippe. *Les Compagnies des Indes orientales. Trois siècles de rencontre entre Orientaux et Occidentaux*. Paris: Desjonqueres, 2006.

Heijmans, Elisabeth. *The Agency of Empire: Connections and Strategies in French Overseas Expansion (1686–1746)*. Leiden; Boston: Brill, 2020.

Jordão, Levy Maria, ed. *Bullarium patronatus portugalliæ regum in ecclesiis africæ, asiæ atque oceaniæ*. 3 vols. Lisbon: Typographia National, 1868–1879.

Keohane, Nannerl O. *Philosophy and the State in France. The Renaissance to the Enlightenment*. Princeton: Princeton University Press, 1980.

Krumenaker, Yves. *L'École Française de la spiritualité. Des mystiques, des fondateurs, des courants et leurs interprètes*. Paris: Le Cerf, 1998.

Lach, Donald F., and Edwin J. Van Kley. *Asia in the Making of Europe, Vol. III: A Century of Advance. Book Three; Southeast Asia*. Chicago: University of Chicago Press, 1993.

Launay, Adrien. *Histoire générale de la Société des Missions Étrangères*. 3 vols. Paris: Téqui, 1894.

McClure, Julia. *The Franciscan Invention of the New World*. London: Palgrave Macmillan, 2017.

McClure, Julia. "The Globalisation of Franciscan Poverty." *Journal of World History* 30 (2019): 335–62.

Marin, Catherine. "Du refus d'un patronat royal à la française: un soutien du Roi et des Grands contrôlé." In *La Société des Missions Étrangères de Paris—350 ans à la rencontre de l'Asie (1658–2008)*, edited by Catherine Marin, 81–94. Paris: Karthala, 2010.

Newitt, Malyn. "Formal and Informal Empire in the History of Portuguese Expansion." *Portuguese Studies* 17 (2001): 1–21.

Patterson, Jonathan. *Representing Avarice in Late Renaissance France*. Oxford: Oxford University Press, 2015.

Pedreira, Jorge M. "Costs and Financial Trends in the Portuguese Empire, 1415–1822." In *Portuguese Oceanic Expansion, 1400–1800*, edited by Francisco Bethencourt and Diogo Ramada Curto, 49–87. Cambridge: Cambridge University Press, 2007.

Phelan, John Leddy. "Free versus Compulsory Labor: Mexico and the Philippines, 1540–1648." *Comparative Studies in Society and History* 1 (1959): 189–201.

Prudhomme, Claude. "Le missionnaire et l'entrepreneur dans les colonies françaises." In *L'esprit économique impérial (1830–1970). Groupes de pression & réseaux du patronat colonial en France & dans l'empire*, edited by Hubert Bonin, Catherine Hodeir, and Jean-François Klein, 149–66. Paris: Société française d'histoire d'outre-mer, 2008.

Quaglioni, Diego, Giacomo Todeschini, et Gian Maria Varanini, ed. *Credito e usura fra teologia, diritto e amministrazione: linguaggi a confronto, sec. XII-XVI*. Rome: École française de Rome, 2005.

Reid, Anthony. *Southeast Asia in the Age of Commerce, 1450–1680. Volume Two: Expansion and Crisis*. New Haven, CT and London: Yale University Press, 1993.

Roth, Denis Morrow. *The Friar Estates of the Philippines*. Albuquerque, NM: University of New Mexico Press, 1977.

Sá, Isabel dos Guimarães. "Ecclesiastical Structures and Religious Action." In *Portuguese Oceanic Expansion, 1400–1800*, edited by Francisco Bethencourt and Diogo Ramada Curto, 255–82. Cambridge: Cambridge University Press.

Santos, Catarina Madeira. *"Goa é a chave de toda a Índia" Perfil político da capital do Estado da Índia (1505–1570)*. Lisbon: Comissão Nacional para as Comemorações dos Descobrimentos Portugueses, 1999.

Smithies, Michael. "Jacques de Bourges (c.1630–1714) and Siam." *Journal of the Siam Society* 81 (1991): 113–28.

Souza, George Bryan. *The Survival of Empire: Portuguese Trade and Society in China and the South China Sea 1630–1754*. Cambridge: Cambridge University Press, 2004.

Teixeira, Manuel. *Macau e a sua diocese*. Macau: Tipografia Soi Sang, 1956–76.

Todeschini, Giacomo. *I mercanti e il tempio: la società cristiana e il circolo virtuoso della ricchezza fra Medioevo ed età moderna*. Bologna: Il Mulino, 2002.

Todeschini, Giacomo. *Ricchezza francescana: dalla povertà volontaria alla società di mercato*. Bologna: Il Mulino, 2004.

Tramontana, Felicita. "Trading in Spiritual and Earthly Goods. Franciscans in Semi-Rural Palestine." In *Catholic Missions in Early Modern Asia. Patterns of Localization*, edited by Nadine Amsler, Andreea Badea, Bernard Heyberger and Christian Windler, 126–41. London: Routledge, 2020.

Van De Cruysse, Dirk. *Louis XVI et le Siam*. Paris: Fayard, 1991.

Vermote, Fred. "Finances of the Missions." In *A Companion to Early Modern Catholic Global Missions*, edited by Ronnie Po-Chia Hsia, 367–400. Leiden: Brill, 2018.

Vignali, Giovanni. *Comento su le leggi di eccezione per gli affari di commercio messe in relazione tra la loro tuttel le leggi di commercio degil stati d'Italia non che delle parti più colte di Europa*. Naples: Vico Figurari, 1855.

Villiers, John. "As derradeiras do mundo: The Dominican Missions and the Sandalwood Trade in the Lesser Sunda Islands in the Sixteenth and Seventeenth Centuries." In *Seminário Internacional de História Indo- Portuguesa,, II Actas*, edited by Luís de Albuquerque and Inácio Guerreiro, 573–86. Lisbon: IICT, 1985.

Villiers, John. "Doing Business with the Infidel: Merchants, Missionaries and Monarchs in Sixteenth Century Southeast Asia." In *Maritime Asia: Profit Maximisation, Ethics and Trade Structures*, edited by Karl Anton Sprengard and Roderich Ptak, 160–70. Wiesbaden: Harrassowitz Verlag, 1994.

Villiers, John. "De um caminho ganhar almas e fazenda: Motives of Portuguese Expansion in Eastern Indonesia in the Sixteenth Century." *Terrae Incognitae* 14 (1982): 23–39.

Vismara, Paolo. "Les Jésuites et la morale économique." *Dix-septième siècle* 237 (2007): 739–54.

Vitullo, Juliann and Diane Wolfthal. "Introduction." In *Money, Morality and Culture in Late Medieval and Early Modern Europe*, edited by Juliann Vitullo and Diane Wolfthal, 1–12. Farnham, UK: Ashgate, 2010.

CHAPTER 11

Regulating the Forbidden

Local Rules and Debates on the Missionary Economy in the Jesuit Province of Paraguay (17th–18th Centuries)

Fabian Fechner

Historical research into the missionary economy has diversified and changed significantly in past decades. My aim is to analyze this change by taking as an example the South American Provinces of the Society of Jesus, with a special focus on the Jesuit Province of Paraguay, a well-documented and polemically discussed case. According to the traditional historiography, the economic efforts of missionary orders were a moral failure and reflected a discrepancy between vision and reality, a violation of the vow of poverty, and a giving in to greed. This historiography was influenced by concepts of confessionalisation and the "Kulturkampf," in which the difference between Catholicism and Protestantism was interpreted as decisive for the German nation-building process.[1] After the 1950s, during the rise of the study of economic history, scholars like Magnus Mörner, Juan Carlos Garavaglia and Nicholas Cushner clearly broke with earlier stereotypes. They opposed traditional biographical, theological or edifying approaches, and proposed instead to understand and reconstruct the missions as economic enterprises. The questions they asked were the following: What were the mission's economic assets and outputs? And, how were missions funded?[2] Moreover, the analysis was based on statistical and numerical

---

1   See some of the best-known traditional works on the Jesuit economy in Kurt Dietrich Schmidt, "Bücherkunde und Anmerkungen," in *Die Jesuiten*, ed. Heinz Böhmer et al. (Stuttgart: Koehler, 1957). There is an excellent introduction to the Paraguayan missions in Guillermo Wilde, "The Missions of Paraguay: Rise, Expansion and Fall," in *Companion to Early Modern Catholic Global Missions*, ed. Ronnie Po-Chia Hsia (Leiden; Boston: Brill, 2018), 73–101. I wish to thank Oonagh Hayes and Alexander Straker for their helpful comments.

2   See this topic in relation to the Asian mission, especially Frederik Vermote, "The Role of Urban Real Estate in Jesuit Finances and Networks between Europe and China, 1612–1778" (PhD diss., University of British Columbia, 2013); Frederik Vermote, "Financing Jesuit Missions," in *The Oxford Handbook of the Jesuits*, ed. Ines G. Županov (Oxford: Oxford University Press, 2019), 128–49; Charles J. Borges, *The Economics of the Goa Jesuits, 1542–1759* (New Delhi: Concept Publishing Company, 1994); James D. Riley, "The Wealth of the Jesuits in Mexico, 1670–1767," *The Americas* 33, no. 2 (1976): 226–66.

© FABIAN FECHNER, 2021 | DOI:10.1163/9789004444195_012

approaches. The most important conclusion of these inquiries was that there was no fundamental difference between Jesuit-owned farms/enterprises and "private" ones.[3] The result of these studies urged historians of missions to reconsider the economics of missionary activity, a topic which the Jesuit writers left out of their apologetic chronicles of the time, and which thus received no scholarly attention.[4]

However, a conflict between the monastic ideal of poverty and financial necessity did exist, and the issue was not simply a struggle between the Jesuits and their external opponents, as contemporaneous printed pamphlets may have suggested. In the anonymous "Abridged Report," for instance, the alleged hidden treasures of the Jesuits in Paraguay are described in detail.[5] Economic activities were a burning topic in Jesuit internal debates as well, and were discussed between various conflicting factions. Those who championed agriculture, handicrafts and commerce in the missions and farms were pitched against those who insisted on a focus on core spiritual responsibilities. The Jesuits were a socially heterogeneous group and had different, even opposing, opinions and perceptions regarding economic questions.

The centre of my analysis will be to understand the attempts to regulate "forbidden" economic activities through continuous dialogue and debate between different administrative levels. My claim is that through dialogue and a local *fait accompli* policy, an illegal practice acquired an administrative and judicial framework. Thus, through collective decision-making processes, the practice of locally drafting legislation and sending it to be approved in Rome,

---

3   See also Herman W. Konrad, *A Jesuit Hacienda in Colonial Mexico: Santa Lucía, 1576–1767* (Stanford, CA: Stanford University Press, 1980).

4   The most influential works are Magnus Mörner, *Actividades políticas y económicas de los jesuitas en el Río de la Plata*, 2nd ed. (Buenos Aires: Hyspamerica, 1985); Juan Carlos Garavaglia, *Mercado interno y economía colonial: Tres siglos de historia de la yerba mate* (México: Grijalbo, 1983); and Nicholas P. Cushner, *Jesuit Ranches and the Agrarian Development of Colonial Argentina 1650–1767* (Albany, NY: State University of New York Press, 1983). These studies are mostly concerned with reconstructing Jesuit economic activities from scarce and unsystematic sources. On the deep economic interests of clerics in the early modern period, see Philip Knäble, "Wucher, Seelenheil, Gemeinwohl: Der Scholastiker als Wirtschaftsexperte," in *Wissen und Wirtschaft. Expertenkulturen und Märkte vom 13. bis 18. Jahrhundert*, ed. Marian Füssel et al. (Göttingen: Vandenhoeck & Ruprecht, 2017).

5   *Relação abreviada da República que os Religiosos Jesuítas das Provincias de Portugal, e Espanha, estabeleceram nos Domínios Ultramarinos* (Lisbon: n.p., 1757). The "Relação abreviada" is attributed to the Portuguese minister Sebastião José de Carvalho e Melo, better known by his later title Marquês de Pombal. Christine Vogel, *Der Untergang der Gesellschaft Jesu als europäisches Medienereignis (1758–1773): Publizistische Debatten im Spannungsfeld von Aufklärung und Gegenaufklärung* (Mainz: von Zabern, 2006).

and the involvement of special procurators in negotiations, an illegal practice could become practically "legal" for a certain local context. This judicial framework was never recorded among the general rules or in printed Jesuit collections, and is only found in local copies of letters from superiors and other kinds of internal correspondence and memoirs. Because of its limited visibility in the historical sources, the internal debate about commercial activities was not well known in studies on missionary economics.[6]

The "economy" as a broader concept only appeared in the eighteenth century and became an umbrella term for all kinds of material and monetary transactions between humans that presupposed a certain rationality.[7] In spite of the belated appearance of the concept that the semantic field "economy" uneasily covers, it is helpful for observing and analyzing manifold economic activities that also contained a surprising number of taboos. Theoretically, the Jesuits had to avoid any explicit intention to gain goods or money. This concern was repeated again and again by the Superior General or the Provincial.[8] The best known opinion on this topic can be taken from Ignatius of Loyola (1491–1556) who enshrined in the *Constitutions* of the Society the notion that "poverty is like a bulwark of religious institutes which preserves them in their existence and good order and defends them from many enemies."[9] Simultaneously, it was stressed that each kind of "scandal" or "scruple" should be avoided. This taboo, this striking fear of economic profit, seems to reflect the tension

---

6   So far, there are only a few attempts to systematically analyze local Jesuit rules and regulations. Markus Friedrich, *Der lange Arm Roms? Globale Verwaltung und Kommunikation im Jesuitenorden 1540–1773* (Frankfurt a. M.; New York: Campus, 2011); Martín M. Morales, "Violencia y misión en la antigua provincia del Paraguay," *Studia Missionalia* 60 (2011): 235–55; Fabián R. Vega, "Las sanciones a las conductas represibles de misioneros en las reducciones jesuíticas de guaraníes (siglo XVIII): Entre el control y la laxitud," *Red Sociales, Revista del Departamento de Ciencias Sociales* 6 (2019): 57–79. See also Markus Friedrich, "Government and Information-management in Early Modern Europe. The Case of the Society of Jesus (1540-1773)," *Journal of Early Modern History* 12 (2008): 539–63.

7   The key term "economy" in this context may seem unhistorical when referring to the early modern period, a time when the term "oeconomia" was restricted to processes of interchange in smaller entities like families. I use the term in order to emphasize the fact that Jesuit activities were clearly of economic nature, although some of the historians sought to obscure it for reasons discussed in this chapter. Peter Spahn, Otto Gerhard Oexle and Johannes Burkhardt, "Wirtschaft," in *Geschichtliche Grundbegriffe. Historisches Lexikon zur politisch-sozialen Sprache in Deutschland*, vol. 7, ed. Otto Brunner et al. (Stuttgart: Klett-Cotta, 1992), 511–94.

8   See Martín M. Morales, ed., *A mis manos han llegado: Cartas de los PP. Generales a la Antigua Provincia del Paraguay (1608–1639)* (Madrid: Comillas, 2005), passim.

9   Ignatius of Loyola, "The Constitutions of the Society of Jesus," in *The Constitutions of the Society of Jesus and Their Complementary Norms: A Complete English Translation of the Official Latin Texts*, ed. John W. Padberg (Saint Louis, MO: The Institute of Jesuit Sources, 1996), 412.

between the profane and the sacred. However, economic profit was tolerated to a certain degree, especially when it was absolutely necessary to secure solid funding of a given enterprise.[10] Semantic subtleties between the permitted and the forbidden appear in the internal documentation. *Renta* was a normal term for the income of a farm, but in some cases it was used as an equivalent for *negoçiaçion*,[11] a term which referred to illegal economic activity that exceeded the normal maintenance (*sustento*) of a Jesuit residence or a college. A parallel term of the profane word *negoçiaçion* was *portería*—where liquors and other products were sold at the gate of a residence, in the manner of a mundane or secular shop.[12]

1   Local Manuscript Rules: Methodological Approach

For the following analysis, my sources are exclusively administrative, internal documents, which directly reflect discussions within the Society of Jesus. Among them are letters from the Superiors General to the authorities in Paraguay.[13] This vertical and hierarchical relationship is the well-known top-down principle of Jesuit government.

Less helpful for this analysis are the published Constitutions and printed decrees of the General Congregations, because it is not clear whether these collections of normative texts were systematically applied in specific cases. Here I am instead interested in concrete local settings: What kind of local and normative knowledge was mobilized in what kind of situations? Furthermore, also less helpful are shipping lists or bills, because these documents especially concern goods and quantities of circulation, but so far, it has been nearly

---

10   This was also the case with the Japanese mission. The Jesuits in Japan were allowed to invest in the silk trade by the General and by the Pope, since the funds coming from Europe were not sufficient. See Hélène Vu Thanh, "Un équilibre impossible: financer la mission jésuite du Japon, entre Europe et Asie (1579–1614)," *Revue d'Histoire Moderne et Contemporaine* 63, no. 3 (2016): 7–30.

11   Morales, *A mis manos*, 126, 434, 505 (*negoçiaçion*); Josef Wicki, ed., "Dois Compêndios das Ordens dos Padres gerais e Congregações Provinciais da Província dos Jesuítas de Goa, feitos en 1664," *Stvdia. Revista do Centro de Estudios Históricos Ulatramarinos da Junta de Investigações Científicas do Ultramar* 43/44 (1980): 419 ("negoceação").

12   Archivo General de la Nación, Buenos Aires, fondo Biblioteca Nacional 69, Libro de Consultas de la Compañía de Jesús 1731–1747 [en la Provincia de Paraguay], hereafter "Libro de consultas."

13   Morales, *A mis manos*; Biblioteca Nacional de España, Madrid, Mss/6976, Cartas de los PP. Generales y Provinciales de la Compañía de Jesús a los misioneros jesuitas de Paraguay, Uruguay y Paraná.

impossible to gain from them precise information about economic and financial structures. It is unclear how many of these documents have survived, and especially in the case of bills, it is very hard to read them.[14]

Of more interest are internal debates within the same province, which can be deduced or read "against the grain" of the vertical communication. There are other types of sources which point to horizontal communication, however, that is to say, debates among administrative Jesuit entities that were capable of making decisions on their own or who would prepare questions for the Superior General in Rome. In the first case, the Provincial's discussions (*consultas*) with his counsellors or so-called "consultors" are the most important. The consultors of the Provincials (*Consultores Provinciae*) were nominated by the Superior General. Every year, they were obliged to write a report for the Superior General about the progress of their province.[15] In the case of the Province of Paraguay, summaries of all the consultations between 1731 and 1747 are preserved in a special register "*Libro de consultas.*"[16]

The core source genre consists of the files of the Provincial Congregations, a special kind of consultative preparation. Normally taking place every three, or in the case of overseas provinces, every six years, forty fathers of a province gathered together at a Provincial Congregation. It was the decisive intermediate authority of the Society of Jesus. The fathers discussed the most important items and needs of the provinces in order to communicate them to the Curia in Rome. Furthermore, the participants of the Provincial Congregations elected temporary provincial procurators who were sent to Rome to

---

14   Teresa Blumers, *La contabilidad en las reducciones guaraníes* (Asunción: CEADUC, 1992); other attempts in Julia J. S. Sarreal, *The Guaraní and Their Missions: A Socioeconomic History* (Stanford, CA: Stanford University Press, 2014); Julia Lederle, *Mission und Ökonomie der Jesuiten in Indien: Intermediäres Handeln am Beispiel der Malabar-Provinz im 18. Jahrhundert* (Wiesbaden: Harrassowitz, 2009). A convincing analysis of shipping lists, focused on wooden sculptures in colonial Paraguay, can be found in Corinna Gramatke, "*La portátil Europa.* Der Beitrag der Jesuiten zum materiellen Kulturtransfer," in *Die polychromen Holzskulpturen der jesuitischen Reduktionen in Paracuaria, 1609–1767: Kunsttechnologische Untersuchungen unter Berücksichtigung des Beitrags deutscher Jesuiten,* vol. 1, ed. Erwin Emmerling et al. (Munich: Technische Universität München, 2019), 191–397.

15   Jerome Aixala, "Consultores de provincia y casa," in *Diccionario histórico de la Compañía de Jesús. Biográfico-temático,* vol. 1, ed. Charles E. O'Neill et al. (Rome: Institutum Historicum Societatis Iesu, 2001), 935.

16   Libro de consultas. This text and other local manuscript rules for the Province of Paraguay will be edited by Guillermo Wilde, Fabián R. Vega and myself in the series "Global Perspectives on Legal History" (Frankfurt/Main: Max Planck Institute for European Legal History).

participate either in a Congregation of Procurators or a General Congregation. Additionally, these provincial procurators provided information to the Jesuit Curia in Rome, the Council of the Indies, and the authorities and merchants in Andalusian harbors, and thus helped them prepare for their coming expeditions. They were part of a dense communication network that was not reduced to written communication, but that included dialogic knots, represented by stationary procurators in Rome, Madrid and Seville, the so-called "General Procurators."[17]

Surprisingly, numerous documents relating to decision-making can be found at this administrative level, while the Superior General hardly ever did more than accept the proposals prepared in the province. Concerning administrative practice, the competencies and prerogatives of these congregations were thus much broader than the mere administrative rules of a "monolithic" Society of Jesus. The internal decision-making process of the congregations was mainly based on requests (*postulata*) supported by the majority of the congregated Fathers and special petitions (*memoriales particulares*), which were suggested by a smaller group, mostly missionaries. The differences between majority and minority proposals clearly reveal Jesuit internal dissent.[18] There were four economic matters which were continuously debated in local contexts and which appear in local documents.

2   Jesuits as Slave Owners and Slave Traders

The highly debated issue of slavery is one of the most distinctive fields where social reality and the application of rules and regulations in the overseas provinces of the Society of Jesus differ.[19] The missions and schools in South America were mostly funded by the profits of the farms, while the core element of

---

17   Paul Oberholzer, "Briefkultur als integratives Element vor der Herausforderung eines globalen Sendungsauftrages im Kontext sich wandelnder Herrschaftskonzepte im spanischen Weltreich," in *Diego Laínez (1512–1565) and his Generalate. Jesuit with Jewish Roots, Close Confidant of Ignatius of Loyola, Preeminent Theologian of the Council of Trent*, ed. Paul Oberholzer (Rome: Institutum Historicum Societas Iesu, 2015). These General Procurators contained the Court Procurators. See Félix Zubillaga, "El procurador de la Compañía de Jesús en la corte de España," *Archivum Historicum Societatis Iesu* 16 (1947): 1–55.

18   Fabian Fechner, *Entscheidungsprozesse vor Ort. Die Provinzkongregationen der Jesuiten in Paraguay* (Regensburg: Schnell & Steiner, 2015).

19   See Sandra Negro and Manuel Marzal, eds., *Esclavitud, economía y evangelización: Las haciendas jesuitas en la América virreinal* (Lima: Pontifica Universidad Católica del Perú, 2005).

colonial agriculture and manufacture was slavery.[20] The rejection of forced labor of the indigenous peoples and the support of African slavery can and has been described as "surely paradoxical."[21] Compared to famous Jesuit apologetic narratives about the lives of the saints, the progress of the missions and theological issues, there is very little mention of African slavery and the moral implications of the slave trade. Alonso de Sandoval's "De instauranda Aethiopum Salute" (On Restoring Ethiopian Salvation) is in that respect an exception.[22] The importance of a phenomenon, which was not systematically documented in the colonial period, is obvious given that approximately 17,275 slaves of African origin worked on Jesuit farms in South America at the time of their expulsion in 1767.[23] The attitude towards slavery was a subject of continuous conflict between Jesuits in Brazil and in Paraguay. Both provinces tolerated and supported Indian forced labor in their *estancias* (farms) and, for Brazil, in *aldeias* (villages). While enslavement of the indigenous Tupí-Guaraní was practiced intensely in southern Brazil, it was strictly rejected by the Jesuits in the missions of Paraguay.[24]

The local documentation reveals that buying and selling slaves was part of the responsibility of the Provincial and his consultors. However, it is hard to find these detailed records elsewhere. These documents even include reasons for buying or selling individual slaves, and they enrich our knowledge of the social history of enslaved Africans and the everyday life of a Jesuit farm or school. One of the main reasons why specific slaves had to be sold was their acts of resistance or general disobedience. It was a "scandal" in Buenos Aires when several slaves in the college rebelled and made plans to flee in June 1732. When discovered, they were sold.[25] One year later, the Provincial Jerónimo Herrán (1672–1743) and his consultors decided to sell "all the blacks who gave poison to

20   David G. Sweet, "'Black Robes' and 'Black Destiny.' Jesuit view of African Slavery in 17th-century Latin America," *Revista de historia de América* 86 (1978); Cushner, *Jesuit Ranches*.

21   Clement J. McNaspy and Jesús Gómez Fregoso, "Esclavitud negra en América I–II," in *Diccionario histórico de la Compañía de Jesús. Biográfico-temático*, vol 2, ed. Charles E. O'Neill et al. (Rome: Institutum Historicum Societatis Iesu, 2001), 1254.

22   Nicole Priesching, *Sklaverei im Urteil der Jesuiten: eine theologiegeschichtliche Spurensuche im Collegio Romano* (Hildesheim; Zurich; New York: Georg Olms Verlag, 2017); Hugo Fragoso, "Sklaverei in Brasilien. Die Haltung der Orden in einer umstrittenen Frage," in *Conquista und Evangelisation. 500 Jahre Orden in Lateinamerika*, ed. Michael Sievernich et al. (Mainz: Matthias-Grünewald-Verlag, 1992).

23   McNaspy and Fregoso, "Esclavitud negra," 1254.

24   Ignacio Telesca, "Esclavos y Jesuitas. El Colegio de Asunción del Paraguay," *Archivum Historicum Societatis Iesu* 77 (2008): 191–211; Fechner, *Entscheidungsprozesse*, 222–23; Cushner, *Jesuit Ranches*, 99–107.

25   Libro de Consultas, Consulta 12.06.1732, fol. 2v–3.

Brother Mareca," and "other slaves who, because they were proud and haughty, could not be kept neither in the college nor on the estates."[26] In some cases, it was considered inappropriate to keep female slaves in the college. In September 1734, during a visit to the College of Tucumán, the Provincial Jaime Aguilar (1678–1746) decided to sell the enslaved Magdalena, because "it is against our spirit [*espíritu*] to keep her inside the house."[27] With the money received from this sale, they planned to buy male slaves. The rules governing the slave trade in relation to the Society of Jesus were not codified in printed documents, neither in the Constitutions nor in the Decrees of the General Congregations.[28] They can be found exclusively in the handwritten local rules, which are very brief and wrapped in casuistry, without sufficient indication of the region or the period in which they were valid. A consultation in February 1733 shows that the sale of a slave without the previous permission of the Provincial was not valid: the rector of the College in Rioja had sold a slave "surreptitiously." It was decided to buy back this individual for 300 *pesos*, and if this were to prove impossible, he should be brought back after a trial that proved "the obvious nullity of the sale."[29] This case hints at illicit slave trading in South America, which was not supported by a Provincial or by another authority in the Society of Jesus. However, though illicit, the relatively high number of cases suggests that slavery was important in the economic system. Connected with smuggling activities, some members of the Society of Jesus not only had the role of slave owners, but were also slave traders. A letter from General Muzio Vitelleschi (1563–1645) for the Provincial Nicolás Mastrilli Durán (1568–1653) reveals that in the years leading up to 1628, some Jesuits in Buenos Aires bought (and eventually smuggled in) slaves for the purpose of resale. Thus, the "good name and reputation of the Society [of Jesus] was damaged."[30] Durán's successor,

---

26   Libro de Consultas, Consulta 18.07.1733, fol. 15. All the biographical data on Paraguayan Jesuits has been taken from Hugo Storni, *Catálogo de los jesuitas de la Provincia del Paraguay (Cuenca del Plata) 1585–1768* (Rome: Institutum Historicum Societatis Iesu, 1980).

27   Libro de Consultas, fol. 27. In some cases, higher numbers of slaves were mentioned in the "Libro de consultas," for example, in January 1739, when sixty slaves had to be bought for the Colegio de la Paz. See Libro de Consultas, fol. 96 r–v.

28   John W. Padberg, Martin D. O'Keefe and John L. McCarthy, eds., *For Matters of Greater Moment. The First Thirty Jesuit General Congregations: A Brief History and a Translation of the Decrees* (St. Louis, MO: Institute of Jesuit Sources, 1994). For the Brazilian case, see Luiz Felipe de Alencastro, "Le versant brésilien de l'Atlantique-Sud: 1550–1850," *Annales. Histoire, Sciences Sociales* 61 (2006): 339–82; Luiz Felipe de Alencastro, *O trato dos viventes: Formação do Brasil no Atlântico Sul, séculos XVI e XVII* (São Paulo: Companhia das Letras, 2000).

29   Libro de Consultas, fol. 8.

30   Morales, *A mis manos*, 388.

Francisco Vázquez Trujillo (1571–1652), was contacted for the same purpose six years later. Obviously the prohibition of the Superior General was respected in Paraguay. However, the Superior General criticized the Provincial of Peru and the Vice-Provincial of Chile for their penchant for buying slaves from ships that purportedly "got lost" (*por extravios*). Thus, the slave owners avoided royal taxation and could sell the enslaved for a cheaper price. The Superior General explicitly ordered the purchase of slaves in town, in spite of the higher price, to avoid "so many risks and gossip," and the Provincial of Paraguay was obliged to notify his two colleagues from the neighboring provinces.[31] In later confirmation of the same information, the rector of the College in Mendoza was included in the group of concerned authorities.[32]

3   Production and Distribution of Goods

In the case of agricultural and preindustrial production, three different stages can be observed. The first entailed very strict rejection by the Jesuit Curia in Rome. In the early years of the Province of Paraguay, a few participants of the second Provincial Congregation (1614) wanted to explore their economic opportunities. Those fathers supporting the economic incentives expressed their doubts in a special petition (*memorial particular*). This particular form could have had two reasons: either the congregated fathers did not place much emphasis on their question, or only a minority of the participants supported it.[33]

Juan de Viana (1565–1623) was the provincial procurator who took note of these questions and who personally communicated them afterwards to Superior General Vitelleschi in Rome. The fathers presented three suggestions. First, they wanted to cultivate wheat and corn in a field belonging to the residence of Buenos Aires. However, the crop was not intended to be wholly for feeding the members of the residence and it was planned that a certain spill over was to be sold as flour in Brazil.[34] Second, a similar solution was suggested for the residence in Mendoza.[35] Third, the Superior General was informed that the missionaries in the Paraguayan *reducción* (mission town) bred cattle, but "only a few" cows, to avoid exorbitant profit. In these three cases, the procurator

---

31   Morales, 467.

32   Morales, 493.

33   Archivum Romanum Societatis Iesu, Rome, Section Congregationes (hereafter ARSI, Congr.) 55, fol. 182r–v, Memorial from the second Provincial Congregation 1614.

34   ARSI, Congr. 55, fol. 182.

35   ARSI, Congr. 55, fol. 182.

requested a dispensation—one of them was already granted, and the two others were under review. We can thus see that the local superiors did not always first ask for permission from authorities higher up and outside the region.

The usual form of reaction to this kind of memorial would be an answer, a *respuesta* written in Spanish. But Vitelleschi did not answer in this way. He chose a more formal mode by emitting a response to the postulate—a *responsum ad postulatum*. Vitelleschi's rejection of all of these suggestions was very strict and harsh. He forbade all three types of economic activity in the missions and residences, because he feared that the fathers in Paraguay might break the vow of poverty. Thus he expressed his *scrupula*.[36]

But how long did these scrupula in fact continue to be valid? The second stage is a surprising shift in the economic policies of the Curia. Only eighteen years after the outright rejection, the Superior General was confronted with various accomplished facts in Paraguay. In the meantime, the Provincial Nicolás Mastrilli Durán had allowed the foundation of soap works in Salta, which is today in north-western Argentina. The gains of this soap production were meant to fund the school (*colegio*) in Salta. In 1632, General Vitelleschi approved this foundation, but added a clear restriction. He suspected mass production with exorbitant profit. That is why he ordered that only raw materials, especially suet, which were produced on Jesuit-owned farms, could be processed in Salta.[37] This decision can be seen as a kind of compromise, halfway between sustention and excess. In another case, in the same year of 1632, some fathers from Paraguay protested against a highly productive weaving mill. Their reasons are unknown, but several fathers wrote a petition against this protest, arguing that this weaving mill was essential for funding the education of the novices there. The Superior General was convinced by this reason, but in this case and some others (for example the selling of a vineyard in Salta), he emphasized that all the financial and economic operations should not arouse suspicion among the public. They ought to be moderate and each of them should be characterized "with evident utility."[38] Two years later, the Superior General repeated his major concerns in a letter to the Provincial Francisco Vázquez Trujillo.[39] With terms like "evident utility," the narrow path between necessary funding and suspicious excess is precisely described.

---

36   ARSI, Congr. 55, fol. 181.

37   ARSI, Congr. 63, fol. 316, Postulate from the fifth Provincial Congregation 1632; the General's answer in ARSI Congr. 63, fol. 318v–319.

38   ARSI, Congr. 63, fol. 299r–v; the General's answer in ARSI, Congr. 63, fol. 301.

39   Morales, *A mis manos*, 494–95.

4   The Infrastructure for Production and the Debate on the Just Price

As noted, the year 1632 was a changing point in relations between Rome and Paraguay over the acceptance of financial and economic enterprises. After a total rejection of economic enterprises, a certain compromise was reached, but always with the exhortation that every kind of excess should be avoided. In a further stage, only formal questions were treated. An institutional framework for the administration of earnings was created and completed between 1637 and 1644. This framework followed a fundamental rule: Only colegios were allowed to earn a surplus from agriculture and manufacturing. The other types of Jesuit residences and missions were not. That is why in some cases, a colegio had to be founded to legally administer the money from financial gains.[40] That was the case in the Guaraní reducción San Ignacio Miní. In 1637, the provincial procurator Francisco Díaz Taño (1593–1677), the consultors of the Provincial and some missionaries debated on the foundation of a new colegio there. Thus, all the gains from the Guaraní reducciones could be registered in a formally correct way. In other cases, economic entities like the cattle farms in the Guaraní missions were to be assigned to already-existing colegios. After the Provincial Congregation in 1644, Superior General Vitelleschi considered this was necessary, so that "each kind of scruple may have an end."[41] Surprisingly, he only saw the recording of the income as a possible stumbling block, and not the fact that with the same decision he approved of each reducción having a farm of its own. This decision replaced the system of a common farm with meadows for all the reducciones.[42]

After an initial phase we can recognize the appearance of manifold economic activities. Adopting this compromise, the province worked well during the following century. In the mid-eighteenth century the economic infrastructure was extended, and from this can be assumed a certain growth and professionalization. Beyond the goods mentioned, such as soap, cattle and woolen materials; after 1726, others, such as mules and especially the famous Paraguay tea (*yerba maté*), began to play an important role in the Jesuit economy.[43] This growth required the development of extended economic networks.

---

40   Olwen Hufton, "Every Tub on Its Own Bottom: Funding a Jesuit College in Early Modern Europe," in *The Jesuits II, Cultures, Sciences and the Arts, 1540–1773*, ed. John O'Malley et al. (Toronto; Buffalo; London: University of Toronto Press, 2006), 5–23. On the funding of colleges, see Ariane Boltanski and Sébastien Malaprade's chapters in this volume.

41   ARSI, Congr. 71, fol. 226v.

42   ARSI, Congr. 71, fol. 223.

43   Cushner, *Jesuit Ranches*; Garavaglia, *Mercado interno*. On yerba maté, see Claudio Ferlan's chapter in this volume.

A new point of intersection for these networks was a more specialized procurator in Lima, the capital of the Viceroyalty of Peru. The majority of the participants of the Provincial Congregation in 1750 demanded this representative for the Province of Paraguay. This new charge was needed to organize the mule trade more efficiently. Up until that point, each year thousands of mules had been bred in Paraguay and sold to intermediaries in Tucumán who then sold the mules in Lima at a higher price. The Jesuits in Paraguay wanted the help of the new representative to sell their mules directly in Lima, in order to obtain the higher price to be had there. The same argument concerned the trade in Paraguayan tea. The Jesuits in Paraguay expected some benefits in the opposite direction as well: they wanted to buy sugar, yarn and other goods directly in Lima. However, the aforementioned charge had a political function as well. The Jesuits were convinced that the additional procurator would negotiate the Paraguayan business with the Viceroy "in a faster, wiser and more successful manner."[44] One example was to get the viceroyal support for the recently-founded missions among the Abipones and the Mocobíes, indigenous groups situated in the central part of the Paraguayan province between the rivers Paraná and Río Salado.[45] The Superior General approved the creation of this new charge immediately and without demur.[46]

Generally speaking, we know quite a lot about the administrative and political network of the Society of Jesus, about interactions between the Curia, Provincials, Provincial Congregations and central procurators in Lisbon, Madrid, Seville and Rome.[47] We do not know much about the local, parallel economic structure, however. There are some details about the provincial procurators who were sent periodically to Europe. Their activities in the Old World were a central part of the overseas mission economy and their names and business are documented in the files of the Provincial Congregations. The procurators who were assigned only on special occasions, on the demand of a province in a certain town, are difficult to trace.[48] This is because they are only occasionally

44   ARSI, Congr. 88, fol. 344r–v.
45   ARSI, Congr. 90, fol. 207r–v; excerpted in ARSI Congr. 90, fol. 209. For information on these two ethnic groups, see Thomas L. Whigham and Jerry W. Cooney, ed., *Campo y frontera: El Paraguay al fin de la era colonial* (Asunción: Servilibro, 2006).
46   ARSI, Congr. 90, fol. 212.
47   See the references in J. Gabriel Martínez-Serna, "Procurators and the Making of Jesuits' Atlantic Network," in *Soundings in Atlantic History: Latent Structures and Intellectual Currents, 1500–1830*, ed. Bernard Bailyn et al. (Cambridge, MA: Harvard University Press, 2009), 181–209.
48   Antonella Romano, "Prime riflessioni sull'attività intellettuale dei gesuiti ai tempi di Claudio Aquaviva. La circolazione delle idee e degli uomini tra Roma, Spagna e Nuovo

mentioned in a few letters or files, and these charges were not created systematically. However, we can assume a parallel network of economic procurators for certain provinces. Maybe the charge created for Paraguay in 1750 was linked to another "special" procurator in Lima. In 1579 the Province of Peru requested a procurator in Lima for the "secular business" in the province (only eleven years after the foundation). His duties were defined in detail, and he had to represent the Society of Jesus in the viceroyal court and in the *audiencia*. It is not known when this plan, which was approved, was realized, but there are certain functional parallels with the later special procurator for Paraguay.[49]

What is the meaning of "extended economic networks"? In 1741, for example, the Provincial and his consultors debated the fact that several thousand heads of cattle were bred in the surroundings of San Carlos, a Guaraní reducción in Paraguay. Their major concern was that the Spaniards who lived nearby should not become aware of the Jesuit herds.[50]

Another of the central issues of the Jesuit economy was the debate over the just price (*precio justo*).[51] In the case of the province of Paraguay, there are many examples of a normative price. These prices were given especially for cattle,[52] horses,[53] cedar wood,[54] donkeys,[55] beef tallow,[56] the famous Paraguayan tea (*yerba maté*),[57] and tobacco.[58] Interestingly, the prices of numerous goods were fixed for a specific place. They were not fixed for a determined period of time, but it was obvious that now and then they could be rearranged. In some cases, it becomes very clear that the prices were suggested by the Provincial, but then discussed during the consultas, possibly in more than one session (*junta*).[59] So it was not an executive and monocratic act imposed by the Provincial or by the Jesuit Curia in Rome, with only one exception: sometimes the Provincial fixed a price during a visitation. But these decisions could

Mondo," in *Strategie politiche e religiose nel mondo moderno. La Compagnia di Gesù ai tempi di Claudio Acquaviva (1581–1615)*, ed. Paolo Broggio (Rome: Aracne 2004), 271–97.

49   Antonio de Egaña, ed., *Monumenta Peruana*, vol. 2 (Rome: Institutum Historicum Societas Iesu, 1958), refer to p. 782 for a concise summary of the procurator's duties.

50   Libro de consultas, fol. 118v.

51   Theodor Mulder, "Economía, Teorías," in *Diccionario histórico de la Compañía de Jesús*, vol. 2, 1180–81.

52   Libro de Consultas, fol. 42, 63, 64v, 117v–118, 141v.

53   Libro de Consultas, fol. 42, 114v.

54   Libro de Consultas, fol. 63.

55   Libro de Consultas, fol. 63, 142v, 144v.

56   Libro de Consultas, fol. 63.

57   Libro de Consultas, fol. 131.

58   Libro de Consultas, fol. 142v, 144v, 146v.

59   Libro de Consultas, fol. 100.

be modified afterwards by a consulta.[60] In general the definition of prices was seen as a complex process, and in some cases the consultors said that it was impossible.[61]

During the consultas, various parameters were followed to determine the price. Two of them are very obvious today because they fit into the modern concept of economy: the added value of transportation for different kinds of goods,[62] and the price for work in the case of manufactured goods, e.g., bells and silver plates.[63] Two other criteria are quite surprising. In some cases, the price was influenced by the needs of the village where the agricultural goods were produced: poorer mission towns could sell for a higher price, and thus the price difference became a certain kind of alms-giving.[64] Finally, the ethnic background of the buyer could justify a higher price, e.g., in the case of Spaniards who wanted to buy goods from the missions.[65] On one occasion, the congregated consultors considered questions of supply and demand and relied for answers on the Jesuit information network. On April 24, 1746, during the juntas in the village of Candelaria, the procurators suggested temporarily ceasing the exportation of yerba maté, "because within a short timespan its value and the estimation [of the tea] had notably decreased, because there is a huge amount of it in Chile and Lima."[66]

5   Manifold Financial Services for Non-Jesuit Merchants

Manufacture and commerce were the basis of the Jesuit missionary economy. Along with the slave trade, the manufacture and distribution of goods, and the debate on just pricing, we can observe a fourth aspect: Jesuit financial services. These services, offered to individuals outside the religious order, normally caused a stir, because they proved that the clerics had entered the field of secular economics, and to good profit. Of course, these cases are not documented systematically because this is the material that scandals are made of. One case from Paraguay can be reconstructed, however, because the Superior General's permission was first sought. He was probably not asked in many other cases.

---

60   Libro de Consultas, fol. 141v.
61   Libro de Consultas, fol. 42.
62   Libro de Consultas, fol. 100, 114v, 146, 146v.
63   Libro de Consultas, fol. 64v.
64   Libro de Consultas, fol. 63v.
65   Libro de Consultas, fol. 145.
66   Libro de Consultas, fol. 166v.

In this case, in 1644, Pedro Carmenato, choirmaster in the Tucumán Cathedral, wanted to send one thousand pesos to Spain. The money was sent in the form of bills of exchange with the procurator Juan Pastor (1580–1658) via Rio de Janeiro and Seville. This transaction was for free, of course. Carmenato did not pay any fees. But in his gratitude, he gave to several charities: 200 pesos for Juan Pastor, 50 pesos for the *colegio* in Rio de Janeiro and 250 pesos for the Procurator of the Indies in Seville.[67]

This transaction was only the tip of the iceberg, as we learn from a well-informed witness, the provincial procurator Simón de Ojeda (1589–1673). He represented the Province of Paraguay in Europe between 1651 and 1658, and reported to the Superior General that it was impossible for Jesuit procurators to keep such financial transactions secret. Thus, the enormous amounts of money transferred to secular individuals and clerics was a reason for the deep mistrust of the Jesuits.[68] With this general remark, Ojeda introduced even more scandalous information. The Jesuit father, Pedro Marín (1586–?), from the Province of Paraguay was, on the one hand, confessor of the *gobernador* in Buenos Aires, that is, of the highest Spanish authority in the homonymous secular province. So far so good. Yet on the other hand, Marín administered the governor's sums to buy slaves from Angola, "almost like an agent," while another Jesuit kept thorough accounts of the slave trade.[69] This might be one of the most telling examples of economic transactions in Paraguay. Although it may not have been an everyday case, it shows the extent to which the financial services of the clerics were requested and offered.[70]

6   Conclusion

The analysis shows very pragmatic solutions in the course of the seventeenth century, when internal debates were not concerned with ethics or morals but with the public image of the Society of Jesus and recording details. In conclusion, the analysis of economic activities in the Province of Paraguay can help in revising any notion of a "monolithic" Society of Jesus.[71] Instead, it hints at the

---

67   ARSI, Congr. 71, fol. 216v, Memorial from the seventh Provincial Congregation 1644.

68   ARSI, Congr. 61, fol. 269, Memorial from the eighth Provincial Congregation 1651.

69   ARSI, Congr. 61, fol. 269, Memorial from the eighth Provincial Congregation 1651.

70   For the financial services offered by the Jesuits in Japan, see Hélène Vu Thanh's chapter in this volume.

71   Vermote, "The Role of Urban Real Estate."

inner dynamics of a supra-regional administration that includes to a certain degree autonomous decision-making far away from the Roman headquarters. At the same time, this analysis can clarify the ways in which the Jesuits were integrated into local society. These results may help in better understanding the relations between "local histories" and "global designs," as Walter D. Mignolo calls them.[72]

Surprisingly, there is no clear strategy from the Jesuit Curia concerning economic activities. In many cases there is a contrast between a local solution and the Roman opinion, but the Curia's voice is not clear or consistent at all. Furthermore, it is not clear what had to be reported to Rome. In their economic activities, the local Jesuits asked before, occasionally they asked afterwards, and in other cases they did not ask at all. In the latter cases, we have no way of knowing what happened.

Bibliography

Primary Sources

Archivum Romanum Societatis Iesu [ARSI], *Congr.* 55, 61, 63, 71, 88, 90.

Archivo General de la Nación, Buenos Aires: fondo Biblioteca Nacional 69, Libro de Consultas de la Compañía de Jesús 1731–1747 [en la Provincia de Paraguay].

Biblioteca Nacional de España: Mss/6976, Cartas de los PP. Generales y Provinciales de la Compañía de Jesús a los misioneros jesuitas de Paraguay, Uruguay y Paraná.

Egaña, Antonio de, ed. *Monumenta Peruana*, vol. 2. Rome: Institutum Historicum Societas Iesu, 1958.

Loyola, Ignatius of. "The Constitutions of the Society of Jesus." In *The Constitutions of the Society of Jesus and Their Complementary Norms: A Complete English Translation of the Official Latin Texts*, edited by John W. Padberg, 18–418. Saint Louis, MO: The Institute of Jesuit Sources, 1996.

Morales, Martín M., ed. *A mis manos han llegado: Cartas de los PP. Generales a la Antigua Provincia del Paraguay (1608–1639)*. Madrid: Comillas, 2005.

Padberg, John W., Martin D. O'Keefe and John L. McCarthy, ed. *For Matters of Greater Moment. The First Thirty Jesuit General Congregations: A Brief History and a Translation of the Decrees*. St. Louis, MO: Institute of Jesuit Sources, 1994.

Relação abreviada da República que os Religiosos Jesuítas das Provincias de Portugal, e Espanha, estabeleceram nos Domínios Ultramarinos [...]. Lisbon: n.p., 1757.

---

72   Walter D. Mignolo, *Local Histories/Global Designs. Coloniality, Subaltern Knowledges, and Border Thinking* (Princeton, NJ: Princeton University Press, 2000).

Wicki, Josef, ed. "Dois Compêndios das Ordens dos Padres gerais e Congregações Provinciais da Província dos Jesuítas de Goa, feitos en 1664." *Stvdia. Revista do Centro
de Estudios Históricos Ultramarinos da Junta de Investigações Científicas do Ultramar*
43/44 (1980): 343–532.

Secondary Sources

Aixala, Jerome. "Consultores de provincia y casa." In *Diccionario histórico de la Compañía de Jesús. Biográfico-temático*, vol. 1, edited by Charles E. O'Neill and Joaquín
María Domínguez, 935. Rome: Institutum Historicum Societatis Iesu, 2001.

Alencastro, Luiz Felipe de. *O trato dos viventes: Formação do Brasil no Atlântico Sul,
séculos XVI e XVII*. São Paulo: Companhia das Letras, 2000.

Alencastro, Luiz Felipe de. "Le versant brésilien de l'Atlantique-Sud: 1550–1850." *Annales. Histoire, Sciences Sociales* 61 (2006): 339–82.

Blumers, Teresa. *La contabilidad en las reducciones guaraníes*. Asunción: CEADUC, 1992.

Borges, Charles J. *The Economics of the Goa Jesuits, 1542–1759*. New Delhi: Concept Publishing Company, 1994.

Cushner, Nicholas P. *Jesuit Ranches and the Agrarian Development of Colonial Argentina 1650–1767*. Albany, NY: State University of New York Press, 1983.

Fechner, Fabian. *Entscheidungsprozesse vor Ort. Die Provinzkongregationen der Jesuiten
in Paraguay*. Regensburg: Schnell & Steiner, 2015.

Fragoso, Hugo. "Sklaverei in Brasilien. Die Haltung der Orden in einer umstrittenen
Frage." In *Conquista und Evangelisation. 500 Jahre Orden in Lateinamerika*, edited
by Michael Sievernich, Arnulf Camps, Andreas Müller and Walter Senner, 167–200.
Mainz: Matthias-Grünewald-Verlag, 1992.

Friedrich, Markus. "Government and Information-management in Early Modern Europe. The Case of the Society of Jesus (1540–1773)." *Journal of Early Modern History*
12 (2008): 539–63.

Friedrich, Markus. *Der lange Arm Roms? Globale Verwaltung und Kommunikation im
Jesuitenorden 1540–1773*. Frankfurt a. M.; New York: Campus, 2011.

Garavaglia, Juan Carlos. *Mercado interno y economía colonial: Tres siglos de historia de
la yerba mate*. México: Grijalbo, 1983.

Gramatke, Corinna. "*La portátil Europa*. Der Beitrag der Jesuiten zum materiellen
Kulturtransfer." In *Die polychromen Holzskulpturen der jesuitischen Reduktionen
in Paracuaria, 1609–1767: Kunsttechnologische Untersuchungen unter Berücksichtigung des Beitrags deutscher Jesuiten*, vol. 1, edited by Erwin Emmerling and Corinna
Gramatke, 191–397. Munich: Technische Universität München, 2019.

Hufton, Olwen. "Every Tub on Its Own Bottom: Funding a Jesuit College in Early Modern Europe." In *The Jesuits II, Cultures, Sciences and the Arts, 1540–1773*, edited by
John O'Malley, Gauvin Alexander Bailey, Steven Harris, and Franck T. Kennedy, 5–
23. Toronto; Buffalo; London: University of Toronto Press, 2006.

Knäble, Philip. "Wucher, Seelenheil, Gemeinwohl: Der Scholastiker als Wirtschafts-experte." In *Wissen und Wirtschaft. Expertenkulturen und Märkte vom 13. bis 18. Jahrhundert*, edited by Marian Füssel, Philip Knäble and Nina Elsemann, 115–37. Göttingen: Vandenhoeck & Ruprecht, 2017.

Konrad, Herman W. *A Jesuit Hacienda in Colonial Mexico: Santa Lucía, 1576–1767*. Stanford, CA: Stanford University Press, 1980.

Lederle, Julia. *Mission und Ökonomie der Jesuiten in Indien: Intermediäres Handeln am Beispiel der Malabar-Provinz im 18. Jahrhundert*. Wiesbaden: Harrassowitz, 2009.

Martínez-Serna, J. Gabriel. "Procurators and the Making of Jesuits' Atlantic Network." In *Soundings in Atlantic History: Latent Structures and Intellectual Currents, 1500–1830*, edited by Bernard Bailyn and Patricia L. Denault, 181–209. Cambridge, MA: Harvard University Press, 2009.

McNaspy, Clement J. and Jesús Gómez Fregoso. "Esclavitud negra en América I–II." In *Diccionario histórico de la Compañía de Jesús. Biográfico-temático*, vol. 2, edited by Charles E. O'Neill and Joaquín María Domínguez, 1254–57. Rome: Institutum Historicum Societatis Iesu, 2001.

Mignolo, Walter D. *Local Histories/Global Designs: Coloniality, Subaltern Knowledges, and Border Thinking*. Princeton, NJ: Princeton University Press, 2000.

Morales, Martín M. "Violencia y misión en la antigua provincia del Paraguay." *Studia Missionalia* 60 (2011): 235–55.

Mörner, Magnus. *Actividades políticas y económicas de los jesuítas en el Río de la Plata*, 2nd ed. Buenos Aires: Hyspamerica, 1985.

Mulder, Theodor. "Economía, Teorías." In *Diccionario histórico de la Compañía de Jesús. Biográfico-temático*, vol. 2, edited by Charles E. O'Neill and Joaquín María Domínguez, 1177–87. Rome: Institutum Historicum Societatis Iesu, 2001.

Negro, Sandra, and Manuel Marzal, ed. *Esclavitud, economía y evangelización: Las haciendas jesuitas en la América virreinal*. Lima: Pontifica Universidad Católica del Perú, 2005.

Oberholzer, Paul. "Briefkultur als integratives Element vor der Herausforderung eines globalen Sendungsauftrages im Kontext sich wandelnder Herrschaftskonzepte im spanischen Weltreich." In *Diego Laínez (1512–1565) and his Generalate. Jesuit with Jewish Roots, Close Confidant of Ignatius of Loyola, Preeminent Theologian of the Council of Trent*, edited by Paul Oberholzer, 757–805. Rome: Institutum Historicum Societas Iesu, 2015.

Priesching, Nicole. *Sklaverei im Urteil der Jesuiten: Eine theologiegeschichtliche Spurensuche im Collegio Romano*. Hildesheim/Zurich/New York: Georg Olms Verlag, 2017.

Riley, James D. "The Wealth of the Jesuits in Mexico, 1670–1767." *The Americas* 33, no. 2 (1976): 226–66.

Romano, Antonella. "Prime riflessioni sull'attività intellettuale dei gesuiti ai tempi di Claudio Aquaviva. La circolazione delle idee e degli uomini tra Roma, Spagna e

Nuovo Mondo." In *Strategie politiche e religiose nel mondo moderno. La Compagnia di Gesù ai tempi di Claudio Acquaviva (1581–1615)*, edited by Paolo Broggio, 271–97. Rome: Aracne 2004.

Sarreal, Julia J. S. *The Guaraní and Their Missions: A Socioeconomic History.* Stanford, CA: Stanford University Press, 2014.

Schmidt, Kurt Dietrich. "Bücherkunde und Anmerkungen." In *Die Jesuiten*, edited by Heinz Böhmer and Kurt Dietrich Schmidt, 258–78. Stuttgart: Koehler, 1957.

Spahn, Peter, Otto Gerhard Oexle and Johannes Burkhardt. "Wirtschaft." In *Geschichtliche Grundbegriffe. Historisches Lexikon zur politisch-sozialen Sprache in Deutschland*, vol. 7, edited by Otto Brunner, Werner Conze and Reinhard Koselleck, 511–94. Stuttgart: Klett-Cotta, 1992.

Storni, Hugo. *Catálogo de los jesuitas de la Provincia del Paraguay (Cuenca del Plata) 1585–1768.* Rome: Institutum Historicum Societatis Iesu, 1980.

Sweet, David G. " 'Black Robes' and 'Black Destiny': Jesuit view of African Slavery in 17th-century Latin America." *Revista de historia de América* 86 (1978): 87–133.

Telesca, Ignacio. "Esclavos y Jesuitas. El Colegio de Asunción del Paraguay." *Archivum Historicum Societatis Iesu* 77 (2008): 191–211.

Vega, Fabián R. "Las sanciones a las conductas reprensibles de misioneros en las reducciones jesuíticas de guaraníes (siglo XVIII): Entre el control y la laxitud." *Red Sociales, Revista del Departamento de Ciencias Sociales* 6 (2019): 57–79.

Vermote, Frederik. "The Role of Urban Real Estate in Jesuit Finances and Networks Between Europe and China, 1612–1778." PhD diss., University of British Columbia, 2013.

Vermote, Frederik. "Financing Jesuit Missions." In *The Oxford Handbook of the Jesuits*, edited by Ines G. Županov, 128–49. Oxford: Oxford University Press, 2019.

Vogel, Christine. *Der Untergang der Gesellschaft Jesu als europäisches Medienereignis (1758–1773): Publizistische Debatten im Spannungsfeld von Aufklärung und Gegenaufklärung.* Mainz: von Zabern, 2006.

Vu Thanh, Hélène. "Un équilibre impossible: financer la mission jésuite du Japon, entre Europe et Asie (1579–1614)." *Revue d'Histoire Moderne et Contemporaine* 63, no. 3 (2016): 7–30.

Whigham, Thomas L., and Jerry W. Cooney, eds. *Campo y frontera: El Paraguay al fin de la era colonial.* Asunción: Servilibro, 2006.

Wilde, Guillermo. "The Missions of Paraguay: Rise, Expansion and Fall." In *Companion to Early Modern Catholic Global Missions*, edited by Ronnie Po-Chia Hsia, 73–101. Leiden; Boston: Brill, 2018.

Zubillaga, Félix. "El procurador de la Compañía de Jesús en la corte de España." *Archivum Historicum Societatis Iesu* 16 (1947): 1–55.

CHAPTER 12

Afterword

For What Is a Man Profited, if He Shall Gain the Whole World, and Lose His Own Soul?

Ines G. Županov

Perhaps in no other moment of history has the Apostle St. Matthew's saying made more sense than today, although it is not only the soul that is in danger, but the whole world, because of the "profits" that go to individual men, but also, to be fair, to humanity.[1] Who would be more competent and far-sighted in formulating such a judgment than an ex-tax collector for the imperial Roman power? Colonial and imperial impositions foster lucidity as much as they destroy lives, in the process of generating riches for the minority while skillfully framing a narrative of some kind of a common good and common destiny for all.[2] The spiritual or ritual specialist actors in any historical moment may find themselves on one or other side of the barricade, but they all participated in and contributed to reflection about what constitutes moral and economic benefit and how they relate to each other.

In this volume, we opened with a still modest chapter on the particular historical moment (the sixteenth to eighteenth centuries) and a set of particular historical actors when the quest for economic profit fueled the most extraordinary endeavor of travel, learning and conquest. The purpose—in the process that engulfed with unequal but steady force the whole planet and most human societies (albeit with a few exceptions)—was always extraction of revenue and creation of value.

All the chapters in this volume address the question of Catholic missionary economy in the early modern period by looking into concrete cases of the

---

1   The full citation in the King James' version: "For what is a man profited, if he shall gain the whole world, and lose his own soul? or what shall a man give in exchange for his soul?" The Latin translation of St. Jerome: *quid enim prodest homini si mundum universum lucretur animae vero suae detrimentum patiatur aut quam dabit homo commutationem pro anima sua.* (Matthew 16:26). For macro-analysis see David Graeber, *Debt: The First 5000 Years* (Brooklyn, NY: Melville House, 2011).

2   St. Matthew's economic spirit, in particular the insight that the rich get richer and the poor get poorer (Matthew 25:29), inspired theories such as Robert K. Merton's "Matthew effect," referring to the cumulative advantage of fame and status (in scholarly community), but which is also applicable to economic capital.

opening, financing, growth and preservation of Christian missions and related institutions such as churches, colleges and other permanent endowments. One of the common and self-evident conclusions is that whatever the strategies employed—from engaging in trade, financial transactions, acquisition and management of landed properties, the use of labor and servitude—and regardless of religious families and denominations, Christian missions were an integral part of the early modern long-distance networks and were driven by capital flows.[3] What is less obvious, requiring more systematic archival research, is how religious institutions, which became active and willing partners in Iberian and European colonial and imperial expansion from the fifteenth century onwards, rationalized and reconciled their participation in global markets, given the diametrically opposed ideals of Christian poverty, anti-usury and anti-profit.[4] The question was posed to, and in a way deflected by the Portuguese Crown and court theologians in the early sixteenth century, Giuseppe Marcocci has argued, by way of a particular institution, *A Mesa da Consciência e Ordens*, established in 1532.[5]

In spite of often scanty sources, medieval historians have evidenced that the economic development of the cities, population growth and the commercial revolution that continued to nourish such growth was accompanied by secularization of human activity.[6] The invention of the notion of purgatory in the twelfth century, as Jacques Le Goff has taught us, transformed the medieval Church into a huge bank (treasure) of merit, a powerful if intangible product, and transformed "good works" into commodities exchanged between traders.[7]

---

3   Steven J. Harris, "Confession-Building, Long-Distance Networks, and the Organization of Jesuit Science," *Early Science and Medicine* 1, no. 3, thematic issue, "Jesuits and the Knowledge of Nature" (October 1996): 287–318. Dauril Alden, *The Making of an Enterprise: The Society of Jesus in Portugal, its Empire and Beyond, 1540–1750* (Stanford, CA: Stanford University Press, 1996).

4   On the canonical ban on trade and business by religious men, see John P. Beal, *New Commentary on the Code of Canon Law* (New York; Mahwah, NJ: Paulist Press, 2000), 378. See also Rômulo da Silva Ehalt's chapter in this volume.

5   Giuseppe Marcocci, *A consciência de um império: Portugal e o seu mundo (Sécs. XV-XVII)* (Coimbra: Imprensa da Universidade de Coimbra, 2012) and "Conscience and Empire: Politics and Moral Theology in the Early Modern Portuguese World," *Journal of Early Modern History* 18 (2014): 473–94. Marcocci's work presents rich evidence supporting the mutually constitutive role of religion and commerce in Portuguese early expansion.

6   Jacques Le Goff, *Time, Work, and Culture in the Middle Ages*, trans. Arthur Goldhammer (Chicago; London: University of Chicago Press, 1980), 30. Cynthia L. Negrey, *Work Time: Conflict, Control, and Change* (Cambridge, UK: Polity, 2012), 14. See also Le Goff's classic statement, Jacques Le Goff, *La Bourse et la vie: économie et religion au Moyen Âge* (Paris: Hachette, 1986).

7   Jacques Le Goff, *The Birth of Purgatory*, trans. Arthur Goldhammer (Chicago: University of Chicago Press, 1984).

The ecclesiastical institutions evolved and changed accordingly, and the divisions (schisms) at the heart of the Holy See caused a particular turn of events that affected European religious geography. It has also been argued that the changes in social mobility were related to the fact that "scholastic capital" became a factor of central importance in vocational success and that in the thirteenth and fourteenth centuries there was a proliferating number of canons, bishops and prelates from modest families, whose careers had been furthered by university studies.[8] In fact, just one such student, Martin Luther, called a spade a spade when he denounced the Church's revenue maximizing effort in the sale of indulgences.

In the sixteenth century, the missionaries had to defend the Church against criticisms of its worldly riches and provide an example of and justification for their own vow of poverty. They had to "enrich" the Church by saving and converting the souls of Christians and non-Christians alike. This is why the Society of Jesus, a newly established order approved to do just that, recruited members from all walks of life and professions, elected on the basis of their skills and piety. The Jesuits invented the blueprint for ideal missionary career and inspired other religious orders, even those, such as Franciscans, who had a much longer missionary tradition.

A famous Jesuit, Alessandro Valignano, had first been a student of law before deciding to switch to an ecclesiastical vocation. Even more importantly, unlike the noble Valignano, the Jesuits opened the door to men from more modest and common families, who were then destined to become surgeons, painters, accountants and merchants. Luís de Almeida not only sacrificed his métier as surgeon and optician, but used his personal inheritance to become a professed Jesuit father and a priest in Japan.[9] However, the tension between "religious" and "secular" spheres (including economics) was clearly spelt out in antagonistic terms within the Society of Jesus from the late sixteenth century onwards, when it became the subject of theological, legal and missionary disputes over what would later be called the Chinese and Malabar rites.[10] The rites controversies have been studied recently from historical, anthropological and epistemological perspectives, but deep below the discursive surface, at the root of the debate, economic and financial problems were brewing. A common

8   Sandro Carocci, "Social Mobility and the Middle Ages," *Continuity and Change* 26, no. 3 (2011): 377.

9   See Hélène Vu Thanh's chapter in this volume.

10   Ines G. Županov and Pierre-Antoine Fabre, eds., *The Rites Controversies in the Early Modern World* (Leiden; Boston: Brill, 2018).

argument was that the method of accommodation was excessively costly, since Jesuits had to employ and pay local interpreters and catechists, who possessed indispensable local knowledge. Investment in building a knowledge base was a rational tool, especially useful at moments when doctrinal innovation was inevitably taking place.[11] More systematic research and in-depth studies focusing exclusively on the financial and economic aspect of the Rites controversies are still lacking and this area was, to our regret, left beyond the scope of this volume.[12]

The opening of the overseas "spiritual market" for Francis Xavier, the very first Jesuit missionary sent to the Indies, was programmatically set in a double register of monetary and non/anti-monetary exhortations. The agents participating in Portuguese colonial expansion very often requested and expected cash from the royal treasury after performing important services for the Crown. Xavier's letter to the Portuguese king, João III, written in Cochin (Kochi) on January 20, 1548, referring to his military experience in the Melaka armada's attack on Aceh the previous year, consists, therefore, of a long list of people he recommends to be favored by royal "*mercês* (grants)" for their military service to the king.[13] In addition Xavier also pleaded for funds to be bestowed on the "Santa Misericórdia do Cochim" for the acquisition of paintings and other expenses, such as stipends for orphan boys and similar, and for the local hospital. In the last paragraph he expressed his own demand. "The last *mercê* that I request Y. H. is that [you] pay me in [the] true love that I have for you, that you bestow your grant on me for the love and service to God Our

---

11   Robert B. Ekelund, Jr., Robert F. Hébert and Robert D. Tollison, "The Economics of Sin and Redemption: Purgatory as a Market-pull Innovation?" *Journal of Economic Behavior and Organization* 19 (1992): 10.

12   Some remarkable studies have been published. See the latest by Frederik Vermote, "Financing Jesuit Missions," in *Oxford Handbook of the Jesuits*, ed. Ines G. Županov (New York: Oxford University Press, 2019). See also Ronnie Po-Chia, Hsia, *Noble Patronage and Jesuit Missions: Maria Theresa Von Fugger-Wellenburg (1690–1762) and Jesuit Missionaries in China and Vietnam* (Rome: Monumenta Historica Societatis Iesu, 2006).

13   Georg Schurhammer and Josef Wicki, eds., *Epistolae S. Francisci Xaverii aliaque eius scripta* (Rome: Monumenta Historica Societatis Iesu, 1996) [hereafter *EX*], vol. 1, 410–17. Xavier wrote three letters on the same day to João III. Georg Schurhammer, *Francis Xavier: His Life, His Times, India (1541–45)*, trans. from the 1963 German edition by J. Costelloe (Rome: Institutum Historicum Societatis Iesu, 1977), vol. 3, 338. On royal "mercês" and the making of Indo-Portuguese emphyteuses in the wake of Portuguese colonization in India and elsewhere see, José Vicente Serrão and Eugénia Rodrigues, "Migration and Accommodation of Property Rights in the Portuguese Eastern Empire: Sixteenth-Nineteenth Centuries," in *Property Rights in Land: Issues in Social, Economic and Global History*, ed. R. Congost, J. Gelman, R. Santos (London; New York: Routledge, 2017), 9–31.

Lord, which should be urgently put in place with great diligence ... do not put this off until the hour of your death."[14]

In another letter written the same day and addressed to Simão Rodrigues, a noble Jesuit who stayed on in Lisbon as a close advisor to João III, Xavier recommended, among other things, that he make the king meditate a quarter of an hour each day on Christ's words recorded in Matthew 16:26.

"For what is a man profited, if he shall gain the whole world, and lose his own soul? Or what shall a man give in exchange for his soul?" Xavier insisted that all this was to be done to "relieve the conscience of the King." Thus, from Xavier's letters it appears that what was flowing between people—the agents of colonization in particular, structured hierarchically within the Portuguese imperium—were not simply pecuniary emoluments but all kinds of non-monetary flows and substances: honors, favors, friendship and love. However, from his correspondence we can gather that Xavier and his co-religionists were keeping careful tabs, as we will see, on the quantities and quality of these exchanged immaterial goods. Even divine retribution helped, since if one were to trust Jesuit hagiographies, those who betrayed Jesuits always ended badly (illness, shipwreck, bankruptcy, etc.).

1   Market

The concept of "spiritual market" is itself somewhat misleading to the extent that the missionary agents did not want to be involved in, or did not want to perceive themselves as involved in exchanging or competing on the market. Christianization was, in theory, not part of a circle of exchange. It was a one way "gift" of "Glad Tidings" to the non-Christians. Just as one cannot buy one's salvation, a mission could not be a work of money, but represented instead a special divine grace, a supra-human, universal agent, outside of the market economy. And yet there is a family resemblance between this supra-human agent, which in fact determines the outcome of the Christian moral economy, and Adam Smith's famous "Invisible Hand" or a mysterious (self-regulating) market force, which is one of the key insights in his 1776 book, *An Inquiry into the Causes and the Wealth of Nations.*[15] Divine will thus blended with Smith's

---

14   *EX*, vol. 1, 416, translation slightly changed from Schurhammer, *Francis Xavier,* vol. 3, 344.

15   Adam Smith, *An Inquiry into the Nature and the Causes of the Wealth of Nations,* ed. Edwin Cannan, 2 vols. (London: Methuen, 1904) [based on the 5th edition of 1789, the last during Smith's lifetime]. Laurence L. Iannaccone argues in her article, "Introduction

secular will for profit and success, in using the market to enrich oneself and to enrich others. The theory is well known: individual ingenuity is stimulated by the division of labor and shored up by commercial and entrepreneurial societies. It is not my brief to argue for or against, nor to provide seamless analogies, or even borrowings between the Christian—Catholic at that—and Smith's moral economy. The parallels are suggestive enough, since the Jesuits, in fact, have a spiritual formula from Loyola's *Spiritual Exercises* that was elucidated in scholarship as "save oneself while saving others," just as commercial agents did, according to Smith, in producing wealth for themselves that intentionally or unintentionally benefited other people.[16] Individual choice, or in Ignatian terms, "discernment of the spirits," becomes a factor of universal salvation, or in Smith's concept, public interest and prosperity.

Missions—material places staffed with missionaries and their local hands (catechists) and acolytes—were such sudden material foundations brought into being from scratch and they sometimes created or increased the wealth of the Church and the locality. However, in the documents, they were also conceived and spoken of in a different, immaterial register. The collection of petitions to the Superior General of the Society of Jesus called *Indipetae*, in which missionary desire to be sent to the Indies was expressed as the highest spiritual goal, took for granted that the Jesuit missions—some actually concretely named, such as Madurai mission or the China or Japan missions—were otherworldly creations.[17] The confirmation of the missionary vocation often came to the Jesuit petitioners in premonitions and dreams, just as the first missionary in Asia, Francis Xavier experienced, while still in Europe—where he dreamed of

---

to the Economics of Religion," *Journal of Economic Literature* 36, no. 3 (1998): 1478, that Adam Smith recognized the existence of a religious market because "self-interest motivates clergy just as it does secular producers. ... The benefits of competition, the burdens of monopoly and the hazards of government regulation are as real for religion as for any other sector of the economy."

16   See the French edition of the *Spiritual Exercises* in Ignace de Loyola, *Écrits*, ed. Maurice Giuliani (Paris: Desclée De Brouwer, 1991), 62–63. On sources and multiple consequences of Jesuit self-reflexivity on this and other similar points, see Pierre-Antoine Fabre, "L'institution du texte fondateur," *Enquête* 2 (1995): 79–93 and Pierre Antoine Fabre, "Une érudition critique: Michel de Certeau vers 1968," in *Fabula / Les colloques, Revisiter l'œuvre de M. de Certeau*, ed. Christian Indermulhe and Adrien Paschoud. URL: http://www.fabula.org/colloques/document4655.php, accessed October 15, 2019. See also, J. Michelle Molina, *To Overcome Oneself: The Jesuit Ethic and Spirit of Global Expansion, 1520–1767* (Berkeley, CA: University of California Press, 2013).

17   Gian Carlo Roscioni, *Il desiderio delle Indie. Storie, sogni e fughe di giovani gesuiti italiani* (Turin: Giulio Einaudi Editore, 2001).

Somnium Xauerij de fubfidio Indis ferendo.

Credimus? an qui amant ipfi fibi fomnia fingunt?

ILLUSTRATION 12.1   Somnium Xaverii de subsidio Indis ferendo (Xaverius's dream of giving
help to the Indian), *Imago Primi Saeculi* (1640), 720

the burden of carrying an "Indian" on his back according to the widely dissem-
inated hagiographic literature and iconography (see illustration 12.1).[18]

"I am completely broken," he cried out in the middle of the night, "do you
know what was brought before my eyes while I slept? That I lifted and carried
on my back, for quite some time, a black Indian like those of Ethiopia."

This image of Francis Xavier carrying a non-Christian on his back, often portrayed in paintings and prints with feathers in his hair, went viral

---

18   Sebastião Gonçalves, *Primeira Parte da História dos Religiosos da Companhia de Jesus e
do que fizeram com a divina graça na conversão dos infieis a nossa sancta fee catholica nos
reynos e provincias da Índia Oriental* [1614], ed. Josef Wicki (Coimbra: Atlântida, 1957–
1962), vol. 1, 45.

in Jesuit hagiographic literature and pictorial representations. Mission was not only a huge financial load; it was costly in terms of the personal energy and strain each missionary had to deploy. Accepting and enduring the load of a mission was enshrined in the fourth vow of obedience: to go wherever needed, and the image also harks back to Christ carrying the cross before his crucifixion.

The pathos of the image was subverted, interestingly, while retaining the external form, in a late eighteenth century satirical British caricature. By reversing the load and the carrier, the image produced an ironic comment on the impeachment trial against India's governor general Warren Hastings. He is portrayed with hands clutching bags of money from colonial plunder while riding on the shoulders of his defender Chancellor Thurlow as he waddles through a sea of blood and dead Indians. The image of a "burden" is obviously highly treacherous and volatile and can serve different purposes. However, a century later, British writer Rudyard Kipling wrote a poem entitled "*The White Man's Burden: The United States and The Philippine Islands*," in which he urged the United States to take up the "burden" of empire, just as the British and other Europeans had done.[19] And thus Xavier's dream is found to resemble very closely the British discovery of their own imperial "costs."

The mission was, of course, a "burden," but it was also a necessity, at least for the Jesuits, and, moreover, it was the only reason why the pope consented to the creation of their religious community. The fourth vow to the pope to accept any mission was a price the Jesuits paid in order to be willed into existence.[20] Even though the burden was heavy, they asked for more. Again, it was Xavier, whose every word or gesture was collected as a relic of his heavenly inspiration, who pronounced the three words "more, more, more."[21] Indeed, they referred to more suffering or a heavier weight, but can be and often were read as a shibboleth and a battle cry to "grow." And grow they did. In terms of membership, the Jesuits who numbered twelve in Paris in 1550, twenty-five in Brazil and thirty in India grew to a thousand in 1556 (in twelve provinces),

---

19   Nicholas B. Dirks, *The Scandal of Empire: India and the Creation of Imperial Britain* (Cambridge, MA: The Belknap Press of Harvard University Press, 2006).

20   On the fourth vow, see John W. O'Malley, *The Fourth Vow in its Ignatian Context: A Historical Study. Studies in the Spirituality of Jesuits*, vol. xv, no. 1 (St. Louis, MO: American Assistancy Seminar on Jesuit Spirituality, 1983).

21   For discussion of Ignatian *mas, magis*, see John W. O'Malley, *Religious Culture in the Sixteenth Century: Preaching, Rhetoric, Spirituality and Reform* (Aldershot, UK: Ashgate, 1993), 12.

five-thousand in 1580 (in twenty provinces) and fifteen thousand in 1626 in four hundred colleges.[22]

Xavier famously left Rome with a torn *roupeta*, a breviary, a crucifix and two books, but in ten years he had succeeded in transforming the existing seminary of Santa Fe in Goa into the Jesuit college, which at the time of his death in 1553 had 450 students.[23] It is therefore safe to claim that the Society of Jesus enriched itself as an institution. Charles J. Borges, a Jesuit historian born in Goa, listed and chronicled the "economics" of the Jesuit "conquest" and loss of Goa in a rather laconic statement:

> The Jesuits worked at gathering funds since the promised Crown subsidies were often either not forthcoming or inadequate. They thus bought lands, received donations and endowments from pious lay folk, got a flourishing palm-grove business going, sub-let lands, accepted pawned goods and mortgages, and helped the State with funds whenever the need arose. In the process, they became powerful landlords and financiers.[24]

To sum up, at the height of the Society's success around 1750 and just before its downfall, the Jesuits had under their helm more than five-hundred colleges/universities in Europe, a hundred more in overseas colonies and 270 missions throughout the globe.[25] Therefore, while the Jesuits and other missionary orders denied or ignored the fact that they were part of the "market" forces, their livelihood depended entirely on the ebb and flow of capital and smart management.

2   Merchants

The Jesuits did liken their role to that of the merchants. By calling themselves the "merchants of the soul (*negoceadores das almas*)," they in fact presupposed

---

22   John W. O'Malley, "The Society of Jesus," in *A Companion of the Reformation World*, ed. Ronnie Po-chia Hsia (Oxford: Blackwell Publishers, 2004), 223–36. Joan-Pau Rubies, *Travel and Ethnology in the Renaissance: South India through European Eyes, 1250–1625* (Cambridge: Cambridge University Press, 2002). See António Boccaro, *O "Livro das Plantas de todas as fortalezas, cidades e povoaçoens do Estado da Índia Oriental (1635)" da Biblioteca Pública e Arquivo Distrital de Évora de António Bocarro e Pedro Barreto de Resende* (Lisbon: Imprensa Nacional-Casa da Moeda, 1992).

23   On Xavier's scant clothing, which even Ignatius found unacceptable, see Schurhammer, *Francis Xavier*, vol. 1, 555–56, fn. 146.

24   Charles J. Borges, *The Economics of the Goa Jesuits, 1542–1759: An Explanation of Their Rise and Fall* (New Delhi: Concept Publishing Company, 1994), 41.

25   Steven J. Harris, "Jesuit Scientific Activity in the Overseas Missions, 1540–1773," *Isis* 96 (2005): 71–79.

the existence of a parallel world of values, wealth and riches.[26] Of course, the comparison with merchants is glaring. It was obvious to the missionaries as well, but it was the Jesuits who dared to exploit it and qualify it by transposing it to a spiritual dimension. The historiography of the merchants is rich and varied, and in the context of early modern European "expansion," they are considered the most important agents of change and development, operating in the widest possible geographical frame. Although it has been argued that in the early modern period, the status of a merchant was somewhat less prestigious than, say, a bearer of aristocratic and chivalric virtues, the riches of the East were able to transform any commoner into an aristocrat.[27] According to Pietro della Valle, the Portuguese in Goa wanted to be considered "gentlemen" even when they were dirt poor. "They all profess Arms, and are Souldiers though marry'd, and few, except Priests and Doctors of Law and Physick, are seen without a Sword. ... [T]he sole dignity of being Portugals sufficing them to value themselves as much as Kings and more."[28] The poorest of the Portuguese *casado* (married man-merchant-settler) dreamt of acquiring a noble status from the profits made in trade or through exploitation of slaves and landed property.

It may still appear puzzling that the Jesuits chose to present themselves as "merchants." In fact, this identity category had also been coupled with another common social category mobilized for the "conquest" of the Indies: that of the soldier. In this double role, they represented the majority of Europeans engaged along with the small contingent of Iberian nobility. The role of merchant-cum-soldier was then upended and qualified to mean that their task was a militant spiritual commerce which also produced "profit" in the soul ("*fazer fruyto em as almas*").[29]

In a letter Xavier wrote from Kagoshima to D. Pedro da Silva da Gama, the Captain of Melaka, thanking him for various favors, among which providing him with the ship to Japan, he presented his and his patrons' deeds as having impact on future "fruits" of global conversion. Again he failed to mention money. However, three years later in the instructions he gave his co-religionist Gaspar Barzaeus in Goa, it was clear that he knew very well the amounts he received. Thus, the noble Captain gave him "200 cruzados to give to the lord of

---

26   Gonçalves, *Primeira Parte da História,* 1–139, and *EX,* vol. 2, 96.

27   On fluctuating urban stratification in Europe, see Christopher R. Friedrichs, *The Early Modern City 1450–1750 A History of Urban Society in Europe* (New York; London: Routlege reprint, 2014).

28   Pietro della Valle, *The Travels of Pietro della Valle to India From the old English Translation in 1664 by G. Havers* [...] (London: Hakluyt Society, 1892), vol. 1, 158.

29   Xavier to the captain of Melaka, D. Pedro da Silva da Gama, Kagoshima, November 5, 1549, in *EX,* vol. 2, 228.

the land in Japão so that we might be better received," and "he kindly lent me 300 cruzados so that I can pay back the 300 cruzados which were given me in Japão for the erection of a church in Amanguche. ... After you have seen this letter, pay within a very short time the 300 cruzados to Senhor Dom Pedro da Silva. ... And these 300 cruzados should be paid from the revenues of the college or from the 2000 cruzados which the King orders to be given each year to this college."[30]

In a word, Xavier could talk money and the "fruits in souls" alternatively or simultaneously as the occasion presented itself. Were these two registers— economic and spiritual—seen as being in contradiction or were they inextricably entwined? Reading Alessandro Valignano's correspondence a few decades later, the impression is that in his everyday administration his mind was endlessly occupied with calculation of sums coming in and out of his account books.[31] And yet he was doing all this with the unique goal of setting up a Christian spiritual empire.

3   Franchise

The discussion about whether or not the Society of Jesus was a corporation according to formal economic definitions is beyond our task in this volume. Some historians, such as Magnus Morner, have argued that the Society of Jesus was as close to a modern chain store as it was possible to be in that period: centralized administration, transnational recruitment of agents, management of agricultural production, and ownership of property-sustained international trade.[32] Charles Boxer wrote in the late 1970s that the Society of Jesus was the true international (multinational) organization, compared to English East India Company (EIC) and the Dutch East India Company (VOC), which were limited by the boundaries of English and Dutch colonial territories.[33] Dauril Alden has contradicted these claims, showing that the economic and commercial importance of the Society of Jesus was too modest to be comparable with the EIC and VOC and making the point that it lacked backing from a centralized

---

30   Schurhammer, *Francis Xavier*, vol. 3, 607.

31   See for example Valignano's letter to the Jesuit General Acquaviva, Cochin, December 20, 1586 in Joseph Wicki, ed., *Documenta Indica XIV (1585–1588)* (Rome: Institutum Historicum Societatis Iesu, 1979), 420–49.

32   Magnus Mörner, *The Expulsion of the Jesuits from Latin America* (New York: Alfred A. Knopf, 1965).

33   Charles R. Boxer, *Portuguese India in the Mid-Seventeenth Century* (New Delhi: Oxford University Press, 1980), 50.

corporate location (Rome).[34] In addition, Jesuits were praised for their rational and efficient information network, although both Alden and Luke Clossey after him, pointed to its fragility and ineffectiveness.[35] Managing a global enterprise, to use Alden's term, was a role into which the Jesuit order stumbled in the second half of the sixteenth century and which was extremely time consuming and difficult without a properly designed managerial blueprint. The *negocios* were thus taken care of one at a time, and what from afar looked like concerted network-building, was in fact trial-and-error, based on the individual assessment of the agents who had to deal with local partners and adversaries.

The chapters in this book address precisely the grain of the economic and social interactions and the different level of accommodation these missionary situations required or allowed for. Integrating local, regional, "national" or semi-imperial, and global settings was what trade corporations did and the missionary "spiritual" trade corporations followed suit in a very similar way. Yet can one say with Liberal and Marxist historians—following Adam Smith—that all trade corporations, missionary included, behaved as capitalist agents desirous of siphoning economic (or spiritual) opportunities into privileged pockets?[36] Was this desire also present behind the Propaganda Fide's fantasist project to establish an Italian East India company at the turn of the eighteenth century?[37] The ultimate plan—admittedly nothing more than epistolary musings—was to take control of Indian missions on the Coromandel coast where the Malabar rites controversy was brewing, partly because of the "national" question, that is, animosity fueled by the Portuguese *padroado's* ecclesiastical monopoly against papal Rome. Free trade, in this and other contexts, was envisaged as a remedy, and the solution for the Roman newcomers in the trading and missionary field.

However, Catholic missionary "corporations" developed a model—not without much contention and internal negotiations—that was in all very similar to that of the East Indian corporations, most notably and successfully for a while,

---

34   Alden, *The Making of an Enterprise*, 668.

35   Luke Clossey, *Salvation and Globalization in the Early Jesuit Missions* (Cambridge: Cambridge University Press, 2008).

36   William A. Pettigrew and David Veevers, "Introduction," in *The Corporation as a Protagonist in Global History, c. 1550–1750*, ed. William A. Pettigrew and David Veevers (Leiden: Brill, 2019), 11.

37   Paolo Aranha, "'Glocal' Conflicts: Missionary Controversies on the Coromandel Coast Between the XVII and the XVIII Centuries," in *Evangelizzazione e Globalizzazione: Le missioni gesuitiche nell'età moderna tra storia e storiografia*, ed. Michela Catto, Guido Mongini, Silvia Mostaccio, Biblioteca della "*Nuova Rivista Storica*" n. 42 (Città di Castello: Società Editrice Dante Alighieri, 2010), 100–101.

the English East India Company.[38] This means that they were conceived as homogenous franchises of royal or papal authority at home, but allowed de facto for a variety of forms of action and a multitude of local partners and collaborators overseas. Catholic missionaries were transporting commodities (a spiritual package wrapped in material goods of various kinds), setting out production outlets (missions and churches), and tapping into or creating consumption markets. In Asia these were mostly settlements along the coast under the often precarious control of the Iberians, then French and other non-Catholic Europeans, but also they ventured inland into kingdoms and empires in India and China. Some material products were commercialized, price attached although not always paid, on different markets, such as sacred paintings, icons, silver chests and chalices, famously made in Goa or in Japan. These artefacts and their "styles" travelled as far and wide as to missions in the Americas and to royal or private cabinets of curiosities in Europe.

The domestic background of these corporations differed for, say, Portuguese Augustinians, French Capuchins, various families of Franciscans, Roman Discalced Carmelites and the Jesuits, and was crucial for the way they operated outside of their headquarters, monasteries or priories and especially in the farthest areas overseas. Their internal constitutions, just like charters of the trade companies, provided a blueprint for acting locally. The Jesuits were in this respect the most mobile and accommodating agents, since their *Constitutions*, published when they were already a missionary order in the four parts of the world, gave them a lot of leeway for local decision making. This was especially the case, since the distances—a letter from China to Europe and back could take seven years—gave the missionaries both an administrative headache and freedom of choice.[39]

The Jesuits lost their corporation and their global enterprise precisely when the domestic support that invested them with authority and vouchsafed for them—Iberian and French monarchs and the pope—blacklisted them on account of their overseas dealings and freedom, or to put it in the language of the major contemporary actors, disobedience. Of course, their local competitors profited from the dismantlement of their properties, rents, churches and

38   Moreover, when in 1678 both the New East India Company and the Society for Promoting Christian Knowledge received their charters, the EIC was forced to define and regulate its relationship with the organized church and to make provisions for evangelization. See Haig Smith, "Religion," in *The Corporation as a Protagonist in Global History, c. 1550–1750*, ed. William A Pettigrew and David Veevers (Leiden: Brill, 2018), 137–62.

39   On Jesuit correspondence see Paul Nelles, "Jesuit Letters," in *Oxford Handbook of the Jesuits*, ed. Ines G. Županov (New York: Oxford University Press, 2019), 44–74.

their established spiritual authority. This is why, for example, the documents and books belonging to the Jesuit Goan Casa Professa were scattered, sold and appeared most notably in the British Library.[40] After the suppression of the order, French Jesuit possessions in Pondicherry, including the leftover Jesuits themselves, were incorporated in the Société des Missions-étrangères and thus preserved and relatively easily reclaimed, at least their archival documents, when the Jesuits returned half a century later.

If one can talk at all about an early modern spiritual "franchise," without falling into anachronism or hyperbole, it is safe to say that the Catholic missionaries can be seen as exporting an expansionist business model created for and by the Catholic Church and based on a commercial paradigm. However, success, especially in Asia, often depended on local enterprising agents who took the product and developed it further, while at times also deflecting it and using it for their own spiritual ventures.[41] Quite concretely, a new religious order founded in Goa in 1685 by the Catholic Goan Brahman diocesan priests—Congregação do Oratório de Santa Cruz dos Milagres (or Oratorians, also called *Milagristas, Padres Bragmanes*, etc.), modeled their behavior on the Jesuit accommodation theory.[42] Just like the Jesuits, they were confirmed by the Portuguese king, and consequently by the pope, because they claimed to be a missionary order that would expand Portuguese Catholicism to "pagan" areas. Subsequently they did become famous missionaries in Sri Lanka after the Dutch takeover of the coastal part of the island and the expulsion of the Portuguese. Thus, the Catholic Goan Brahmans were seen by the Portuguese authorities to be a fifth column working on future Portuguese re-conquest.

---

40   The history of the sale of Jesuit collections and manuscripts is still to be written. See E. Denison Ross, 'The Manuscripts Collected by William Marsden with Special Reference to Two Copies of Almeida's "History of Ethiopia," ' *Bulletin of the School of Oriental Studies* 2, no. 3 (1922): 513–38. See also Henry Hosten, "The Marsden MSS and Indian Mission Bibliography," *Bulletin of the School of Oriental Studies* 3, no. 1 (1923): 129–50.

41   On Hindu-Christian sects in South India, see an older but classic statement in Susan Bayly, *Saints, Goddess and Kings: Muslims and Christians in South Indian Society, 1700–1900* (Cambridge: Cambridge University Press, 1989). Syncretic sects were mushrooming within the contact zones and some persist to this day. There is a considerable scholarship on "hidden Christians" in Japan, and various other syncretic cults in Africa, America and Oceania.

42   Ines G. Županov, "Goan Brahmans in the Land of Promise: Missionaries, Spies and Gentiles in the 17th-18th century Sri Lanka," in *Re-exploring the Links: History and Constructed Histories Between Portugal and Sri Lanka*, ed. Jorge Flores (Wiesbaden: Harrassowitz and the Calouste Gulbenkian Foundation, 2006), 171–210. They were accepted by the Oratorians of St. Ph. Neri because the Jesuits were unwilling (without a real consensus on the issue!) to accept local converts into their order.

This turned out to be a vain dream of an exhausted and moribund empire. Nevertheless, their mission was the closest to the "franchise" model: Indian missionaries selling a Roman brand of spiritual power. In fact, in spite of many and different setbacks, this was the winning model for the Catholic Church. It is usually called the indigenized, or even, in the newer Jesuit parlance, the inculturated Church.

4   Money and Spirit

Made of the same invisible substance, (the value of) money and spirit— *spiritus sanctus*—cohabited and cooperated in the early modern world. The classical Christian theory holding that where there was more money there was less spirit was acknowledged but not practiced. From the missionary perspective, money and all it could buy, was a means of financing their religious and humanitarian projects—churches, seminaries, schools, hospitals, orphanages and similar—and of acquiring a toehold in the unchristian communities. From the chapters in the volume, we can glimpse the enormity of this task, since in spite of promises by their major institutional patrons, kings and popes, they were left to fend for themselves. Hence their inventive, creative financial schemes, some successful, other failed. Perhaps the most successful feature of the Jesuit financial model was the fact that they were socially savvy and were able to engage various social groups as benefactors, from the poorest of the poor to the richest members of the mercantile and aristocratic societies. Their reputation for being well connected, and part of a large transnational corporation also made them appear "trustworthy" for financial operations such as loans and borrowings. Their creditors had to learn the hard way that Jesuit spiritual and financial empires did not neatly coincide. There simply was no organized and centralized financial safety net provided by the Society of Jesus, since each mission, even each Jesuit, was an independent financial agent. In the long run, it is possible that the famous Lavalette affair—in which he managed to bankrupt, and hasten the ban of, the Society of Jesus in France—was one of the massive nails in the coffin of the Society of Jesus in the early modern period.[43] The debts Lavalette contracted as a superior of the Martinique mission by dealing with colonial associates

---

43   D. G. Thompson, "The Fate of the French Jesuits' Creditors under the Ancien Régime," *The English Historical Review* 91, no. 359 (April, 1976): 255–77. The article tells a fascinating story of Jesuit debt management taking half a century to settle and involved various Ancien Régime and post-Revolution institutions.

and speculators in France reveals the whole structure of financial speculation that went on in the latter half of the eighteenth century. The Society of Jesus, a spiritual-cum-financial treasury had lost all credit and landholdings by 1761. How they recovered all this and made another start in the early nineteenth century requires a further volume.[44]

Bibliography

Primary Sources

Gonçalves, Sebastião, S.I. *Primeira Parte da História dos Religiosos da Companhia de Jesus e do que fizeram com a divina graça na conversão dos infieis a nossa sancta fee catholica nos reynos e provincias da Índia Oriental* [1614]. Edited by Josef Wicki. Coimbra: Atlântida, 1957–1962.

Loyola, Ignace de. *Écrits*. Edited by Maurice Giuliani. Paris: Desclée De Brouwer, 1991.

Schurhammer, Georg, and Josef Wicki, eds. *Epistolae S. Francisci Xaverii aliaque eius scripta*. Rome: Monumenta Historica Societatis Iesu, 1996.

Valle, Pietro della. *The Travels of Pietro della Valle to India from the old English Translation in 1664 by G. Havers* […]. London: Hakluyt Society, 1892.

Wicki, Joseph, ed. *Documenta Indica XIV (1585–1588)*. Rome: Institutum Historicum Societatis Iesu, 1979.

Secondary Sources

Alden, Dauril. *The Making of an Enterprise: The Society of Jesus in Portugal, its Empire and Beyond, 1540–1750*. Stanford, CA: Stanford University Press, 1996.

Aranha, Paolo. " 'Glocal' Conflicts: Missionary Controversies on the Coromandel Coast Between the XVII and the XVIII Centuries." In *Evangelizzazione e Globalizzazione: Le missioni gesuitiche nell'età moderna tra storia e storiografia*, edited by Michela Catto, Guido Mongini, Silvia Mostaccio, 79–104. Biblioteca della "*Nuova Rivista Storica*" n. 42. Città di Castello: Società Editrice Dante Alighieri, 2010.

Bayly, Susan. *Saints, Goddess and Kings: Muslims and Christians in South Indian Society, 1700–1900*. Cambridge: Cambridge University Press, 1989.

Beal, John P. *New Commentary on the Code of Canon Law*. New York; Mahwah, NJ: Paulist Press, 2000.

Boccaro, António. *O "Livro das Plantas de todas as fortalezas, cidades e povoaçoens do Estado da Índia Oriental (1635)" da Biblioteca Pública e Arquivo Distrital de Évora de António Bocarro e Pedro Barreto de Resende*. Lisbon: Imprensa Nacional-Casa da Moeda, 1992.

---

44   For pertinent analysis see Greaber, *Debt*, 361–391.

Borges, Charles J. *The Economics of the Goa Jesuits, 1542–1759: An Explanation of Their Rise and Fall.* New Delhi: Concept Publishing Company, 1994.

Boxer, Charles R. *Portuguese India in the Mid-Seventeenth Century.* New Delhi: Oxford University Press, 1980.

Carocci, Sandro. "Social Mobility and the Middle Ages." *Continuity and Change* 26, no. 3 (2011): 364–404.

Clossey, Luke. *Salvation and Globalization in the Early Jesuit Missions.* Cambridge: Cambridge University Press, 2008.

Dirks, Nicholas B. *The Scandal of Empire: India and the Creation of Imperial Britain.* Cambridge, MA: The Belknap Press of Harvard University Press, 2006.

Ekelund, Jr., Robert B., Robert F. Hébert, and Robert D. Tollison. "The Economics of Sin and Redemption: Purgatory as a Market-pull Innovation?" *Journal of Economic Behavior and Organization* 19 (1992): 1–15.

Fabre, Pierre-Antoine. "L'institution du texte fondateur." *Enquête* 2 (1995): 79–93.

Fabre, Pierre-Antoine. "Une érudition critique: Michel de Certeau vers 1968." In *Fabula / Les colloques, Revisiter l'œuvre de M. de Certeau,* edited by Christian Indermulhe and Adrien Paschoud. URL: http://www.fabula.org/colloques/document4655.php, accessed October 15, 2019.

Friedrichs, Christopher R. *The Early Modern City 1450–1750: A History of Urban Society in Europe.* New York; London: Routledge reprint, 2014.

Graeber, David. *Debt: The First 5000 Years.* Brooklyn, NY: Melville House, 2011.

Harris, Steven J. "Confession-Building, Long-Distance Networks, and the Organization of Jesuit Science." *Early Science and Medicine* 1, no. 3, thematic issue, "Jesuits and the Knowledge of Nature" (October 1996): 287–318.

Harris, Steven J. "Jesuit Scientific Activity in the Overseas Missions, 1540–1773." *Isis* 96 (2005): 71–79.

Hsia, Ronnie Po-Chia. *Noble Patronage and Jesuit Missions: Maria Theresa Von Fugger-Wellenburg (1690–1762) and Jesuit Missionaries in China and Vietnam.* Rome: Monumenta Historica Societatis Iesu, 2006.

Hosten, Henry, SJ. "The Marsden MSS and Indian Mission Bibliography." *Bulletin of the School of Oriental Studies* 3, no. 1 (1923): 129–50.

Iannaccone, Laurence L. "Introduction to the Economics of Religion." *Journal of Economic Literature* 36, no. 3 (1998): 1465–96.

Le Goff, Jacques. *Time, Work, and Culture in the Middle Ages.* Translated by Arthur Goldhammer. Chicago; London: University of Chicago Press, 1980.

Le Goff, Jacques. *The Birth of Purgatory.* Translated by Arthur Goldhammer. Chicago: University of Chicago Press, 1984.

Le Goff, Jacques. *La Bourse et la vie: économie et religion au Moyen Âge.* Paris: Hachette, 1986.

Marcocci, Giuseppe. *A consciência de um império: Portugal e o seu mundo (Sécs. XV-XVII)*. Coimbra: Imprensa da Universidade de Coimbra, 2012.

Marcocci, Giuseppe. "Conscience and Empire: Politics and Moral Theology in the Early Modern Portuguese World." *Journal of Early Modern History* 18 (2014): 473–94.

Mörner, Magnus. *The Expulsion of the Jesuits from Latin America*. New York: Alfred A. Knopf, 1965.

Molina, J. Michelle. *To Overcome Oneself: The Jesuit Ethic and Spirit of Global Expansion, 1520–1767*. Berkeley, CA: University of California Press, 2013.

Negrey, Cynthia L. *Work Time: Conflict, Control, and Change*. Cambridge, UK: Polity, 2012.

Nelles, Paul. "Jesuit Letters." In *Oxford Handbook of the Jesuits*, edited by Ines G. Županov, 44–74. New York: Oxford University Press, 2019.

Roscioni, Gian Carlo. *Il desiderio delle Indie. Storie, sogni e fughe di giovani gesuiti italiani*. Turin: Giulio Einaudi Editore, 2001.

Ross, E. Denison. 'The Manuscripts Collected by William Marsden with Special Reference to Two Copies of Almeida's "History of Ethiopia." ' *Bulletin of the School of Oriental Studies* 2, no. 3 (1922): 513–38.

O'Malley, John W. *The Fourth Vow in its Ignatian Context: a Historical Study. Studies in the Spirituality of Jesuits*, vol. xv, no. 1. St. Louis, MO: American Assistancy Seminar on Jesuit Spirituality, 1983.

O'Malley, John W. *Religious Culture in the Sixteenth Century: Preaching, Rhetoric, Spirituality and Reform*. Aldershot, UK: Ashgate, 1993.

O'Malley, John W. "The Society of Jesus." In *A Companion of the Reformation World*, edited by Ronnie Po-chia Hsia, 223–36. Oxford: Blackwell Publishers, 2004.

Pettigrew, William A. and David Veevers. "Introduction." In *The Corporation as a Protagonist in Global History, c. 1550–1750*, edited by William A. Pettigrew and David Veevers, 1–40. Leiden: Brill, 2019.

Rubies, Joan-Pau. *Travel and Ethnology in the Renaissance: South India through European Eyes, 1250–1625*. Cambridge: Cambridge University Press, 2002.

Schurhammer, Georg. *Francis Xavier, His Life, His Times, India (1541–45), vol. 3*. Translated by J. Costelloe. Rome: Institutum Historicum Societatis Iesu, 1977.

Serrão, José Vicente and Eugénia Rodrigues. "Migration and Accommodation of Property Rights in the Portuguese Eastern Empire, Sixteenth-Nineteenth Centuries." In *Property Rights in Land: Issues in Social, Economic and Global History*, edited by R. Congost, J. Gelman, R. Santos, 9–31. London and New York: Routledge, 2017.

Smith, Adam. *An Inquiry into the Nature and the Causes of the Wealth of Nations*. Edited by Edwin Cannan, 2 vols. London: Methuen, 1904.

Smith, Haig. "Religion." In *The Corporation as a Protagonist in Global History, c. 1550–1750*, edited by William A Pettigrew and David Veevers, 137–62. Leiden: Brill, 2018.

Thompson, D. G. "The Fate of the French Jesuits' Creditors under the Ancien Régime." *The English Historical Review* 91, no. 359 (April 1976): 255–77.

Vermote, Frederik. "Financing Jesuit Missions." In *Oxford Handbook of the Jesuits*, edited by Ines G. Županov. New York: Oxford University Press, 2019.

Županov, Ines G. "Goan Brahmans in the Land of Promise: Missionaries, Spies and Gentiles in the 17th-18th century Sri Lanka." In *Re-exploring the Links: History and Constructed Histories Between Portugal and Sri Lanka,* edited by Jorge Flores, 171–210. Wiesbaden: Harrassowitz and the Calouste Gulbenkian Foundation, 2006.

Županov, Ines G., and Pierre-Antoine Fabre, eds. *The Rites Controversies in the Early Modern World.* Leiden; Boston: Brill, 2018.

Index of Names, Places, Concepts

East India Companies 7, 20, 35, 135–136, 140, 146, 248, 254, 298–300
encomenderos (*encomienda*) 145, 25–26, 73–76, 79–81, 83, 85
Este, Alessandro (cardinal of) 187
Eu 190, 193
Europe 1, 3, 5, 7–14, 19, 21–22, 25, 28, 31, 35–36, 51, 55, 64, 71, 73, 78, 80–81, 98–99, 113, 124–126, 128, 134–136, 138, 140–141, 144–146, 183, 211, 217, 222, 237–243, 246–247, 261, 280, 283, 289–290, 293, 295–297, 300

farms 197, 216, 219–220
  estancias 26, 38, 83, 275
  haciendas 15
  in Japan 107, 115–116
  in Paraguay 38, 83, 270, 272, 274–275, 278–279
Ferdinando VI (king) 90
Figueiredo, Belchior de 101
Fonseca, Pedro 214, 229
France 31–32, 142–143, 183, 185–186, 190, 196, 207–208, 217, 222, 237, 246, 248, 258, 260–262, 302–303
Francesco Maria di San Siro O.C.D. [Antonio Gorla] 137
franchise 298
Franciscans 14, 35, 237, 290, 300
  in Japan 9, 18, 24–25, 61, 165
  in Palestine 16
  in the Philippines 31, 60, 163, 166, 172
  Nagasaki martyrdom 31, 61, 165
  rivalries with the Jesuits 19, 60
Fróis, Luís 100–101, 108, 112, 114
Fuan 173–175
Fujian (Hokkien) 31, 156–163, 166–167, 169–171, 173
Funai 100
Funamoto, Bernard 60
funding 3, 12, 34–38, 125, 132, 190, 240–243, 269, 272
  alms 18, 36, 133, 135–137, 139–141, 229, 255–256, 282
  annuities 32, 187, 189–191, 193–196, 200
  Carmelites 29, 133, 137, 141
  donations 9, 13–16, 26–28, 32–33, 53, 55, 57, 97–109, 111–112, 114–120, 143, 189–190, 193, 195–196, 199–202, 226, 239–243, 263, 296

from the *Propaganda Fide* 29, 127–131
  insufficient 132–133, 139, 141–142, 145–146, 186
  Jesuits 3, 24, 32, 34, 53, 58, 184–185, 190–192, 198, 274, 278, 291, 296
  See also patronage; mounts of piety
Fuzhou 174

Gago, Baltasar 100
Gama, Vasco de 7
Genoa 188, 190
Gévaudan 32, 184
gift economy 29, 135
Gion festival 101
Gnecchi-Soldo, Organtino 111
Goa 11, 15, 24, 28, 126, 137, 139–140, 143, 254, 296–297, 300–301
go-betweens 49, 165
  interpreters 10, 30, 47, 50, 55, 58, 63, 65, 156, 158, 168, 244, 291
  Jesuits as 24, 49–50
  lay 211
  mediators 23–24, 30, 48, 50, 52, 55–56, 61–63, 65–66, 158, 161, 165, 171
  See also brokers; procurators
Gonzague, Louis de (Duke of Nevers) 186
Gonzague, Charles de (Duke of Nevers) 189, 200
Grado, Lorenzo de 78
Granada 155, 209
Gregory XIII (pope) 132, 251
Gregory XV (pope) 127
Guangdong 97
Guangxi 97
Guairá 71, 76
Guise, Henri de Lorraine (duke of) 190
Guo, Bangyong 173–174

Hachirao 110, 118
Hainan 97
Hault (family) 194–195
Hakata 27, 100–101, 113
Herrán, Jerónimo 275
Hinami 105
Hirado 102, 108, 165, 175
hitojichi 115
Hōshōji 104, 118
Hizen 98
Holy Office 30, 141–142, 225

Printed in the United States
By Bookmasters